A TOUCHSTONE BOOK
Published by Simon & Schuster
New York · London · Toronto · Sydney · Tokyo · Singapore

UNDER GOD

Religion and American Politics

GARRY WILLS

TOUCHSTONE
Simon & Schuster Building
Rockefeller Center
1230 Avenue of the Americas
New York, New York 10020

Copyright © 1990 by Garry Wills

Designed by Nina D'Amario/Levavi & Levavi
Manufactured in the United States of America

3   5   7   9   10   8   6   4   2

3   5   7   9   10   8   6   4   2   Pbk

Library of Congress Cataloging-in-Publication Data

Wills, Garry, date.
Under God : religion and American politics / Garry Wills.
p.   cm.
Includes bibliographical references and index.
1. Presidents—United States—Election—1988
2. Christianity and politics.   3. Church and state—United
States.   4. United States—Politics and government—1981-
1989.   5. United States—Church history—20th
century.   I. Title
E880.W54   1990   90-44624
322'.1'0973—dc20   CIP

ISBN 0-671-65705-4
ISBN 0-671-74746-0 Pbk.

A leatherbound signed first edition of this book
has been published by The Easton Press.

ACKNOWLEDGMENTS

This book developed from my reporting of the 1988 presidential campaign. Walter Isaacson, then the Nation editor for *Time*, proposed that I write three cover stories on the 1988 election, along with ancillary articles for the magazine. That project was supported by managing editor Henry Miller and then–assistant managing editor Richard Duncan. *Time* also sponsored the *Frontline* television show on the candidates that I wrote and narrated, "The Choice." Donald Morrison edited *Time*'s book on the election, *The Winning of the White House, 1988*, for which I wrote the introduction. To these people, and those in *Time*'s local bureaus and research department (under Ursula Nadasdy de Gallo), I am grateful for the help that went into the first stage of this book.

At *Frontline*, David Fanning produced "The Choice," and Sherry Jones directed, with the assistance of Elizabeth Sams. Thanks to their expert work, "The Choice" won a Peabody Award for Excellence in Broadcasting.

When it became clear to me that religion would become the focus of my further work on the 1988 election, I traveled to the institutions whose archives proved so helpful—Bethany Nazarene College in Oklahoma City (where Gary Hart studied for the ministry), the Nazarene Archives in Kansas City, Chicago Theological Seminary (where Jesse Jackson studied for the ministry), New York Theological Seminary (where Pat Robertson studied for the ministry), Elim Bible Institute in Lima, New York (where Randall Terry was trained), and Christian Heritage College in San Diego (where the Institute for Creation Research was begun).

Editors were helpful in letting me try out ideas in their magazines while working on the book, especially Robert Silvers at *The New York Review of Books*, who showed special interest in the project. I am also grateful to Alex Kaplan of *Wigwag*, Byron Dobell of *American Heritage*, Elliot Kaplan of *GQ*, and Terry Zintl, Walter Isaacson's successor as Nation editor at *Time*. I am grateful to Dean Lawrence Dumas and the history department of Northwestern University for a two years' leave of absence to complete the book. My agent, Ted Chichak, to whom the book is justly dedicated, orchestrated the whole project. My editor, Alice Mayhew, sped it along. Natalie Wills was my first reader and most percipient critic. John C. Wills again helped with the research. The bulk of the book was typed with speed and accuracy by Joan Stahl.

Scripture passages, unless otherwise indicated, are from the New English Bible.

To Ted Chichak
agent and friend
for over twenty years

CONTENTS

CONTENTS

CONTENTS

INTRODUCTION

THE LEARNED HAVE THEIR SUPERSTITIONS, PROMINENT AMONG THEM A belief that superstition is evaporating. Since science has explained the world in secular terms, there is no more need for religion, which will wither away. Granted, it has been slow to die in America. Even Marx noticed that, in the 1850s. But he explained it by the raw state of this country: "the feverish, youthful movement of material production, which has to make a new world its own, has left neither time nor opportunity for abolishing the old spirit world."[1] The funeral, he was sure, had been delayed, not canceled. Yet when Communist regimes were given their own sudden funeral in 1989, an American preacher (Andrew Young) remarked: "When they come out from behind the Iron Curtain, they are singing 'We Shall Overcome,' a Georgia Baptist hymn."[2] And he did not mean the Soviet Georgia.

In a time of reviving fundamentalisms around the world, some Americans have rediscovered our native fundamentalists (a recurring, rather than cumulative, experience for the learned). It seems careless for scholars to keep misplacing such a large body of people. Nonetheless, every time religiosity catches the attention of intellectuals, it is as if a shooting star had appeared in the sky. One could hardly guess, from this, that nothing has been more stable in our history, nothing less budgeable, than religious belief and practice. Religion does not shift or waver; the attention of its observers does. Public notice, like a restless spotlight, returns at intervals to believers' goings-on, finds them still going on, and, with expressions of astonishment or dread, declares that religion is undergoing some kind of "boom" or revival. But, as Seymour Martin Lipset observed, statistics tell the story of "a continuous 'boom' in American religious adherence and belief."[3] Revivalism does not need to be revived. Revival is, like respiration, the condition of its life. Apparent fluctuations in the nineteenth century had more to do with inchoate reporting methods than with oscillation in the things reported on.[4]

Technology, urbanization, social mobility, universal education, high living standards—all were supposed to eat away at religion, in a wash of overlapping acids. But each has crested over America, proving itself a solvent or a catalyst in other areas, but showing little power to corrode or diminish religion. The figures are staggering. Poll after poll confirms them:

> Nine Americans in ten say they have never doubted the existence of God.
> Eight Americans in ten say they believe they will be called before God on Judgment Day to answer for their sins.
> Eight Americans in ten believe God still works miracles.
> Seven Americans in ten believe in life after death.[5]

When Cardinal O'Connor of New York mentioned exorcisms in his diocese, he was widely ridiculed in the press. Yet 37 percent of Americans believe in a personal devil. Fifty percent believe in angels—as opposed to the 15 percent who believe in astrology.[6] Cardinal O'Connor is joined in his views by well over twice the numbers that join Nancy Reagan in consulting astral charts.

Practice conforms to profession. About 40 percent of the American population attends church in a typical week (as opposed to 14 percent in Great Britain and 12 percent in France).[7] More people go to church, in any week, than to all sports events combined. Over 90 percent of Americans say they pray some time in the week.[8] Internationally, "Americans rank at the top in rating the importance of God in their lives. On a scale of 1 to 10, with 10 the highest, Americans average a rating of 8.21, behind only tiny Malta (9.58)."[9]

One would expect that something so important to Americans would affect their behavior as voters. And, as a matter of fact, no non-Christian has ever been elected president of the United States. No non-Protestant was elected until 1960, when some took the acceptance of John Kennedy to mean that religion would thenceforth matter less to the voters. But if that is true, why did a majority of Americans say, in 1987, that they would not vote for an atheist as president?[10] Some may have exaggerated their own tolerance when a majority said it would vote for a Jew, but educated people probably *under*reported their resistance to an atheist. What emerges from this and similar questions is that the electorate wants a president who observes his (or, eventually, her) religion. President Eisenhower was, as usual, close to his constituents' instinct when he said that people should practice their faith, "and I don't care what it is."

Candidates have intuited enough of these truths to put in church time during their campaigns, even the secular Michael Dukakis resuming his exiguous ties to the Greek Orthodox church. Yet his coolness in this area was in striking contrast to the easy religiosity of Ronald Reagan—a contrast that, no doubt, had something to do with their differing successes at election time. People seem to trust the person who shares their moral values. In fact, Paul Kleppner, in a sophisticated study of polling data, found religious styles more predictive of voting patterns in the Populist Era than were the normal data studied (economic, class, regional, etc.).[11] George Gallup and Jim Castelli claim that the same thing would prove true today if analysts framed the right hypotheses: "Religious affiliation remains one of the most accurate, and least appreciated, political indicators available."[12]

But most political commentators show acute discomfort when faced with the expression of religious values in the political arena. That was demonstrated when Gary Hart's adultery became an issue during the 1988 presidential campaign. It is obvious that religion influences one's view of adultery—77 percent of Protestants think "extramarital sex is always wrong," as opposed to 71 percent of Catholics and 46 percent of Jews.[13] But when there was a reaction against Hart, analysts had to "legitimate" this hostility on anything but the obvious grounds. As a *New Republic* editorialist put it: "The revelation of salacious details [was] justified on the basis of news values or competitive pressures [between networks and publications] or insight into 'character'—in short, on any remotely plausible basis except disapproval of adultery (which violates an elite social taboo against moralism)."[14] Voters are allowed to like or dislike a candidate for the way he looks, or his television skills, but not for his recognition of the dominant moral attitudes of his society.[15]

President Reagan was constantly praised as "a great communicator" without giving enough emphasis to *what* he was communicating. He *communicated* religious attitudes (despite his absences from church on Sunday); he *communicated* appreciation of the conventional family (despite his own family's messy interrelationships). He would pray at the drop of a hat—as when he prayed for a soap opera character's deliverance from the indignities imposed on her by the show's writers.[16]

The right wing regularly deplores "liberal bias" in the media, trying to count how many Democrats there are in the working press, as opposed to the percentage in the electorate at large. It could more tellingly reflect on the number of churchgoers in the national press, as opposed to the general population; or on the uneasy way journalists talk about religion, as opposed to the frequency of reference among ordinary people. Some of the glibbest persons in the nation are oddly tongue-tied when the Bible is brought up. And editors seem to prefer inarticulacy on the subject. Major papers and networks encourage reporters to acquire expertise in the law or economics, but I have not heard of any editor asking reporters to brush up their theology. Religion writers at most papers are kept in their Saturday-edition ghettos. In covering six presidential campaigns, I do not remember seeing a single religious writer on any campaign plane—not even on Pat Robertson's in 1988, and certainly not on Jesse Jackson's in 1984 or 1988. (James Wall, the editor of *The Christian Century*, was on Jimmy Carter's campaign plane in 1976, but as an aide to the candidate, not as a journalist.)

Religion embarrasses the commentators. It is offbounds. An editor of the old *Life* magazine once assigned me a book on religion with the remark that I was the only "religious nut"—his term for a believer—in his stable of regular reviewers. At an Operation Rescue rally, a journalist joined a group of other reporters with the breathless announcement that antiabortionist Randall Terry was telling bloodthirsty stories about murder and dismemberment to avenge a rape. She did not know, though Terry had named the passage (Judges 19), that he was telling a Bible story, the tale of the Levite's concubine.

One reason editors tend to shy at political coverage of religion is their fear that this will somehow breach the wall of separation between church and state. Since the Constitution mandates this division, journalists and others seem to think voters should maintain their own hermetic division between religion and politics—and if they do not do so, it is better not to know about something so shameful. Because schools are not allowed to sponsor prayers, it is somehow an enlightened act to turn the other way when candidates pray aloud (as they always do).

If religion intrudes too obviously, as in the case of Pat Robertson's campaign, this is treated as an anomaly. It is given special coverage by an outsider. "Call Martin Marty" is the editor's easiest recourse for the special case. (Where narrowly Catholic or Jewish views are at issue, the call to Marty may be alternated with calls to Richard McBrien or Arthur Hertzberg.)

The severest test to this self-restraint in the coverage of religion at campaign time was Jimmy Carter's candidacy. He was the nominee of a major party—and, in 1976, the winning contender. Yet he disconcerted many liberals by using "backward" language. It seemed vaguely Dogpatchish for him to say he was "born again"—though all baptized Christians are, in some sense, born again according to Scripture passages like John 3.3–7:

> Unless a man be born over again he cannot see the kingdom of God. . . . No one can enter the kingdom of God without being born from water and spirit. . . . You ought not to be astonished, then, when I tell you must be born over again.[17]

It is true that evangelicals put a special stress on the concept of rebirth, using it to describe the psychological experience of being saved—and that, too, was considered an oddity in Carter, though evangelicals make up the largest number of Christians in America, and 40 percent of the population called itself "born again" in response to a 1989 survey.[18]

How did such a sizable part of the population escape, for so long, the notice of journalists and political analysts? Partly this was the result of elitism. Evangelical believers are, as a whole, less educated and affluent than members of the significantly named "mainline" churches. Many people accepted *mainline* as a term indicating the predominant, if not quite the "mainstream," churches. But the word was appropriately borrowed from Philadelphia's term for the artery extending into the city's fashionable suburbs. The main*stream* of American religion has always been evangelical. George Marsden, the best student of the subject, calls evangelical Protestantism "the dominant force in American life" during the nineteenth century, when it made up the "unofficial religious establishment" of our politics.[19]

Nathan O. Hatch has traced the role experiential religion played in the democratization of America.[20] The revival has been the distinctively American religious experience (much as jazz is the most distinctive American musical form). To the extent that other religions take on an American character, they tend toward revivalism. That explains why a Quaker family like the Nixons could attend one of evangelist Paul Roder's revivals, where the young Richard was saved, making him, later in life, more clearly the disciple of Billy Graham than of George Fox.[21] The Catholic scholar Jay P. Dolan has noticed the way his church acquired revivalistic touches in the preaching of parish "missions," mounting by way of hellfire sermons (often delivered by the Passionist Fathers, a revivalistic religious order) to long lines at the confessionals replicating the files of sinners making their "decisions for Christ" at the end of a Billy Graham rally.[22]

The evangelical Billy Graham has been, over the years, the most admired man in America. He is always high on the list of people given that title on surveys, and he stays there as other leaders come and go. He has been in the top ten uninterruptedly for thirty-five years. During the decade of the 1980s, he averaged third on the list, flanked by Pope John Paul II (number two) and Jesse Jackson (number three). In fact, religious figures made up a majority of the top ten, since the two American presidents named (Ronald Reagan and Jimmy Carter) were known for their religiosity, as was the Catholic leader in Poland, Lech Wałesa.[23]

Though Billy Graham represents the broad stratum of religious experience in America—something politicians have recognized and tried to use over the years—commentators continue to neglect or dismiss the elements of that experience: revivalism, biblical literalism, millennial hope (for the Second Coming of Christ). Yet these have profoundly influenced our politics, right down to the shape given to political rallies and national conventions. When, as always happens, new millennial sects proclaim that the end of time is near, these are not seen as the latest manifestations of a central theme in our history—the apocalyptic spirit that drove American settlers to grapple with the devil's instrument in the wilderness. The religious rhetoric of the millennium was more useful to orators of the American Revolution than were maxims of the Enlightenment.[24] The millennium proved just as serviceable in the Civil War, whether to fill with apocalyptic smoke Julia Ward Howe's "Battle Hymn of the Republic" or to steer war toward a "peaceable kingdom" in Abraham Lincoln's writings. So, when the followers of Elizabeth Clare Prophet gathered in 1990 to go underground at the world's rending, they were as American as apple pie—or as violence.[25]

Yet there is a reluctance to explore the America that can produce a Mrs. Prophet as frequently as a Dr. King. I remember when, in the 1960s, journalists were trying to report on black militants. In attempts to understand the movement from the inside, works supposed to be revelatory were studied with intensity—Frantz Fanon's *Black Skin, White Masks* or *The Autobiography of Malcolm X*. With Fanon, people were willing to follow recondite musings on negritude, and with Malcolm to juggle complex African and Islamic loyalties. But it seems too much to ask journalists to read the Bible (of all things) in order to understand a Pat Robertson or Jesse Jackson—or even a Dr. King.[26] I know from experience that it is considered a little kooky for a journalist even to know what "premillennial dispensationalism" is—though that is the most important concept in modern fundamentalism. Fundamentalists are not so numerous as evangelicals, but they are a sizable part of the larger evangelical family, and have many ties to other members of that family. And no group making up a fifth of the population can safely be ignored by anyone trying to understand America.[27]

Yet people who will not learn the intricacies of evangelical eschatology were reporting, in the 1960s, on the "death of God" fad that titillated elite divinity schools. That notion actually led some to think there was a falling off from religion in the 1960s, though religious profession and observance generally held steady.[28] There has been a decline in mainline religions over the last three decades or so—but that affected the less populous denominations (e.g., Episcopalians, who make up only 2 percent of the nation, or Presbyterians, 3 percent). Evangelical churches, the big ones (like the Baptists, 20 percent of the nation), were growing.[29]

An evaporation of belief toward the top of the socioeconomic scale occurs regularly in America. Doctrine thins out there—as among Unitarians early in the nineteenth century, or theological liberals early in the twentieth. This is seen as a betrayal of belief by those lower in the scale, who often compensate with a renewal of their own fervor—as the fundamentalists did in responding to theological liberals. Part of the evangelical "resurgence" of the 1970s was a matter of new voices being heard as the elite denominations fell silent on religion, learning to speak in more secular terms.[30] The religious vote has been, increasingly, an evangelical vote, a fact that helps explain the tendency of recent presidents to proclaim themselves born again—Ford, Carter, Reagan, Bush.

In 1988, some thought that scandal among televangelists was bringing to an end this "revolt" of the so-called moral majority.[31] But the surprising power of the flag issue in George Bush's campaign came from the Pledge of Allegiance that Dukakis refused to support, though it contains the words "under God," the religious Right's rallying cry in public schools where other references to the Deity are banned. I begin my book by looking at the play of religious issues around candidates in the 1988 campaign. Even Gary Hart, the "mystery man" of that election year, can only be understood by investigating his strict religious training.

The strength of evangelicals in our modern political culture surprised many because the evangelicals were supposed to have disappeared from politics after the Scopes trial of the 1920s. Much of our recent history has been distorted because the real issues and outcome of that trial have been misunderstood, as I argue in part two.

The Scopes trial turned on biblical beginnings, the story of creation still being fought for in an age when Ronald Reagan and Marilyn Quayle defend "creationism" against Darwinian evolution. Even more heated controversies have surrounded the scenario of biblical endings—the apocalypse, or cosmic showdown, around Christ's Second Coming. The Second Coming, as one of the fundamentalists' five fundamentals of faith, is often presented as an extreme or aberrant view in our modern culture. Yet "biblical prophecies" of a climactic battle over Israel found a hearing in Ronald Reagan's White House, and best-sellers like Hal Lindsey's *The Late Great Planet Earth* instructed ordinary people in views that remained secrets hidden from the intellectuals.

Just as all believing Christians are "born again," so all orthodox believers hold that they live in the "end time." At a minimum, the Christian Scriptures say that Jesus brought the final dispensation to history. There will come no later prophet or lawgiver to establish a different relationship between God and man. The final covenant was sealed in Christ's blood. Religious history has, in that sense, nowhere to go beyond the New Testament, so far as Christians are concerned. Cardinal Newman described the orthodox view:

> But when once the Christ had come, as the Son over His own house, and with His perfect Gospel, nothing remained but to gather in His saints. No higher Priest could come, no truer doctrine. The Light and Life of men had appeared, and had suffered, and risen again; and nothing more was left to do. Earth had had its most solemn event, and seen its most august sight; and therefore it was the last time. And hence, though time intervenes between Christ's first and second coming, it is not *recognized* (as one may say) in the Gospel scheme, but is, as it were, an accident. For so it was, that up to Christ's coming in the flesh, the course of things ran straight towards that end, nearing it by every step; but now, under the Gospel, that course has (if I may so speak) altered its direction, as regards His second coming, and runs, not towards the end, but along it, and on the brink of it; and is at all times equally near that great event, which, did it

run towards, it would at once run into. Christ, then, is ever at our doors; as near eighteen hundred years ago as now, and not nearer now than then; and not nearer when He comes than now. When He says that He will come soon, "soon" is not a word of time, but of natural order. This present state of things, "the present distress" as St. Paul calls it, is ever *close upon* the next world, and resolves itself into it. As when a man is given over, he may die any moment, yet lingers; as an implement of war may any moment explode, and must at some time; as we listen for a clock to strike, and at length it surprises us; as a crumbling arch hangs, we know not how, and is not safe to pass under; so creeps on this feeble weary world, and one day, before we know where we are, it will end.[32]

All Christian theology has been permeated by this theological version of "the end to history." The Lord's Prayer is an eschatological prayer. But early Christians thought not only that they were living in the last age, but that this age would end *soon*. Much of the fear and exaltation of the earliest Christian letters centered on this expectation. Believers wrote about it in a kind of frantic code, and from that language some of the most bizarre aspects of American religion have taken their rise. It is a forbidding subject, in a secular age; yet no one can understand evangelicals' emotional temperature without addressing it. When the Quayle family's interest in a fundamentalist preacher (Colonel Robert Thieme) came into the news during the 1988 campaign, odds and ends of his preaching were printed, with no real attempt to see how they were structured, or how closely they were related to the whole fundamentalist endeavor.

I was told by some early readers of my manuscript that modern readers are not prepared to venture into the hermetic world of Christian apocalypse described in parts three and four. But I refuse to think that secularists are less intelligent than the evangelicals themselves, who seem to have no trouble grasping the concepts explained to them by Hal Lindsey, Jerry Falwell, or Colonel Thieme. What the willed ignorance about religion reflects is a refusal to see the connection between Christian doctrine and politics—though people were willing to study black-power doctrine, even of a recondite sort, in the hope of understanding black activists' relation to our politics. In fact, millennialism and black politics have been related ever since black Protestants formed their own version of the end of history in the nineteenth century—a matter I consider in part five.

The winding down of the cold war has cooled evangelical rhetoric about a final battle in the Middle East; but no part of our history has gone for long without a fresh application of the patterns of apocalypse. And the ending of a century in the year 2000 (or, as some more accurately put it, in 2001) is bound to create that feeling of history taking a corner that always stimulates apocalyptic thinking. Mrs. Prophet's followers in Montana are a first harbinger of what promises to be another apocalyptic decade, as omen-haunted as the 1890s.[33] The way to cope with biblical zealotry is not to match it with secular ignorance, producing muddle. An understanding of Christian prophecy will be more needed, not less, in the next few years, as "signs of the times" are read by everyone under the impending deadline of a millennium.

The hope of new life in a new century will almost certainly stimulate mystical aspirations of the sort now fostered by "New Age" movements. Some evangelicals see in this "false religion" itself a sign of the apocalypse. History will culminate in the forging of "one world" under a diabolic "angel of light." In any chain bookstore one can find dozens of titles in the New Age section—and, sure enough, there are to be found, now, in evangelical bookstores, three dozen or so works "exposing" the dangers of New Age religion. Even the threat of peace breaking out after the cold war tends to frighten millennialists, who denounce one-worldism, whether represented by the "godless" UN or the "apostate" World Council of Churches. A European Community containing ex-Soviet elements is the kind of "false peace" against which the religious Right is always well armed. Indeed, New Age eschatology unites a number of the fundamentalists' old villains—evolution, through the alleged influence of Teilhard de Chardin in New Age thought; the "mind control" of psychiatry and "Deweyite" education; and papal Rome, through the ecumenical work of Catholics with Eastern believers.

But the century's end may be more marked by domestic than international conflict. Already the makings of a "cultural war" are present in the religious attacks on pornography, homosexuality, abortion, and the eroticism of rock music and television. We hear again the old myth that the Roman Empire was sluiced to its ruin in a slither of lubricity. And the dying of one age is bound to encourage some cult of decadence—a development already present in 1990 studies like Camille Paglia's *Sexual Personae* and Elaine Showalter's *Sexual Anarchy*, both of which examine Oscar Wilde's fin-de-siècle dandyism.

In parts six and seven I look at the religious activism of those opposing pornography and abortion in the frame of family values and the preservation of civilization. The assault on the National Endowment for the Arts shows that this political battle did not end with the Meese Commission's attempt to control pornography. The struggle for a nation's soul is under way, with the new millennialism as a kind of deadline set for all sides.

I end the book where the riddle of American politics is first posed—with the separation of church and state. Neither Jefferson nor Madison thought that separation would lessen the impact of religion on our nation. Quite the opposite. Churches freed from the compromises of establishment would have greater moral force, they argued—and in this they proved prophets. The first nation to disestablish religion has been a marvel of religiosity, for good or ill. Religion has been at the center of our major political crises, which are always moral crises—the supporting and opposing of wars, of slavery, of corporate power, of civil rights, of sexual codes, of "the West," of American separatism and claims to empire. If we neglect the religious element in all those struggles, we cannot understand our own corporate past; we cannot even talk meaningfully to each other about things that will affect us all (and not only the "religious nuts" among us).

PART ONE

Sin and Secularity

◇ O N E ◇

New Moral Language

PREACHERS AND POLITICIANS WERE STUMBLING OVER EACH OTHER IN THE 1988 campaign. Televangelist Jim Bakker, whose support had been sought by George Bush, was caught in a sex scandal. When a second televangelist, Jimmy Swaggart, was also caught, Pat Robertson complained that this was too much: Bush's aides must have set Swaggart up, to discredit a brother of the cloth who was seeking the presidency. Gary Hart had got into the act, though he is not a preacher, when philandering drove him from the campaign. It did not seem fair. Swaggart, accepting the charges of kinky voyeurism, returned to his ministry, rebaptized in his own copious tears. Hart merely had normal sex with a willing woman, and his wife claimed she did not mind. If she did not care, said Lee Hart, why should others.

Swaggart, however, dealt with his offense in a framework of moral discourse he shared with his followers. Journalists miss the point when they keep asking, after each new church scandal, if a preacher's fall has shaken the believers' faith. Sin rather confirms than challenges a faith that proclaims human corruption. The drama of salvation is played out against the constant backdrop of original sin.

Hart lacked a comparable moral vocabulary for dealing with—what?

He would not, until late (and by way of an aside), call it sin. He treated his difficulties less as originated by himself than as created by intruders. Nor did he have a defined set of followers who could explain what he had done. He had to forge a special language for himself, in the midst of his ordeal. That was his real problem, as his experiments with different responses indicated.

At first he relied on simple denial. Nothing, he assured us, happened. Journalists had seen him enter his Washington home with a comely young blonde; but then (in his version) the two exited, almost immediately, and unobserved. He denied spending a night with her, or having sex. The vigor of the denial implied that there would have been something troubling, politically if not morally, had the charge been true.

Then, when it came out that he had spent an earlier night with the same woman on a boat that sailed from Bimini, Hart released equally detailed and exonerating information—the boat had been kept out of harbor by a closed customs office; sleeping arrangements had been sexually segregated; his continuing relation with the woman had been consultative (he needed her expertise on celebrity campaigners). The category of political or moral sin was still implicitly accepted, but—the argument went—it had been wrongly applied to innocent behavior.

When these first two lines of defense proved untenable, Hart moved to a third one. He could no longer maintain (a) that nothing happened, or (b) that something happened but it was innocent. He now took the position that if anything happened, it was not a subject the media had any right to notice. At first he claimed that journalists had not collected enough evidence; now he said they could not, by right, collect any evidence at all. The argument was still a moral one, but the onus had been shifted. Whatever Hart's conduct, the media had exceeded their moral warrant to inspect the lives of public men. There are plausible arguments in Hart's favor here. One: that the media had agreed not to "invade the privacy" of candidates before. Two: that if they had, in exceptional cases, noticed sexual misconduct, they should not have done so—from respect for a candidate's right to privacy, or from the lack of a public right to know such things, or from the social benefits of observing such a ban (irrespective of rights on either side).

Hart appealed, at various times, to each of these arguments. Other presidential candidates—and presidents, for that matter—had sexual lives not held up to public scrutiny. His family's peace had been violated. The journalists had stooped to undignified and untraditional measures. The charges did not affect his ability to serve, even were they true. The level of public debate was pulled down, discourse muddied, and "issues" obscured, all because the media had not observed the ban Hart advanced, now, as a social imperative.

These were all *moral* arguments, each with some force; but there were counterarguments as well, which left the matter unresolved. By jumping from one to another, Hart complicated his position. If, moreover, a person disagreed with just one of his arguments, the others were in danger of being discounted. The moral discourse frayed out, constantly making new evidence relevant. Was it true, for instance, that the media had refused to discuss the private lives of politicians in the past? Sexual charges had been raised against Thomas Jefferson, John Quincy Adams (of all people), Andrew Jackson, Grover Cleveland. Had this been permissible then, but reprehensible now—or reprehensible (because hypocritical) in all the cases? Such a complex position, whatever its other merits, did not *settle* the moral question, as did Swaggart's use of a preestablished pattern of repentance.

It is hard to make nuanced distinctions in the midst of a campaign. Trying to sort out moral arguments, while keeping fuzzy the facts under discussion, had debilitated Hart by the time he left the race in May of 1987. New evidence of his activities was being investigated, by *The Washington Post* among others, even as he argued that such investigations were morally impermissible. Even four months after his withdrawal, when he appeared on Ted Koppel's *Nightline* show, Hart had trouble explaining why real moral concerns in politics (like the Iran-Contra scandal) should be divorced from pseudoissues (like the people he spent his private time with).

When, in December of 1987, Hart reentered the presidential race, he decided to revert to a simpler moral language, having tested the futility of more sophisticated approaches. At the first public debate he joined, he confessed: "I probably should have said in that [*Des Moines Register*] interview that I'm a sinner. My religion tells me all of us are sinners." But this was obviously a concession with which he did not feel comfortable. By the new moral standard he was proposing (at least part of the time), it made him a hypocrite. So he did not remain consistent to it, but returned to his attack on the press, making even grander claims about the sex lives of the presidents. "I won't be the first adulterer in the White House," he told *The Des Moines Register*. He offered Ted Koppel such examples as George Washington and Thomas Jefferson, and his followers implied that a leader would not be much of a man if he lacked an active sex life. The actor Warren Beatty urged Mrs. Hart to tell reporters, "If you want a monk for president, you don't get me as first lady."[1] By a spectacular reversal of the values assumed in Hart's own first denials, marital fidelity was now presented as a disqualifying feature: Would you rather have Richard Nixon than Gary Hart?

This was edging toward an entirely new moral argument, which some of Hart's supporters thought was the only way to end hypocrisy on all sides. Hart, they felt, should have answered questions about his being an adulterer with this challenge: "Yes, I am. So what? That has nothing to do with political qualifications." That is what many people actually feel—including Hart himself. His momentary pose as a penitent was not convincing, even to himself. In this case, the truth might actually be the best defense. His base of support, insofar as he had one, was not united on a *religious* position, like Jimmy Swaggart's congregation.

But this approach, even if one agreed with its assumptions, was not likely to accomplish what Hart needed in immediate terms. It would not preclude further discussion, precisely *because* it was a new position for a candidate to be taking in public. As the first candidate of Adulterers' Lib, Hart would be expected to *discuss* his novel situation—just as the first Catholic candidate, or black candidate, or female candidate was expected to comment on the timing of his or her emergence on the public scene. The idea of a Catholic's running for president is acceptable now. No one raised that as an issue for Alexander Haig or Bruce Babbitt in 1988. But the issue was strong enough to contribute to Al Smith's defeat in 1928 and to make John Kennedy face a panel of skeptical Protestant ministers in 1960. In the same way, Geraldine Ferraro had to defend her position as a female candidate for vice-president in 1984 and Jesse Jackson as a black candidate for president in both 1984 and 1988. The newer their claim, the more time they had to spend explaining it.

That adultery should be irrelevant was a new political stand in 1988, as could be proved by the very historical examples Hart had cited. There is no evidence of adultery in George Washington's life.[2] Most scholars deny it in Jefferson's life as well—but it certainly was alleged against him in the 1804 campaign, and was considered a relevant argument against his presidency.[3] John Quincy Adams was accused unjustly of pimping for Czar Alexander I while serving as the American minister in St. Petersburg, and Andrew Jackson was accurately accused of having lived in adultery with his own wife (the adultery was inadvertent, since her divorce was not completed for the first four years of her second marriage to Jackson).[4]

The most famous sexual charge brought during a presidential campaign was of no use to Hart at all. In 1892, Grover Cleveland admitted that he might have fathered an illegitimate child. But he told the truth about this youthful indiscretion (which did not involve adultery), and a panel of leading clergymen declared that he had acted honorably in caring for a child that was only possibly his.[5] The electorate, given all the facts by a cooperative candidate, approved his actions and chose him as president.

Later cases of presidential philandering—Warren Harding's and John Kennedy's—were kept secret at the time precisely because it was acknowledged they could hurt the men's electoral chances. John Kennedy even wrote a note early in his 1960 campaign complaining that he would have to give up his "poon days" for election purposes.[6] Though he did not abide by this wry resolution, he did break off a White House affair with Judith Exner when his brother pointed out its dangers.

Gary Hart knew well the trouble a candidate's private life can cause. He managed George McGovern's 1972 campaign and later wrote a book about the vetting of Thomas Eagleton for possible scandals in his background. He overheard Frank Mankiewicz, McGovern's aide, ask Eagleton: "Now, Tom, is there anything in your background that we ought to know about, you know, like dames . . . ?"[7] Eagleton's problem was not "dames," but the suppression of his medical record, which included electric-shock treatments. But Hart saw, up close, the price Eagleton had to pay for hiding problems from his own political allies. Nonetheless, he acted just like Eagleton when supporters asked him, repeatedly before the 1988 race, if he was being sexually indiscreet. He assured them unequivocally, in many different confrontations, that stories about his "womanizing" were (at least currently) false. If Hart was disturbed by media hypocrisy, that was nothing to the reaction he caused among his own female supporters, whom he had deceived when recruiting their support.[8]

Some felt that Hart, whatever his indiscretions, deserved a measure of sympathy in a year when the media seemed to change the rules of scrutiny overnight. After Watergate and other scandals, a new suspicion of politicians, coupled with the technological resources for pursuing inquiry, had made it difficult if not impossible to maintain a dignified public posture. Cameras of the Cable News Network, if not those of network or local news, seemed to be at every caucus and little rally, picking up things like a snappish response to questions about Senator Joe Biden's law school grades.

After Judge Douglas Ginsburg had been nominated to the Supreme Court, he was forced to withdraw his name from consideration, in part because it was discovered that he had smoked marijuana as a young law professor. Since this happened during the presidential campaign, the question about substance abuse was put to the candidates (or anticipated by them). Bruce Babbitt and Albert Gore admitted they had used marijuana, though at younger ages than Ginsburg's last reported use. This was the same campaign in which it came out that the two preachers running for president, Pat Robertson and Jesse Jackson, had sex with their wives before marrying them. Does the public need to know this kind of thing?

Some even said there was a kind of "generational vendetta" taking shape, to bar from higher office those who came of age in the sixties, when relaxed social constraints led to experiment in what were called "different life styles." The raising of "the character issue" in 1988 seemed more a *cultural* issue: As Depression-era radicals were punished for leftist political associations in the 1930s, "kids" of the 1960s might see their youthful high jinks return to haunt respectable later careers.

But before we succumb to pity for politicians, we should remember that there have always been generational tests for them. After World War II, it was almost impossible for men of a certain age to win political office if they had not worn the uniform of one or another branch of the armed forces. John Kennedy was still trying to use this ban against Hubert Humphrey fifteen years after the war ended. Conversely, in the nineteenth century, men who *had* worn Confederate uniforms were excluded from federal office—especially on the federal bench—after the Civil War.

More recently, generations of Southern senators, brought up with the notion that keeping blacks in their place was not only an allowable but an admirable social goal, woke up in the 1970s to find that the rules of the game had been changed. A new generation of Southern politicians arose, less blatantly racist.

Most generational tests reflect an opening up of politics rather than a closing off of the approaches. Gary Hart was wrong when he said that George Washington's sex life would exclude him from election if he were running today. But one thing certainly would exclude him—his slaves. For the first four decades of our existence as a country, from the time of Washington through that of Andrew Jackson, holding slaves was no barrier to being elected president. But before slavery became illegal, that practice became unacceptable in a president. The political rules changed in a way no one can regret.

It is absurd to say that a new puritanism has straitened entry into politics at our highest level. In 1988, not only were two Catholics running for president (a thing unthinkable for most of our national history); so, briefly, was a woman (Representative Patricia Schroeder). So was a black. So were candidates who supported gay rights. In fact, at lower levels, gays were winning and holding office.

The president himself was, in 1988, a man who had been divorced and remarried, a handicap that Nelson Rockefeller found crippling as recently as 1964. There is more curiosity about candidates' private lives precisely *because* so many different kinds of people are now being considered for an office that used to be restricted to white male heterosexual Protestants (and those men *married*, but only once). In the "old days," voters could assume a set of stable values in the candidates, reflected in the limited social options for those seeking the presidency. We still informally limit the range of realistic choice—there has been no serious Jewish candidate for president yet, nor any gay candidate. But the field is not nearly as confined as in the past. The choice of past leaders was made within a framework of trust assured by the lack of significant differences in social convention.

That situation is changing, not because the American people are becoming less tolerant—quite the reverse. In fact, the openness to new possibilities is what has introduced confusion. Gary Hart's need to find a new moral language exemplifies the problem modern politicians face, at many levels, because of the rapidity of moral change in American society. Some changes have outraced the law, creating a gap between the society's stated norms and generally acceptable conduct. Public reaction showed a tolerance for early experiment with drugs in the cases of Gore and Babbitt, though there are still laws on the books against that activity (laws that explain the harsher attitude toward a law professor or a judge who breaks the laws). Liberal candidates like Michael Dukakis and Jesse Jackson supported gay rights, though homosexual activities are still illegal in some states.

In this flux of changing values, it is hard for a candidate to give the kind of unspoken assurances that were traditionally provided by a president. Our leaders have not normally been chosen for their brilliance, but for their stability. People want leaders whose responses are predictable, not erratic, who reflect a social consensus, who *represent* more than they *enlighten*. That explains Ronald Reagan's popular defense of "old values." He did not really take people back to the past, but he made a dizzy rush toward the future less disorienting. He did so by clinging uncritically to notions that reassured people, despite their lack of practical impact. Neither the sexual nor the drug revolution was reversed, or even held static,

by the Reagans' exhortation to "say no," but these developments were
made somehow endurable by being treated as anomalous. Reagan made
it possible to live with change while not accepting it.

Gary Hart offered "new ideas" to the public already seasick with novelty. He offered technical solutions to problems felt to be moral. He did
not have a conventional political base or a reassuringly familiar background. All this was true of him even before the evidence of erratic
private behavior and deceptive public statement was added to his burden.
It is true that new social programs must be forged for the situations that
confront Americans; but arguments for those programs must be *moral* in
order to elicit the kind of trust presidents need to be effective. Hart found
he had to articulate ethical arguments for keeping the press out of his
life. But he started from a position—including an initial profession of
conventional morality—that made it hard for him to look credible as the
castigator of an immoral journalism.

How *does* one invent a new moral discourse for handling modern
sexuality, chemical stimulation, and the relationship of one generation
to another? The long history of the Temperance movement, Prohibition,
and modern driving penalties shows how difficult the country has found
its public treatment of alcohol. New pills and drugs of all kinds just add
to this problem rather than replacing it.

Feminism, gay rights, abortion, adolescent crime, the responsibility
for the aged, all raise complex new occasions for judgment that make it
hard for any politician to find the kind of consensus that used to settle
moral questions in a comparatively early and easy way. The modern
politician cannot weep and exhort in terms as recognizable as Swaggart's.
While the pulpit is yielding to the lectern, religious creeds to secular
programs, the appetite for moral guidance has not disappeared. In many
cases, it has been sharpened. It was not moralism that did in Hart, but
morality, or the quest for it. He had not defined himself as a responsible
agent. He could not be equitably judged while he was *changing* the
norms of judgment so rapidly. The American people, as they have proved
with men as different as Jimmy Swaggart and Richard Nixon, can be
almost too ready to forgive sinners. What they find it hard to forgive is
sinlessness.

Other politicians, in moral and political trouble, go back to the core
of their supporters, to those people with a past commitment to them,
with a stake in what happens to them, with whom they share a common
language. Thus Richard Nixon could always fall back on the anti-Communist Right, or Edward Kennedy on the Boston Irish. You know a

politician is finished when even an appeal to his base is ineffective, as when Jimmy Carter was rebuffed by the South.

In the fall of Gary Hart we saw what happens to a politician under fire who never *had* a base. How can one have a base if one does not have a background? Hart resembled the character in Aristophanes who "hung his thought in mid-air, and dealt with off-the-ground matters" (*Clouds* 228–29). He not only suspended himself from some invisible hook; he kept switching hooks. He seemed to come out of nowhere, losing here a year and there a name, changing handwriting as often as hairdos, resembling Warren Beatty at one moment, John Kennedy at the next. He was a mystery man admiring mystery men. His romanticized description of George McGovern in 1972 was a self-portrait.

> Throughout the nomination race he had few to advise and fewer still to heed; like a sea captain born to his craft, he carried his most trustworthy compass and sextant in his head, trusting neither polls nor sage outdated advice, never canvassing the crew to determine which way to sail, but reading the mood of the political ocean by the roll of the deck under him.[9]

We get a remarkably similar picture of the hero in Hart's spy novel:

> Connaughton was a singular man who enjoyed the company of others but who used his privacy—his aloneness—as a bird uses the air. His aura of separateness made him seem, to those around him, strong but elusive.[10]

George McGovern was the beneficiary, in 1972, of a unique concatenation of party reform and political accident. The Democrats had suffered an upheaval that made the choice of delegates to their national convention an uncertain process. Insurgent, challenged, and unpredictable elements entered the process. Then the assassination attempt on George Wallace removed the one factor that might have given cohesion to the party: If, as seems likely, a healthy Wallace had entered the national convention with more delegates than any other candidate, a stop-Wallace movement would have formed around a more conventional figure than McGovern. As it was, the outcome of the convention depended on a tricky series of rulings on the delegate challenges supported, rejected, or betrayed by the McGovern team. Shrewd operators, above the fray, could manipulate delegates in this unprecedented and unpredictable scene.

Some, notably Jeane Kirkpatrick, have argued that the McGovern campaign became a captive of New Left special interests in 1972.[11] But Hart, as McGovern's campaign manager, says he fought successfully to keep McGovern the exploiter, not the victim, of these causes. "Each

special-interest group or caucus seemed to want to possess the campaign,"
he wrote. [12] Hart and his colleagues were ready to abandon the insurgents
who got troublesome. The best instance of that was a feminist challenge
to the disproportionately male delegation from South Carolina. The
McGovern forces might have won that challenge (as they had promised),
but only by a vote that fell within a "window" of percentages that would
affect voting rules later on.

> If we could keep the vote out of that "window," the Chair's ruling could
> not be challenged, we could raise the 1,433 votes necessary to win Cali-
> fornia, we would get our 151 delegates back, and we would win the
> nomination.

Thus:

> The stop-McGoverns would try to throw that South Carolina vote in the
> "window" [by a close vote], challenge the Chair's definition of a majority,
> carry that vote—since their 151 Californians could vote on that question—
> and replace it with a ruling that our 120 [California] delegates couldn't
> vote on the challenge. We would lose the California vote and lose the
> nomination. [13]

These words show how narrowly procedural was McGovern's victory.
When it became clear to Hart that the South Carolina challenge could
be won only narrowly enough to fall within the window, he gave orders
to delegate leaders to start shaving votes for it, so that the women would
lose by a broad enough margin to be "outside the window." The trick
was to shave the votes so gradually that it would not be obvious, alerting
the other side to complementary maneuvers that would put the vote back
"in the window." (Also, the women should not realize what was happening, and denounce McGovern for the maneuver.)

Rick Stearns, the delegate counter for McGovern, boasted of this crucial moment in the nomination: "There were perhaps 250 people on the
[convention] floor who had a good idea of what was going on. There
were another 50 or 60 who had a pretty *complete* idea of what was going
on. And then there were about 20 who *knew* what was going on." [14]
McGovern, given this merely procedural victory over his own bemused
party, lost badly in the general race; but Hart blames that loss on the
Eagleton affair. His own first experience in politics—he had never gone
to a national convention before the one he manipulated in 1972—fostered
his belief that a "gypsy-guerrilla" campaign can defeat entrenched forces
by a combination of "new ideas" and brilliant maneuvers. [15] Technological
wizardry, not large moral commitment, could win political wars at home.

As a senator, he would argue for a similar "high-tech" approach to foreign policy.

When Hart entered politics for himself—as a senator from Colorado in 1975—he did it as a comparative loner on Capitol Hill, contemptuous of the "old politics," looking for bold plans, engaging in eccentric enterprises (like the writing of spy novels), and speaking for a "new generation" (the obsession of his old partner from the McGovern campaign, pollster Patrick Caddell). Even in his novel, the hero is a noble misfit in the diplomatic corps, who finds and conspires with a similarly heroic woman among the Soviet translators. The two make arrangements for their respective peoples and governments (who are incapable of understanding what their benefactors are doing for them).

Hart's unconventional politics seemed to work, in 1984, when he unexpectedly won a string of early presidential primaries. But then, as he stepped into the glare of publicity around a presidential candidate, people began to look at the unexamined blanks in his résumé. He was asking voters to reject an outworn "old politics" and listen to a new generation. It is time, he said, to heed "our voices." *Whose* voices? Who were the *we* he spoke for? He had even presented the McGovern campaign, in his 1973 book, as the emergence of a "new generation" on the scene—though McGovern, like most candidates in the last three decades, was a World War II veteran.

The Caddell youth-vote strategy targeted "baby boomers" born after World War II, who came into the system during the sixties. But Hart was born in 1936, grew up in the fifties (in circumstances he did not want to dwell on), and took no part in the major struggles of the sixties. He had no record on civil rights before he met George McGovern in 1970. He had neither served in Vietnam (he was attending law school after his divinity-school deferment) nor demonstrated against it. The only political background he supplied for this period in *Who's Who* was some volunteer work in Kennedy campaigns—John's in 1960 and Robert's in 1968.

Hart did represent a new generation, all right—one that came out of nowhere. He was only nine years younger than Walter Mondale, yet he was trying to make that age difference a generation gap. Indeed, he tried to make the gap, not tremendous already, a little larger by pretending that there was a *ten*-year difference: He had altered his birth date for *Who's Who*.

That might have passed for inadvertent except that he had altered his name, from Hartpence to Hart—which might have passed, as well, except that he gave an explanation for the change (family pressure) that his family would not confirm. The mystery man was creating the wrong kinds of doubt about himself. If these changes had taken place so recently—like his handwriting experiments, which usually go with an adolescent's search for a personal style—what had taken place in his *real* adolescence, back in the terra incognita of the 1940s and 1950s?

When it was learned that, during this period, he had belonged to a strict religious denomination, the Church of the Nazarenes, there should have been nothing surprising about that. The ranks of our politics have regularly been filled by the sons of ministers, or by people who studied for the ministry themselves. (That was true of McGovern himself.) And smaller religious denominations have been well represented in presidential contests. George Romney was a Mormon. Ronald Reagan grew up active in the Disciples of Christ, and his 1976 choice as running mate, Richard Schweicker, was a Schwenkfelder. But these candidates never tried to hide their background. They were at ease in talking about it. They made the normal political use of their hometowns, the practiced recollections of boyhood. That is one aspect of establishing a political base.

Hart, professing an unwillingness to indulge such "old politics," deprived himself of a platform from which to explain himself. A Gatsbylike evasiveness about his past made people suspect something shameful in it. When charges of cheating in high school were made, he disdained to respond. When his religion was presented as something weird, he neither came to its defense nor discussed his present views of it. He inadvertently made himself a powerful symbol of the problem presented by a secular politics cut off from its past moral vocabulary. He was not merely inventing himself, moment by moment, but improvising an entire political morality without any help from traditional forms of ethical and religious discourse.

⟡ T W O ⟡

Holiness and Gary Hart

MOST POLITICAL REPORTERS ARE UNCOMFORTABLE WHEN DEALING WITH religion. With care they can avoid revealing outright boredom or clear bias; but ignorance is harder to conceal. Thus Gail Sheehy could write of Gary Hart's religion: "The truly singular feature of the Nazarene sect [*sect* and *cult* are properly distancing terms] is that its members believe one can, and should, achieve perfection in this life."[1] Actually, perfectionism is a recurrent Christian phenomenon, from the early ascetics to the utopian communities of the New World. It is especially prominent in Methodism and other Protestant communities, and it is absolutely central to the American religious tradition.

Christian perfectionism shows what impact a single word in the Bible can have. Twice the Gospel of St. Matthew uses the term *teleios* ("inclusive") to show how an ethic of love should go beyond mere observance of the law, or beyond love only for those who return one's love.[2] In that context Jesus says to his disciples, "You should be inclusive [in accepting others], as is your Father in heaven" (Matthew 5.48). Many translations, from the time of St. Jerome's Latin version, have rendered the word *teleios* as "perfect"—be as *perfect* as the Father—setting Christians the impossible task of a Godlike perfection.

The word by itself would not have encouraged such a lofty ambition if the broad Christian theology of redemption did not favor it. This theology says that Jesus, "the second Adam," undid with a redemptive act the ravages inflicted by the first Adam's "original" sin. Some Christians have, persistently, taken that to mean that the redeemed can live like Adam before his fall—as if they came fresh from their Maker's hands, with no flaws. Thus the "Adamites" of the fifteenth century, like the earlier Brethren of the Free Spirit, considered themselves entirely "sinless."[3]

The Protestant view that unmediated grace floods the soul at conversion led to high expectations about the later conduct of "visible saints." John Wesley, the founder of Methodism, wrote a book on what he called "entire sanctification." Against this background, a wave of revivals in nineteenth-century America formed a Holiness Movement, since it meant to produce *manifestly* holy lives. One Anglo-American form of this movement was called Keswick spirituality, from the name of the English town where its founding conference occurred in 1875. Keswick spirituality became—through many channels, including the widely used Scofield Bible of 1909—the fundamentalist norm in America.[4]

How far one could go in aspiring to perfection was a matter of mutual challenge for developers of Holiness theology. Adventurous types split off from Methodist and other perfectionist churches, launching themselves on even stricter programs. One of the most visible of these was the Salvation Army, begun in England but extended around the world, and taken up with great enthusiasm in America. William Booth, the founder of the Salvation Army, had his moment of epiphany in an urban slum. Outside London's Blind Beggar Tavern in 1865, he began to call sinners away from their drink-ruined lives.[5] The saintly would win over the fallen by proving their immunity to sin even on the hellish new ground offered by the Industrial Revolution.

In the fourth century, Christian heroes went into the wilderness to confront demons, in ascetical contests that achieved detachment from the flesh. In the nineteenth century, ascetics would go into the demonic filth and din of the poor urban areas, carrying the joy of salvation, playing on cymbals and drums, celebrating in the midst of despair. They waged *war* on drink as the fourth century had warred on pagan celebrations.[6] The military discipline General Booth added to this movement was like the bow-tied decorum Black Muslims exact from themselves as they wage a religious crusade against drugs and other scourges of late-twentieth-century slums. In such circumstances, paradoxically, "entire sanctification" often seems to be the only practical form of improvement. What David Harrell has written of America's Pentecostal churches was true of the earlier Holiness Movement:

> The moral and ethical problems which the church struggled with, and which often divided the pentecostal subculture, were real issues in the world of tenant farms and mill town slums. The church's moral code was a strenuous guidebook for lifting oneself from squalor. Sanctification meant that "all our members are required to be patterns of frugality, diligence, faith and charity, taking up the cross daily, and true to the abiding baptism of the Holy Ghost." If some of the regulations of the church seemed stringent, they were demanded by the ferocity of the battle. Pentecostalism was bred in a society in which moral lapses and sexual promiscuity constantly threatened to undermine the family; Steinbeck's Jim Casey was a figure well known to pentecostals. Most pentecostals knew the pleasures of sin as well as the ecstasy of salvation, and they knew the Devil must be tightly bound.[7]

In nineteenth-century America, the discipline of the frontier could fade directly into urban problems, as in early Los Angeles, that desert crossroad of several worlds, where a Holiness preacher named Phineas Bresee launched the Church of the Nazarenes. Bresee was a "Come-Outer," one of those who called for people to leave the everyday churches—even the supposedly perfectionist Methodist church in which he had been a precocious young leader—and achieve entire sanctification by living on perpetual "mission" to the poor. From Bresee's first salvation meeting, held in Red Men's Hall in October 1906, the Nazarene movement spread quickly, first up the West Coast, then back toward Methodism's ancient base in the Mississippi Valley. In 1907, it merged with a similar mission that was spreading from New England urban centers, the Association of Pentecostal Churches. The Pentecostal Nazarenes, after their union effected in Chicago, were a national force. A year later, they incorporated a rural movement from the Southwest, the Holiness Church of Christ, joining old-South and rural congregations with urban and Northern ones in a momentous meeting at Pilot Point, Texas.[8] The Come-Outers were coming together. In 1915, eight Scottish churches joined the Nazarenes to make the movement international—it is now very active in Africa.[9] Bible schools were formed to train Nazarenes for missions, foreign and domestic. But the church aimed at permanent improvement in the believers' living conditions as well. Unlike some narrower enthusiasts, the Nazarenes endeavored against great odds to establish liberal arts colleges.[10] They would train laymen to deal with

sophisticated worldlings, as General Booth's army faced the harsh world
of the slums.

A good example of this educating force in Nazarene holiness was the
career of Sylvester T. Ludwig (1903–1964). He was born to two ministers
who had helped create the Nazarene community. His father had been a
leading Methodist preacher until Bresee ordained him in the Nazarenes.
His mother was equally famous among the Free Methodist preachers.
When they joined their ministries, they became a single entity, "Theodore and Minnie." "That was their name," says church historian Charles
Edwin Jones, "you never said one without the other."

Most Americans are acquainted only with the tawdrier side of husband-
wife preaching teams—the parents seen through a captive child's eyes at
the beginning of Dreiser's *An American Tragedy*, or the hedonist pair,
Jim and Tammy Bakker. Yet nothing could be farther from the energy
and imagination of Theodore-and-Minnie than the puffy self-indulgence
of Tammy Faye or the worldly pout and self-pity of Jim Bakker. Evangelism is of its nature individualistic, and it tends to isolate "star" preachers
unless they can form a family base for their ministry. This makes not
only for a more inclusive message, but for continuity when the children
of the marriage take up their parents' work. That is what happened with
Sylvester T. Ludwig, the only son of Theodore-and-Minnie.

S. T. Ludwig was marked out, from his birth in 1903, for service to
the Nazarenes. He took college degrees both from a Christian college,
Olivet, and from secular Northwestern University. He studied for his
doctorate at the University of Kansas, but his gift for administration led
the Nazarenes to press offices on him before he could become a scholar.
He went from principal of Bresee Academy in 1926 (when he was twenty-
three) to president of Bresee College in 1927. In 1936, by a two-thirds
vote of the quadrennial general convention, he was made general secretary
to the international church. In 1942–44 he was president of the church's
main liberal arts college, then called Bethany-Peniel, before resuming
the general secretary's office for the rest of his life.[11]

S. T. Ludwig had two daughters who showed some of the initiative of
their grandmother, the famous Minnie. Nazarenes, like other Holiness
groups (including the Salvation Army), expected leadership of women
long before that was the norm in our society. The egalitarian concept of
perfection for everybody crossed boundaries of gender as well as class in
the formation of their clergy. The daughters of S. T. did not become
preachers, but leadership was expected of them. One, Martha Ludwig
Keys, became a two-term congresswoman from Kansas. The other, Ole-

tha, went to the leading Nazarene college, Bethany, where her father had been president, and became the winner of the school's outstanding student award in her first year. Actually, she was a co-winner. The school paper, *The Reveille Echo*, said on its front page for September 29, 1955: "All-round freshman awards were presented to Oletha Ludwig and Gary Hartpence at the all-school banquet." For the next three years, these classmates would be the unofficial prince and princess of the campus, often in the papers and the yearbooks, leaders of social and academic events. In their senior year, full-page studio portraits of the two faced each other in the part of the yearbook devoted to those who were listed in the *National Students Who's Who* (a distinction the two had shared for three years). The couple's engagement, in their junior year, became the talk not only of the campus but of the whole Nazarene community. In the fall of their senior year, the faculty, students, and a caravan of neighboring Nazarenes convened after dinner to see a mock celebration of the forthcoming event. Under the picture of the "wedding party" in the school paper (for November 8, 1957), one reads:

> To the consternation of the weeping Mrs. Ludwig (Lorrence Owens), her daughter (Betty Jo Blystone) was given in "alimony" by a spry Dr. Ludwig, portrayed by Bob Snodgrass. The "bride" and "groom" [played by friends] rushed from the "altar" only to encounter great difficulty when the groom's feet became entangled in the bride's train. (The ensuing tumble brought an end to the farce.)

The joke was all the richer because the prospective groom (conventionally portrayed in the skit as "reluctant") was such an intensely serious young man. The same school paper that reported this farce was the vehicle for monthly communiqués from Hartpence in his office as president of the student council. These columns tended to scold fellow students for frivolousness. Preparing them to vote for his successor, he told readers on May 2, 1958, not to be swayed by personality, but to look for self-sacrifice and prayerfulness in candidates:

> First of all, this being a Christian college, we should elect those who will benefit our school spiritually. Here words about religious matters never substitute for attendance at early prayer meetings. After all, candidates for office are always not what they are built up to be.

Though he would come to resent "the character issue" in 1984 and 1988, it was something he understood in his early twenties, during his first period of leadership. One of the themes Hartpence stressed in his newspaper sermonettes was the duty of using one's God-given intellectual talents. On February 28, 1958, he wrote that his fellow students should

> sacrifice a few personal pleasures to attain the level of knowledge which God expects and of which they are capable. Those who hold to the idea that God's call upon their life excludes them from the necessity of maximum output in life and learning are not facing scriptural truth.

The idea of Christian education seems to have made Hart, the Holiness Protestant, surprisingly sympathetic to the founder of the Jesuit order, Ignatius of Loyola. In a five-thousand-word term paper on the Jesuits, he described the conversion of St. Ignatius, and added:

> He realized that his life must be given in service to mankind and the church rather than spent in solitude. In addition to this he realized that to be an efficient instrument he must acquire a better education.[12]

In this essay we gét a first glimpse of the ideal of enigmatic leadership that appears in Hart's book on McGovern and in his spy novel. "He [Ignatius] possessed some mysterious force which drew men to him and to his goals and purposes." The ideal followers of Ignatius also bear a resemblance to the McGovernites who were to answer orders without question at the 1972 Democratic convention: "The Society [of Jesus] had inherited the motivation of soldiers who fill in ranks of fallen men in the front line unquestioningly and seemingly automatically." In the Philosophy Club that was Hart's major interest during his four years at Bethany, he was known as "Plato Hartpence," and Charles Edwin Jones, who was at Bethany during those years, now says: "Gary never wanted to be president. He wanted to be Philosopher King."[13]

The Philosophy Club had some outstanding students, led by a Nazarene teacher, J. Prescott Johnson, who was trying to shake the complacency of others while questioning dogma himself. He argued that Christians could take part in—in fact, could take credit for—much of the "existentialism" that preoccupied professional philosophers in the 1950s. The postwar malaise of Europe—the memory of collaborating regimes, of the Holocaust, of colonial powers being restored—had led to a revolt against the optimistic rationalism of modern technocracies. According to Johnson, the subjective experiences of nausea, absurdity, and irrationally free acts had for their surprising prophet the nineteenth-century Danish theologian Søren Kierkegaard, who had radically reconceived man's fallen state as one of "dread," and the theology of grace as a gratuitous "leap of faith."

On a campus that resisted worldly fashions, Johnson, the faculty "liberal," could claim that Kierkegaard was more Protestant than the Calvinist church of Denmark he tried to reform—a perfectionist in his own way, an ascetic of risk and spiritual adventure. This line of argument may not have convinced his faculty peers (who later drove him off the campus), but it exhilarated his students, especially Gary Hart.

Hart attended Johnson's philosophy classes, seminars, and evening meetings of the Philosophy Club (of which he became president). When Johnson went to teach courses at the University of Oklahoma, Hart commuted to that campus and took the courses. There is a picture of Professor Johnson's famous Kierkegaard seminar in the Bethany yearbook, with Hart at the end of the table. Charles Edwin Jones says, "We were all expected to be little Søren Kierkegaards." Professor Johnson attracted the best, or at least the most questioning, students. Several members of his Philosophy Club went on to be scholars or pastors. Two from Hart's time have committed suicide. Few of "Dr. Johnson's boys" remained Nazarenes.

When Hart went to the Yale Divinity School after graduating from Bethany, it was with a desire to become a Christian scholar, like Prescott Johnson. He was accompanied by his roommate, Charles Harper, a childhood friend of Oletha Ludwig's who is now a Congregationalist pastor in Boston. Later, another Bethany friend joined them—Tom Boyd, now a Presbyterian pastor in Iowa. The Bethany graduates had all married fellow Nazarenes (as was the pattern at Bethany), but they were intellectually restless young people. The barriers that Holiness doctrine reared against the world stood in the way of their sampling the cultural explosion of the 1960s. These questing Nazarenes risked such "existential" acts, for them, as going to the movies. Charles Harper now says, "In the context of the time, this was a major deviation"—especially for the daughter of S. T. Ludwig. Charles Edwin Jones told me: "The Nazarene church is like a Catholic religious order, and the prohibitions are like an order's vows." The prohibitions set the "perfect" apart, not only from the world, but from ordinary Christians.

The Hartpences no longer wanted to be set so far apart. When Charles Edwin Jones, on a visit to New Haven, asked for them at their rooming house, a foreign student told him there were no such people there as Oletha and Gary Hartpence. Oletha had become Lee, and Hartpence

had become Hart. Gary was exploring the religious side of literature—
he wanted to be a writer. And, for the first time, he became interested
in politics—he wanted to be a lawyer. He entered the world during the
world-upsetting sixties.

Kierkegaard, according to W. H. Auden, believed that one cannot go
from intense Christianity back to mere worldliness:

> No one, believer or not, who has once been exposed to Christianity can
> return to either the aesthetic or the ethical religion as if nothing had
> happened. Return he will, if he lose his Christian faith, for he cannot
> exist without some faith, but he will no longer be a naive believer, but a
> *rusé* one compelled to excess by the need to hide from himself the fact
> that he does not really believe in the idols he sets up.[14]

Kierkegaard, a reluctant celibate, was fascinated by the figure of Don
Juan, especially by Mozart's version of the myth, *Don Giovanni*. He
considered Mozart's opera a *Christian* vision of sensuality—not merely
the natural pagan sensuality, diffused through life and at home there.
Christianity, by declaring war on sensuality, drove it into a pure and
compacted form, a distillation of its essence as deprived of spirit. Don
Giovanni is an Antichrist—Kierkegaard makes him thirty-three at the
time of his death (the age at which Kierkegaard himself expected to die).
Christ is incarnate spirit; Don Giovanni is not merely flesh incarnate
(which is a tautology), but an incarnation of the "*spirit* of the flesh,"
demonic though amoral.[15]

In the stages of erotic immediacy Kierkegaard traces in Mozart, Cher-
ubino yearns out toward a future love, and Papageno settles for a gratification that has antecedents and consequences; but Don Giovanni lives
in the actual moment of seizure, never looking back or forward, fulfilled
only in the constant repetition of the same mastery of others. He is
"unfinished" because inexhaustible, always starting over again. He is "an
individual who is continually being formed but is never finished."[16] His
staff cannot fathom him, just (like the puzzled Leporello) keep on count-
ing.[17] The objects of his mastery are ciphers in this sequence: "Mozart
has purposely kept Zerlina as insignificant as possible."[18] Donna Rice is
the Zerlina of our story. Zerlinas become interesting only when Don
Giovanni is finished with them. Then they become a threat because they
"have a consciousness that Don Giovanni lacks"—the apprehension of
consequences, the ability to look forward and back. Don Giovanni lives
in no such arc of rising or declining expectation. His encounters with
women are like those of a pebble skipping over water—the pebble has

no thought of stopping, and when it does it sinks.[19] For Kierkegaard, the water is Christian dread—it actually sustains the joy of sensuality by repulsion, speeding the pebble on its way, for a while. I asked Prescott Johnson if Kierkegaard's parable did not seem to suggest aspects of Gary Hart's post-Christian life. "Yes, I know," he said.

John Updike, a student of Christian hedonism, has long been fascinated by Kierkegaard. He quotes a classmate of the young Kierkegaard who said his father's "home was wrapped in a mysterious half-darkness of severity and oddity." Kierkegaard himself said: "As a child I was strictly and austerely brought up in Christianity; humanly speaking, crazily brought up."[20] Gary Hart's mother was well liked and active in her earlier days, teaching Sunday school; but she ended her life an invalid, immobilized with her Bible. His father moved the family through fifteen homes, rehabilitating them for a local real estate man. This involved three changes of schools for the young Gary. Itinerancy is in the spirit of Methodism, but itinerancy as mission, not as flight. Once anyone felt the *enabling* sacrifices of asceticism as *crippling*, they would repel. Already at Bethany, according to Professor Johnson, Hart thought the Nazarene scheme of life an imprisoning one.

As the 1960s began, Hart told his Bethany classmate Tom Boyd, "My life is slipping away from me." He was twenty-three, and he still had the young years to live that he had lost among the Nazarenes. The Kennedys, looking younger than they were, offered an image of fun-loving service. The celebrants of sixties energy warned against trusting anyone over thirty. After consistently putting his proper year of birth (1936) on school forms and other documents up to the point when he had turned thirty (1967), he just as regularly put the wrong date (1937) on every form and statement afterward. Don Giovanni lives in a present of his own constant recreation.

Kierkegaard, living with the guilt of his religious parent (the father in his case), said he felt bound, "like a bird whose wings have been clipped, yet retaining the power of my mind undiminished, and its undoubtedly exceptional powers."[21] He was manipulative of others, yet he was always manufacturing crises with them—with his fiancée, the newspapers, the bishops, his church. He could not work within the church system he hoped to reform. He expected to be martyred, and criticized those—even Luther—who did not push their defiance of the world far enough to be destroyed by it.[22] He was, as Updike puts it, afraid of succeeding.

Friend after friend of Gary Hart has said to me, in surprisingly similar words, "He must not really have wanted to be president." His manipulative skills, honed in the McGovern campaign but always there, were not used to calculate for his own safety. Instead, he needed risk, the perpetual remaking of himself in action, the rush and refusal to explain, the ideas thrown out as a proof of mastery, the affectless expertise; the anger at not being accepted, yet the expectation that he would not be.

In December of 1989, Howard Oliver, a Nazarene who has remained the Harts' friend, remembered a conversation that had taken place just the day before in the Harts' home: "We were noticing how much better Gary took his treatment in the campaign than Kitty Dukakis had. Lee said she had mentioned this to Gary, and he told her, 'But remember: We never wanted to be president.' " Any attempt to understand Gary Hart has to begin with the religion he tried to hide and reporters consistently misunderstood. Other politicians have all his ambition, but not the simultaneous renunciation. Some people defended Hart by saying no one is perfect; but much of Hart's past kept asking him to be.

Hart represents one aspect of modern America, the combination of a pietistic youth with a technological maturity, and an unacknowledged fissure between the two. No one yearned more to be worldly yet to keep himself above the run of common politicians. Would-be rake and moralist, spy and philosopher king, Hart was closer to the pulse of American history than he was willing to let on—and that is why we did not let him in.

❖ T H R E E ❖

Fatal Composure

People somehow fend off righteousness.
EURIPIDES, *Hippolytus* 93

INSTRUCTED TO HUMANIZE HIMSELF IN THE 1988 RACE FOR PRESIDENT, Governor Michael Dukakis went before audiences in Iowa with the repeated deadpan announcement that he had been chosen one of America's ten sexiest men by *Playgirl* magazine. This claim, which would have made an audience uneasy if Gary Hart advanced it, provoked laughter when it came from the buttoned-up Dukakis.

According to the crowd's response and his own mood, Dukakis tried, at times, to tease more laughs out of the story. His wife, he would add, did not think this listing very funny—and people in the crowd thought *that* was funny. If people were still with him, he would add that he felt complimented by this distinction until someone—in some tellings it was an aide, in others his daughter—deflated him by saying, "Y'know, they chose *George Bush* for that two years ago." On a good day this would get the best response of all. George Bush was still, in September of 1987, the "wimp" in Reagan's shadow, with no separate identity. For the next ten months George Bush would continue to look weak, trailing Dukakis by as much as seventeen points in the polls. Eventually, Roger Ailes and others provided Bush with an identity. But no one ever did make Dukakis sexy.

Some politicians are plagued with rumors that they have sex with women other than their wives. Dukakis would rejoice if others concede that he had sex *with* his wife. He went out of his way to bring the subject up. Early in the Iowa campaign, when I flew back to Boston with him, there was only one other journalist on the plane. Dukakis told us a rambling story about a time when protesters came to demonstrate at his home in Brookline. The funny thing, he kept suggesting by periphrasis, was that he was making love to his wife while these politically ardent people called out to him under his window.

When the governor and Kitty, separated for individual campaigning, met in Chicago to walk in the St. Patrick's Day parade, Dukakis told her amorously: "Tonight, if I'm asleep, wake me up. Don't let a moment go by." She answered, mordantly, "Your microphone's on." But she would revive the story even as she grimaced at it. Later, at her house, I said that I had seen her in that parade, and she remarked, "Oh, yes, that was the day Michael told me to wake him up if he was asleep. My daughter told me she was *so* embarrassed."

The humanization of Michael had to begin at the most basic level. Yes, he was interested in people—though not in stories about them. No gossip around him. No books about people. "I have never seen my husband read a novel," Kitty said, "unless you count Nick Gage's *Eleni* as a novel." (*Eleni* is a story, based on fact, about a Greek-American who goes back to the old country on a family mission of revenge.) Dukakis would rather read a statistical report than a biography. The book that influenced him most, Henry Steele Commager's *The American Mind*, is a historical report shaped as a program for action.

As a Massachusetts politician who does not swear, smoke, or drink, Dukakis seemed too good to be true. His handlers searched for flaws the way other teams seek out virtues in their candidate. Concupiscence for his own wife may not be much of a concession to the flesh, but there was little other warmth to put on display. The campaign seized on one other weakness, or what could be painted as a vice: Nick Mitropoulos, Dukakis's engaging early scheduler, told every comer worn old stories about the candidate's worn old clothes. Almost with relief, he said it: "The man is *cheap.*" Dukakis rides the subway—not to rub elbows with the people, but to save a dollar. This trait had the force of myth by the time of the Democratic convention in Atlanta, where his ancient snowblower became an icon in the film introducing Dukakis's acceptance speech.

Why this rather desperate search for imperfections in a man with no overwhelming personal claims to greatness? The managers of Dukakis's campaign knew—they had learned it from people's reactions—that there is something infuriating about claims of perfect rectitude. In a state where politics is sometimes a bad word, Dukakis's passion for clean government had worked for him at the outset. Yet he risked becoming so antiseptic that healthy growth as well as fungus would be blighted in his presence.

In his first term as governor (1974–78), Dukakis took every occasion to contrast his meritocratic approach to governing with the pattern of deals and favors he meant to replace. His attitude was that of Euripides' tragic hero: "I can handle uncorruptible friends, those too delicate to put others up to wrong, or to respond in kind when wrongs are done to them" (*Hippolytus* 997–99). In fact, Dukakis proved to be too pure even for his own band of friends and allies, who had helped him carry a reform movement to victory. He took a priggish glee in denying supporters even legitimate roles in government. Hassell (Hackie) Kassler, a friend who started out in politics with Dukakis, was denied a judgeship for which he was qualified; Dukakis meant to prove he would lean over backward rather than do even expectable favors. F. X. (Fran) Healey, who deserted another candidate to help Dukakis in an earlier campaign, was told to forfeit either a government contract or Dukakis's friendship. After some bitter experience of the latter, Healey took the former while he could.

Dukakis is perhaps too ready to impress on others his skill, independence, and probity—traits he came by so naturally that he treats them as unquestionable. He grew up in proud Brookline, which dates its village history from the Revolution, and which has resisted Boston's efforts to engulf it for more than a century. It is a place of aspiring professionals from all ethnic backgrounds. It welcomed Michael's parents, Panos and Euterpe Dukakis, who came to America from Greece knowing no English and having no money. Panos learned English rapidly enough to proceed through Harvard Medical School toward a successful obstetrician's practice. He died leaving million-dollar trusts to his wife and his son.

Euterpe Boukis Dukakis, after arriving in Haverhill, Massachusetts, at the age of nine, sped through high school with honors, became one of the first Greek women to leave home for college, perfected the accentless English her son imitates, and became a high school teacher of Latin and French.

Theirs was a loving but demanding home. The children, Michael and his older brother Stelian, were expected to achieve at least as much as their parents had. When Stelian mysteriously failed, attempted suicide in college, and lived his short life in and out of care for his mental health, this was treated as a family disgrace. The suicide attempt was not discussed, and Michael managed to suppress all memory of it.

Michael prospered under the challenges that proved too much for Stelian. His mother remembers his first words as *monos mou*, Greek for "all by myself." In the competitive Brookline schools, he was a good student, athlete, musician, and class politician. He rejected the obvious school—Harvard, just across the river from Brookline—to attend meritocratic Swarthmore College. He excelled there, not with the brilliance that picks things up easily, cramming at the last minute, but by maintaining a predetermined schedule of study. He boasts that he never stayed up all night in order to study—or for anything else. He did not yield to diversions or passing impulse. In the same way, he ran his one Boston Marathon, underage, and portioned his resources out in a steady pace that put him in the top third of the runners.

After service in Korea and politically active years at Harvard Law School, Dukakis rose through the political ranks as part of a reform group anchored in Brookline, making his name in the legislature with a typically unglamorous change in the accident-insurance laws. He was not an ideologue during the marching and protesting sixties, and he steered clear of the busing controversy that divided Boston in the 1970s. He saw politics as a managerial art, not a conflict of emotional causes or committed personalities.

When, as governor, Dukakis emphasized fiscal probity and cut all government programs, including those for the poor, he lost many of his liberal supporters, those who had backed reform but had other goals in mind as well. Dukakis expected to win them back by the expertise he demonstrated in the remainder of his first term: he felt little challenge when a clownish ex–football player ran against him. Dukakis did not think anyone could seriously prefer Ed King to the demonstrably competent incumbent, so he campaigned mainly by governing in an exemplary fashion. When this led to his rejection at the polls, he was not only surprised for himself, but disappointed in the voters.

He took the loss hard. It upset his assumptions about the meaning of public service. It was clear that the populace, even when given a government worthy of it, was not capable of recognizing what really matters. If people can go from a Dukakis to a King, is there any reason to want the people's esteem? They are clearly not qualified to judge excellence.

Dukakis had an ancient Greek sense of excellence (*aretē*) precisely because he did not grow up with the gritty reality of actual Greek boys playing around him. His mother told him ancient Greek myths as his bedtime stories. He was shocked when, as an adult, he finally visited Greece and found it a dirty unclassical place. His was a Greek history of imagined achievement. He once dismissed the story of a Greek gangster with the impatient denial, "A Greek would not do that." The classical ideal was not intermediated, for him, by the florid Byzantine liturgy of the Greek Orthodox church, which has been the principal organizational support for most Greek immigrants to America. Panos and Euterpe quickly succeeded themselves out of the community that relied on that adhesive force. Michael married outside the church, did not baptize his children in it, and was technically "excommunicated" when he ran for governor and president, though few Greeks wanted to remember that fact in the access of ethnic pride they felt over Dukakis's success. As Charles Moskos, the Greek-American historian, puts it, "Greeks were hoping Michael would erase the shame they felt over the fall of Spiro Agnew, the first Greek to rise so high in political life." As for Michael's separation from the church, Moskos notes realistically that all the most successful Greeks in politics had married outside the faith—not only Agnew and Dukakis, but Paul Sarbanes, Paul Tsongas, and John Brademas. Agnew, in fact, was an Episcopalian named Ted until national politics made it expedient to resume his Greek first name. John Brademas is a Methodist. Dukakis, who grew up in Brookline and entered politics in a circle largely Jewish, married a Jewish divorcée who also did not discover her own heritage until it became politically useful to her husband. Their children were raised observing the Orthodox Easter and Yom Kippur as cultural dates on the calendar, but Kitty said in 1987, "None of us is very religious."

For Dukakis, being Greek was a matter of family pride and internalized goals. Panos Dukakis was an Anatolian Greek (from the region of Troy), and *his* father was from Lesbos, the island of antiquity's greatest lyric poets, Alcaeus and Sappho. Michael grew up speaking Greek with his grandmother, who lived with his parents. The brothers of Panos would gather at this successful doctor's home for family reunions. Stelian and Michael had a code language they could turn to when they did not want other boys to understand them. In these circumstances, at least, there was not only *monos mou* but *oi thyo mas* ("we two"). Dukakis used Greek with his aide Nick Mitropoulos when he did not want journalists to understand him during the 1988 campaign. Greek was a secret language for the initiates around him.

Panos Dukakis met Euterpe in America because of Euripides' play *Hippolytus*, in which Panos was playing the lead during a college production. When Jules Dassin made a movie adaptation of *Hippolytus* (*Phaedra*, starring Melina Mercouri), Panos and Euterpe went to see it as a way of remembering their first meeting. Euripides' *Hippolytus* is the classic story of a man too good for his own good. (Panos, who played the role, is short for Panayotes, "all holiness.") As someone who "keeps higher company than his fellow men" (19), the hero is ill equipped to deal with those whose standards are lower than his own. As he says: "I have no crowd-pleasing tricks, but make sense only to the few who are my peers—just as, conversely, men not esteemed by the wise can make music before crowds" (986–89).

This hero is crippled by a moral paradox—his intemperate temperance, an unmoderated moderation. The word that describes his virtue, *sōphrosynē*, means, etymologically, "sound-mindedness"—and how can one's mind be *too* sound?[1] But as the play's earthy nurse (who might have strayed out of *Romeo and Juliet*) says, "The consistent life trips up instead of comforting. . . . Not every warp in your house can be trued back into line" (261, 468–69).

Hippolytus' appetite for asceticism takes the form of a fanatical devotion to the virgin goddess Artemis. He prefers mystical communings with her during the hunt to intercourse with his fellows. Aristotle said the unsociable human is something below or above humanity—and Hippolytus is drawn away in both directions.[2] When his life is in danger, he calls out to his horses, not the goddess, for help (1240–41).

The paradox in Dukakis's case is made more striking when we notice that Aristotle describes the unsociable being as *apolitical* (outside the *polis*). Politics is the one thing that has interested Dukakis all his adult life. But it is a rather desiccated ideal of politics, without the glow of personal exchange that attracts heartier types to this calling. Politics for Dukakis is programs, not people; reform, not the normal; administration, not human satisfaction. That explains the quiet contempt he felt for ordinary Boston pols, and the careful distance he kept from the Kennedy machine in Massachusetts. (When John Kennedy was killed, Dukakis wrote in his weekly column for the Brookline *Citizen* that the only useful tribute Massachusetts citizens could pay the dead president was to pass the reforms Dukakis was sponsoring in the state legislature.)

Dukakis's pinched ideal of politics is like Hippolytus' narrow ideal of self-containment, which makes of *sōphrosynē* mere "fastidiousness," on which he prides himself: "There is no man living, say what you will, more fastidious than I" (994–95).[3] When Hippolytus is struck down by Aphrodite, the goddess of passion, he learns that his "fastidiousness offended her" (1402). His words might be those of Dukakis when he looked around at other politicians: "Look at this, Zeus! Here am I, righteous toward the righteous gods, none more fastidious in the world, and I go to my recognized destruction, my life in utter ruin, all my righteous acts toward other human beings futile" (1363–69).

Kitty Dukakis called the 1978 loss "a public death," and her son said it disoriented his father in a way he had not seen before. But Dukakis quickly took charge of his own life again, and his campaign managers would later use the experience to humanize their candidate. He cited his defeat to show he did not think himself infallible. He and his mother even quoted Aeschylus about wisdom coming through suffering. It later became a commonplace that "Dukakis II" emerged a different man from his defeat. In the concentration on this redeeming loss, few remembered that he had lost political races before (in 1960, 1966, and 1970, as well as in 1978). He had left office before, giving up his legislative seat for an unsuccessful run at the lieutenant governor's spot. This was not the first or only setback in his career, and his response to it was not as wrenching as some have made it. When he lost the lieutenant governor's race in 1970, he went back to a law practice with emphasis on public works. After losing the governor's seat, he went to Harvard's Kennedy School of Government to set up a program on local government administration. He was still a programs-and-reform man, though with a broader recognition of the usefulness of compromise.

Dukakis gave little evidence of soul-searching. He did not reforge his own basic values. His own exaggeration of the change he underwent just left him open to unscrupulous allegations by the Bush camp that he had psychiatric help in this period. In fact, he did not seek counsel, religious or personal. He changed his timetable for enacting programs. As Congressman Barney Frank, a longtime friend-foe, put it, "His personality has not changed so much as his public posture. He is very intelligent, and I think he just sat down and said, 'These behaviors are not appropriate, and therefore I will behave in this way.' I think he said the words, though you may not get the music. It was an intellectual decision to behave differently."

His principal new form of behavior was hiring a young lieutenant, John Sasso, to make political deals of the sort forbidden to friends in Dukakis's first term. With Sasso's more conventional style of favor-dealing and infighting, Dukakis won back the governor's post from a scandal-ridden King administration, and became successful enough in his second term to be rated by his fellow governors the most effective state executive in the nation. A rising economy for his high-tech state let Dukakis turn "the Massachusetts miracle" into his platform for the presidency.

But Dukakis did not so much lose his rectitude as give Sasso an exemption from it. Dukakis did not want to know everything Sasso was up to, as he did not want to know exactly how much Kitty Dukakis smoked, spent, swore, drank, or took pills. Kitty had been his one indulgence. Sasso made it two. The Dukakis reluctance to know exactly what Sasso was doing on his behalf led to the first great stumble in the 1988 campaign, just as Dukakis was making an impact with his smooth money-raising for the long haul. Sasso sent newspapers the tape of a rival candidate's unacknowledged use of a British politician's rhetoric. Dukakis claimed his campaign had nothing to do with "the Biden tape," but in vague terms, the product of his long habit of refusing to press Sasso for possibly embarrassing details. Vague as Dukakis was in his denials, Sasso could not let him misrepresent the situation in a way that would be revealed shortly. Sasso offered to resign, and even then Dukakis tried to retain him. Outrage inside the campaign as well as out made Dukakis reluctantly accept Sasso's resignation. He reversed himself again when he called Sasso back later in the campaign. His dependence on Sasso was made clear by the campaign's lack of imagination during his absence.

Dukakis's need for a Sasso, for some escape hatch from his own self-containment, is like Hippolytus' involvement, against his nature, with Phaedra, the stepmother who falls in love with him. Hippolytus rejects her, but with a violence and rash oath that involve him in her death, so that the Chorus sings that he must "learn to maintain his fastidiousness, in the future, coupled with her contamination" (739–40). And even Hippolytus comes to admire Phaedra's suicidal attempt to rescue her reputation: "She was fastidious in death who could not be so in life" (1034).

Not that Dukakis is capable of the tragic insight Hippolytus reaches in that description of Phaedra's death. Greek tragedy is a no-win game. They do not play it at the Kennedy School. Dukakis never knew what hit him in the 1988 campaign. Since his emotions were not triggered in expectable ways, Republican functionaries mocked him as weird, remote, and cold. George Bush referred to him as "the Ice Man" during a debate. Marilyn Quayle called him "a little man from a little state." Bush's media adviser, Roger Ailes, referred to him as "mean," "ruthless," and "narcissistic." A TV ad showed Dukakis cruising around in a tank with a sappy grin on his face, an earth-touring extraterrestrial. Truly vile charges about his mental health were circulated at the Republican convention.

Cruel as these attacks were, Dukakis seemed to give them indirect confirmation by his lack of indignation, his flabbiness of response, his refusal even to see that there was a problem in his intellectual bearing. He brushed all such matters off, saying people were too intelligent to be concerned with "atmospheric" things. He seemed to believe his own claim that people care only about "issues," not personalities.

And then, in the second and final presidential debate, Dukakis provided more evidence than his enemies could have invented that he is tone-deaf on human matters. He answered with an eerie serenity—more proper, as Aristotle would say, to a god or a beast than to a man—when asked whether he would alter his stand on capital punishment if Kitty Dukakis were raped and murdered. The question was the first of the evening, posed by the inappropriately named "moderator" of the interrogative panel. Bernard Shaw's journalistic colleagues on that panel— all women in this case—had urged him not to ask the question, or at least not to particularize it by using Kitty's name. Shaw was adamant. The issue that had been raised was Dukakis's very humanity. Kitty was the channel through which that humanity had been almost officially expressed by Dukakis and everyone around him. She was the hostage he had given to mankind's ordinary condition. If he could not show feeling here, where would he?

The point of the question, though not its fierce articulation, had been anticipated. The "Willie Horton ad," publicizing the rape committed by a man out on furlough from a Massachusetts prison, had emphasized Dukakis's lack of sympathy for the victims of crime. To counter this, his aides made Dukakis rehearse over and over a personal response to any question about crime and its victims. Dukakis would mention his father, mugged in his office by criminals seeking drugs. He would mention his brother, killed on his bicycle by a runaway driver (probably drunk—it was St. Patrick's night in Boston). He would place himself at the side of victims, speaking for them. If the questioners gave him no opportunity to do that, he was to bring it up himself, so important was it to counter the misperception that he does not care about people who are assaulted.

And then Bernard Shaw gave him a perfect occasion to respond. People in the audience gasped at the question that Shaw's fellow panelists thought too brutal. It was itself a kind of assault, linking a particular woman by name with the fantasy of rape. The next day, on Dukakis's campaign plane, the actress Debra Winger said of this question, "You know, if you tell an audience to imagine performers on the stage as naked, everyone will do it." Shaw had, in effect, invited the world to imagine Kitty Dukakis being raped. Yet Dukakis, in a voice as equable as an accountant's, gave a completely impersonal answer on the failure of capital punishment as a deterrent, adding his characteristic assurance that everyone knows his record on this issue. If he had rehearsed to give the *worst* answer to any question about crime's victims, he could not have done a more thorough job. The campaign was over from that moment. Any hope Dukakis had of establishing human contact with the voters was dispelled by his fatal composure, his self-containment, his *sōphrosynē*.

Did he freeze, just lose his way; or was this a deliberate refusal to "stoop," to indulge in the crowd-pleasing "personalities" Dukakis always considered unworthy of a life in public policy? His contempt for the blarney and sentiment of Boston pols was built so firmly into his own self-image that he could not indulge in behavior even he must have known was appropriate in this case. This was not a personal expression he could delegate to John Sasso. He was called on to reveal emotion directly, not through his surrogate, and he could not, not even for Kitty. There is a zombielike consistency to the man, admirable on its own strange terms.

By the end of the race it was hard to remember how strong Dukakis had appeared when he launched his campaign based on demonstrable "competence." Then he had seemed, as so often before, the inevitable Michael. He is quick and decisive in policy debates because he moves nimbly on a mental map, all of whose parts are equally clear to him. His map does not blur in places, or fade off at the edges. It does not border on large areas of mystery, suggesting (in the words at old maps' margins) that "here be monsters." Monstrous things, like his brother's suicide attempt, are simply *off* the map, not uncertainly placed there. Even Kitty, in some of her aspects, was off Michael's map. If he did not admit to them, they were not there.

There is a certain increase of efficiency, an elimination of friction, in simply ignoring irremediable things. On Dukakis's Lear Jet back to Boston, early in the long campaign, he talked with Dave Nyhan of *The Boston Globe* about the fear of flying. For Dukakis, it was a nonsubject. "Have any of you," he asked, including Nick Mitropoulos and me in the question, "even once thought of dying on this trip?" Nyhan promptly said, "As a matter of fact, I have." Dukakis was surprised. "Really? I never think of dying." That would be a wasted effort. There is no government program to eliminate death.

At that moment it occurred to me that Dukakis was the first truly secular candidate we had ever had for the presidency. Not a "secularist" as Pat Robertson would define that term, not a militant *against* religion, but someone entirely free *from* religion. For him it is simply irrelevant, like death and other intractable matters. Even Gary Hart had, for a long time, known the terrors of religion, whatever his later attempts to obliterate their memory. Dukakis was simply untouched by them. Other politicians have used religion somewhat cynically, manipulating Billy Graham or Cardinal Spellman, but with at least some residual sense that they were dealing with explosive human material. Nixon seemed to have a soul, even if a damned one. John Kennedy took a happy-go-lucky approach to his religion, but he had a sense of humor (often allied with a sense of mystery), and he relied on his Irish gods of luck (the ones who most betrayed him in the end). Some politicians are so inclusive in their religiosity as to turn druid if the trees of their native state are threatened. They will rely on anything to shorten the electoral odds, even the odd god or imp or omen. They are all, on St. Patrick's Day, devout to leprechauns. But Dukakis is not haunted by even the minor deities of Greece, neither dryad nor hamadryad.

It was this blindness to the blinder forces in other human beings that left him so vulnerable to Republican dirty tricks in 1988. Much of their assault on him relied on religion, a force he did not even know was in play. The deep hostility to the American Civil Liberties Union, a ferocity inexplicable to him, had been fostered by religious groups because of the ACLU's role in outlawing school prayer. The pledge to the flag was dear to some because it invokes God.

The failure of Dukakis to respond on these points was an even deeper symptom of his problem with the American people than was his weird answer to Shaw's question about Kitty. At least he and his aides knew, by late in the campaign, that there was a problem to be addressed in the Willie Horton ad. About the religious animus behind the flag and ACLU questions they remained in the dark. God was not in their computer. They did not realize what other people will stoop to when it comes to using God for political advantage. Hippolytus, at first, had too high (and distant) an opinion of the gods to think they could take any delight in destroying a man—till one of the gods destroyed him.

⬥ F O U R ⬥

Jeremiad:
The Extreme Center

THE SECULARISM OF MICHAEL DUKAKIS WAS MORE NOTICEABLE IN 1988 because other candidates made such open appeals to religion. In fact, two of those running were ordained ministers—Pat Robertson and Jesse Jackson. Though both were from the South, they seemed to represent opposite extremes, Robertson the rightwardmost Republican and Jackson the leftwardmost Democrat. This very fact demonstrated the broad stratum of religion underlying American culture. While Bush was making a successful appeal to religiosity at the center of the 1988 campaign, both of the less "moderate" candidates were institutionally more tied to churches.

The difference between the two men's situations was that Robertson's credentials stood in a continuum of religiosity that extended toward and past the center now occupied by Bush. Jackson, though his appeal to religious tradition was as legitimate as Robertson's, was comparatively isolated among Democrats, disconnected from the center of our culture by the intervening secularity of the Dukakis campaign. Journalists and other analysts tended to treat him in purely secular terms, as a spokesperson for blacks, for civil rights, for the disadvantaged; or just, vaguely, for "the Left." Robertson, somewhat to his dismay, was *never* considered apart from his religious past.

Yet, while Robertson played down the piety of his TV show, Jackson was unabashed in his use of preachy talk. Most journalists, however, treated this as so many jazz riffs on his basically "leftist" message. While asking what Jackson "really wants," they kept looking for what he was "really" saying *under* the ornamental flourishes of Scripture language. If reporters had not shown a determination to keep Robertson boxed into his religious past, and an obliviousness to Jackson's religious rhetoric, the similarities of the two preachers would have been more frequently noticed. I alternated coverage of them in the period leading up to the "Super Tuesday" primaries, and was able to trace similar themes, terms, and even identical passages of Scripture turning up in their talks. Certain parts of their speeches could have been interchanged with no one being the wiser.

Both men called for a moral revival in America, a return to family values, a toughening of school discipline, a war on drugs. More than any others in the race, they concentrated on the schools—as each, for his own purpose, had done for years. Jesse Jackson spent much of the 1970s touring inner-city schools, trying to raise morale in depressing circumstances, calling for self-discipline, study, and parent involvement. Pat Robertson had launched a large literacy program as part of his (quite justified) attack on the public schools' poor record, as well as to legitimate the movement toward private Christian schools that promise a "disciplined, drug-free, crime-free" atmosphere for learning. All candidates, admittedly, mouth truisms about our future resting on the preparation of our young, but these two preachers did not happen on this ritual just for campaign purposes.

In fact, both made special efforts, during the race, to address the needs of the inner city. Pat Robertson actually opened his presidential run with an event in the Bedford-Stuyvesant neighborhood of Brooklyn. He brought in a choir and made music on the street, recalling urban efforts of the Holiness Movement. He came to rally saints in the midst of sinners. There was a compensatory motive for this symbolic action: Robertson had to address the fears of blacks, to counter the suspicion that his campaign was just a polite later rerun of George Wallace's. But the gesture was not entirely artificial. Robertson had begun his Christian ministry with some tentative preaching in Bedford-Stuyvesant. He was, in ways few gave him credit for, returning to his Holiness roots, to the early period of fervor just after his baptism in the Spirit. This did not prevent him from using the hecklers who greeted his effort, in later accounts of that event, to tell shocked followers how devils had mocked the saints. Holiness groups have always taken opposition to their mission as a sign that the forces of evil are opposing them—this was the way Puritans interpreted Indian wars when America was colonized.

Jackson went into bedeviled territory too. He spent a night in the Nickerson Gardens project in Watts, where gang wars and drugs threaten everyone's life, but especially the lives of the young. The morning after he had listened to the grievances of those living there, he met with representatives of the regnant gang. The meeting was private, but Jackson's aide Bob Borosage relayed to me what was said, and I confirmed his quotes with Jackson.

The gang leaders, though impressed with Jackson's audacity, did not think he could do anything for them. One of them claimed, "If you talk long enough, strong enough, bright enough about black folk, they gonna kill you, like they did King and Malcolm." According to Jackson, "I told them I don't worry 'bout what THEY gonna do. I don't want you worrying 'bout THEM. I don't want YOU to kill me. If you do that, I die twice. You killin' me every time you sell drugs, buy weapons, shoot each other. You stoppin' everything I try to do. You in a muddy hole, and nobody can get you out but yourselves, not even Jesse Jackson."

It was his old lesson to the high schools, but delivered to people who stand constantly, as he does, in the shadow of death, and both sides knew it. No other politician could talk to them quite like this: "I been in a muddy hole, and I know the way out, and I can help you. But only you can do it. I can get you jobs, but only you can show up on time, not drunk, not high. You know the song? 'Momma may have, Pappa may have, But God loves the child that has his own. . . .' "

Still challenged by the gang to show he could *do* something, Jesse improvised. His aides called Mayor Tom Bradley's office in downtown Los Angeles, and Jackson took the neighborhood toughs to present their demands for job training in Nickerson Gardens. Jackson, precisely because he was at the left edge of the spectrum of candidates, had to show, on the one hand, that he can bring his core constituents into the political process while, on the other hand, convincing those followers that they can actually accomplish something for themselves by addressing (and implicitly supporting) elected officials. Thus even an "extreme" candidate works to legitimize authority. Simply by seeking rewards from the system, a candidate endorses the system and discourages action outside it.

The same was true for Pat Robertson at the other end of the spectrum. He was calling on Christians who had earlier given up on worldly tactics, urging them to become involved in politics, promising that they could make an impact on the godless forces that were massed against them in the media, the bureaucracy, and the courts. Despite his own distrust of secular reporters, Robertson's campaign forced him to court them, answer their questions, and put compensatory stress on his nonreligious credentials, as lawyer, as businessman, as television executive. He had to convince doubters that he was not so extreme as to lie beyond the rational bargaining that goes into a political campaign, and he had (indirectly) to urge his followers to support him in the effort by their own motion toward the political mainstream. So, ironically, he promoted in his own world a measure of that "secularization" he usually deplores. The preacher had to become a businessman in order to become a politician.

This is not to say that either man abandoned the religious base of his moral protest. They simply softened the edges of their pulpit oratory. Both denounced "the world" in its evil aspect—Washington as held captive, in Robertson's view, by godless humanists, or, in Jackson's view, by corporate greed. But Washington had to be presented as *redeemably* bad, or there was no sense supporting a candidate to go there. In Robertson's case, the Washington of *Ronald Reagan* could not be presented as godless. In Jackson's case, the moral message could not be made a merely racial protest against "the *white* power structure." Both men were gingerly in their choice of targets, though vigorous in preachments once limited foes had been identified. Jackson attacked only corporate "barracudas," not businessmen in general. Robertson was careful not to make his attacks on crime, the schools, and teenage illegitimacy look as if they were aimed at blacks. In a compensatory effort to disarm suspicion, he attacked abortion as a form of genocide against blacks!

In one of the neat reversals that mark our political system, the real extremism of the 1988 campaign was voiced at the winning *center* of the political spectrum. While Jackson and Robertson were being exquisitely diplomatic on the subject of race, the Republicans launched their lurid campaign ads using the convicted black rapist Willie Horton as a symbol of Dukakis's blindness to the threat in our midst. The Bush supporters were not talking simply about a matter of internal Massachusetts practice. They were using fear of criminals as a national issue. Yet the Reagan administration, of which Bush was a highly visible part, had presided over the nation while this threat, or the perception of it, grew so intimidating.

Here is the paradox at the heart of so many others: While the "outside" candidates had to show respect for the political system in their bid to be admitted inside, the incumbents were free to attack "government" with a relish not at all lessened by the fact that they *were* the government they excoriated. At regular intervals, as if waking from a trance, journalists discover that politicians become popular by attacking "politics," that the same people who say America is God's country lament that its administration is the source of evil—that a Ronald Reagan can offer as his credential for governing a contempt for government.

This pattern is woven from an interplay of causes both recent and remote in our history. Among the more recent causes is the combination of an electorate drastically expanded in this century with a two-party system that makes for a politics of compromise. With no electoral rewards offered to small, ideologically defined parties (as in the parliamentary system), many voters feel no pressing motive (or appropriate means) for expressing a distinct view by casting a vote. Voter turnout is accordingly low, and the task of candidates who have compromised on the larger issues is to ignite *some* symbolic passion to increase turnout. Those who can experiment with greatest safety in this inflammatory politics are precisely the ones at the center of the process. Rhetoric that would be destructive along the fringes of a party can be indulged as largely a matter of gestures by people whose positioning makes them seem humdrum unless they rave a bit. So the racial rabble-rousing of 1988 came from the "extreme middle," from a Bush camp that was initially considered too bland even by its Republican supporters.

The effort to rouse voters from apathy less by overt political disagreements than by covert appeals to passion makes for a politics of contentless fervor. Voter lethargy is lashed as a form of obduracy like the "hardheartedness" assailed by religious preachers, who are often concerned less with creeds than with making people *care* about virtue. In their sermons, sin is attacked more than doctrinal error. In such nonintellectual fervor, as in more direct ways, the modern political convention is derived from nineteenth-century revivals:

> The most enduring legacy of the camp meeting was in the realm of politics. The political rally was more than a secular counterpart to camp meetings. It was an actual borrowing of camp-meeting methods by American political party structures, and the nominating convention of today is probably the closest thing to an evangelical nineteenth-century camp meeting that most Americans experience.[1]

It is appropriate that the greatest speech at any political convention was delivered by the lay preacher William Jennings Bryan. He acquired his speaking skills sitting in the front row ("the anxious bench") at revivals. As he rightly said himself: "I commenced speaking on the stump when I was only twenty, but I commenced speaking in the church six years earlier—and I shall be in the church even after I am out of politics." Bryan was only thirty-six when he addressed the 1896 Democratic convention in Chicago, and it was not ludicrous, yet, for Vachel Lindsay to rhyme this way on his name:

> Prairie avenger, mountain lion,
> Bryan, Bryan, Bryan, Bryan.[2]

Bryan came to the Democrats that year with a cluster of bold proposals— an income tax, recall of elected officials, abandonment of the gold standard—and was not timorous about presenting them:

> We have petitioned, and our petitions have been scorned; we have entreated, our entreaties have been disregarded; we have begged, and they have mocked when our calamity came. We beg no longer; we entreat no more; we petition no more. We defy them.[3]

The "we" Bryan spoke for was the people, but especially the people of the West (he gestured westward as he referred to those he championed) and the people on farms:

> You come to us and tell us that the great cities are in favor of the gold standard; we reply that the great cities rest upon our broad and fertile prairies. Burn down your cities and leave our farms, and your cities will spring up again as if by magic; but destroy our farms and the grass will grow in the streets of every city in the country.[4]

Like Martin Luther King, Bryan referred to American tradition in advocating change. Both men appealed to Jefferson. Both described the American continent rhapsodically as itself calling for change. Both appealed to ancient ways. When Bryan spoke of the West, it was a place "where they have erected schoolhouses for the education of their young, churches where they praise their Creator, and cemeteries where rest the ashes of the dead."[5]

Most important, both orators relied on religious language to advance their cause. Bryan called his errand a "holy" one:

> With a zeal approaching the zeal which inspired the crusaders who followed Peter the Hermit, our silver Democrats went forth from victory unto victory

until they are now assembled, not to discuss, not to debate, but to enter up the judgment already rendered by the plain people of this country.[6]

Although both men came with a healing rhetoric, they were also denouncers of sin. For Dr. King, it was racial hatred that was crucifying his people. For Bryan, it was the gold standard insisted on by Eastern bankers that was turning America's prairies into deserts:

Having behind us the producing masses of this nation and the world, supported by the commercial interests, the laboring interests, and the toilers everywhere, we will answer their demand for a gold standard by saying to them: You shall not press down upon the brow of labor this crown of thorns, you shall not crucify mankind upon a cross of gold.[7]

This revival language led to a revival experience in the crowd that heard Bryan. Tearful conversions and confessions of sin occurred:

One of his [Bryan's] followers who was sitting in the gallery reported the behavior of a nearby gold Democrat who had been sneering at every friendly reference to the silver cause. When Bryan finished his appeal the gold Democrat lost control of himself and literally grabbed hold of me and pulled me up from a sitting to a standing position on my chair. He yelled at me, "Yell, for God's sake, yell," as Bryan finished his speech.[8]

Vachel Lindsay, who was sixteen that year, thought Bryan was America's savior:

I brag and chant of Bryan, Bryan, Bryan
Candidate for president who sketched a silver Zion. . . .[9]

The power of religious language in our politics is suggested not only by the resemblance between Bryan's oratory and that of Dr. King but by the fact that Peggy Noonan—speechwriter to Mr. Reagan and Mr. Bush— used Lindsay's poem on Bryan to set the mood for her speeches at more recent conventions.

Preachers need devils. President Reagan inveighed against the "evil empire." Bryan treated gold as a devil, much as he treated rum when he was promoting prohibition. The sinner needs to be rescued from the threat of an evil that breathes down on him. A crisis is always at hand. This aspect of our political language is derived not only from revivals but—even farther back in our history—from the jeremiads of New England meeting times. The jeremiad, like the diatribe of classical rhetoric, was less a genre of oratory than a style of thought, one used in the sermons of the Puritan calendar (especially the sermons preached on Election

Days). As the name (given to these sermons by Perry Miller) would indicate, the preacher denounced like an ancient prophet the people's defection from its contract (*foedus*) with God, a defection that can free God from honoring his promises in the contract.

The negative tone of such sermons made Perry Miller argue that there was in fact a rapid decline from the Puritans' original fervor, though later historians have challenged his view.[10] The form itself is denunciatory, and it reflects an original *theory* of grace more than the actual loss of grace. Since God's saving grace cannot be merited in Calvinist theology, all the soul can do is *prepare* itself for grace by lamenting its own insufficiency. In the revival formula that Shaw mocked in *Major Barbara*, the only way to become a saint is to proclaim oneself a sinner. Thus, in an America that has retained its sense of being chosen and historically blessed, there has always been a tendency to stress each generation's personal unworthiness for the inscrutable blessings God has showered on the country. Sometimes this awareness of national guilt has reached great depth, as in Lincoln's second inaugural address. More often it gives us the attacks on "government," or on the current administration, or on "higher-ups."

Thus George Bush, though speaking from his own high place of power in the national government, could express the fear that patriotism was under attack, the flag was being desecrated, the godless ACLU was gaining power, and criminals were being sheltered in this home of the brave. The people were being led astray. It was time to recall them, revive the ancient spirit of the country, silence the voice of the tempters. The most centrist figure of the 1988 campaign was licensed to become the most hysterical in his rhetoric. As denouncers of guilt, the professional preachers were pushed aside by that orator born again at the last minute, George Jeremiah Bush. But for this his managers had to supply him with a preacher's devil. The name of the new devil was Horton.

❖ F I V E ❖

A Theology of Willie Horton

POLITICAL DEVILS COME IN MANY GUISES. FOR WILLIAM JENNINGS BRYAN, early in his career, the devil was gold. He personalized his fight against what he called "that child of ignorance and avarice, the gold dollar."[1] Later, he would make evolution the threat to salvation. And, of course, he was always opposed to demon rum. When he was secretary of state to Woodrow Wilson, no alcoholic beverages were served at diplomatic functions in Washington.

For Bryan, these "devil's tools" were not metaphors. They were instruments used by a literal Satan. In the increasingly secularized twentieth century, politicians moved away from dogmatic beliefs of that sort, but turned the devils of politics into metaphors that were no less powerful for being partly unconfessed. Woodrow Wilson is a good type of the secularized preacher in modern politics, who found an absolute evil and shaved the truth to fight so preternatural an enemy. He went on crusade against the demon submarine.

As secretary of state, Bryan carried on what even his critics called a "gallant fight for neutrality."[2] As his first task in the State Department he had created a worldwide network of treaties calling for arbitration, cooling-off periods, and protected neutrality to prevent the onset of war.

He saw this structure threatened by Wilson's tilt, against his declared neutrality, toward England, and especially by his willingness to let Americans travel without warning on British vessels carrying arms. "A ship carrying contraband," Bryan wrote, "should not rely upon passengers to protect her from attack—it would be like putting women and children in front of an army."[3] When 128 Americans died after a German submarine sank the contraband-carrying *Lusitania*, Bryan wanted to follow the fact-finding procedures prescribed in the treaty Germany had signed with America, to warn Americans about travel on belligerent ships, and to pair a protest to Germany with an inquiry into the suspicious loading of the *Lusitania*. Wilson rejected all these measures as weakening the force of the moral cry he meant to issue against the evil submarine, a weapon which violated even values "which Germany has always stood for."[4] Wilson did not want troublesome doubt about the facts in the case to interfere with the moral polarities of good and evil. He wrote to Bryan:

> I am inclined to think that we ought to take steps, as you suggest, to prevent our citizens from traveling on ships carrying munitions of war. . . . I am sorry to say that, study as I may the way to do it, *without hopelessly weakening our protest*, I cannot find a way [italics added].[5]

Nothing must be done that "might operate as an exemption from responsibility" resting on one clear malefactor. Such steps might indicate "uneasiness and hedging," and Wilson had already decided "to put the whole note on very high grounds."[6] In the best study of the *Lusitania*'s sinking, Thomas A. Bailey and Paul B. Ryan note that Bryan's principles "were subsequently written into the neutrality legislation of the mid-1930s—one war too late. As was often the case in domestic affairs, Bryan was a generation ahead of his time."[7] But Wilson could not be neutral on what he considered a moral issue. Bryan resigned over the *Lusitania* note, knowing that this ended his distinguished political career.[8] Thenceforth Wilson glowed with agreement when his new wife referred to Bryan as "that traitor."[9] Dissent over the facts is not a luxury one can afford when facing the devil.

The moral purist in this case, the one who let moral fervor blind him to the facts, was Wilson, not Bryan. The secretary of state had a more vivid belief in the devil, but also a more conventional view of the devil's role. He could read the cargo manifest of the *Lusitania* with as sharp an eye as any Puritan shipowner in the Salem yards. It was Wilson, the secular preacher, who wanted to concentrate evil in one place so he could expel it forever. The protest against submarine war was harsh because it was meant to *end* submarine war, like all of Wilson's warlike acts. Wilson's view is a perfect example of what Andrew Delbanco calls

> the transformation of the idea of sin from the self-critical Augustinian meaning that it briefly sustained in prerevolutionary England into the self-righteous form that it has chiefly assumed in Protestant America: sin as excrescence, disease—the threatening other—against which the community of purist selves builds barricades.[10]

Evil as the threatening other has taken many forms in American politics. In our early history, it was that Whore of the Devil, the Church of Rome. More recently, it has been Communism. But for many voters in 1988, it was crime.

Crime is not as concrete an object of fear as a submarine, a battle, or a foreign country. *Crime* is a term that covers lawbreaking of every type, committed by lawbreakers of every class. But increasingly in our politics it has become a code word for the threat of the drug-afflicted poor in our inner cities. The more different from "us" the criminals are made to seem, the more distant from "average" Americans, the harder it becomes to cope with the conditions that foster crime—unemployment, demographic imbalances, urban obsolescence, drug traffic, improper police administration. But, also, the more different the objects of fear become, the more useful they are politically. As victims of social conditions, they might nag at the conscience or even stimulate the imagination of political reformers, but as devils they prove too handy to the moralists, who bring on social war by denouncing it, much as Wilson wooed physical war by castigating it.

Some things only the apparently high-minded get away with. Imagine the reaction if Pat Robertson had used an ad centered on a black criminal like Willie Horton. When Bush's advisers created their ad strategy, their man's centrist position in the political continuum gave just enough plausibility to the claim that they were discussing crime, not tickling racial prurience.

It was a thin enough pretense, even without the ancillary use of Willie Horton's brutish features in a lowering photograph. The overt charge was that Michael Dukakis could not safely be allowed into the White House after his record of letting this killer go on furlough and rape an innocent woman. But presidential candidates who make crime a national issue are always suspect, since law enforcement depends mainly on state and local courts, police, and mores. If furlough programs were dangerous, then Bush and his principal, Ronald Reagan, were guilty of presiding over a nation in which almost all states had been furloughing criminals over the eight years of their administration, and the federal prison system had itself released a man who committed rape and murder in 1987. Thirty-five states grant first-degree murderers furloughs. Reagan, as governor of California, had a program that resulted in two murders by those out on furlough. The escape rate in Massachusetts was low, the rehabilitation rate high. The Massachusetts program had been instituted by a Republican governor and upheld by the state supreme court. What could one make of a single criminal's abuse of a program most experts in penology considered a benefit to the community?

That depended, in this case, on the rather hysterical coverage given the Willie Horton case by a Massachusetts paper, *The Lawrence Eagle-Tribune*. In an extraordinary campaign to repeal the furlough program, the paper ran more than 250 stories, editorials, or commentaries dealing with Willie Horton, whose picture was often reprinted in conjunction with the most demonizing information about him, some of it false. At least four times the paper alleged, on its front page, that, in the crime for which he was serving time when granted a furlough, he had not only stabbed his victim but "cut off the youth's genitals, put them in his mouth and then spit them out."[11] The paper later printed an admission that this story was not true; it had been accepted without confirmation from an overheated state legislator's denunciation of Horton. (Actually, the jury that convicted Horton had not even been able to confirm that Horton was the assailant wielding the knife—though the paper continually asserted that he was.)

No allegation against Horton was wild enough to be treated skeptically by the *Eagle-Tribune*. A dozen times before correcting itself the paper printed the false claim that the woman he raped while on furlough was pregnant—according to one story, in an advanced state of pregnancy. It was clear that the paper was evoking a kind of mythopoeic response with these stereotypical images of the sex-crazed black rapist. A reporter on the case said of a colleague: "Susie and I became obsessed by the story. We would go to lunch and take the Horton file." The paper won a Pulitzer Prize in 1987 for its massive coverage of the case—an award later criticized by Alexander Cockburn in *The Nation* and by Steve Burkholder in the *Washington Journalism Review*.

Nor did the paper give up on the Horton case after leading the public clamor to get first-degree murderers removed from eligibility for parole. During the primary in New Hampshire, just across the state line from Lawrence, the paper's reporters repeatedly asked Dukakis about Horton, with no impact on Dukakis's New Hampshire victory. The local audience was apparently saturated with the vendetta against Horton.

But Horton was still a stranger on the national scene. Senator Albert Gore had heard of him and raised the furlough program in a debate before the New York primary, attacking Dukakis for his "weekend passes for convicted criminals" like Horton. It was from this one mention that the Bush researchers caught on to the story. They used it on a test group of pro-Dukakis voters assembled in Paramus, New Jersey, by Bush's pollster, Robert Teeter. Only then did the potential of the Horton story become clear. In later tests Horton emerged as what Lee Atwater called "the silver bullet" for destroying Dukakis's image as an effective governor.[12] The use of the black rapist set the terms for discussing Dukakis's attitude toward crime. In this way it led to Bernard Shaw's question about Dukakis's response if his wife were raped.

The unvoiced part of that question was: What if your wife were raped *by Willie Horton*—by the Black Rapist who haunts the cellar of the public imagination, with endless violations imaginable in any one actual crime (the *Eagle-Tribune*'s wild embroidering about mutilation, genitals in the mouth, or an unborn baby assaulted during a woman's advanced pregnancy)? The Black Rapist is deeply seated in America's iconography of evil. Rape was the quintessential racial crime, for which the quintessentially frightened response of lynching was largely reserved. This archetype of rape screens out the reality, the expectations, and the reporting of rape. Fear of black rapists promotes the misunderstandings that let other rapists get away with their crimes. As Catherine MacKinnon argues, from the statistics of rapes reported and unreported:

> The rapes that have been reported are the kinds of rapes women think will be *believed* when we report them. They have two qualities: they are by a stranger, and they are by a black man. These two elements give you the white male archetype of rape. . . . [But] rapes by strangers are the least common rapes women *experience*. . . . Most rapes are by a man of the woman's race and by a man she knows: her husband, her boss, an acquaintance, or a date [italics added].[13]

Since so many people assume that rape is an interracial crime, intraracial rape (by far the more common kind) is underreported.[14] Women, who anticipate with good cause the skepticism of law-enforcement officials in any case, are especially deterred from reporting cases of the "wrong" kind of rape, the kind they are most likely to suffer. It was not an accident, as Lee Atwater liked to claim with an almost straight face, that the Bush campaign chose a rape, not just any crime, when creating a fear of "permissiveness," and even less an accident that it chose a black rapist rather than a white one. As Roger Ailes said, leering up out of his "foul rag and bone shop of the heart," the real choice was whether to show Willie Horton with or without a knife in his hand. It was a sign of the almost diabolical cleverness of the campaign that the ultimate Willie Horton question was asked by a black man, Bernard Shaw.

In Puritan lore, the devil was often known as the Black Man, and that is how he figures, obsessively, in Hawthorne's *The Scarlet Letter*. Witches are said to meet the Black Man in the woods for their evil rites. Pearl, the daughter born of Hester Prynne, is hypnotically drawn to talk about the Black Man, until her hidden father, the Reverend Dimmesdale, breaks the spell and rescues the innocent white girl from the fear-fascination that seems to draw her toward the Black Man.

The devil from our past haunts American literature, merging with Melville's confidence man. In politics especially, he wears many disguises. "Willie Horton" was a product of communal fears. As "horror movies" repeatedly demonstrate, the plausibility of the supernatural is retained longer by hellish than by heavenly images. If you put together communal fears and cynical campaign managers' skills, the result is a mixture of myth and fiction that becomes the artifact "Willie Horton." Pat Robertson would not have been allowed to present him as a literal devil, any more than William Jennings Bryan could have *exorcised* the German submarine. But the vague religiosity of a Wilson makes of submarines what the born-again ruthlessness of George Bush did with Willie Horton. No question about it, there was evil involved.

Playing to Win

MANY THOUGHT, EARLY IN 1988, THAT GEORGE BUSH HAD ENTERED THE
race for president severely debilitated by his niceness. Sketch after sketch
of his background emphasized the prep school ethos of "service" to which
he had been trained. He cited that code himself when accused of being
namby-pamby in his loyalty to President Reagan. So other people were
as surprised as Michael Dukakis when Bush campaigned with a kind of
vicious glee on issues that seemed "ungentlemanly," accusing his opponent of deficiencies in patriotism, family feeling, and—most subtly
but effectively—religion.

Those who thought Bush might be excessively prim had not paid
enough attention to his earlier campaigns, or even to his maneuvers
toward the Republican nomination in 1988. Bush had entered politics in a John Birch corner of Texas, and first ran for office with
Barry Goldwater at the top of the Republican national ticket. After that
he had been Richard Nixon's protégé, never a role for developing nice
scruple. He was the front man who fought off "Red China" in the
UN while Nixon and Kissinger were forging a secret alliance with that

country. He was the Republican national chairman denying all charges during Watergate. He protected Gerald Ford's right flank at the CIA by letting hard-line outsiders come in and second-guess the agency's estimates.

The wonder was that Bush kept looking so clean through this succession of dirty jobs. This was partly the legacy of his father, Prescott Bush, the patrician Republican senator from Connecticut. Prescott's son imbibed the correct enthusiasms at Andover, but he was also a fierce competitor on Andover's soccer field. A famous photograph has kept alive the memory of his prowess at baseball—a sport he also played at Yale—but he was best at the rough-and-tumble of Andover's traditional sport. The bible on athletics at Andover records that "Poppy Bush's play throughout the season ranked him as one of Andover's all-time soccer greats."[1]

In political mythology the Kennedy family was obsessed with sports, playing tag-team touch football through the decades. But next to the Bushes, the Kennedys were sports dilettantes. One of Bush's middle names is Walker, after the uncle who established golf's Walker Cup. Senator Prescott Bush was a fanatical golfer. Dorothy Bush, his wife, was fanatical in all her sports. When Barbara Bush played tennis with her mother-in-law, the elder Mrs. Bush would switch to her left hand, spot her daughter-in-law several points, and still win. Told, earlier, that George would marry this Barbara, Dorothy Bush remained confident that he would not: "She won't play net." Bush once injured his shoulder going for a tennis shot while Barbara was his doubles partner. "His mother said it was my ball to hit, and it happened because I didn't run for it," Barbara later explained.[2]

The Bush family tradition is maintained among the president's children, who speak of a mysterious Ranking Committee that handicaps all the relatives on their prowess in various sports. Jeb Bush says its proceedings are as secret as those of Skull and Bones, his father's Yale secret society.[3] Whatever its mechanics, it produces results. When tennis pros Chris Evert and Pam Shriver went to play tennis with Bush's sons at the White House, they expected to breeze through their games with these amateurs. Instead, the Bushes won. Chris Evert was depressed.[4]

Barbara Bush claims that the great influence on her husband was not his father, the unflappable senator, but his competitive mother, who was as concerned about appearance as about winning. When Barbara's hair started going gray, it was her mother-in-law who, for a period, insisted

that she dye it.[5] Bush, for all his well-attested amiability, does not like
to lose at anything. William Sloane Coffin found that out at Yale when
Bush, a visitor during his time as UN ambassador, played game after
game of squash, determined to win one. But the great testimony to Bush's
fighting spirit is his war record, the fifty-eight missions he flew while
losing four planes out from under him. Some wimp.

Two reporters—Judy Bachrach and Marianne Means—got a glimpse
of Bush's determination during his vice-presidential campaign of 1980.
A television producer on his plane had taken to mocking him, and at
one point was straddling the aisle, his feet on the opposite armrests, not
letting the candidate get through. Bush quietly took him by the balls and
steered him out of the way. Pete Teeley, Bush's press secretary at the
time, tried to persuade the reporters not to print what they had seen, but
Bachrach did.[6]

Bachrach's coverage of the 1980 campaign, for *The Washington Star*,
was highly critical of Bush. When I mentioned that to Bush eight years
later, in his White House office, he burst out: "Judy Bachrach used to
drive me up the fucking wall, with her bent pelvis and mink over her
shoulder. But now, who cares?" Then he brought up criticism of him
by Garry Trudeau, in his *Doonesbury* comic strip: "But I see this week
he's even going after Donald Trump. So, it's one person one week,
another the next." Besides, he said, who is Trudeau (a Yale graduate) to
be making fun of Ivy Leaguers? "And George *Will*! Who *cares*?" (Will
had called him a lapdog.) He was heating up as he went over his list of
grievances. Ironically, he had said shortly before that only Barbara remembers any attacks on him. "I told her, 'Guess who I saw the other
day at the Houston convention—Joe Blow!' [She said,] *'Joe Blow!*
Don't you remember what he said about you in 1964?' I don't remember
stuff."

Knowing just how well he remembers gives special point to the single-
mindedness with which Bush pursued his prize in 1988—his last chance
to win the office he had been seeking for years. (Ten years earlier, Barbara
Bush calmly told a surprised Nancy Bush Ellis, "You know your brother's
going to be president of the United States, don't you?")[7] In 1980, the
right-wing *Union Leader* of Manchester, New Hampshire, had helped
Bush lose his "big mo" (momentum) in that state's primary by attacking
him for complicity in Watergate. Yet five years afterward, a good three
years before the next New Hampshire primary, Bush was at a dinner for
the late publisher of the *Union Leader*, praising William Loeb for being

"outspoken." Bush's strategists had told him he could only get the Republican nomination by a long effort to counteract right-wing Republican suspicions of him. Despite all the service he had done for Richard Nixon and the Goldwater wing of the party, he was not forgiven for his Eastern ties and his assaults on Reagan before becoming his running mate.

The right wing has disproportionate weight in the early stages of the Republican nominating process. According to his own backers, Bush had to pay humiliating court to this most reactionary sector of the party—and the earlier he did it, the better. There would always be time to move to the center, once the Southern primaries were past.

So Bush went to right-wing religious gatherings, wooed hard-liners, and emphasized his Reagan credentials all through Reagan's second term. Just a year after his address at the Loeb dinner, Bush went before the New York Conservative party to say of that state's governor, Mario Cuomo, "He's telling us to be ashamed to stand up and be proud of this great land." Then, showing what he would be capable of two years later when discussing prison furloughs, Bush characterized a Cuomo recommendation for clemency this way: "I can tell you one thing about the difference between a liberal politician and a conservative one: Governor Reagan kept cop-killers in jail." Even George Will, the conservative columnist, was hoping, after this dinner, that Bush "got the demagoguery out of his system."[8]

Yet Bush was paying court to evangelists Jim and Tammy Bakker in that same period, hoping for an endorsement from them while they were still in their glory days of running Heritage USA, the patriotic theme park. Reagan had won evangelists away from Jimmy Carter, one of their own, in 1980, capturing the electorally important South. That region stayed with him in 1984, though he had not pushed very hard for causes like prayer in school. Now the evangelicals, feeling powerful, were ready to make harder demands—even, in 1988, to run one of their own. It was time for Reagan's party to deliver.

Bush, who had earlier been equivocal on abortion, and whose wife was known to be pro-choice, made all the right noises as he negotiated for Jerry Falwell's support (which he won), Pat Robertson's neutrality (which he did not), and Jim Bakker's favor. The Falwell campaign was the most public, but the Bakker one was the most serious. In 1985, while setting up a meeting between Bush and Bakker, two people who would be closely involved in Bush's election—Pete Teeley and Ron Kaufman—met with the staff of Bakker's PTL organization, after which Teeley became a paid lobbyist for PTL. He received $120,000 in consulting fees before Bakker was exposed for paying blackmail to Jessica Hahn.[9]

When Bush met with Bakker, he told reporters that he watched Jim and Tammy Faye on television "from time to time." This was his season for truckling to the religious Right. Despite Reagan's sympathy in belief with the evangelicals, he had deftly sidestepped invitations to call himself "born again." But Bush, a product of the prototypical High Church atmosphere of Andover, used the formula that means so much to those who share it: "Jesus Christ is my personal savior."[10]

It was this period, leading up to the 1988 election, that seemed to seal Bush's reputation as a wimp—the charge leveled at him on *Newsweek*'s cover. That is one way to look at his early campaigning. The other way is this: He had finally got *religion* by the balls. South Carolina, where he made his profession as a born-again Christian, was the state where he broke Pat Robertson's 1988 challenge, on the eve of "Super Tuesday," a Southern event he would sweep. Besides, he was doing the very things that would, later in the campaign, lead people to call him ruthless and vicious. He was, throughout, playing to win.

When Bush surprised Dukakis and others by the ferocity of his attacks in the fall of 1988, he was pursuing the same themes he had been working since 1985—patriotism, religion, law and order. What was surprising to Bush's own people was the durability of those themes. Appeals tailored to the early part of the process kept eliciting such favorable response that they were kept on the calendar long after they had been scheduled for retirement. Polls showed they were still "working," to the elation of Roger Ailes and Lee Atwater, who were ready to move their candidate into the center when that proved necessary, but found he did better with "comparative" (negative) campaigning. People did not so much like "the new George Bush" as they liked seeing Dukakis get roughed up.

The flag issue was the perfect example of this. At last, almost adrift in a sea of flags, Bush moved on, while never quite abandoning this issue. To Dukakis, and most of the press, it remained a mystery how the flag could ever become an *issue* in the first place. Partly this was a matter of style. Some people love the rituals of patriotism—the sense of community created by playing "The Star-Spangled Banner" at the ballpark. Others, who cultivate a dissenter's independence, have a low threshold of tolerance for such rites. The difference in attitudes was made clear to Bill

Kovach of *The New York Times* when he went to Georgia to edit the
Atlanta *Constitution*. He felt uncomfortable, at lunches and dinners,
saying the Pledge of Allegiance as earlier generations had said grace before
meals. It was the symbol of a clash in temperaments that would make
his stay in Atlanta so short.[11] Politicians like Dukakis find regional customs
like that embarrassing. George Bush relishes them.

But the semireligious pattern of saying the pledge is a clue to what was
really at stake when the flag issue was raised in 1988. To Arthur Schlesinger, talk about "blasphemy" toward the flag is a sign that some people
are sacralizing the secular. But to the religious Right, the flag is *not* a
secular symbol. That was guaranteed, for them, during Dwight Eisenhower's presidency, when "under God" (Lincoln's phrase from the Gettysburg Address) was added to the Pledge of Allegiance. In fact, in
independent Christian schools a Christian Pledge of Allegiance is recited
that reveals the full impact of the two words that matter most to these
believers in the more generally recited pledge. This one begins: "We
pledge allegiance to the Christian flag, and to our Savior, for whom it
stands . . ."[12]

Why do believers make so much of "under God" in the pledge? For
a reason that never occurred to the secularists around Michael Dukakis.
Since the removal of prayer from public schools, the pledge is the one
place in almost every school's daily regimen where God can still be
mentioned in connection with national loyalty. To evangelicals—who
are dismayed when Christmas symbols are removed from public places,
who fear even for the mention of God on coins and public buildings—
the words in the pledge are a bastion they must rally to defend. Prayer
may be forbidden, but one act of homage is still allowed—in fact, in
most places, required. Dukakis had acted in Massachusetts only to protect
teachers from being compelled to say the pledge. But his connection with
the American Civil Liberties Union allowed his critics to claim that he
endorsed that body's stated aim of *removing* the words "under God" from
all uses of the pledge. (National Policy Number 84 of the ACLU reads:
"The insertion of the words 'under God' are [sic] unconstitutional and
should be forbidden.") Dukakis, not understanding the link between the
flag and his ACLU membership, was insouciant about attacks on his
patriotism—just as he seemed insensitive to people's violation by criminals.

This insensitivity looked sinister to his religious critics, who could not
believe he was ignorant of the battle waged around the words in the

pledge. Dukakis, they thought, had good reason to know what was at stake. He was not a mere bystander at the struggle that had been going on for decades over patriotic and religious symbols—he was a participant. What organization had been most active and effective in removing crèches from courthouse lawns? What organization, for that matter, was to the fore on abortion? Who deserved most credit for taking prayer out of schools? Who always showed up when it was time to defend pornography in court? The villain in morality play after morality play lived through by religious activists, for as long as any of them could remember, was the American Civil Liberties Union; and Dukakis was "a card-carrying member" of that organization.

When George Bush accused Dukakis of belonging to the ACLU, that struck most people in the press as the equivalent of discovering that Dukakis was on the board of a local museum. In the secular press, the ACLU is covered mainly for its maverick defense of unlikely candidates for civil rights, like the Ku Klux Klan. But on the right, the ACLU is considered a very prominent agent in twentieth-century history. Look for anything that has gone wrong in "Christian America," and the ACLU has been making it go wrong, according to the evangelical Right. The ACLU created "the Scopes trial," which broke America's leading evangelical, William Jennings Bryan. It has been more effective than the Communist party precisely because it looks more acceptable. It is more pervasive than groups that deal with only one issue (like the National Abortion Rights Action League) or one profession (like the National Education Association) or one constituency (like the National Organization for Women) or foreign policy (like the Council on Foreign Relations). It is strong in single areas, but its influence extends to the whole range of political issues that matter most to dedicated evangelical Christians—abortion, private education, prayer in schools, gay rights, pornography, the *Miranda* laws, the teaching of evolution, testing for AIDS, capital punishment.

Some Christian activists know the ACLU only from its involvement in whatever issue concerns them most (e.g., abortion). But the better informed and the more active such people are, the more comprehensive the ACLU appears to them, the more coordinated with all parts of the effort to rid America of religion. Even poorly educated believers tend to know more about the ACLU and its founder, Roger Baldwin, than do more secular college graduates. (In the same way, right-wingers otherwise ill-informed had a surprisingly detailed knowledge of all the charges against Dr. King that were circulated for years by J. Edgar Hoover.) Thus, in concentric circles out from the core of religious hard-liners, *ACLU* has become a swearword for many only vaguely on the right. Edwin Meese, Reagan's White House counselor and later his attorney general, called the organization "a criminals' lobby"—a charge that seemed extreme to the secular press but was only a mild version of what is said about the group by right-wingers. When Joseph Scheidler, the antiabortion activist, claimed that his free-speech rights had often been infringed, I asked him if he ever thought of appealing to the ACLU. He acted as if I had suggested an alliance with the devil. "I would not accept their help if they offered it." (The ACLU *has* offered help to antiabortion activists, some of whom accepted its services.)

All this would have hurt Michael Dukakis even if there were nothing to the charges that the ACLU is opposed to religion. Its official position neither favors nor opposes religion; it simply calls for the separation of church and state according to constitutional prescription. Yet in fact the ACLU pursues this goal in ways that sometimes suggest a deeper grudge against religiosity in general. This is not surprising. The religious Right is "the enemy" in the eyes of ACLU leaders. At the biennial meeting of the national organization in 1989, the ACLU was feeling besieged—the *Webster* case had just been decided by the Supreme Court, offering an apparent rebuff to those who defend abortion as a right. Addressing the assembled affiliates in Madison, Wisconsin, Ira Glasser, the ACLU's executive director, said it was time to imitate the street tactics of the antiabortionists, and president Norman Dorsen said that it was no coincidence that the hardest resistance the ACLU met on issue after issue came from organized religion—not only on abortion, but on teaching evolution in the schools and on gay rights: "Religious values are, up front, the basis of the way our government operates."

The ACLU takes the measure of its enemy from the fact that so many Christian groups have been formed in recent years to act as little anti-ACLUs: the Christian Legal Society, the Washington Legal Foundation, the Rutherford Institute. These bodies imitate ACLU tactics in bringing suit where Christians' freedom of speech is limited—and they have been able to find stunning cases of that occurring. For instance: In Omaha, Nebraska, fifth-grade students were allowed to read a book of their own choice after assigned work was done. When a student took out his Bible, he was told he must remove it from the building, and he could not check out the Bible in the school library for his own perusal.[13] When a valedictorian at a Louisiana high school planned to speak about the importance of religion in her life, she was censored. She could have criticized church and state and school, but she could not speak her own mind on religion.[14]

Excesses like these, well chronicled in Nat Hentoff's indispensable column on free speech in *The Washington Post*, are the result of frightened teachers' overreaction to the Supreme Court's prayer decisions. The ACLU is not responsible for such free-lance absurdities. Nor is its national coordinating office in charge of all that its state affiliates do. Yet the organization as a whole has tried to prevent religious groups from meeting in schools under the provisions of the equal-access bill passed by Congress in 1985, which allows extracurricular clubs, even those that study the Bible, to use the same facilities that bird-watchers and ham-radio enthusiasts do.

A certain paranoia on both sides haunts the troubled border between church and state in the public schools. Liberals find invocations before football games a misuse of school loudspeakers.[15] Believers find themselves gagged even when expressing voluntary opinions, which are supposed to be guaranteed by the First Amendment. The Bush campaign was able to exacerbate this struggle, calling on the advice of William A. Donohue, the sociologist who wrote the right wing's favorite book on the subject, *The Politics of the American Civil Liberties Union*.[16] Donohue, for instance, gave the campaign the useful political charge that the ACLU would keep "kiddie porn" legal.

This is one of those quixotic and legalistic positions of the ACLU that the public finds hard to understand. It comes from the general principle the ACLU has adopted that "all definitions of obscenity are meaningless because this type of judgment is inevitably subjective and personal." Thus pornography as such should not be criminalized, no matter what its content or the age of those represented in it. Of course, murder is not protected just because the killers are making a "snuff film," and child abuse can be prosecuted under laws against physical or emotional exploitation, regardless of whether the abuse is filmed. But the ACLU's guidelines on protecting children sound as dry and legalistic as Dukakis's response to the question about Kitty's being raped. The child's abusers can be prosecuted, after the fact, "*when* such a [filmed] use [of a minor] is *highly* likely to cause: a) *substantial* physical harm; or, b) *substantial* and *continuing* emotional or psychological harm" (italics added). Most people are readier to presume that it is not good for kids to be filmed as sex objects.

No wonder the ACLU was constantly on the defensive during the 1988 campaign. If Willie Horton was that year's devil, the ACLU could be presented as all the devils' defenders. In fact, next door to Michael Dukakis's home state of Massachusetts, the ACLU was defending witches that year, as ministers of a genuine religion.[17] For many Americans, the coldly technological "Massachusetts miracle" was not only godless but the enemy of God.

⊹ S E V E N ⊹

Secular Innocence

MICHAEL DUKAKIS, WELL EDUCATED IN OTHER WAYS, WAS NOT PREPARED to deal with religious ardor. Asked which book most influenced him, Dukakis regularly mentioned Henry Steele Commager's *The American Mind*. He read it shortly after its appearance in 1950, when he was in high school. For a man whose preferred reading would, in later years, be project papers, this volume was something to stir the imagination. It sings the praises of the Tennessee Valley Authority and describes public planning as a special expression of the American genius.[1]

Commager argues that the American mind is pragmatic, optimistic, and secular. He castigates as un-American-minded any "irrationalists"—a hospitable category that includes people as different as Ernest Hemingway and Henry Adams (p. 120). Artists are especially prone to irrationalism, whose leading indicators are "an obsession with sex" (pp. 122–23), a "rejection of the concept of normality" (p. 124), and a glorification of "subhuman louts" (p. 125). Instead of busily building dams and setting up government programs, artists—people who succumb to the lure of Gertrude Stein—bog us down in "the quagmire of futility" (p. 128). Having given up on science (like Henry Adams), such people easily become pessimists (p. 138), retaining practically no American Mind at all.

For Commager, religion is clearly as irrational as modern art, but he is comparatively benign in his description of it. It puzzles him, by its anomalous perdurance in a people as rational and secular as those who possess the authentically American Mind. But religion does not disturb him as much as dirty poems. He decides, to his relief, that people do not really mean it when they say they believe in the old creeds: "For three hundred years Calvinism had taught the depravity of man without any perceptible effect on the cheerfulness, kindliness, or optimism of Americans" (p. 162).

If it seems strange that Commager can get so worked up about an assault on reason mounted by e. e. cummings (p. 121) while remaining tranquil about religion's "flight from reason" (p. 165), that is because he cannot imagine that anybody would take a preacher as seriously as a poet. For him, "no American could believe that he was damned" (p. 163). All real Americans have "preferred this life to the next" (p. 163), so their religious professions are a cover for something else—luckily, for something quite useful: "The church was, on the whole, the most convenient and probably the most effective organization for giving expression to the American passion for humanitarianism" (p. 168). When the church is not being useful, it is neutered; so support for it is harmless: "The church was something to be 'supported,' like some aged relative whose claim was vague but inescapable" (p. 166). A meaningless religion is a rather nice thing to have, since it does not interfere at all with dam-building, and it gives people something to do with their spare time.

Almost forty years after Commager defined the American mind, Arthur Schlesinger, Jr., returned to the task and found the same qualifying traits. In a widely publicized address at Brown University, Schlesinger argued that secularity is the leading characteristic of Americans: "The American mind is by nature and tradition skeptical, irreverent, pluralistic and relativistic."[2] Yet Schlesinger, unlike Commager, is nervous about religion, which some people in 1989 were taking altogether too seriously. Schlesinger sets the canons of Americanism in an exclusive way. We are told who are "the two greatest and most characteristic American thinkers"— Emerson and William James. We are told who was the "most quintessential of American historians"—George Bancroft (no doubter of American virtue, like Henry Adams). We are told what is the (one and orthodox) "American way"—"Relativism is the American way." We are even told what is "the finest scene in the greatest of American novels"—the point when Huck Finn decides to help Nigger Jim escape. In fact, we are told that this scene "is what America is all about."

Like a nativist facing immigrant hordes, Schlesinger multiplies the defining (and excluding) social signs of "our sort." Our sort have no truck with "reverence." We are committed to "our truth." Even relativism helps us to keep up standards here: "For our relative values are not matters of whim and happenstance. History has given them to us." They are like descent from the *Mayflower.* "People with a different history will have different values. But we believe that our own are better for us." How lucky, then, that history did not give us religious values. It is not enough that pragmatic, irreverent relativism be a high ideal for Americans to aspire to. It must be a "given," like the liberalism Louis Hartz, the consensus historian, said was the American situation (rather than its creed).[3] It is something one need not argue for, since one cannot escape it in any event: Our values "are anchored in our national experience, in our great national documents, in our national heroes, in our folkways, traditions, standards."

Schlesinger obviously has a different understanding of America's "folkways" than did the author of "the finest scene in the greatest of American novels." Twain's novels, and especially the one Schlesinger cites, are filled with folk superstition, religion, prejudice, and dogmatism. Even in the scene offered (rightly) to our admiration, Huck does not escape the presumptions of the entire culture around him. In fact, Huck at his supreme moment performs an act Professor Commager called impossible for any real American—Huck not only believes in hell, but believes he is going there now that he is helping Jim. He defies, while still believing in, "the American way" of everyone around him, the way of sin and damnation.

Huck cannot escape, even in rebellion, the categories of the circumambient religious culture (which Twain clearly thought *was* America's culture). Schlesinger, in the grip of an even stranger blindness, cannot see the circumambient culture. He is an American historian for whom much of American history simply does not exist. If religious figures pop up here and there, from the time of Jonathan Edwards to that of Flannery O'Connor, they are freaks or sports, somehow not as truly American (or truly great) as Emerson or William James. The demon-haunted world of Melville, Hawthorne, Poe simply ceases to be American in the world where Commager's TVA is the secular icon. Even Twain gets into the canon by a perverse misreading of his central scene's deepest irony.

Commager and Schlesinger are to American history what Michael Dukakis was, in 1988, to American politics. Much of American (indeed, of human) experience is off their mental maps. They have a serene provincialism, dismissive of the ordinary torments of people less optimistic, irreverent, and pragmatic than they. Those people are not simply treated as if they did not matter. They are not visible. America's encounters with religion are, for these learned men, what Kitty Dukakis's pill-taking was, something too embarrassing to be adverted to.

In 1959, the British novelist and scientist C. P. Snow stirred up a famous controversy by saying that the intellectuals of the developed world were split into "two cultures"—scientific and nonscientific—that no longer spoke each other's language. Many objections were made to Snow's argument, some almost as silly as the argument itself, but the best answer to it is contained in Snow's own presentation, which has the form of unwitting self-caricature. What Snow presents as a tragic gap between cultures is the difficulty Cambridge dons of different disciplines had in talking shop across the "high table" of Snow's college in Cambridge.[4] It seems not to have occurred to him that his two factions of academia represent aspects of a single thin stratum in much larger "cultures"— English, British, Western. Seen in that context, their interdisciplinary squabbling—however unfortunate—was, in the fullest sense, intramural, walled off from larger worlds, of which (whether they recognized it or not) they were also members, yet from which their psychological distance was greater than any that could be measured across the dons' table when the port was going round.

In one way, Snow's perspective is broader than Commager's or Schlesinger's. He at least admits two factions into his dining room. He clearly favors one, the scientific, but he admits the existence of another, however much he might deplore it.[5] For Commager and Schlesinger there is only one "real" American culture, with scattered exceptions that rate not even a seat at their American equivalent of the "high table" where the American Mind communicates with itself.

Without using Snow's unfortunate language of cultures, one might conclude from Commager and Schlesinger that there are, in the great amalgam of American culture, two attitudes toward religion that would like to be mutually exclusive. The religious try to extrude, as invaders of God's country, those who question religion's centrality in public life. Reciprocally, and somewhat unexpectedly, pragmatic "Americanists" make their own attempts at excommunication. Nor is this confined to the world of professors like Commager and Schlesinger, or politicians like Dukakis. Some journalists also think there is something un-American about religion, as they demonstrated in a 1988 flap—what a *New York Times* reporter called "a form of low-intensity intellectual warfare"—over the appointment of a president to the New York Public Library.[6] Professor Schlesinger gave his address at Brown University at the installation of the school's new president—Vartan Gregorian, who had vacated the library post. The library board had appointed six persons to a search committee, and then approved the committee's recommendation—the Reverend Timothy S. Healy, S.J., at the time president of Georgetown University, though he had held high office (vice-chancellor for academic affairs) in a secular academic institution (City University of New York) for seven years. Journalists like Gay Talese and Jimmy Breslin objected to the appointment of a Jesuit priest, not reflecting perhaps that they were instituting a religious test where there had been none before. Their warrant, Talese said in a letter to the *Times*, was that Vartan Gregorian had been not only successful but "unquestionably secular."[7] Henceforth, apparently, anyone of questionable secularity would be disqualified. The test would presumably be: Is the prospective librarian at least as secular as Dr. Gregorian? If he were secularer, that would be a bonus.

Noting that Father Healy had taken the customary religious vows, including one of obedience, Talese asked: "Obedience to whom? To his church? Or to those who disagree with his church?" It seems fairly obvious that, whatever the reach of Father Healy's vow, it did not commit him to "obey" enemies of his church. Was Talese suggesting that it should?

It was mentioned, at the time, that voters had been able to install John Kennedy in the White House and Robert Drinan (a Jesuit) in the House of Representatives without observing a religious test; but Healy's critics, who now included the novelist Joseph Heller, said that the librarian's post was even more sensitive than that of the president of the United States. The latter has only nuclear destruction at his disposal. The former can favor or disfavor ideas.[8]

I do not suppose any New York City librarian, even the exemplarily secular Gregorian, has been entirely neutral about moral values, nor has that ever been considered a condition for upholding free speech. If Healy's critics were not demanding so entire a neutrality in the librarian (a ludicrous position it would be an insult to attribute to them), and if they were not just expressing anti-Catholic bigotry (which it would also be unworthy to suspect in them), they must have been saying that a librarian should typify the American Mind as defined by Commager and Schlesinger—relativist, pragmatic, and *nonreligious* (or non-meaningfully religious, in Commager's terms). The only values such a librarian could espouse would be the quintessentially American values of these professors—certainly not the aberrant, irrational values that Professor Schlesinger fails to find anywhere in "our" tradition, documents, and folkways.

Once one has taken this position on the presidency of the New York Public Library, it seems captious to say one should not hold it, as well, for such a political office as the presidency of the nation. The chief executive has in his custody all the amendments, not merely the first; and he, even more than the librarian, should adhere to—if not, in fact, typify—the pragmatism that is his country's orthodoxy. By expecting an adherence to that orthodoxy, we will have reversed colonial America's first (pre-Constitutional) demand of officeholders, that they take religious oaths upholding at least a minimally Christian creed (as defined by the community), substituting a kind of "irreligious test," demanding the safeguard of a minimal secularity (one that would reach the benchmark of, say, Dr. Gregorian's).

This informal demand, rarely spelled out so specifically as in the case of the New York Public Library appointment, is what modern evangelicals call the standard of "secular humanism." But, for their own legal purposes, the evangelicals do not call this position irreligious. They call it a religion. Thus anyone trying to impose it is guilty of establishing a religion. In their zeal for the First Amendment, the secularists, it is claimed, undermine the First Amendment, and the evangelicals must come to the rescue of the Constitution![9]

What the evangelicals now call a religion would never have met their ancestors' definition of belief in God. For immediate tactical advantage, the believers rely on people they normally treat as enemies, the social scientists, who define religion as anyone's most comprehensive symbol-system. If the secularists' most comprehensive symbol-system does not include God, the argument goes, then their very godlessness becomes their religion. But that would not have been enough for a modern secularist to meet the old religious test of political office—he could not have sworn that he believes in God *because* he does not believe in Him. And evangelicals who suddenly express a preference for Clifford Geertz's anthropology—over, say, Increase Mather's theology—as a test of religion are acting in bad faith.[10] We can see that when they oppose tax exemptions for "secular humanists."

Yet we should not let the opportunism of the assault on "secular humanism" as a religion distract us from the problem posed by secularity as an irreligious *requirement* in modern society. Is it true that the only way to be sincerely neutral toward religion in public office is to have no religious beliefs in private life? If so, then John Kennedy was not really acceptable *as a Catholic* in the presidency. He was acceptable only to the degree that he did not really believe in his religion (as, Commager assures us, no *real* American does). This, certainly, is going beyond any expectations of the Constitution's framers. They did not suppose that the absence of religious oaths for holding office entailed, logically, irreligious officeholders.

Clearly, in our society, two large groups are talking past each other. One fails to see legitimacy in religious values not comprehended by the American Mind. The other fails to see legitimacy in irreligion: If secularity is really religious, then it is diabolic—a plot against God, not mere indifference to Him. Thus, when school textbooks steer as clear as they can of religious subjects, Pat Robertson does not see in this the work of timorous publishers trying to avoid subjects about which state school boards can be nervous. For him, it is the result of a great conspiracy against God:

> And one of them [a humanistic schoolteacher] said, "So what if Johnny can't read? We will have him for sixteen years, and we will be able to drive from him every vestige of the Christian superstition."[11]

On the other hand, when Frances FitzGerald, in her book *America Revised*, describes how publishers' timorousness and school boards' importunacy determine the content of our schools' history texts, she concentrates on the shifts in attitude toward social groups (blacks, women, Native Americans) and political issues (Reconstruction, Cold War, Vietnam), but does not notice the odd silence of such texts on the huge and embarrassing role of religion in our history. Even the controversy on evolution receives only passing reference.[12] To her, the real issues are ethnic, political, and economic. No wonder that when she came to write about evangelicals in her book *Cities on a Hill*, she found Jerry Falwell's old-time gospel comparable with the Rajneesh cult, or a retirement community in Sun City, Florida, or a gay neighborhood in San Francisco.[13] To put Falwell in this company of recent eruptions shows no sense of the depth or continuity of evangelical belief.

Secularists, unlike C. P. Snow's scientists and their foes, are not confined to a donnish little world. They speak in large part for what right-wing politicians call the "Eastern establishment." They are heavily represented in the communications industry and in the "new class" of intellectual mediators that has come under attack from neoconservatives.

Warned by the wreck of Snow's grandiose terminology, we would do well not to call this secularist bias a "culture." It is one way of looking at American culture, a prejudice about it, which is paired with the opposite prejudice, that of religious people who cannot recognize a legitimate secularity (one not the declared *enemy* of religion). Most classes and regions of the country have some people affected by these two prejudices. One might suppose that they simply represent the forces of modernity and of tradition; but in that case one would expect the traditions to be fading and the modern attitudes to be prevailing, as surely as modern technology is prevailing in our life.

Yet Michael Dukakis, the first truly modernist candidate in our politics, as trustful of secular values as of technology, was a man isolated from his fellow citizens, while George Bush was accepted by ordinary Americans as their spokesman, despite his elite (verging on effete) background. The secularist prejudice may be useful to those wanting to get ahead in certain fields; but in politics one does better to cultivate, as have all our recent presidents, the religious prejudice.[14] No one did that more than George Bush in 1988.

PART TWO

Bible Beginnings

❖ E I G H T ❖

The Superman Trial

THE ACLU AND THE RELIGIOUS RIGHT HAVE THE AIR OF FATED ANTAGO-
nists. The case that brought the ACLU its first great public recognition
was the one that discredited the most important evangelical politician of
this century, William Jennings Bryan.

In 1925, the state of Tennessee passed—in a diffident, almost tentative
manner—a law forbidding state schools to teach evolution in their biology
courses. The state-approved textbooks already contained the arguments
for evolution. Bryan himself, who had indirectly inspired the law, tried
to alter it before it was passed, and disagreed with its strategy. It was not
exactly the ground he would have preferred to defend.

The ACLU, which had been founded in 1920, after its predecessor
organization defended conscientious objectors during World War I, was
still a small operation with a one-person research staff in 1925—Lucile
Milner going through newspapers to find items concerned with civil
liberties. She read about the Tennessee law and brought it to the attention
of the union's founder, Roger Baldwin, who committed funds to challenge the law. But the ACLU had no friends, yet, in Tennessee from
whom it could learn how best to proceed. It had no recourse but to
advertise in the state's newspapers that it would support any teacher who

made a "friendly challenge" to the law. The result was a scramble by various local publicists who, for their own reasons, wanted to sponsor such a contest. Dayton won this competition, with a defendant, John T. Scopes, who claimed (rather shakily) to have broken the law. The ACLU, following its normal practice, wanted to hire an unthreatening team of local lawyers, but since it was announced that William Jennings Bryan would be helping the prosecution, John Scopes overruled his advisers and accepted an offer to be defended by the famous lawyer (and ACLU member) Clarence Darrow.

The resulting "monkey trial" was a comedy of errors in which nothing was exactly what it appeared to be. It was, in many respects, a nontrial over a nonlaw, with a nondefendant backed by nonsupporters. Its most famous moment involved nontestimony by a nonexpert, which was followed by a nondefeat. The law, it has been noticed, would have outlawed Tennessee's own state-approved textbooks if anyone had taken either the law or the texts seriously enough to look closely at them, whether singly or in conjunction. Governor Austin Peay said, at the time of signing the bill, that he would not sign it if he had any idea that it was going to be enforced:

> After a careful examination I can find nothing of consequence in the books now being taught in our schools with which this bill will interfere in the slightest manner. Therefore it will not put our teachers in any jeopardy. Probably the law will never be applied. It may not be sufficiently definite to admit of any specific application or enforcement. Nobody believes that it is going to be an active statute.[1]

The doctrine of evolution *was* "in the books now being taught." The students who testified that it was taught to them had to go back and check the text to find it there, and Scopes did not admit until after the trial that he probably missed teaching the classes covering evolution.[2] The teaching was *only* in the books, and Scopes (who never testified) seems not to have committed the act for which he took the blame or credit.

The legal question in the trial was the state legislature's right to establish the school curriculum, which was upheld by the court in its conviction of Scopes, and then upheld by the state's supreme court. But Darrow's aim at Dayton was to discredit fundamentalists, and with the help of his friend, the journalist H. L. Mencken, he did that in a famous bit of testimony that was never heard by the jury or entered into the trial record.

Bryan foolishly let himself be called as an expert witness on the Bible, and the judge let this occur though he doubted its relevance and ruled it irrelevant after one session. By that time, Bryan wanted to continue the diversion, so he could repair the damage done by Darrow's surprise maneuver in calling him to the stand; but the other prosecutors told him this digression undermined their real case. The prosecutors won in court, but Bryan's name was forever dishonored.

Thanks to Mencken and to *Inherit the Wind*, a 1950s play that continually re-creates (quite inaccurately) the famous trial on stage and on the screen, Bryan is now best known as the fuddled biblicist of Dayton, looking like a beached whale himself as he tried to explain Jonah's mode of transportation. It was the sad end to a career launched with the "Cross of Gold" speech at the Democratic convention of 1896. For thirty years after that, Bryan was the most important figure in the reform politics of America, three times the party's nominee for president, a kingmaker at the convention that chose Woodrow Wilson, and, after that, Wilson's secretary of state. No other populist agitator had Bryan's impact. His wife listed with justifiable pride the many reforms, later adopted, that he had championed in their embattled earlier stages—women's suffrage, the federal income tax, railroad regulation, currency reform, state initiative and referendum, a Department of Labor, campaign fund disclosure, and opposition to capital punishment.[3] His campaigns were the most leftist mounted by a major party's candidate in our entire history. Nor was his a merely sentimental leftism. As Robert Cherny points out:

> The middle of Bryan's career, from 1900 to 1910, reveals few instances where he reduced a complex issue to a simple one. His 1908 platform was one of the longest and most complicated up to that time. While he might have dramatically argued that private monopoly was intolerable, he posed a variety of solutions, including government ownership, licensing, and anti-trust action.[4]

Edward Larson exaggerates, but in the proper direction, when he writes, "Probably no other American, save the authors of the Bill of Rights, could rightly claim credit for as many Constitutional amendments as the Great Commoner."[5] It is one of the tragic turns of American history that this man who in so many ways extended the Bill of Rights should have been steered by character and accident into a deadly clash with the organization set up to protect the Bill of Rights.

How did the great populist reformer, the crusader against big business, war, and oppression, become the ridiculous figure of Dayton? Some have argued that Bryan declined into religion as his political career faded, but the best students of his life find religion as important to him at the outset of his career, and at the peak of his political influence, as at the sad performance on the courthouse lawn in Tennessee.

It is true that there was a physical decline in Bryan. His body was ravaged by diabetes when he went to Dayton—a condition he was trying to control with an inadequate diet, which led to his intermittently fierce attacks on food, the subject of much jesting by Darrow.[6] When Bryan died of diabetes one week after the trial, lachrymose followers said that his heart had broken. Darrow volunteered: "Broken heart nothing; he died of a busted belly."[7]

But there had been a hardening of Bryan's position on evolution over the years. He had not been convinced, in 1904, that man evolved from animals, but "I do not mean to find fault with you [his audience] if you want to accept the theory. . . . I shall not quarrel with you about it."[8] It was clearly a matter of legitimate debate for him, and even as late as 1920 he did not want to *forbid* the teaching of evolution, merely to treat it as one biological theory. The biblical account of creation did not rule out, at this stage, scientific accounts at their own level.[9] In fact, Bryan's original position was the one that modern "creationists" retreated to after the school prayer decisions of the early 1960s—neutrality regarding the various accounts of human origin. Florida had earlier passed a law in accord with Bryan's recommendations, one in which neither the biblical nor the scientific account could be taught as exclusively true, a statement of policy with no criminal penalties attached.

Bryan, though he accepted the plea to prosecute in Tennessee, did not like the criminal aspect of the case, and offered ahead of time to pay any penalty the court inflicted on Scopes. The ACLU was not looking for a criminal trial either. In its original advertisement it spoke of a "friendly challenge" to the law that would not risk the teacher's job—an attempt to bring a civil charge of unconstitutionality against the state. Instead, the local publicists agreed with Scopes to get him arrested, forcing the state to bring criminal action. Already the case was off the rails for both sides.

The court would not let Darrow produce expert witnesses before the jury to discuss the scientific consensus regarding evolution. In a brilliant move, Darrow got the judge (but not the jury) to hear Bryan testify as an expert on whether evolution in fact was irreconcilable with the biblical account. Darrow, contrary to later impressions, argued that it was not. He wanted to make Bryan fall back on biblical literalism as the only way of maintaining opposition between the Bible and science—and he succeeded beyond even his own hopes.

There was reason for his hopes to have been modest. Bryan was not, in most ways, a biblical literalist. Even in his exchange with Darrow, he admitted that the seven "days" of Genesis could have been seven ages. That was a highly respectable view in the evangelical circle Bryan belonged to—the view set forth, for instance, in the influential Scofield Bible.[10] Bryan, after all, was a man whose career typified the "social gospel" denounced by the right wing of evangelicalism. He never had the anti-Semitic or anti-Catholic views of some fundamentalists (for whom Jews were Christ-killers and the pope of Rome the Whore of Babylon). Bryan had worked easily with secular Democrats in his presidential races. He did not let St. Paul's words on the place of women keep him from supporting women's suffrage. His optimistic populism was not hampered with the extreme anti-Pelagianism of those oppressed by the doctrine of original sin. He was a Presbyterian moderate in the theological controversies of the time, and had even collaborated with the liberal William Sloane Coffin (Senior) to head off a fundamentalist takeover in his church's general assembly.[11]

Then why did Bryan become so obsessed (for he surely was) with evolution? The answer was evident back in his earliest references to the view, when he said he had nothing against it as a scientific theory. He did raise this warning: "We must be careful how we apply this doctrine of the strongest."[12] Bryan feared what came to be known in the next decade as "*social* Darwinism"—the idea that human society is an arena of struggle in which the strongest prevail, the fittest survive, and poor "misfits" must be neglected in the name of progress through "betterment of the race." Modern scholars have attacked the metaphor involved in social Darwinism and questioned whether it was ever as influential as a right-wing justification for the powerful as generations of social and cultural historians have claimed.[13] But many great scholars, most notably Richard Hofstadter, shared that misconception (if it was one) with Bryan, and there *were* important Americans who read Darwin the way Bryan feared people would—including both of Bryan's most famous adversaries in Dayton.

H. L. Mencken made his first ambitious claim upon public attention in 1908, when he published *The Philosophy of Friedrich Nietzsche*, which argues that the Nietzschean "superman" (*Übermensch*) is precisely the Darwinian "fittest" who rises above the weak crowd of history's rejects. Mencken summarizes and endorses Nietzsche's teaching thus:

> There must be a complete surrender to the law of natural selection—that invariable natural law which ordains that the fit shall survive and the unfit shall perish. All growth must occur at the top. The strong must grow stronger, and that they may do so, they must waste no strength in the vain task of trying to lift up the weak.[14]

Nothing could be more opposed to Bryan's populist belief that progress will come only from the moral support of the weaker. As he framed the question of evolution: "When reform comes in this country, it starts with the masses. Reforms do not come from the brains of scholars."[15]

Bryan's populism was simplistic, but it is not easy to claim that it was more simplistic than Mencken's antipopulism. Mencken was a literalist—in ways later scholars have derided—in applying Darwin to human ethics. Even in human history,

> the struggle for existence went on among the lions in the jungle and the protozoa in the sea ooze, and . . . the law of natural selection ruled all of animated nature—mind and matter—alike.[16]

Mencken was unflinching when he drew the social and political consequences of his doctrine. The superiorities already won—of men over women, of whites over blacks, of gentiles over Jews, of the elite over the mob—must be retained and built on in the name of progress. Since men are stronger than women, women "cultivate cunning" in order to circumvent men, becoming "shrewd, resourceful, and acute; but the very fact that they are always concerned with imminent problems [because of their physical weakness] and that, in consequence, they are unaccustomed to dealing with the larger riddles of life, makes their mental attitude essentially petty."[17]

Bryan's had been one of the strongest voices for women's suffrage. Mencken considered that reform a defeat for the hope of rule by the stronger: "The net result is that feminine morality is a morality of opportunism and imminent expediency, and that the normal woman has no respect for, and scarcely any conception of, abstract truth."[18] In the past, Mencken argued, men submitted to women, or were beguiled by them, to protect offspring in the conventional family, which made it "necessary for the stronger sex to submit to the parasitic opportunism of the weaker."[19] But in the future, the conventional family must yield to eugenic and rational schemes, dispelling the myths that served female cunning—for example, "the good old sub-Potomac doctrines that a woman who loses her virtue is, *ipso facto*, a victim and not a criminal or *particeps criminis*, and that a 'lady,' by virtue of being a 'lady,' is necessarily a reluctant and helpless quarry in the hunt of love—those ancient and venerable fallacies."[20] For Mencken, "the hunt of love" is scarcely a metaphor. It *is* the Darwinian world Bryan denounced as one where man "hunts for prey with the savage loathing of a beast."[21]

Mencken, in service to the idea of a master code (*Herrenmoral*), presents Jews as the type of the very opposite ideal, a slave code (*Sklavenmoral*). Jews, like women, are cunning in the attempt to make weakness overcome strength.[22] Their moral code was framed to protect the weak, condemning, for instance, "the quite natural act of destroying one's enemies."[23]

Bryan did not share Mencken's anti-Semitism. In fact, the distinguished lawyer Samuel Untermyer, the vice-president of the American Jewish Congress, agreed to join Bryan at the appeal stage of the Scopes trial.[24] On blacks, Bryan's record was not as good, as one might expect from a Democrat whose base was in the South as well as in the West. Few populists could afford to oppose their poor white constituents with regard to the segregation patterns of the time. But at least Bryan had no scientific *doctrine* of black inferiority. For Mencken, blacks *must* be repressed to let the stronger whites develop their genetic superiority. In fact, the oppression of blacks was one *sign* of the white man's superiority:

> In the southern states the educated white class—which there represents, though in a melancholy fashion, the Nietzschean first caste—has found it easy to take from the black masses their very right to vote, despite the fact that they are everywhere in a great majority numerically.[25]

Mencken's error about the numbers of blacks "everywhere" is itself a product of fear, which means that—though he calls superiority in the South a "melancholy" excellence because the whole area is so retrograde—the maintaining of that slender margin of superiority is crucial to progress from the depths of such a swamp.

When World War I broke out in Europe, many critics of Germany tried to blame Prussian militarism on the philosophy of Nietzsche. Mencken obliged them by turning their attacks into a boast. In 1914, he argued that Nietzsche had supplied the philosophy for modern Germany's ruthless efficiency, in which Mencken took an ethnic pride. Nietzsche had taught the Germans that

> Christianity and brotherhood were for workingmen, soldiers, servants, and yokels, for "shopkeepers, cows, women, and Englishmen," for the submerged chandala, for the whole race of subordinates, dependents, followers. But not for the higher men, not for the superman of tomorrow.[26]

This was the rationale for Bismarck's bureaucracy of experts.[27] And now, in the war, "the streams of parallel ideas coalesce. Germany becomes Nietzsche; Nietzsche becomes Germany."[28] The title Mencken gave his article was "The Mailed Fist and Its Prophet."

Ironically, one of the Americans most convinced of Nietzsche's role in Germany was William Jennings Bryan. He had tried to maintain a strict neutrality toward Germany while acting as secretary of state; but as soon as he left office he began to heed his fellow evangelists, who already had reason to distrust Germany as the source of biblical "higher criticism." Now, with a nativist fervor, they linked the ruthless scientism Mencken praised with the teachings of Darwin as extended to human relations by Nietzsche.

Thus, by one of the less-noticed twists of modern religious history, opposition to evolution served a number of fundamentalist needs. It became a pressing doctrinal concern at the very time when it could simultaneously give Christian motivation to those supporting America's participation in the war, extend the appeal of evangelical causes, and ratify the patriotism of its preachers. "Evolution became a symbol. . . . German barbarism could be explained as the result of an evolutionary 'might is right' superman philosophy."[29]

Bryan became the principal spokesman for this position.[30] It served his needs, too, at a time when he had closed off a more conventional political career by his resignation from the State Department. By the end of the war, Bryan was citing the work of an evolutionary biologist who had written a high school textbook with Darwinian doctrine—Vernon Kellogg, who in conversation with Germans in Belgium heard evolutionary doctrine being used to justify German aggression. Kellogg's book *Headquarters Nights* (1917) and Benjamin Kidd's *The Science of Power* (1918) were the kind of *moral* (rather than scientific) works Bryan used to attack the superior attitudes of undemocratic "supermen."[31]

If there was a philosophical naïveté in Bryan's treatment of Nietzsche, it was matched by others' willingness to blame a wide variety of evils on the Germans. Bryan's words were no more naive than those of a man who (in 1924) defended criminals because their minds had been poisoned by Nietzsche in college:

[Nietzsche taught that] man has no obligations; he may do with all other men and all other boys, and all society, as he pleases—the superman was a creation of Nietzsche, but it has permeated every college and university in the civilized world. . . . His very doctrine is a species of insanity. . . . His own doctrine made him a maniac.

This deleterious doctrine, which destroyed its own container, is omnipresent in its menace:

More books have been written about him than probably all the rest of the philosophers in a hundred years. More college professors have talked about him. In a way he has reached more people. . . . No other philosopher ever caused the discussion that Nietzsche has caused. There is no university in the world where the professors are not familiar with Nietzsche, not one. . . . I will guarantee that you can go down to the University of Chicago today—into its big library—and find over a thousand volumes on Nietzsche, and I am sure I am speaking moderately.

Nietzsche, it is admitted, may not bear the "responsibility for the war" that has been assigned him, but he "believed that sometime the superman would be born, that *evolution* was working toward the superman" (italics added). Here it is claimed not only that Nietzsche's doctrine is potentially corrupting (indeed, liable to craze its holder) but that it actually corrupted the killer who was exposed to it in college.

Is there any blame attached because somebody took Nietzsche's philosophy seriously and fashioned his life on it? And there is not any question in this case that it is true. Then who is to blame? The university would be more to blame than he is.

If exposure to Nietzsche could inflict such damage on the morals of a college student, then the citizens of Tennessee might understandably hesitate to expose even younger students to the moral doctrines of Darwin, who was considered the inspirer of Nietzsche. Indeed, Bryan would have been well advised to use the very passages just quoted in his argument at Dayton—which, in fact, he did, since the author of the preceding passages was Clarence Darrow, arguing for leniency in the sentencing of his clients, the teenage "thrill killers" Nathan Leopold and Richard Loeb.[32]

When Bryan quoted Darrow's own words that "the university would be more to blame," Darrow quoted from a later part of his plea to the jury, which said "the universities are not to blame." Who was, then? The matter was dropped in Dayton, but in Chicago Darrow blamed the system of education that does not allow close attention to each student's needs. In that case, a teacher would have recognized that Nietzsche "belonged to older boys" than Nathan Leopold, who "should never have seen it at that early age." Leopold had gone young to college; and Darrow, the defender of academic freedom, makes an exception for those too young to hear profane doctrine—a point which should have told on Bryan's side where high school teaching was at stake.

Of course, Darrow did not believe his own argument in the famous Chicago murder case. He was himself an enthusiastic Nietzschean of the Mencken sort. He had a stock Nietzsche lecture that he took out on the Chautauqua lecture circuit when he needed money.[33] His attack on crazy foreign ideas, on experts, on professors as corrupting good American youth—his exaggerated description of all those *books* absorbing the attention of all those philosophers—was a populist pose assumed to impress the jury. And it did. But Darrow was no populist. As he said of Nietzsche in his lecture, "His idea was that whatever a majority believed must necessarily be untrue."[34]

The man who had to feign a populism he did not hold while pleading for Loeb and Leopold could let his real feelings show in Dayton. In Chicago he had deplored the lack of close supervision for the eighteen-year-old Leopold. His more usual attitude was expressed during the Scopes case:

> Strange how anxious old folk are apt to be over the children. The main reason for this is that children do not act like the old people.[35]

In Dayton, Darrow meant to ridicule and humiliate Bryan: "My object, and my only object, was to focus the attention of the country on the programme of Mr. Bryan and the other fundamentalists in America."[36] He was addressing the nation, not the local audience: "We knew that it was hopeless to fight again for a verdict in Tennessee so long as it remained in its present stage of civilization."[37] The "stages of civilization" treatment of the South was one Mencken was already famous for.

The Scopes trial, comic in its circus aspect, left behind it something tragic: It sealed off from each other, in mutual incomprehension, forces that had hitherto worked together in American history. Bryan's career had been a sign of the possible integration of progressive politics and evangelical moralism.[38] That seemed an incongruous union to Darrow and others, who meant to end it by destroying fundamentalism. Science demanded nothing less. For the forces of the ACLU, the Scopes trial was what Mencken labeled it—the monkey trial. For Bryan, it was the superman trial, a defense of the populace against secular experts. The trial itself ended in spectacular irrelevancies; Darrow and Mencken departed thinking they had won a victory. Amid all the misunderstanding that surrounded this trial, that was the greatest error of all.

Scopes: Who Won?

THE SCOPES TRIAL IS ONE OF THE BEST EARLY EXAMPLES OF WHAT WOULD later be known as a "media event." Not only was the trial heavily covered; it changed its nature to accommodate the coverage. The judge let radio lines be brought into the courtroom, and held up the proceedings to let photographers get better shots of them. More words were cabled abroad than had been devoted to any earlier event. When the crowds could not fit inside the courthouse, the judge moved the whole trial out onto the lawn—Bryan's infamous testimony occurred alfresco. On the edges of the leafy square, exotic preachers, freak shows, and peddlers gave the gathering an eerily appropriate touch of old camp meetings. Evangelicalism went to its ordeal in a setting like that of its earlier triumphs.

The *Baltimore Sun* papers sent to Dayton the unusual number of five reporters, led by Mencken, the most famous journalist of the day. Westbrook Pegler and Joseph Wood Krutch were also on hand. *The New York Times* ran the trial on its front page every day. When the scientists brought to Tennessee were not allowed to give their testimony to the court, they held little seminars for newsmen clustering around the trial's fringe. The point of a "media event" is not simply that it is heavily covered, but that coverage is more important than what is officially going on. The real trial, it was agreed, was taking place in the newspapers. Things the jury was never exposed to got the heaviest emphasis around the nation.

That was the way Henry Mencken had planned it. Mencken knew Darrow, from having published a piece of his in *The American Mercury*, and by chance they were together in Richmond when news reached them that Bryan would be arguing for the Tennessee law. Mencken urged Darrow to break his rule against volunteering his services. From that time Mencken remained Darrow's "Consulting Man" (as he put it) on the trial.[1] Between them they could beat back "the massed forces of darkness."[2] They had other allies in the press, like Watson Davis, who syndicated science news to various papers; Davis helped collect experts who would testify for Scopes.[3] Modern evangelists are usually being paranoid when they say that the media are out to destroy them; but that would have been an accurate description of Mencken's work behind the scenes at Dayton. It was he who realized that the real trial would take place outside the courtroom. As he told Darrow in Richmond, "Nobody gives a damn about that yap schoolteacher [Scopes]. The thing to do is make a fool out of Bryan."[4]

Mencken at Dayton was more an impresario than a reporter, more Darrow's colleague than his critic. When this kind of thing happens today—for example, when George Will helps coach Ronald Reagan for a debate and then evaluates the performance for a network—most journalists protest the abuse. But Mencken is still celebrated for his activity in Dayton. His admirers even believe that he (with Darrow's help, of course) delivered "the final mortal blow" to Puritanism in America when he discredited Bryan.[5] Mencken himself put it more personally when he used to say of Bryan, "Well, we killed the son of a bitch."[6]

Darrow was just as convinced that he had won the "real" trial in Dayton, though he lost (as he had expected) in narrowly legal terms. He had not come to get his client off (his customary mission), but to indict by ridicule those who would prosecute him on such a charge. He had contempt not only for the judge but for the jury, telling them they *had* to convict, letting them know he wanted nothing more than to get the case out of this courtroom, before judges better qualified to deal with scientific matters. When the judge informed him that he should "always expect this court to rule correctly," Darrow said on the record: "No, sir, we do not. We expect to protect our rights in some other court. Now, that is plain enough, isn't it?" Later, when the judge protested, "I hope you do not mean to reflect on the court," Darrow answered, "Well, Your Honor has the right to hope."[7]

Darrow thought he had made the judge and other officials so much an embarrassment to the local community that even Tennesseans, though he called them barbarians, could not continue such disgraced men in office. The thoroughness of Darrow's victory was measured not only in the Baltimore press but at the Tennessee polls:

> Judge Raulston, not easily daunted, achieved some further glory through speechmaking in fundamentalist churches on the evolution question as he saw it. He was eminently qualified; he had never read a line on the subject, and very little on any other, and had held that to teach evolution was a criminal offense in Tennessee and therefore presumably wicked everywhere. But there was no great rush at the box office to attend his lectures, so he went back to his home town in Tennessee, and when his term expired he ran for re-election, but was defeated for nomination. Later he tried to get the nomination for governor of the State as honor and glory for having served the Lord, but was beaten in that lofty ambition. So it was "back to the mines," and he resumed trying replevin cases and collecting bills for the town merchants.
>
> The county superintendent of schools who had employed Mr. Scopes also ran for office in the autumn after the case was tried. He circulated his cards through the State which bore the glorious emblem "Prosecutor of John T. Scopes." But Tennessee once more proved itself ungrateful; he was not nominated. Dayton and Tennessee had gained all the notoriety out of the case that it deserved. So the county superintendent, whose name I believe was White, though it may have been Smith or Jones, or even Black, also returned "to the mines," although I believe that he was a carpenter, or perhaps a plumber.[8]

But better students have found the electoral aftermath of the case quite different from the picture Darrow gives us. It helped rather than hurt most major figures to have been involved in prosecuting Scopes: "Tennessee Governor Peay was re-elected in 1926, lead prosecutor Thomas Stewart was elected to the U.S. Senate, and local prosecutor S. K. Hicks was elected to the state House of Representatives."[9]

Darrow seems incapable of seeing that the *moral* argument against *social* Darwinism (the kind of argument about social conditioning he had used in the Leopold-Loeb case) was not touched by ridicule of the Genesis account in his exchange with Bryan. This is all the more surprising since he shaped the trial precisely as a morality play. For this purpose he diabolized Bryan, treating him as evil rather than pitiful. Bryan was not only "the idol of Idiotdom." More despicably, "he had reached a stage of hallucination that would impel him to commit any cruelty that he believed would help his cause."[10] The authors of the play *Inherit the Wind* wanted to accept this view, but could find nothing in the court record to justify it; so they invented a character, a young woman in love with Scopes, whom Bryan could bully and victimize. How far this is from the facts can be seen in Scopes's own sympathetic treatment of Bryan in his book. He still found in him, even in his final days in Dayton, traces of the most eloquent speaker he had ever heard, and he never doubted his sincerity.[11]

Darrow, like Mencken, used the trial as a vehicle for affecting public opinion. But that did not mean appealing to what Mencken called "the booboisie." It was *enlightened* opinion that mattered. Both men, for all the cynicism of their poses, had a touching faith in the power of scientific evidence, once vindicated by argument, to make its own way in the world. This led Darrow to take the gamble of bringing in outside experts to testify—which was not only an affront to local pride but a relatively risky new procedure in the law.[12]

The role of experts was a hotly debated issue in the 1920s. Robert and Helen Lynd argued in their classic study, *Middletown*, that modern life had become too complex for ordinary householders to get along without the help of experts. The model for such a division of labor was the scientific bureaucracy Mencken celebrated at the beginning of World War I:

> [Wilhelm] Koch rid Germany of typhoid fever by penning up the population of whole villages and condemning whole watersheds. It was ruthless, it was unpopular, it broke down and made a mock of a host of "inalienable" rights—but it worked.[13]

That insouciance about penning up people for their own good is hard for a politician to affect in America. To the populists it was anathema. And even such a mildly progressive Democrat as Woodrow Wilson, in his first campaign for president, had to flatter the people:

> What I fear is a government of experts. God forbid that in a democratic country we should resign the task and give the government over to experts. What are we for if we are to be scientifically taken care of by a small number of gentlemen who are the only men who understand the job?[14]

This, of course, had long been Bryan's doctrine: "According to our system of government, the people are interested in everything and can be trusted to decide everything."[15] But during World War I Wilson had been forced to turn to experts, the normal result of war in the modern age—which led to a reaction against their sudden prominence in the turbulent postwar years.[16] Through it all, Bryan had remained true to his populism. He drew its radical consequences in religion as in politics: "The one beauty about the word of God is that it does not take an expert to understand it."[17] By tying Bryan up on basic questions about the biblical account of creation, Darrow thought he had demonstrated that it *does* take an expert to understand the Bible. But Americans were even less prepared to accept that view than they were the need for a "knowledge elite" in politics. When neoconservatives fashioned an attack on the "elitist new class" in the 1970s, they were returning to a question Mencken and Darrow thought they had settled in 1925.

If Darrow misunderstood the impact of his summoned experts on the populace at large, he was also mistaken in a matter closer to his own expertise. He repeatedly said that his only aim in the Scopes case was to get the process out of the state court and into the federal courts. That was the goal of the ACLU, too; but most members of that organization, who had not wanted Darrow in the first place, thought he was going about it the wrong way. At the appeal level in the state courts, the union again tried to have Darrow removed from the case. He was going far in the newspapers but not in the courts, they feared; and they were right.[18]

Darrow let it be known that Tennessee could not be trusted to decide its own fate "so long as the State remained in its present stage of civilization."[19] So the state appeals court decided to show the big-city lawyer that it, too, had tricks to play. Relying on a technicality in the sentencing procedure, the court overthrew Scopes's conviction, leaving Darrow no case to take up to the Supreme Court. Scopes was free of his fine, and Darrow's hands were tied—just what the ACLU officers had feared. The publicity had backfired, scaring the state court into its defensive maneuver. In the opinion of the chief justice of the court, "We see nothing to be gained by prolonging the life of this bizarre case."[20] Darrow had made it bizarre; that was what derailed it.

Of course, his client—as was usual—got off. But that was the last thing he wanted at this stage. Scopes was acquitted; but the law under which he had first been convicted still stood—and would stand for another forty-two years. One of Darrow's colleagues took comfort that no one else would be indicted under the law. But the more important fact is that there would be no need to enforce the law. The textbooks were altered: No other Scopes would find in Tennessee's books what Scopes had— not for decades, at any rate. Publishers all across the nation took alarm from the Scopes trial and began a very efficient purge of Darwin from high school texts.[21] Just as the lawyers and journalists left Dayton, laughing and congratulating themselves that they had slain fundamentalism, the teaching of evolution was starting its decline in America, one from which it would not recover until the 1960s.

Almost everything about the Scopes trial has been misrepresented, and it is the "educated" part of America that accepted the distortions. The "experts" were the ones who believed that evolution had triumphed in Dayton. Only careful study of what was actually taught before and after the Tennessee trial has led to a revision of the history. Ferenc Morton Szasz presents the new opinion:

> The Scopes trial is often seen as the high point of the Fundamentalist controversy, but this view is open to doubt. Because of the reputations of the men involved, it received the most publicity, but instead of being the apex, it was really just the beginning of the concerted antievolution agitation. The trial proved that an evolution law could be passed and upheld, and pressure on many of the legislatures increased after 1925 until the peak year, 1927, when such laws had been introduced in thirteen states. Most failed to pass, and Rhode Island relegated theirs to the Committee on Fish and Game, but Mississippi and Arkansas put antievolution laws on their books. California allowed the teaching of evolution only as "theory." The governor of Texas, Miriam "Ma" Ferguson, personally saw that evolution was eliminated from the school textbooks. Even more effective, and impossible to uncover, were the actions by the various local school boards.[22]

The real story was what was happening in the schools, and scientists had no idea about that. Darwinism had silently crept into texts in the late nineteenth and early twentieth centuries. In the late 1920s and early 1930s it just as quietly crept out, and those in the scientific community did not notice it. "Educators dominated the biology textbook market from the start. Biologists did not abandon the field after Scopes; they simply did not enter it until 1960."[23] It was not Scopes that put evolution in the schools, but *Sputnik*. The Soviet space satellite caused a widespread fear that Russians taught science more efficiently than Americans. American experts, who thought they had "settled" Bryan, finally took a look at what Americans were actually being taught; and what they were being taught about the origin of mankind more often assumed the Genesis account than Darwin's.

This came as a great surprise to the better-educated parts of America. They were as unaware of anti-Darwinism persisting in the schools as Michael Dukakis was of resentment against the ACLU in large parts of the electorate. In fact, the two prejudices at play around the Dukakis campaign took their modern shape in the aftermath of the Scopes trial. Bryan always called the East "enemy country," and the press did everything it could to justify his presumption of hostility. But animosity matters less than basic misunderstanding. Mencken and others took silence on the part of the "boobs" as a concession of defeat. Darrow even thought the Tennessee voters had joined him in mocking their own officials. It was a blindness that would haunt many lesser men to our own day. No ignorance is more securely lodged than the ignorance of the learned.

✧ T E N ✧

Refighting Scopes

IN THE LATE 1950S, AMERICANS HEARD AN UNCHARACTERISTIC NOTE IN their political discourse—self-doubt. The beep from *Sputnik* as it circled Earth was a constant reminder that some brains were busying themselves on other than American priorities in what we had come to think of as "the American century." Reported deficiencies in our schools led to the wry fear that "Johnny can't read (but Ivan can)." Among the learned a deadlier myth was being spread by leaks—that the Soviet Union enjoyed a superiority over the United States in nuclear missiles (a charge John Kennedy would bring into the open during the 1960 campaign).

Only ninety miles from our border, a Soviet satellite of a different sort was defying America's control of its own hemisphere. Kennedy also made campaign use of this humiliation in what he called "Cuber." At home, President Eisenhower seemed to get the worst of both worlds by hesitating over enforcement of the Supreme Court's *Brown* decision and, none-theless, sending in federal troops to desegregate an Arkansas high school. The benevolent hero of World War II looked as if he were exercising as little control over the nation as over his syntax. Senator Kennedy called for a new generation of leaders, born in this century, to get America "moving again." (Queen Victoria was still on her throne when Dwight Eisenhower was born.)

Americans are not very good at self-doubt; so the election of Kennedy was taken as a sign that the country could once more "bear any burden" to restore its supremacy—in Cuba, in Southeast Asia, and even on the moon. The famous inaugural address—"Ask not what your country can do for you"—encouraged some people to do generous, sometimes foolish, things for their country, abroad (in the Peace Corps or the Green Berets) and at home (in civil rights and free-speech agitation). And the euphoria of the time took an ironically secular turn—ironically, because John Kennedy, elected with help from Catholic urban machines (most notably Mayor Daley's in Chicago), had frightened some evangelicals, who thought the pope would rule America from Rome. But Rome gave us, instead of the pope, a new Caesar. Robert Frost called Kennedy's a renewed "Augustan age." Robert Bellah, in the profoundest reaction to the classicism of Kennedy's inauguration, revived Rousseau's entirely Roman notion of a "civil religion." Bellah's concept can move in different directions, like the Greeks' two-headed snake, the amphisbaena: Later it would be used to reintroduce religiosity into political talk, but in 1966 (at the last moment before Vietnam shattered Kennedy's palladian realm of dreams), it marked a search for sturdier civic gods of intellect and duty beneath the smarmy piety indulged around Eisenhower.[1] American evangelicals, who had braced themselves for an Irish Catholic presidency, were hit instead by a secularizing religion of the state that had its own rites and sacred symbols (touch football, PT-109 tie clips), even its own religious order (the Peace Corps).

In the brief moment of self-doubt before this new wave of euphoria, the nation's intellectual elite had taken a panicky look at what was actually going on in American schools. Post-*Sputnik* money generated new kinds of textbooks in the physical and social sciences. These texts tried to make American children more worldly-wise, in order to make them more responsible for the world. One cannot train future Peace Corps volunteers in ignorance of the cultures they will be serving. Those aware of the "cultural lag" in America's schools—where creationism, ethnocentrism, and cartoon versions of American history had undergone little challenge—tried to make up for lost time, in the sixties, by massive shots of cultural awareness. Not only foreign cultures but indigenous Americans' patterns of living were introduced into formerly all-white schoolbooks. Blacks, Native Americans, and Eskimos were studied; American history began to include more about Mayan, Aztec, and other cultures that are part of our hemisphere's past.[2]

The religious Right found it hard to resist this onslaught of federal money introducing new (often Darwinian) texts into the schools, since the emphasis on science was given an anti-Communist justification in the congressional funding debates. American schools had to modernize in order to catch up with the Russians. Yet, even so, hard-liners felt that their brethren who accepted the new texts were falling into a devil's trap.

There was much to frighten them in the 1960s. Terrain they had quietly held for decades was overrun from many directions. Desegregation of schools challenged all the religious justifications established for a "paternalistic" control of Southern blacks. Even more direct attacks on religion followed with dizzying rapidity. In 1962, an ecumenical public-school prayer was struck down in New York (the *Engel* decision). In 1963, Bible reading and the Lord's Prayer were outlawed in public schools (the *Schempp* decision). In 1966, Arkansas finally overthrew the quiet ban on teaching evolution (the *Epperson* case). In 1968, the *Epperson* decision was upheld, and in 1973 abortion was legalized nationwide (the *Roe* decision). These were acts of "the Warren Court," the same panel of judges that had desegregated the schools—confirming fundamentalist suspicions that the highest court in the land was engaged in a *Kulturkampf* against established mores. The assaults on federal judges mounted by George Wallace (and imitated in 1968 by Richard Nixon) were interpreted by secular analysts as a naked appeal to racism. But many citizens who were only indirectly allied with racists (by a conservative fear of too-rapid change) found themselves agreeing with criticism of Earl Warren's Supreme Court. Even some liberals feared the Court would destroy its own influence by getting too far ahead of the society's consensus on matters like abortion.

A tidal wave of change seemed to make all institutions of authority falter during the sixties. Churches, schools, the military, the Court, America's moral claim on other countries, past and present policy, patriotism—all were under siege. Flags were burned along with draft cards. The planning of college commencements became a branch of riot-control theory.

What concerned even secular analysts seemed to galvanize the religious Right. Its leaders read a deeper significance into activities they considered not only diabolic in themselves but perhaps the prelude to history's "end time." The contraceptive pill and feminism seemed to make chastity obsolete. Long hair and unisex clothes weakened the taboos on homo-eroticism. Technological advances put screaming rock music, video pornography, and demonstrators' walkie-talkies in the hands of adolescents. Blow after blow disoriented the guardians of religious authority, a particularly stunning series in the agitated decade that ran from 1962 (the year of the *Engel* decision) to 1973 (the year of the *Roe* decision). Religious people who had learned to be content with their quiet hold on local institutions found even that realm imperiled. Community pressure had kept girlie magazines off newsstands, even mildly sexy movies out of theaters, sales of condoms under the counter, into the fifties. In the sixties, nudity in movies, in magazines, on the stage, broke those informal agreements that had produced the effects of censorship without the overt machinery of repression.

People who felt their home space violated had to go on the attack. They saw their enemies as conscious conspirators against their peace: The ACLU was in league with the federal courts, from which it exacted rulings favorable to its long-range program. The bureaucracy implemented the resulting decisions—Robert Kennedy and Ramsey Clark in the Justice Department, the lobbyists and teachers of the National Education Association in Congress and in classrooms.

As if in fulfillment of Bryan's dark fears, it was *social* Darwinism that entered the textbooks in the 1960s and 1970s. What disturbed parents was not, primarily, biology textbooks teaching evolution, but the new anthropology series that connected Darwinism with social and moral relativism. The harbinger of this approach was in the schools by 1963, a set of texts produced with federal aid by the American Institute of Biological Sciences—and religious conservatives denounced this "atheistic" series.[3] But the most innovative program was still to come. The National Science Foundation gave five million dollars to a firm headed by Jerome Bruner of Harvard, who devised a curriculum for the social sciences considered as a unit. The result, called MACOS (*Man: A Course of Study*), was to be taught in the fifth and sixth grades.

By the time MACOS textbooks reached classrooms in 1970, they had become a perfect example of everything traditionalists hated about the use of their schoolrooms as laboratories for reshaping the minds of children. The whole subject of cultural anthropology was new at the elementary level. Why introduce it to children at such early ages? This seemed like trying out, on the young, fads that were even younger than they.

The MACOS program followed a "quest" method, giving students material from different cultures and encouraging them to ask how human groups organize themselves, set patterns of conduct, respond to environments, and invent traditions.[4] All these looked like subtle ways of questioning the authority of absolute truths. Since religion was played down, to keep schools in conformity with constitutional bans on teaching religion, the books seemed implicitly atheist. It was also learned that the privileged can more blithely compare their own conduct with that of "primitive" cultures than can people with an insecure purchase on their own dignity in the social order.

Given the content and methods of the series, frightened parents feared that the program was introduced so early for the purposes of indoctrination. Protests against MACOS tapped a vein of animosity in 1970. Local communities rose up, linked their efforts with others, found champions in Congress (Representative John Conlan of Arizona) and the press (columnist Jack Kilpatrick), caused an abrupt plunge in the use of the texts, threatened the very existence of the National Science Foundation, and brought about the passage of inhibiting new rules for federal treatment of school curricula.[5] This was a first, encouraging sign to the religious Right that it could mobilize its forces on a national basis.

When Jimmy Carter was elected president in 1976, many secular commentators first became aware of the evangelical activists, and assigned them a disproportionate role in Carter's unexpectedly rapid rise. Carter himself was closer to the mark when he gave credit to Dr. Martin Luther King for taking the stigma off Southern politicians in the national arena. Evangelical discontent with Carter's liberalism would prove in 1980 that he was never an authentic representative of their grievances. Carter was that rare Southerner who could, for a moment, alleviate the Democrats' presidential problem with the South. He was a genuine Southerner (Bible school teacher, military academy graduate, peanut farmer with a gothic family) who could speak, nonetheless, to blacks and Northerners. Even then, he lost the white Southern vote to Gerald Ford, squeaking by with the black vote and enough whites willing to suspend their suspicion out of local pride, at least for one election. Carter was always going to be a one-term president.

The political energies of the religious Right turned without a struggle from Carter to Reagan, disillusioned by Carter's flaccid approach to Communism, his disinterest in the "social issues," his "relativistic" internationalism. For them, Andrew Young's courtship of third-world countries from his seat at the UN was a nightmare out of MACOS, replacing America as the moral arbiter of the world with a scramble of heathen outsiders as exotic as their costumes.

Ronald Reagan came to reassure these people that "we're number one." He spoke their language of God and country, of finding the answer to all life's problems in the Bible. He encouraged the private Christian schools, which people established to escape the "indoctrination" planned by school boards. He attacked the MACOS program by name. He had cooperated, as governor of California, with that state's director of state education, Max Rafferty, who was a national hero to the Right for his opposition to "relativistic" modern forms of education. Rafferty's *Suffer, Little Children* (1962) was one of the books that formed the little canon of conservative guides in the 1960s. Others were Barry Goldwater's *Conscience of a Conservative* (1960), John Stormer's *None Dare Call It Treason* (1964), and Phyllis Schlafly's *A Choice, Not an Echo* (1964). Ronald Reagan, who entered politics in 1964, in the state where conservative ferment was most evident—where, for instance, the new John Birch Society put a member into the United States Congress—absorbed into his rhetoric elements from all these books. He had campaigned with Goldwater and Rafferty and Schlafly, and he would cite them in his radio and newspaper commentaries. People who observed the religious scene only casually were surprised that ardent believers would desert their studiously biblical fellow Baptist, Jimmy Carter, to vote for Reagan in 1980. The greater wonder, for those familiar with the religious priorities of the Right, was that Carter had ever won the evangelical vote. Jerry Falwell said he had been deceived by Carter. Evangelicals vented on Carter all the rage and disappointment of a supposed betrayal. They felt the secular menace had grown under his stewardship.

Reagan had cultivated politically active evangelicals. He was far closer to the range of their concerns than Jimmy Carter had ever been. Carter, though a sincere biblical believer, was a liberal in theology as well as in politics, not a fundamentalist when it came to matters like evolution. He experienced no tension doing scientific work as a nuclear engineer. But Reagan would tell evangelicals, by the time he ran for president in 1980:

> [Evolution] is a theory, it is a scientific theory only, and it has in recent years been challenged in the world of science and it is not yet believed in the scientific community to be as infallible as it was once believed. But if it was going to be taught in the schools then I think that also the biblical theory of creation, which is not a theory but the biblical story of creation, should also be taught.[6]

That kind of assurance the religious Right would never have won from Jimmy Carter. At a time when apocalyptic prophecies were taking on new urgency in the evangelical community, Jimmy Carter gave his 1977 address at Notre Dame downplaying the Communist threat—as opposed to Reagan, who would treat the Soviet Union as "the evil empire." None of the Right's particular targets was singled out for attack by Carter—the federal courts, the ACLU, the National Education Association, the feminists. All of them were assailed by Reagan, who even promised to abolish the federal Department of Education. Reagan was pro-life and Carter pro-choice.

It was time, religious leaders had decided, for a counterattack, on many levels—in the schools, in the courts, in local, state, and federal politics. Some made their cause abortion, some school prayer, some creationism. There was debate about which was the most vulnerable point in the liberal citadel. With the *Roe* decision of 1973, abortion, not a traditional concern of evangelicals in the past, became almost overnight a focus of resentment at court "interference" with the family. If a young girl could get an abortion without her parents' knowledge or consent, then the "kidnapping" of children by public school teachers had been completed.

Others turned to more traditional concerns, like the old war, never quite lost until the sixties, against evolution. The quiet success in keeping Darwin out of textbooks was no longer possible after the *Epperson* decision; but a whole new generation of Bible scholars, legal activists, and even scientists was ready to take up the battle again in public debate. The continuity with Bryan's effort was most evident in the rehabilitation of George McCready Price, the Seventh-Day Adventist who taught himself geology in order to refute Darwin. When Darrow had asked Bryan for the name of a single scientist who opposed evolution, Bryan rather shamefacedly brought up Price's name, only to have Darrow laugh it away. But Price deserves some kind of award for creative imagination, and for economy of argument: He countered all the Darwinian arguments with one simple chess move of the mind.

The challenge to biblical chronology was built on the layers of fossils that extended time dizzyingly backward, far beyond any calendar furnished by scriptural genealogies. But what if the layers that seemed the work of centuries, slowly heaving new layers of earth over ancient ones, were created by a catastrophic event that not only destroyed all life but jumbled the slain beasts in an earth harrowed and seethed and sifted as in some giant Mixmaster? Then the strata of fossils would not record the slow buildup of life on earth but the sudden crushing of a doomed world and the churning of its rubble in the kind of apocalypse people now connect with nuclear catastrophe.

For Price, the Deluge was just that catastrophe—not the gentle "Noye's Fludde" of medieval imagery, a longish rainfall. The forty days of storm were just the heart of the maelstrom. For over a year the world, cracked, erupted, awash, would have been uninhabitable; the chosen remnant tossed on the "ark" was as out of touch with the continuing destruction beneath the waters as if it were on a modern spacecraft circling Earth, with all signals to the home base going unanswered.

For Price, the important text was not so much the first chapter of Genesis but the seventh. Noah's time, not Adam's, was relevant to the geological evidence of the earth's antiquity. All traces of the innocent and fallen Eden were effaced by the Deluge, which created a disorderly new world appropriate to man's second fall into sin and punishment. Adam had merely been driven out of Paradise; but his sinful descendants brought the world crashing down around them. Cosmic evil—all later storms, droughts, earthquakes, tidal waves—were but aftershudders of this great rending.

Even Bryan did not bank heavily on Price's daring theory. But fellow Adventists took it seriously enough to make corrections in it; they tried to bring it into conformity with the stratigraphic record being developed by geologists. And Price kept on living and cranking out booklets on his theme (he died in 1962, just as Darwin was reentering elementary textbooks—he had completed his ninety-second year and several hundred books).[7]

One of those books stirred the mind of a young scientist named Henry M. Morris, who decided to take his doctorate (at the University of Minnesota) not in the expected areas of biology or geology, but in hydraulics.[8] If Genesis 7 was the key text, not Genesis 1, Morris would have to understand the engineering aspects of water damage. He became a respected scholar in his field, the author of a widely used college textbook, and chairman of the civil engineering department at Virginia Polytechnic Institute (1957–70). But meanwhile he had been putting together a team of other scientists, some eminent though in unexpected ways—for example, the horticultural geneticist Walter Lammerts—who would study aspects of flood technology. After the publication of his major book in 1960 (*The Genesis Flood*, written with theologian John C. Whitcomb), Morris became the organizer of various groups of Deluge scientists who worked their own specialty, off from the mainstream of conventional geology. As radical opponents of the regnant paradigm, they liked to quote Thomas Kuhn on the way science neglects what its practitioners do not expect to see.

With money raised by the popular evangelist Tim LaHaye, Morris set up Christian Heritage College in San Diego to provide a liberal arts education fully in accord with the Bible. On the campus at first, but then moved to its separate laboratory facilities, the Institute for Creation Research gave Christians with higher degrees the opportunity to conduct experiments in, for instance, meteorology—to test computer models of pre-Deluge and post-Deluge atmospheric pressures. Along with such conventional lab work as carbon dating, the ICR equipped several expeditions to find the remains of the vessel in which Noah rode out the end of the world. "Noah's ark," by this hypothesis, was one of the world's great engineering feats—tough enough to be battered by tremendous forces on the outside while carrying a huge and mobile cargo. (It had to contain dinosaurs and their forage for a year.) Those who go through the ICR's Museum of Creation can see a model of the ark used in an educational movie made on the Flood—it had to be as long as one and a half football fields, at least three stories high, and with labyrinthine chambers. It is unlikely that this largest wonder of the ancient world could disappear without a trace. Dr. Morris's son had already, with the permission of the Turkish government, explored by helicopter and infrared camera the Ararat region. If even a small portion of the ark remains, it will furnish the pious with many more splinters than the True Cross ever did.[9]

So far has George McCready Price's hypothesis made its way in the modern world. A different kind of expertise brought the new "creationism" into courtrooms. After the *Epperson* decision accomplished what the Scopes trial had not, Christian lawyers tried to find ways to teach creation without teaching religion. The first attempts were brilliant but inconclusive. A clever student on *The Yale Law Journal*, Wendell Bird, tried to use the ACLU's own logic against itself. Civil liberties lawyers had said that schools could not force students to take positions against their religion—for example, make Jehovah's Witnesses say the Pledge of Allegiance. Then why should believers in creation have to give Darwinian answers on biology tests? If it is answered that Darwin does not exactly *proscribe* all belief in creation, then why not *teach* Darwin that way, as a scientific hypothesis alongside which different kinds of hypotheses are entertainable? American politics had adopted an "equal time" approach to broadcasting the differing views of parties and candidates. Why not observe a similar "fairness doctrine" in educational matters? Polls showed that people responded favorably when the question was posed this way, and two states—Arkansas and Louisiana—passed new laws based on the Bird argument for "equal time." Twenty-three such bills were introduced in state legislatures during the 1970s, prompting Morris and his allies to proclaim that the 1980s would become "the Decade of Creation."[10]

But Bird's arguments were shot down by the Supreme Court's rulings on equal time in Arkansas (*McLean*, 1982) and Louisiana (*Aguillard*, 1986). Bird had made the tactical mistake of beginning with the *religious* views of dissenters from Darwin. The parallel with Jehovah's Witnesses did not stand up, since the Supreme Court had not said that teachers must, in deference to Witnesses' conscience, teach as an equal "hypothesis" that the flag is a graven image.

Bird, still resourceful, recast his strategy. The Supreme Court had found in the legislative record of the Arkansas and Louisiana bills that religious belief was prompting the champions of the creation "hypothesis." But what if creation could be advanced, entirely apart from religious views, as a valid scientific position? Science, after all, is what scientists do; and Morris's colleagues, all academically credentialed scientists, were doing patently scientific acts at their spectographs, microscopes, and computers. So now Delugism, divorced from the Bible, presented itself as "creation science"—as opposed to creation theology, creation myth, creation exegesis, or creation story. As long as scientific arguments can be advanced, based on a choreography of scientific acts, to argue an "abrupt-appearance" cosmogony (some form of the "big bang" theory, give or take billions of eons here or there), who can prevent science teachers from presenting their entertaining, if not convincing, theory? Advocates of academic freedom always have a problem when it comes to *proscribing* views or establishing one orthodox opinion.[11]

This is the approach that "creationists" are now taking to the problem of creation. And, as an option to teachers encouraged by local school boards, it could make the *McLean* and *Aguillard* decisions as hollow a "victory" as *Scopes* proved in the 1920s. The creation story is not going to go away as a political issue, for the obvious cultural reason that the Bible is not going to stop being the central book in our intellectual heritage.

PART THREE

Bible Endings: "Premil"

❖ E L E V E N ❖

Fundamentals

BRYAN, IN THE TENNESSEE COURTROOM, WAS FOLLOWING A DEEP INSTINCT of American culture, to reject "expert" (Augustinian) readings of Scripture in the name of down-to-earth (Lutheran) "facts, ma'am, just the facts." Fundamentalists have trouble with the "facts" of the creation story in Genesis. Bryan tried, in his answers to Darrow's questions, to repeat that he accepted the story "as it is given"—that is, at whatever level intended.[1] His lack of interest in paleography Darrow equated with ignorance of the Bible.

> DARROW: Do you know there are thousands of books in your libraries on all those subjects I have been asking you about?
> BRYAN: I couldn't say, but I will take your word for it.
> DARROW: Did you ever read a book on primitive man? Like Tyler's *Primitive Culture* or Boas or any of the great authorities?
> BRYAN: I don't think I ever read the ones you have mentioned. . . .
> DARROW: You don't care how old the earth is, how old man is, and how long the animals have been here?
> BRYAN: I am not so much interested in that.[2]

Bryan was trying to argue for a moral, even metaphysical, truth in Scripture, as opposed to scientific explanations—as he indicated when he said the word *day* did not have to be literal.[3] But for Darrow there was only one kind of knowledge, literal description, and he kept raising narrative points of inconsistency, to Bryan's evident discomfiture:

> DARROW: "Upon thy belly thou shalt go, and dust shalt thou eat all the days of thy life." Do you think that is why the serpent is compelled to crawl upon its belly?
> BRYAN: I believe that.
> DARROW: Have you any idea how the snake went before that time?
> BRYAN: No, sir.
> DARROW: Do you know whether he walked on his tail or not?
> BRYAN: No, sir, I have no way to know. [Laughter][4]

St. Augustine, more skeptical than Darrow about the narrative devices of Genesis, says that God knows better than to talk to snakes, and that the sacred author was describing the symbol through which Eve fell as appropriately insinuative (*serpens*), appealing to appetitive nature (the belly), and given the mocking nutrition of dust. Neil Forsyth explains Augustine's developed thought on the serpent this way:

> Its breast, Augustine suggests, is pride, which puffs the heretics up; its belly represents carnal desire, which they falsely attribute not to themselves but to the powers of darkness; they eat the earth in their curiosity to search out spiritual secrets with an earthly eye.[5]

The last important stage of Augustine's intellectual journey toward Christianity could not be completed until St. Ambrose's allegorical way of preaching from the Bible removed Augustine's own disgust at that book's crudity.

For Augustine, the tale of creation is, on its surface, a mass of self-contradictions. Darrow points to the most famous difficulty in the account's own logic—that, for the first three days of the creation week (Darrow says four), "they had evening and morning without the sun." Even before that, Augustine ticked off the impossibilities: God "says" "Let there be light" when there is no one to say it to, no atmosphere to vibrate with the sound of any voice, no language in which to do the talking. Augustine dismantles the elements of the story back and back till each aspect of it is pulverized:

> If God spoke through some created stuff to say, "Let light be," how can light be the first creature, since something had to be created through which

he could say, "Let light be"? . . . Or was it from inchoate stuff that God formed physical sound by which he could pronounce, "Let light be"? If so, some physical sound was created, given some form before light. But if that is the case, then there was already *time* as a vehicle for sound, with different moments for the syllables to succeed each other. And if time preceded the creation of light, in what time was the voice created that sounded the words "Let light be"? To which day should we assign that time?[6]

Taking the "days" of creation literally is so obviously silly, so obviously not meant to be acceptable to any careful reader, that Augustine refuses to call the material sense the "literal" sense of Genesis. It is a no-sense. How, for instance, could God make an earthly day without its concomitant night on the other side of the globe?

When it is night with us, the sun is lighting those areas of the world it circles between its setting and rising in our place; so at any of the twenty-four hours during which the sun completes its circuit, there is day in some places, night in others. How can we possibly confine God to one spot, where he will be in night, while somewhere else the light has departed from him?[7]

Rather than treat seriously this no-sense, Augustine takes as the first and intended (literal) sense a stretching of language to deal with a mystery beyond it—the explosion of eternity into time by a single continuing act of creation. It was an act in which all the structural patterns (*rationes seminales*) of every created being were already contained.[8] No created (even angelic) intelligence could comprehend this dazzling proliferation of forms. Attempts at understanding it, not so much sequential as partial, are described as different "takes" on the blinding flash of energy—each flare of vision yields to the next (by a kind of dimming out) until the seventh day of God's "resting" pours the continual energy of being through the formed world. Augustine describes the receiving minds of the six "days," or "takes," on God's single act as angelic in his literal commentary on Genesis and as human in his *City of God*—he considered the two minds analogous.[9] God's unreadable mind could not act in separate stages, as if it were not finished the moment it acted.

Luther dismissed this mystical reading of the creative act as mere "allegory."[10] But for Augustine the six days are not just a rhetorical trope. They are unlike the figurative language of the curse on the snake. To say that Christ is a shepherd is a metaphor; but to say that he is light is literal, since physical light is a "shadow" of the real light spoken of in

Genesis. The Protestant Reformation opposed such exalted readings of the Scripture, since they were derived from Greek exegetical techniques developed by scholars like Origen. Alexandrian Christians used the Bible to achieve a superior insight into sacred things, accessible only to disciplined scholars. It is significant that Augustine's first act after his conversion was to go off and form a study group retired from ordinary life. As he put the matter:

> Cosmic theology, so called, is not a thing one discusses with anyone who happens by. It is not popular entertainment or politics, the province of actors (who present naughty tales about the gods) or office-holders (who desire naughtier things than the gods provide and end up with devils instead).[11]

The reservation of theory to scholars validated the privileges of a priestly caste, against which many Reformers would rebel.

The most successful rebellion, Martin Luther's, though it drew heavily on Augustine's theology of salvation by grace, had little sympathy for his way of reading Scripture. All the mathematical symbolism left over from late Platonism was too esoteric for the "plain reading" being opened up to laymen as the Bible was made more available to them in their vernaculars. There was a genuinely democratic impulse in the Reformation, however compromised it became by alliance with German princes, Genevan theocrats, and English Tudors. Even when this theology was not democratic, it remained individualistic.

The plain reading of the Reformation was joined, in ways important to America, with the "common sense" of the Enlightenment, especially in its Scottish (Presbyterian) form. Evangelicals to this day trace their heritage from Francis Bacon and Thomas Reid, the English forerunner and the Scottish completer of a scientific attack on "metaphysical" constructs of the mind. Exact observation of the outer world was the complement to a literal reading of Scripture. Newton read the book of Nature as Luther read the Epistles of Paul. A rhetoric forged against the surmises of medieval Scholastics is still being applied, with an astonishing continuity of terms, against the "hypotheticals" of modern evolutionists. Post-Newtonian science is untrue to the plain sense of observable phenomena, just as "figural" readings of Scripture were untrue to the daily needs of the lay reader. That is why the creationists consider Darwinism, with its hypothetical mutations and "missing links," not *real* science, not the kind you observe, describe, and form predictions from, as Newton did in establishing the planetary motions. Newton liked things you could observe and measure. He was fascinated by the dimensions of Noah's ark.

Newton's seeking the literal meaning of biblical prophecy was as appropriate as Jonathan Edwards's scrupulous study of the spider's habits. Literalism came as a liberation after centuries of priestly mystification. This was not only a genuine enlightenment; it is something peculiarly American. It helps explain the mystery of America's double heritage, from the Reformation Puritans and from Enlightenment philosophes. What looks like a contradictory coupling was still a natural alliance in the seventeenth and eighteenth centuries. Insofar as the Enlightenment was religious, it was clearly Protestant—Voltaire admiring the individualistic Quakers, each with his or her own "inner light"; Benjamin Franklin developing his secularized Puritanism of self-scrutiny and improvement; the British deists testing God's claims by reason (confident he could meet the test). And Puritanism on its materialistic side was down-to-earth, antimystical, a *measuring* religion, good at keeping books, interested in *results*. This is the American tradition, in politics as well as religion. William Jennings Bryan may have been the last authentic embodiment of all its aspects on a national scale.

Noble as the tradition was, it had its characteristic shortcomings. If Augustinian speculation tended to evaporate up into celestial hierarchies, the down-to-earth school could go very far down, indeed, into gritty detail. Darrow no less than Bryan showed the conditioning of his past as he attacked the Bible in the same literal terms Bryan was using to defend it. In the quibbles over the snake's mode of locomotion, one gets the feeling that both men are hugging the ground and eating dirt.

Thus scriptural literalists had to argue that only the author's original ("autograph") text of any book in the Bible was "inerrant." Copyists' errors in later transcripts do not count. Variant readings in divergent families of manuscripts are not included in the original grant of revelation. But one wonders why, if God intended a revelation, he could preside over the first transcription of his words but let accident intervene to blur his message. Nietzsche asked, for that matter, why God's grammar was so bad in presumably original readings from a text like Revelation. Kierkegaard seriously answered that God used bad Greek for the same reason that he chose untutored fishermen as his disciples—to manifest divine strength through human weakness. But where does one draw the line at being "a fool for Christ"? This was as real a question for Kierkegaard as it would prove for Bryan. American Protestants are, like Orthodox Jews, a people of the Book. If the Bible is just another piece of profound literature, on which an Augustine can play brilliant variations, why is it any more "revealed" than the writings of Tolstoy or of William Blake?

That was the question that evangelicals asked, at the beginning of this century, when faced with "liberal" readings of Scripture that reconciled it with Darwinism. Figuratively construing the Bible was, for them, an offense like "loose construction" of the Constitution. Indeed, political conservatives' belief in an "original intent" behind all the language of the Constitution is often derived from the school of biblical exegesis that adhered to the "literal" meaning of scriptural texts. That the battle over the Bible's meaning was so slow in reaching its modern climax is a testimony to the strength of the "plain reading," common sense, and democratic opposition to esoteric doctrines. This was not simply "anti-intellectual," as one can see in the hardy learning of the literal interpreters known as the Princeton School of theologians.[12] All through the nineteenth century this Presbyterian redoubt theologized for the mainstream (majority) evangelicals of America. It was only when this conservative bastion began to entertain liberal views that the Presbyterian General Assembly took the momentous step, in 1910, of spelling out five "essentials" that must, at a minimum, be held by teachers of the faith.

Despite the fact that Presbyterians subscribed to the Westminster Confession (1647), there was always a certain resistance, in evangelical circles, to imposing creeds. Creeds seemed more appropriate to the "high churches," with their sophisticated dogmas like transubstantiation. Besides, the need for a creed to supplement one's reading of the Bible suggests that Scripture alone is not a sufficient guide to faith.

But historical "higher criticism" of the Bible, combined with Darwinian science and secular commercialism, frightened the Presbyterians into drawing up their "five points" of 1910, to distinguish true believers from false professors of the faith. These were the points:

1) the inerrancy of Scripture;
2) the virgin birth of Jesus;
3) the substitutionary atonement;
4) the bodily resurrection of Jesus;
5) the authenticity of miracles.

Other evangelicals felt a need to declare what was required of supernatural faith. For five years (1910–15) they published a mass-circulation series of books called *The Fundamentals*. In 1918, a World's Christian Fundamentals Association was formed. But it was not till 1920 that the term *fundamentalist* was invented for those trying to preserve the fundamental truths of Christianity.[13] And those truths were often listed as five in number—the original Presbyterian list, with one difference: Instead of miracles listed as number five, Christ's Second Coming (before the millennium) was substituted.

The five fundamentals were not meant to be exhaustive—divine creation, for instance, is not on the list—but to be rallying points for those who still took the Bible as inspired in a special way. The virgin birth, for instance, was not chosen because of any Protestant devotion to the Virgin Mary. Early Christians had debated the cosmic significance of Mary as *Theotokos* (God-Bearer to the world) and debated her place in the economy of salvation. The fundamentalists meant something more plain and direct when they put the virgin birth among their five points. The Gospel of Luke said that Jesus was not born as an ordinary man, any more than he had suffered a usual death. The fundamentalists would not form speculative constructions around that report. They just insisted that the divine Word be taken at face value.

It was the same with the Resurrection. The learned fundamentalist J. Gresham Machen, arguing with an "accommodationist" conservative theologian, said it was not true to the simple report of Christ's resurrection to imagine how the apostles' mentality would "translate" events into what they considered a resurrection:

> According to the assumptions of modern thought, Machen pointed out, scientific history could only talk about "the belief of the disciples in the resurrection." Machen, on the other hand, in accordance with Common Sense Realism, assumed that what we know about in history is not the *idea* of the event (which is in the present) but the event itself (which is in the past). . . . Machen saw it as a question of scientific Christianity versus "modern anti-intellectualism."[14]

Those who started entertaining "hypotheses" about how the Resurrection could have been reported, understood, constructed psychologically, or evolved textually were making the plain words irrecoverable in their real challenge. God can do wonders, and he can tell man that he has done them. Trying to explain them away makes man the judge of God's Word, when that Word should judge him. Ronald Reagan showed he was using the believers' own language when he called Darwinism a "theory," and contrasted it with Genesis, "which is not a theory but the biblical story of creation."

Point three of the five points could have been the most sticky, involving believers in "hypothetical" theology. All it said on its face was that "Jesus died for our sins." But the nature of Christ as man and God is implied in such propitiation, and that nature had tied the Greek councils of the fourth century into metaphysical knots. It is proof of the antimetaphysical habit in American Protestantism that the "plain sense," however mysterious, of point three caused no major problem. The real time bomb was hidden in point five of the amended fundamentals, that which has to do with Christ's Second Coming (the first one being at the Nativity, when Christ was incarnated).

The problem did not arise over any disagreement that Christ would come again "in clouds" to judge the living and the dead. And the problem was not so much the timing of the second Advent as its scenario. Different books of the Jewish and Greek Bibles give contradictory (or incredibly complex) stories about how the "end time" will approach, be delayed, involve loss as well as triumph, sway back and forth in cosmic battle, bring forward a false Christ, and produce attendant circumstances to giddy the soberest "plain reader." No wonder Hunter Thompson regularly uses the Book of Revelation (ready to hand in his motel bedstand, thanks to the Gideons) to embody drug visions. It is a book of clustering animals with multiple eyes and wings and claws—the iconography of the Reformation as illustrated by Dürer.

The beginning of history has, in the Bible, a kind of folktale simplicity (despite the troublesome doubling of some events, like Eve's creation). St. Augustine was attacked for imparting an alien sophistication and complexity to his cosmic speculations. But it is precisely the *literal* reading of history's end that involves Bible readers in heavy detective work. Luther called the Augustinian treatment of Genesis allegorical fantasy. Augustine, by contrast, thought attempts to save a literal meaning for the apocalypses involved Christians in "laughable imaginings."[15] Creation science might be science fiction, but the end time turns easily into horror tales, with personifications of evil stalking the scene.

Even the language used is swollen and alien-sounding. Eschatology is the treatment of "last things" (*eschata*). The Greek term has not been turned into Latin, as *apocalypsis* (unveiling) became *re-velatio*. If the Latin for *eschata* had been used (*ultima*), we would call those who deal with the end time *ultimists*, an altogether more handy term than *eschatologists*.

Since Revelation says there will be a thousand years (millennium) of rule by saints at the end of time, we have people clumsily called millenarians or millennialists. The Greek term for a thousand (*chilias*) gives a simpler form, *chiliasts*, for which there used to be a handy Latin equivalent, *miliasts*.[16] That term dropped from normal usage; but it should be revived—among other things, to avoid the efforts to make arbitrary distinctions between millenarians and millennialists. These get especially troublesome when we learn that there are *pre*millenarians/millennialists/miliasts as well as *post*millenarians/millennialists/miliasts.

Paradoxically, the most "fundamentalist" end-timers (who should be the simplest in their reading) are known by the most tongue-twisting title: *premillennial dispensationalists*. These people think Christ will come in the clouds before the millennium begins (not after), though they split on the question whether he will raise his saints into the clouds before, during, or after the time of tribulation that precedes the millennium.

It is easy to make fun of the hairsplitting and text-juggling that goes into the effort to reconcile scriptural hints and threats of the terrors to come when the world is given its last disciplining. Michelangelo and Verdi could make great drama of these cataclysmic images; but it is hard to make a convincing timetable for them, though that has not discouraged the devout and the ingenious over the centuries. Interpreting Revelation is a parlor game in Dostoyevski's *The Idiot*, in which Lebedev has puzzled out the fact that *wormwood* refers to the Russian railway system. Contemporary Christians have made a more astounding discovery—that *Chernobyl*, the site of a nuclear accident in 1986, means "wormwood" in Russian—a piece of fundamentalist lore that intrigued President Reagan, who asked friends if they knew how to translate *Chernobyl*, then informed them, portentously, that it meant "Wedgwood."[17]

How did people who set out to preserve commonsense reading of the Bible get tangled in such obscure details? They could hardly avoid it, since the plain sense is the wildest one where eschatology is concerned. The early Christian literature describes a cosmic showdown in terms quite specific, however confusing. The horrific details are all there—in fact, there are too many of them, and they seem to cancel each other out, or to describe the last battle in images at war with each other as well as with the normal rules of language. Early Christians felt the ground thrill beneath their feet with the first tremors of a cosmic showdown. Apocalyptic visionaries wrote to each other in a code of signs and portents. The whole universe was ticking and groaning like a house about to collapse. People were so alert to the signals of ruin that they had to be calmed, told that the end, though approaching, was not yet upon them.

St. Paul told the Thessalonians that things would get much worse before the day of final wrath and rescue. His assurances were themselves so dark that his riddles have never been satisfactorily unraveled:

> And now, brothers, about the coming of our Lord Jesus Christ and his gathering of us to himself: I beg you, do not suddenly lose your heads or alarm yourselves, whether at some oracular utterance, or pronouncement, or some letter purporting to come from us, alleging that the Day of the Lord is already here. Let no one deceive you in any way whatever. That day cannot come before the final rebellion against God, when wickedness will be revealed in human form, the man doomed to perdition. He is the Enemy. He rises in his pride against every god, so called, every object of men's worship, and even takes his seat in the temple of God claiming to be a god himself. You cannot but remember that I told you this while I was still with you; you must now be aware of the restraining hand which ensures that he shall be revealed only at the proper time. For already the secret power of wickedness is at work, secret only for the present until the Restrainer disappears from the scene. And then he will be revealed, that wicked man whom the Lord Jesus will destroy with the breath of his mouth, and annihilate by the radiance of his coming. But the coming of that wicked man is the work of Satan. It will be attended by all the powerful signs and miracles of the Lie, and all the deception that sinfulness can impose on those doomed to destruction. (2 Thessalonians 2.1–10)[18]

St. Paul begs one of the early churches he founded not to be carried away by fear. But then he fills the sky with fearful shapes of vast evils to come, paradoxically vague and precise. What is "the secret power of wickedness," which St. Jerome translated as *mysterium iniquitatis*, and what restrains it? St. Paul says he has explained this to the people who are forgetting it. If his hints here are any indication of what he told them earlier, we cannot be surprised that the message was hard to keep straight.

Yet the cosmic urgency of this passage is meant to be homeopathic— Paul is trying to "talk people down" from the hysteria of immediately anticipated doom. That is the atmosphere we must recapture if we are to understand early Christian writings. It is common, even now, to think there was some "simple gospel of Jesus" that Paul and other mystagogues elaborated on or obfuscated. This was the Enlightenment view exemplified by Jefferson, who thought he could cull the original story of Jesus from the Gospels by removing all the miracles and "metaphysics."[19] But the earliest Christian documents, Paul's letters from the 50s of the Common Era, are eschatological, descriptive of the last disaster, dark with symbols, breathless with impending disaster. The Gospels, written after the destruction of the Jewish Temple (70 CE), are a later attempt to arrange portents around a single person's life and death. The story begins in mystery. Early prayers like the Our Father embedded in Matthew and Luke are eschatological. Pre-Pauline hymns, like that contained in Philippians 2.6–11, are cosmic. Theology precedes biography; mystery yields only with effort to history. Paul, whose letters precede the Gospels, is a calming, demystifying influence, a step in the direction of the Gospels, not a wild departure from them. The four Gospels are like the seven days of creation as Augustine understood them—four fuzzy "takes" on what had first been just a blur of light. The same thing can be seen, in lesser form, around other holy men whose miracles are the first things attested about them—the Baal Shem Tov or St. Francis. Ecstasy precedes analysis. The "plain fact" is not recoverable from some Jeffersonian original "report."

If Christianity began with "ultimists," so did America. Cotton Mather thought the early settlements on this continent could only be understood theologically, as a series of wonders and portents. He called the history of his country "Christ's Great Deeds in America," *Magnalia Christi Americana*. Modern fundamentalists are not going all the way back to early Christianity, without any intervening stops. They are going, in the first place, back to the foundation (fundamentals) of European government on this continent. To make even this shorter trip toward "basics" is to enter a world of signs and prophecies. It returns us to the terror and exaltation of people mounting above history to meet their Maker in the air—which is the spirit in which the settlers of America launched themselves toward the unknown.

✦ T W E L V E ✦

America's Miliast Founders

THE PERIOD OF AMERICA'S SETTLING WAS A TIME OF GREAT MILIAST ENTHU-
siasms. The best minds in Europe were on the lookout for the Counter-
Christ (Antichrist) and other signs of impending catastrophe. As Hugh
Trevor-Roper said:

> It is an interesting but undeniable fact that the most advanced scientists
> of the early seventeenth century included also the most learned and literal
> students of biblical mathematics; and in their hands science and religion
> converged to pinpoint, between 1640 and 1660, the dissolution of society,
> the end of the world. . . . [Thus] the Scottish mathematician Napier of
> Merchistoun . . . invented logarithms in order to speed up his calculation
> of the number of the Beast.[1]

The New World played a great part in these speculations. The gospel
had to be preached to the entire globe as one of the conditions of Christ's
second Advent. That is what many of the settlers had in mind as they
took the "good news" to what was considered the last infidel region. Influential miliasts like Joseph Mede, Milton's teacher at Cambridge, thought
Armageddon, the final battle, would be fought in America. The New

World would be history's last stage. Going there meant volunteering for history's showdown. The apocalyptic Enemy would be waiting for the settlers. As William Cranshaw, preaching to members of the Virginia Company, warned them: "We go to disinherit him of his ancient freehold, and to deliver out of his bondage the souls which he hath kept so many years in thralldom." No wonder, as Perry Miller says, the first settlers saw "in every distress the hoof of the devil."[2] One of the miracles God had to accomplish in giving his forces a beachhead in such hostile territory was to clear a spot where the Puritans could settle. Whole Indian villages were wiped out by a plague in 1611 and 1612, so that—as Cotton Mather put it—"the woods were almost cleaned of those pernicious creatures, to make room for a better growth."[3]

Charles Francis Adams later expressed shock at the pious way Mather welcomed the hand of God dealing death to whole Indian populations.[4] But the "realistic" view of the settlers was that they needed God's miracles on their side since the Indians so clearly had the devil working for them. Captain John Smith had reported to Europe in 1612 that, among America's natives, "their chief God they worship is the Devil."[5] The Indian "powachs," or medicine men, were witches in service to the devil; their animals were diabolic "familiars."[6] The devil had recruited them in a clever countermove to thwart in the New World what he could not stop in Europe—the progress of learning and the Reformation.

Joseph Mede published his influential *Key to Revelation* in 1627, where he revealed the devil's strategy. This enemy of mankind had marshaled, from those parts of the world untouched by the gospel, the last pagans who might halt the Puritans' progress.[7] Others made of the Indians the lost tribes of Israel, returning to the Jews' ancient work of opposing Christ.[8] But none doubted they were part of the great cosmic struggle between the forces of light and darkness. Cotton Mather traced the pattern:

Three most remarkable things which have borne a very great aspect upon human affairs did—near the same time, namely at the conclusion of the fifteenth and the beginning of the sixteenth century—arise upon the world: The first was the resurrection of literature. The second was the opening of America. The third was the reformation of religion. But [just] as probably [provably], the Devil, seducing the first inhabitants of America into it, therein aimed at the having of them and their posterity out of the sound of the silver trumpets of the gospel then to be heard through the Roman [Romish] Empire. If the Devil had any expectation that, by the peopling of America, he should utterly deprive any Europeans of the two benefits, literature and religion, which dawned upon the miserable world, one just before, the other just after, the first famed navigation hither, 'tis to be hoped he will be disappointed of that expectation.[9]

The settlers of America had undertaken a "mission into the wilderness," but Cotton Mather reminded them that the biblical "wilderness" is not an area uninhabited but the dwelling place of devils—like that desert in which Jesus was tested.

> When our Lord Jesus Christ underwent his humiliation for us, this point was very considerable in it: he was carried into the wilderness, and there he was exposed unto the buffetings and outrage of Azazel. The assaults that Satan then and afterward made on our Lord Jesus Christ, producing a most horrible anguish in his mind, made such a figure in his conflicts for *us* that they were well worthy of a most particular *pre*figuration [in the Azazel story of Exodus . . . and] there has been too much cause to observe that the Christians who were driven into the American desert, which is now call'd New England, have to their sorrow seen Azazel dwelling and raging there in very tragical instances. The devils have doubtless felt a more than ordinary vexation from the arrival of those Christians, with their sacred exercises of Christianity, in this wilderness. [Italics added.][10]

The treatment of the inhabitants encountered in America was colored by this miliast urgency. The Indians, instruments of the devil, were being used to try the saints and to undo God's work. Even friendly overtures were likely to be part of a larger strategy to disarm the Christians, as William Bradford concluded after one attempt at better relations:

> Also, as after was made known, before they came to the English to make friendship, they got all the Powachs of the country, for three days together, in a horrid and devilish manner to curse and execrate them with their conjuration, which assembly and service they held in a dark and dismal swamp.[11]

Since the devil's intelligence system was behind the Indians' actions, one had to expect the worst in dealing with them.

The miliast edginess about standing on the brink of the world, facing an incalculable Enemy, contributed to most of the things that strike later observers of New England as hysterical or overwrought. To take just three examples, there was an eschatological aspect to the treatment of Thomas Morton's maypole, Salem's witches, and Canadian Jesuits.

Thomas Morton, a learned fur trader, bought pelts independently from the Indians, and got his intelligence about Massachusetts authorities from restive or runaway indentured servants. There were many reasons for "movement" Calvinists, conducting their experiment under a welcome discipline, to dislike his free-lance activity. But when, in 1627, he raised an old English maypole in the New World, his foes seemed to go berserk. They have been ridiculed for the reactions of a prissy Malvolio, but we have to remember that he was dealing with Indians, whose rites were considered devilish. Also, the maypole was a Catholic remnant in England, and Catholic "New France" (Canada) threatened New England with its Indians converted by the Jesuits. A sign of the end time would be the raising of abominable rites. William Bradford called the new idol a "Dagon" that God meant to be destroyed by some new Samson (dwarfish Miles Standish in fact performed the job).[12] John Winthrop wrote of the episode: "The habitation of the wicked shall no more appear in Israel."[13]

Perhaps no episode has received more isolated attention than the Puritans' execution of accused witches, especially those of Salem in 1692. But we should remember that the fear and persecution of witches was a prominent feature of seventeenth-century religious life—itself an indicator of miliast expectations: It was prophesied that the powers of darkness would be "loosed," given free rein, toward the end of time.[14] There was a stretched anticipation of this evil incursion—nowhere more than in America. Where could apocalyptic signs be more convincing? Besides, the "internal" witches had a ready network of external support from the devils directing the Indians in their campaign against the gospel community. George Lyman Kittredge put the case succinctly:

> There was a very special reason why troubles with the powers of darkness were to be expected in New England—a reason which does not hold good for Great Britain or, indeed, for any part of Western Europe. I refer, of course, to the presence of a considerable heathen population—the Indians. These were universally supposed to be devil-worshipers, not only by the Colonists but by all the rest of the world; for paganism was nothing but Satanism. . . . The presence of all these devil-worshiping neighbors was a constant reminder of the possibility of danger from witchcraft. One is surprised, therefore, to find that there was no real outbreak until so late in the century.[15]

One does not have to agree with that final sentence to realize that "the danger within" was anticipated because witches were seen as manipulated by the constant enemy without.[16] Cotton Mather said it was "sagamores" who directed their subversion of the godly community, "horrid sorcerers and hellish conjurors and such as conversed with demons."[17] It was to clear themselves of "going soft" on diabolism that the towns renewed their covenant promises with such fervor during Indian wars, systematically eliminating all sympathy for the devil's ways. A general subversion was feared, a falling away at the very time when the saints must be steadiest for the last assault: "Such is the descent of the Devil at this day upon ourselves, that I may truly tell you the walls of the whole world are broken down! The usual walls of defense about mankind have such a gap made in them that the very devils are broke in upon us."[18]

If the devil had brought Indians to America to be his allies, other troops volunteered for service with him in the climactic struggle of history, notably the French Catholics who brought a corrupt religion from the Old World to the New in the early seventeenth century. All the Reformers agreed that the Papacy would play a key role at Armageddon, under one of its many scriptural symbols—as the Scarlet Woman, the Whore of Babylon, or the Beast. Christopher Hill argues that "the Beast" had become such a technical term for the Catholic abomination, by the beginning of the seventeenth century, that Shakespeare and others had to increase their use of the less common term "animals" to mean ordinary beasts of the field.[19] The worst emissaries of this evil power, the Canadian Jesuits, had made alliance with the devil-worshipers of the New World, teaching them their antigospel. This fear would become most intense during the French and Indian War; but even before it, one Jesuit missionary, Sébastien Rale, was so successful in converting Indians to worship the French Antichrist that the Massachusetts authorities thought it a godly act to send assassins out to capture his scalp. The scalp was carried into Boston, in 1727, to "the great joy and exultation of the people of Massachusetts."[20]

"False religion" of almost any kind was felt to be a manifestation of the devil's war on several fronts to defeat the New England experiment. Thus "heretical" Quaker women were examined for the devil's marks, in the procedure used for witches.[21] Keeping the gospel uncontaminated was so important during this last training time for history's great final encounter with the Enemy that Perry Miller could write of New England: "To allow no dissent from the truth was exactly the reason they had come to America."[22]

This theological rigor entered into what now seems an appalling cruelty toward Indians. Most settlers had been commissioned to convert and "save" the souls of infidels not previously exposed to the gospel. But destruction of the Indians' own evil rites, by which the devil controlled them, seemed a necessary first step to many of the Protestant settlers. Even comparatively tolerant settlers—the kind we would call "enlightened"—were convinced that Indian religion was diabolic. John Smith, Thomas Morton, and Roger Williams all agreed on that.[23]

The fear of contamination by ungodly forces compelled settlers to isolate themselves from Indians in ways that made proselytizing difficult, as Robert Beverley admitted in his early history of Virginia.[24] The apparent exception just confirms the rule. John Rolfe married Pocahontas; but he had to get special permission from the governor, after assuaging theological fears that she was being used as a pawn of the devil. Rolfe assured his superior that he was properly suspicious in his dealing with this woman of a "curst generation [race]." He assumed her charms were "wicked instigations hatched by him who seeketh and delighteth in man's destruction." He would not violate God's law "against the sons of Levy and Israel for marriage of strange wives," except that Pocahontas's entire sympathy with the Christians against her own people led him to risk "this dangerous combat," hoping to turn the devil's normal tactic against the devil, to "His [God's] glory, your [the governor's] honour, our country's good, the benefit of the plantation, and for the converting of the irregenerate to regeneration." He even quoted Calvin's *Institutes* in his favor—which shows that the theological rigor of New England was at home in Virginia as well.[25]

Other Indians, even the Christians, were best kept at arm's length, in "praying villages" treated as pacification and buffer communities.[26] If the attitude toward Indians was fearful verging on hysterical in the best of times, war turned those feelings genocidal. In King Philip's War, said Cotton Mather, it was by "the evident hand of God" that the saints "extinguished whole nations of the savages."[27] If one was entering the battles that would end time itself, one must "naturally" extinguish evil. Modern preachers like Jerry Falwell, who have anticipated Armageddon in nuclear terms, are very close in spirit to the founders of this country, which has at times muted or secularized its millennial heritage but never entirely lost it.[28] The sense of mission, of a manifest destiny, was millennial at its root, and miliasm reasserts itself often in our history, not least in our own time.

◇ T H I R T E E N ◇

Reagan and "the Prophecies"

IT IS OFTEN THOUGHT, WITH SOME REASON, THAT AMERICA'S ORIGINAL miliast vision was deflected, during and after the American Revolution, into more secular versions of American mission and manifest destiny.[1] But religious belief in an impending and literal millennium (thousand-year reign) continued strong into the nineteenth century, and became more widespread among the populace (as opposed to elite speculators like Cotton Mather and Jonathan Edwards).[2] The French Revolution, which overthrew the Scarlet Woman of Rome and was then recaptured by her, was a seismic event that called up many scriptural interpretations.[3] More important to Americans was the wave of revivals that occurred around the turn of the century, known as the Second Awakening. This launched movements like the Disciples of Christ, a community in which three future presidents were brought up—James Garfield, Lyndon Johnson, and Ronald Reagan. The journal edited by the Disciples' founder, Alexander Campbell, was called *Millennial Harbinger*. It is no wonder President Reagan felt so comfortable with biblical language about the end time whenever he met with fundamentalists.[4]

The new government established by the Constitution is a work of the eighteenth-century Enlightenment, but it organized a country that was "revived" in its biblical fervor. Ernest R. Sandeen writes that "America in the early nineteenth century was drunk on the millennium," and Nathan O. Hatch says of the same period: "Judging by the number of sermons, books, and pamphlets that addressed prophetic themes, the first generation of United States citizens may have lived in the shadow of Christ's second coming more intensely than any generation since."[5]

Thanks to a publicist named Joshua V. Himes, much of the miliast strain in American thought focused on the quarter of a century that evangelist Edward Miller devoted to preparing his country for Christ's Advent in 1843. "Millerites" suffered a great disappointment in that year, but those aching for catastrophe cannot be soothed by continuity.[6] Some Millerites "spiritualized" the Second Coming, saying that it *had* happened for believers, in their spirit world, and that later implementation in the physical world would follow automatically.

New prophets took up Miller's role in keeping the clock for the end time. One was Ellen White (1827–1915), prophetess of the Seventh-Day Adventists. In states of almost continual ecstasy, she was a radical on matters like abolition, and she taught a kind of holistic medicine that made health food sacramental. She attracted to her Battle Creek headquarters vegetarians like Sylvester Graham and Dr. John Harvey Kellogg, who would improve America with the literal "soul food" of their graham crackers and cornflakes. Another prophetic adventist was Charles Taze Russell (1852–1916), who founded what became the Jehovah's Witnesses, a stubborn group that would test the American Constitution in more than 150 state supreme court cases and 30 cases in the United States Supreme Court, significantly expanding American liberties.[7]

But the most important miliast thinker of modern times was a British preacher whose name few Americans recognize. J. Gordon Melton claims: "Probably no Christian thinker in the last two hundred years has so affected the way in which English-speaking Christians view the faith, and yet has received so little recognition of his contribution, as John Nelson Darby."[8] An Anglican priest who rebelled against ecclesiastical formalism, Darby lived with his vision of the end so intensely that he would not establish institutions meant to last. His followers gathered in various types of "assemblies" and "brotherhoods" (e.g., the Plymouth Brethren), too aware of this world's transience to build church structures. But some who did found Bible empires—mainly Dwight L. Moody— took their theology from Darby, as did Cyrus Scofield in his annotated Bible, which was brought out by the Oxford University Press in 1909. Many American preachers had heard Darby in his visits to their country (the most important tours were in the 1870s) or at the annual Niagara Bible Conferences held in Ontario from 1883. Thus, when the five points of fundamentalism were established in the teens of this century, there was surprisingly broad agreement on what was said about the fifth point, Christ's Second Coming.

Eschatology was Darby's specialty. He put together in an economical scheme all the apparently conflicting sayings about the end time. In various places biblical texts say that there will be a last battle but that Christians will be spared it; that the Antichrist will be both reined in and released; that a great Trial (or tribulation) will occur, but also a great Reign of the Saints. In what order, in what relationship to each other, are these things to happen?

Darby solved one set of nagging problems by getting the Christians out of the way right at the beginning of the final sequence. They would be swept up (rapt) before any of the other things occurred. This "secret rapture" was thus the first of the last things. Darby's text for this seizure was Paul's first letter to the Thessalonians, our earliest Christian document (written about seventeen years after the death of Jesus):

> We who are left alive until the Lord comes shall not forestall those who have died; because at the word of command, at the sound of the archangel's voice and God's trumpet-call, the Lord himself will descend from heaven; first the Christian dead will rise, then we who are left alive shall join them, caught up in clouds to meet the Lord in the air (1 Thessalonians 4.15– 17.)

Only with these preliminaries out of the way can the great Trial (tribulation) begin. This is described in Paul's *second* letter to the Thessalonians, whose authenticity has been questioned, among other reasons, because it seems to conflict with the simpler ending described in the "Rapture" passage. It is hard to fit all the parts together, but Darby convinced most modern fundamentalists that he had done it.

It is Darby's timetable that makes most modern fundamentalists premillenarianists—"premils" in the slang of the Bible schools. They believe that Christ will come and be joined with his church before the millennium begins (or any of the troubles leading into the thousand-year rule). "Postmils," obviously, believe Christ will come only *after* this end time, when history disappears into eternity. The "Rapture," though it solves problems for literal interpretation of the Bible, is a bit of a stumbling block for modern audiences, despite the huge sales of books expounding Darbyism—foremost among them Hal Lindsey's works (the best known of which is *The Late Great Planet Earth*). Preachers like Jerry Falwell bring a comic defiance of the world to their exposition of this doctrine:

> You say what's going to happen on this earth when the Rapture occurs? You'll be riding along in an automobile; you'll be the driver, perhaps; you're a Christian; there'll be several people in the automobile with you, maybe someone who is not a Christian. When the trumpet sounds, you and the other born-again Christians in that automobile will be instantly caught away, you'll disappear, leaving behind only your clothing and physical things that cannot inherit eternal life. That unsaved person or persons in the automobile will suddenly be startled to find that the car is moving along without a driver, and suddenly somewhere crashes. Those saved people in the car have disappeared. Other cars on the highway driven by believers will suddenly be out of control. Stark pandemonium will occur on that highway and on every highway in the world where Christians are caught away from the world.[9]

That would be the first shock of the world's tribulation, one that would widen into world struggle. American fundamentalists of the 1980s argued that America would be debilitated by the Rapture since Ronald Reagan, Vice-President George Bush, and much of Congress, rapt away as Christians, would be *hors de combat*; but Russia, ruled by atheists, would retain its leadership. It would be the assignment of others to oppose the Antichrist. Jews must lead this opposition, "coming back" to God in a struggle that will convert to Christianity those it did not kill. Nuclear war is often seen as the probable Trial, but Hal Lindsey smiles and says he does not worry about that, because "I ain't gonna be here."[10]

Those not familiar with fundamentalism are often shocked to hear how widespread is belief in this Darbyite rapture, taught at centers of fundamentalist orthodoxy like the Dallas Theological Seminary and popularized not only by the prodigiously successful books of Hal Lindsey but by popular preachers like Tim LaHaye and Charles Swindoll. But fundamentalists can argue that they at least keep the eschatological aspect of Scripture meaningful in their lives. Other professing Christians, more "respectable," seem to shut out that large element of their Bible. They even say the Lord's Prayer (or Our Father) without realizing that they are praying for the Rapture. This Jewish-Christian prayer was old enough to come down to us in three early versions, in the Gospels of Matthew and Luke, and in the *Didachē* ("Christian Teaching") of the second century. It was a basic prayer probably accommodated to different communities' uses. (One variant of the form, in Luke, seems to have been recited at baptisms.)[11] Matthew's form, which has more liturgical balance

than Luke's, looks toward the end (*eschaton*), when God's kingdom will
be finally vindicated:

> Our Father of the Heavens:
> Your Name be honored,
> Your Reign established,
>
> Your aims fulfilled,
> on earth as in heaven.
>
> Give us this day,
> bread of the Coming Day.
>
> And cancel our moral debts
> as we have canceled others'.
>
> And keep us from the Ordeal
> by rescue from its Evil Lord.[12]

The Bible scholar Raymond E. Brown has summarized the evidence for
"the *Pater Noster* as an eschatological prayer."[13] When the community
asks, at the end, to be preserved from the Trial (*ho Peirasmos*), this is not
personal "temptation" but the testing final ordeal of the world, as in
Revelation 3.10: "I will also keep you from the Ordeal [*Peirasmos*] that
is to fall upon the whole world and test [*peirasai*] its inhabitants." In the
first three (synoptic) Gospels, Jesus tells his followers on his last night:
"Pray that you may be spared the Test" (Mark 14.38, Matthew 26.41,
Luke 22.40, all with *Peirasmos*).

The customary rendering of the last line of the Lord's Prayer, "But
deliver us from evil," takes as neuter a genitive that could be—and should
be, according to New Testament parallels—masculine (the Evil One, *ho
Poneros*). In John's Gospel, Jesus, speaking for his disciples, asks the
Father "to keep them from the Evil One [*Poneros*]."[14] In the First Epistle
of John, Christians are said to have "mastered the Evil One [*Poneros*]."[15]

The first two couplets of the prayer ask for the fulfillment of God's
plans for the kingdom. The last two ask that the Christian community
be prepared and saved in the birth-agonies of that kingdom. The central
couplet is mysterious because it uses an adjective for bread ("daily" in
the English formula) that has no earlier Greek use. The same word is
used in all three early forms of the prayer (Luke, Matthew, and *Didachē*)
and seems to be the accepted equivalent of some technical (eschatological)
word in Aramaic, one for which none of the Christian communities
could find a better Greek word. Etymologically the word (*epiousios*) can
mean "being-on" or "coming-on." St. Jerome took the first sense and

translated it as *supersubstantialis* (being-over the normal bread). Others just take it to mean "at hand" (daily). But a better case can be made for "coming-on," with a reference to the future banquet of the eschatological kingdom.[16] The Christian meal anticipates that last feast "even today." Jesus is presented as anticipating that feast in his last supper: "Never again shall I drink from the fruit of the vine until that day when I drink it new in the kingdom of God" (Mark 14.25; cf. Matthew 26.29, Luke 22.16).

The Lord's Prayer seems intimately connected with the last night of Jesus' life—the pledge of a feast in the kingdom, the warning against *Peirasmos* in the garden, Jesus' prayer that his disciples be saved from the *Poneros*. The couplet of the prayer about God's will being done on earth as in heaven is very similar in Greek to Jesus' prayer of submission in the garden: "My Father, if it is possible, let this cup pass me by. Yet not as I will, but as thou wilt" (Matthew 26.39). Jesus prays to escape his own *Peirasmos*, but knows that he cannot. This scene, in which Jesus grasps the enormity of the death he is about to undergo, is similar to his testing (*Peirasmos*, Luke 4.13) in the desert, when he foresees the ordeals of his ministry.

In the garden, as in the desert, Jesus grapples with the Enemy of mankind. This is "the hour when darkness reigns" according to Luke (22.53), when "the Prince of this world approaches" according to John (14.30).[17] Christians are involved in this cosmic confrontation by their identification with their leader. They do not have to repeat what he already suffered for them—in that sense they can ask to be exempted from the *Peirasmos*.

St. Augustine argued that the last days were actually begun when Christ died and rose. There will be no further dispensation now that the age of Grace has replaced the age of Law (which replaced the age before the Law). The eschatological symbols refer to the stakes at issue in the souls of those who die into Christ's life by baptism.[18] In a sense, modern adventists took a modified form of this Augustinian eschatology when they "spiritualized" the Second Coming after 1843.

But why, after all dates disappoint, do some people still try to puzzle out a timetable for end-time events? One reason is the urge to scrutinize current events through the magnifying lens of Scripture. New signs appear that *must* have been foretold. The Christian Right in America has had a scriptural "reading" of modern history ever since 1948, when Jews forged a homeland they could return to. St. Paul, in his letter to the Romans (11.25–27), had quoted Isaiah and Jeremiah to claim that Jews will be regathered and saved. Darbyites have made that one of the conditions, and therefore one of the signs, of the completion of history. When the city of Jerusalem was reunited in 1967, that too was a sign that the Temple can be rebuilt.

The other sign of the end, the Antichrist, took visible shape for these Christians in the Communist empire—which is why they were so excited when Ronald Reagan referred to that as "the Evil Empire" and "the focus of all evil in the world." A leader who would recognize that was, for them, another sign. Detail after detail could be put together. Gorbachev's forehead birthmark became "the mark of the Beast" from Revelation (13.17). Ezekiel 38 and 39 suggested that the last war would begin with an invasion from the north; Falwell sought etymological linkages between Russian and biblical names. The invaders would come for "spoil," and all you had to do was take off that word's first two letters to get the reason for Soviet invasion of the Middle East.[19] When it became known that *Chernobyl* was Russian for "wormwood," fundamentalist excitement reached Reagan again, who passed on the watchword slightly altered.

It is hard to know how seriously Reagan takes "all the prophecies" that are supposed to be coming true in our time. When asked in 1984 what he thought about Armageddon (a subject on which he had been warned to be circumspect), he showed agnosticism only about the date of the event, not about the event itself: "No one knows whether those prophecies mean that Armageddon is a thousand years away or the day after to-morrow. So I have never seriously warned and said we must plan according to Armageddon."[20] He changed the street number on the house he moved to after leaving the White House because it was the number of the Beast (666). On the other hand, Reagan is fascinated by astrology and the Shroud of Turin.[21] He likes good stories, which he usually interprets in his own optimistic way. It has been almost half a century since the state of Israel was formed; Gorbachev, the Beast, became Reagan's friend, the reformer; the Evil Empire begins to look like a paper tiger.

Yet the end of a century is approaching, which tends to heat miliastic brains. New signs can always be found by those who look for them, and the Darbyite establishment has been refining its tools for more than a century. They will not lose heart at this late date—the later the better for them. Those Christians who ignore entirely the eschatological language of their heritage are, in effect, ceding the Bible to those who at least take it seriously. Those who make too much of the dark words about conflict and the hour of darkness are strengthened in their determination when they see other Christians making nothing of them at all. When the Supreme Court declared against public school recitals of the Lord's Prayer, some observers wondered why the fuss was being made over such an "inoffensive" formula (it does not even mention Jesus or one specific doctrine from the Christian creeds). But it was so important to the early Christian church that *only* initiates could be taught the prayer. [22] Whatever else the Bible may be, it is hardly "inoffensive."

❖ F O U R T E E N ❖

Fundamentalism and the Quayles

THE RAPTURE, CONSIDERED IN ISOLATION FROM THE REST OF JOHN NELSON Darby's approach to the Bible, is bizarre. But Darby convinced the main body of fundamentalists by a more basic doctrine—that of "dispensations." Christians generally have believed in at least two dispensations ("parcelings-out") of history, corresponding to the two eras of conventional chronology: Before Christ, and the Years of Our Lord. St. Paul had contrasted God's dealings with mankind "under the Law" and in the freedom of the Spirit.

But Darby, trying to fit all aspects of the Bible into a single literal reading, knew there were dispensations before the Law was given to Moses on Sinai—there was, for instance, the period before the Flood (when God was not restricted in his mode of punishment) and after the Flood (when his concordat ruled out further retaliation by water). In fact, Darby thought the Bible account required at least seven different dispensations, if God's treatment of mankind was to be interpreted properly. Each "arrangement" continued stable until a catastrophe ended it and inaugurated a new regime.

First, there was the time of innocence in Eden, ended by the fall.

Second, there was the time when mankind was on its own, until it brought down on itself the punishing Flood.

Third, the time of temporarily chastened humanity, ending with the attempt to scale heaven by the tower of Babel.

Fourth, the period of God's promise to Abraham, which ended with the captivity in Egypt.

Fifth, life under the Mosaic Law, which came to an end with Christ's first arrival on earth and the catastrophe of his death.

Sixth, the time of grace, which will extend to the coming of a searing Tribulation (*Peirasmos*).

Seventh, the thousand-year rule (millennium) that culminates history and will itself be ended by the Last Judgment.

Seven is a good biblical number, and, though some fundamentalists have refined or reconfigured the specifics of the dispensations, most keep Darby's large scheme. Apparent contradictions in the Bible are reconciled by their having occurred under different dispensations. Also, primitive or repugnant things (like Solomon's polygamy) can be excused according to the dispensation, God accommodating his demands to different contractual relations with his people. In these and other ways, dispensationalism allowed for new sophistication and nuance within literal readings. It was the task of fundamentalist scholars, at places like Dallas Theological Seminary, to develop these subtleties. Under their guidance, Bible study did not have to be anti-intellectual.

Some commentators, lumping all fundamentalists together, treating them as equally ignorant and irrelevant, were surprised to hear that one of the most dogged modern dispensationalists, Robert Thieme of Houston, has a "tape ministry" (mailing cassettes of his sermons around the world) that has gone into the homes of Dan Quayle's parents and in-laws. James Quayle, the vice-president's father, is a secular newspaper editor, and the Tucker family, Marilyn Quayle's family, is educated. Only obscure and uneducated people, it was thought, can attend to simpleminded homilies.

Whatever else he may be, Robert Thieme is hardly simpleminded. He places such emphasis on study of the Bible that he refuses to do ordinary pastoral counseling. The true counselor of the human heart is the text of the Holy Book itself. "The Bible is the only accurate discerner of what you think."[1]

Even attending a service or a lecture in Thieme's Houston church is meant to be a private encounter with Scripture. He instructs people not to talk with others or to make bodily motions that might distract them. Fidgeters are advised to sit in glass booths around the edges of the auditorium, where tape recorders can be plugged into direct feeds, to keep a clear record despite any distractions. A pastor who was once part of Thieme's community says, "He'll throw you out if he catches you whispering." The services could not be further from the popular image of evangelical worship. Thieme is contemptuous of halleluia shouters. He wants no response from his audience but absolute silence and concentration. He resorts to no oratorical showmanship himself. His only prop is a scratch pad that projects his writing—the original Hebrew or Greek terms he is explicating from the Scripture—onto a screen behind him. People copy the foreign words into notebooks, or hold up their tape recorders to catch every syllable. Younger members, of whom there are many, use Magic Marker brighteners to highlight the texts in their large Bibles, as Thieme gives them each noun's case, gender, and number and each verb's mood, tense, and person. It is an endless class, convened six times a week, for which there is no exam.

Thieme spells out the English transliteration of each word as he writes it, and explains to his audience that he is doing this for the thousands of people listening in as he speaks. He wears a little box on his chest that transmits his services into loudspeakers—and also into recorders that make tapes elsewhere in the building. These cassettes are then sent out to subscribers and to dozens of groups around the country listening in by telephone relay. Cells of Thieme enthusiasts meet to hear him work his way, book by book, through the Bible, and individuals listen to the tapes in their homes, some of them daily. Local pastors complain that these "tapers' churches" are considered replacements for fellowship with churches on the spot. Every month or so Thieme goes out to address the members of these cells in their own regions. Not that they get much more than they would from hearing his tapes. When Dan Quayle's parents went to one such gathering, they were too awed to address the great man. "No way I would have gone up and said hello," Quayle's mother told reporters.[2]

It is much the same in his own church. There are no closing hymns following the lectures; people just file out, and Thieme disappears into his office. When I tried to go up to the office door, I was intercepted by an usher who said Thieme was busy. Thieme later told me he does not believe in "glad-handing" after services or lectures.

Most of us had never heard of Robert Thieme until we learned of his connection with the Quayles and Tuckers. Marilyn Quayle's parents were devout followers; they played the tapes for their daughters as they were growing up. Two of Marilyn's sisters still listen to the tapes, one of them regularly and enthusiastically. The vice-president's parents listened to the tapes at least once a week and attended annual conferences where Thieme appeared. Marilyn Quayle became cautious about Thieme and his tapes during the 1988 campaign, but she said as late as September of that year that she and her husband "listened to them when we visited my father." She explained, "I do find Thieme *very* good and enjoy listening to his tapes."[3] *Enjoy* is an odd word to use for these pedantic lectures on dogma. As the Reverend Joe Layton Wall, a onetime follower of Thieme who wrote his doctoral dissertation on him, told me, "You either listen to those tapes carefully or you do not listen at all." They are not background music. "There can be no halfway attitude on R.B.'s tapes."

Thieme has been a controversial figure among fundamentalists for three decades, drawing heavy criticism and producing many influential disciples. He began as the bright light of Dallas Theological Seminary. After Army Air Forces service in World War II, he continued his doctoral studies at Dallas, where he was marked by his teachers as a kind of Bible quiz kid, learned in Hebrew and Greek. But before he finished his doctorate, Thieme went to the Berachah church in Houston, instantly fired its board, and subjected its congregation to rigorous lectures that seemed to be a combination of graduate seminar and military briefing (of the sort he had delivered as an officer at Luke Field). He started a local radio show, answering questions on the Bible, and began building his own systematic theology, in imitation of his Dallas mentor, Lewis Sperry Chafer, who published eight volumes of theoretical dogmatics.

Thieme attracted curious young Bible students, who wanted more than the vague cheerleading they were likely to get from the pulpits of ill-educated preachers. Many of his students went on to become graduate Bible students (some at Thieme's alma mater) after exposure to his philological exegesis of Scripture. Thieme says that he has sent about six hundred people on to higher degrees, though even his adoring assistant, Katherine (Katie) Tapping, admits that Thieme is a high estimator. But there is no denying that two of the most read and oftenest cited evangelical authors today began their studies in Thieme's auditorium. Hal Lindsey, the best-selling pop eschatologist, dedicated his 1989 book, *The Road to Holocaust*, with these words:

To my spiritual father, Col. Robert B. Thieme, Jr., whose systematic teaching of God's word and personal encouragement changed the entire direction of my life. If I have any crowns in heaven, it will be because of him. Thanks, Dad.

And Charles Swindoll, another writer with a huge national following, went, like Lindsey, to Dallas Theological Seminary after being converted in Thieme's church. He is now the head of the First Evangelical Free Church, of Fullerton, California, where he runs his national ministry through books and radio. If Thieme had no other claim to influence, he would be an important figure in late-twentieth-century religion through the impact of these men.

For anyone with a sense of America's religious history, Thieme is a fascinating figure, a kind of walking museum of theological views. On the question of salvation through grace alone, rather than through good deeds, Thieme would fit right into John Winthrop's Boston, as Calvinist as any Puritan in that seventeenth-century settlement. Human merit, he argues, cannot undo the ravages of original sin; only the "imputation" of Christ's redeeming act can lift a person out of the worldly order that is Satan's realm.[4]

Thieme is so close to that original American theology that the troubles of Winthrop's Boston are being played out again in Houston's Berachah church. Anne Hutchinson, who was driven out of Boston for heresy in 1638, so emphasized reliance on the Spirit—rather than on human "works"—that she condemned most Massachusetts preachers as belonging to an order of external works, the "law" from which grace delivers true believers. This antilaw position was called antinomianism, and it comes up frequently in Christian communities that place heavy emphasis on grace.

If human acts cannot save, they cannot damn either. Grace sets the believer apart from the world. This attitude can veer off in opposite directions—toward ascetic isolation from the world, or toward uncontaminated traffic with the world. Thieme is opposed to asceticism on principle—he calls it a way of doubting God's saving grace. "It is impossible to sin inside the divine dynasphere" (which grace forms around the believer).[5] Hal Lindsey follows him in this, treating "guilt trips" as one of Satan's best techniques.[6] In Thieme's system, the saved person may sin, but can instantly "rebound" into grace by a simple acknowledgment of the sin. This doctrine has led theologians at Bob Jones University and other fundamentalist centers to charge Thieme with preaching license, and to suspect that his emphasis on privacy is a way of keeping his conduct from scrutiny.

For Thieme, even responding to such charges would be sinful, a betrayal of the privacy in which the Spirit works for the saved. He has for years refused to give interviews. The religion editors at both Houston newspapers say they have never spoken with him, though he did respond in writing to questions submitted beforehand by the *Houston Chronicle* in 1979.[7] He was unavailable when the Quayle connection came to light in 1988.

When I first asked for an interview, I was told he was too busy studying Scripture to talk with anyone. He does churn out an amazing number of tapes and self-published books, the only material on display in his church's library. Only when I convinced his son Bobby—who is being groomed to take over the ministry—that I was seriously interested in Thieme's theology, and not just in detached political statements that have been given wide circulation, did he set up an interview. When I asked Thieme why he so rarely quoted other theologians, he said he was too busy with his own system to pay attention to other theories. While hardly a page of his work passes without a reference to his own writings, the only other author he cites with regularity is Lewis Sperry Chafer, a man recently attacked in a book that has divided the evangelical community: In *The Gospel According to Jesus*, John MacArthur blames Chafer for the antinomian element in modern evangelicalism, which emphasizes a consciousness of being saved over virtuous conduct.

When Thieme quoted another professor from Dallas Theological Seminary, the man told Thieme that the quotation, printed out of context, distorted his meaning.[8] That may have confirmed Thieme in his self-referential ways. A man who will not even talk to his own congregation is not likely to spend much time with people from outside it. Since his lectures are so like classroom presentations, I asked him whether, as a teacher, he did not want to have some interchange with his students. He said he had entertained questions at one time, but gave up the practice because too many questions were irrelevant. Now he takes written queries from his congregation, but on the condition that they be anonymous, observing "the doctrine of privacy."

During my own interview with Thieme, which lasted two hours, he was flanked by four members of his staff, who did much of the talking: his longtime secretary, Katie Tapping, now the executive vice-president of his ministry; Bobby Thieme; the editor of Thieme's publications; and a female staffer who distributes the tapes (thirty thousand cassettes each month). All those present were quick to intervene in defense of Thieme's positions. His secretary, who has been with him for twenty years, contradicted or corrected him at times, but mainly described Thieme's intellectual prowess, a subject that seemed to fascinate him, no matter how long she dwelt upon it. She answered for him so often that at times he could hardly get back into the conversation ("Just a minute, hon . . .").

A hale seventy-one years old, Thieme has a military bearing and a voice that reflects his affluent California upbringing rather than Texas. I began by asking him about his relations with other churches. Houston is a beehive of evangelical Christianity, with huge churches and an active network of pastors and believers, but Thieme and his people keep to themselves. He told me this was from no hostility to others—he is simply too busy, and so are his followers. His son explained that the schedule at Berachah is so full—four night classes a week and two church services on Sunday—that those who attend do not have time for any other church activities, even in their own congregation.

Yet it is clear from his writings that Thieme is not ecumenical in his approach to other religions. Harsh enough toward his own people, whom he calls stupid from the lectern, he has criticized revivalists as systematic invaders of privacy: "Instead of bringing revival, public confession can burn down an entire church."[9] Charismatics, who boast of healing and other gifts, are satanically inspired when not impostors. "Tongues" is mere babbling, since the Holy Spirit, descending on the young Christian church at Pentecost, used languages understood by their hearers.[10] Baptists offer a ceremony that is worthless without (and unnecessary with) the "dry" baptism of the Spirit that comes from "intellectual assent to Bible doctrine."[11] Even "religion" is a tool of the devil, since it convinces people that a system of works is what matters, and not grace: "Remember, religion is the worst thing that ever hit this world! . . . Religion is the devil's ace trump."[12] Thieme calls his work a Bible ministry, a fellowship of the Word. Though he must call Berachah a church by its constitution, he does not like the term *Reverend*. It is not biblical. He is a pastor, though he is rarely called that. Some call him "Doctor," though he has no right to that title. Most settle on "Colonel Thieme," in deference to his frequently mentioned military experience.

About Catholics Thieme was cautious in the interview after I told him I am one. But his writings have, again, the air of a museum, in which American Puritans considered the pope the Whore of Babylon. The Catholic sacrament of confession is a sin against privacy. Priesthood itself is a violation of the "royal priesthood" of each believer, who alone has custody of his or her own soul. In Catholic countries "religion has abused Mary" by an act of idolatry. In the struggle of the last times, Satan will set up a revived Roman Empire as the Great Whore, an event prefigured by the fact that "millions of our own countrymen consider a man in Rome as the highest person on earth."[13]

Of Jews, the more strictly observant they are, the more they prove "the evil of religion."[14] The real revelation to Israel was of grace despite works, and it involved a foreknowledge of Christ's saving act. So even Adam and Eve were saved by their acceptance of Christ's doctrine (a fact symbolized by their clothing themselves in the skins of animals, whose blood had to be shed in creating the leather).[15] Daniel believed in Jesus.[16] David seems to be Thieme's favorite biblical character, the one he defends most ardently, lashing out at the "stuffy, sanctimonious" people who cannot understand "his energetic lust for life." Despite his sin in murdering Bathsheba's husband, "David never lost a single special blessing that had come to him down the pipeline," including all his wealth, since "once a person believes in Christ [sic], that individual is saved forever."[17]

David also wins Thieme's admiration as "a perfect combat soldier" because he had "no qualms about killing the enemy." Nor would David condescend to answer criticisms, brushing off the envious remarks of his brother Eliab. David even shared Thieme's love of hunting. Despite ancient Israel's lack of safari equipment, like "a .357 H and H Magnum," David "bagged himself a lion!" In Thieme's view, David is the model Christian.[18]

The congregation at Berachah is told that it can substitute "Jesus" for "Jehovah" in the Jewish Scripture, which is just a foreshadowing of the "grace-connection" Jesus would establish with every true believer. The "saints of the Old Testament" saw what was being promised in their prophecies, and were saved by that. Perhaps this explains something Marilyn Quayle told talk-show host Larry King when he asked about the status of Jews in her religion.

> MR. KING: If you're Jewish, [are you] condemned to hell just on the nature of the fact that you don't accept Christ as a savior?
> MRS. QUAYLE: But all Jews have the opportunity to believe in the prophecies of the Bible.
> MR. KING: But if they don't?
> MRS. QUAYLE: Then that's a problem they should deal with within their faith.[19]

When the Quayle connection came out during the 1988 campaign, there was a rush to see what political positions Thieme had espoused. They are typically Texan, anti-Communist and procapitalist. But

Thieme's son justly said, "This is no Jerry Falwell operation." Thieme has retained the traditional evangelical opposition to a "social gospel," and he scorns all "activists," refusing to endorse political candidates or take part in organized political movements. He has never, to his knowledge, met the Quayles. Mrs. Tapping knew Nancy Northcott "by name," but did not know she is Marilyn Quayle's sister. When political references are made in Thieme's talks—to, say, the immorality of a progressive income tax—they are usually asides. His interest is in doctrine.

The doctrine has political implications, of course. According to Thieme, the world is under the devil's rule. The devil is always trying to improve his realm by utopian schemes, hoping to make humans content with merely natural good things. In this the devil's principal allies seem to be the United Nations and the National Council of Churches. (Thieme makes the most imaginative attack on the UN I have ever heard, finding it prefigured in the collaboration of the Roman and Jewish nations in the murder of Christ.)[20] All attempts to improve the devil's environment are points won for the devil, which makes Thieme attack any form of social improvement—except, inconsistently, capitalism, which he praises, even though he thinks it improves the worldly condition. The believer escapes the devil's environment by living at the end of a "grace pipeline" that, like a glassblower's pipe, forms a bubble of protection around him or her.

This is the classic premillenarian ("premil") view—that our age, like all prior ones, will end with a catastrophe; there is nothing the believers can do about that. Private salvation is the pressing task. The cartoon character who walks with a placard—"Repent, the End Is Near"—sums up this position. But Thieme expounds it with his own terminology for the dispensations and their meaning. He adds an eighth dispensation to the classic seven, making of Christ's lifetime, from Nativity to Crucifixion, a separate dispensation (the Age of the Hypostatic Union).[21] Thieme borrows some of his terms from modern therapy and self-help, and some from the Scholastic theologians whose late faults he typifies—a dry approach to intellect, endless definitions and subdivisions.

For Thieme, God created the world on the model of the scene that opens the Book of Job, where Satan bets God that he can make Job curse. It was to accept such a dare that Adam was put in Eden. If Adam and Eve had not fallen, they would have borne no children; the two alone were sufficient for God's contest with the devil. "There was no ovulation in the Garden of Eden," Thieme says. Sex was purely recreational, and the first humans probably enjoyed it every day of their thousand-year life before the fall. (For symmetry, Thieme would like to have history begin *and* end with a millennium of earthly goods.) Although Eve did not ovulate in the Garden, God had foreknowledge of the fall, so he provided her with a womb from the outset. Thieme, like many biblical literalists, brings his own form of science to doctrines like the virgin birth. When a woman's ovum sheds twenty-three of its forty-six chromosomes before being fertilized, that purged ovum is the only untainted bit of human stuff left over after the fall. So the Holy Spirit, by impregnating Mary, provided Jesus with an uncorrupted nature.[22] Thieme is more engrossed in these speculations than in crusading against Communists.

Thieme is no more a feminist than he is an ecumenist, though his most famous opinion on sex is not as outlandish as it has been made to look out of context. He argues that there is a right man for every woman and vice versa—a view that a predestinarian almost necessarily takes. Calvin would have understood. Although Thieme believes that the man should more often be the initiator of sex within marriage, he can be vitriolic about women who do not respond warmly enough: "Some women think, once they are married, they can go into limbo."

But one cannot understand Thieme unless one recognizes that sex and politics are less important to him than his intellectual system. Every theological issue is, for him, a matter of right doctrine. Holding that doctrine by an intellectual act is the only path to salvation. Study of doctrine is the prime religious duty, the entire nurture of the soul (an entity Thieme locates in the cranium). The scriptural "heart" is, he holds, the right lobe of the brain. Everything else in a human should serve this mental center, exempting true believers from storms of emotion. Thieme even substitutes "right lobe" for "heart" in his scriptural paraphrases, making God "see into the right lobe."[23] Where your treasure is, there is your right lobe. Thieme's aloofness, his certitude, his unwillingness to engage in "glad-handing" or "sensitivity sessions," come from this total involvement in his own intellectual system. His repeated attacks on "subjectivity," his praise of objectivity as the principle of poise, often sound like Ayn Rand's, and he has quoted with approval Nathaniel Branden, Rand's biographer and an apostle of her principled selfishness. Thieme's practical attitude looks like Randism *cum* God (ridiculous as that would have sounded to Rand herself).

Thieme ministers to a genuine desire for some intellectually respectable approach to religion among evangelicals. Too often they have suffered from ranting in their pulpits, from vague references to Scripture and an unexamined reverence for it. The congregation of Berachah, which seems to be stable, neither growing nor shrinking, is surprisingly young—many in their twenties or thirties—suggesting a period of intense study (at Thieme's four lectures a week) that slacks off in time. Those attending are well but not lavishly dressed, like young professionals. These are educated believers—like Marilyn Quayle, who told John McLaughlin that she believes in creationism, as opposed to evolution, and in Noah's ark. [24]

For people like this, Thieme holds out the promise, at least, of giving God service from his own great masterpiece, the human mind. Yet this is precisely where Thieme betrays his followers. His entire importance is, by his own decision, as an intellectual guide. Yet on the first night I went to one of his lectures, he made three errors in his Greek (one of case, one of accent, one of aspiration); on the second night, he made two (of accent and of spelling). When I talked to him about the Lord's Prayer, I asked what he made of its famous crux—the meaning of *epiousion*. He bluffed, turning on a tape in his mind, going through his spiel on the Lord's Prayer, touching on every phrase except the one I had brought up—this from a man whose brief biography on the back of his books stresses how many years he studied Greek and Hebrew. I cannot judge his (or anybody's) Hebrew; but if it is no better than his Greek, it is a sham.

What does it matter? No one in his community knows the difference, as he spends hours forming Greek or Hebrew characters on his projected scratch pad, telling people that this is a "peal imperfect" and that an "aorist of finality." For them, he might as well be speaking in the "tongues" he derides as babble. That is the point. This foe of mystification is himself a mystifier, who has formed a cult around the legend of his learning. He never got his doctorate at Dallas Theological Seminary; he says he was too busy with his church in Houston. But at the church he was too busy to see the members of the congregation. What was he busy at? Studying the Scripture, he says. He was too busy studying the Scripture to write learnedly about Scripture. He does not submit his writings to his peers, or encourage intellectual intercourse with them. He rejoices in pedantry, in the paraphernalia of learning, but will not submit to the discipline of real learning. When he went to Houston, he told people he had received and turned down a Rhodes scholarship. When *The Houston Post* printed this claim, Rhodes people assured the paper that there was no record of the award. Thieme explained that he was told he would have got a scholarship if he had applied.

His claims of intellectual achievement will not bear scrutiny. That, and not any of the rumors about personal "license," is probably the real reason for his insistence on "privacy"—which gives him intellectual unaccountability. Even his military background is elusive as one searches for its basis. On the backs of his books he used to claim, with reference to his noncombat service in World War II, "Prior to his release he was *in charge of* all Army Air Forces cadet military training" (italics added). When I asked what that means, the editor of his publications said that this is no longer printed on the books; his son said it did not mean he personally trained all cadets; and Katie Tapping said, "No, no, no, no, no, no, no." Looking over at "Bob," she said, "What we meant is that you had written the books." The books turned out to be two training manuals. Thieme vaguely says he wrote all of the Army Air Forces training manuals and then produces a letter from 1943 saying that he wrote two of them, one on military etiquette and the honor code and one on strategy. It is interesting that he was careful enough to get a superior's letter saying that he had written the anonymous manuals, and that he can only produce evidence for the two. Of these two, Mrs. Tapping says, in front of the Colonel, "I thought that these were remarkable in that they were done by a very young man of twenty-four and his knowledge even then of history I thought was stunning, and I think the way he expressed himself was marvelous. It was, I think, very inspirational."

The manual on etiquette, the only one Thieme has retained, is twenty-four pages long and covers items like the proper mode and time of saluting and whether keeping one's shoes shined should be considered part of the honor code. Considering Thieme's later emphasis on grammar, it is amusing to read, "Aviation Cadets and commissioned personnel use the second person in official conversation. In answering the telephone, identify your organization and then yourself: 'Aviation Cadet Detachment, Aviation Cadet Brown speaking.' " Luckily, winning the war did not depend on knowing the difference between the second person and the third. But if it did not, then what was Thieme's great contribution to the victory he seems to remember as his Davidic moment? The bits of history that moved Mrs. Tapping so deeply are celebrations of Confederate heroes and imperial conquerors. We get this interesting glimpse of a secular David: "Soldiers like Sir Henry Havelock saved British India from the ravages of the Sepoy mutiny because they had the strong conviction of character to prepare for trouble in spite of slanderous slurs and sarcastic implications [sic] of fellow officers."

Even Thieme's adoring circle knows when to brush away some of the Colonel's pretensions. When he suggests that he has a million "tapers,"

Mrs. Tapping chimes in, "No, no, no, no, no, no, no." When he claims that two members of his family signed the Declaration of Independence, including Benjamin Harrison ("in the line running through Eleanor of Aquitaine"), she laughs at this as if it were a family joke, and says to me, "It goes too far back to give it any notice. Don't write that down."

Perhaps Thieme once had intellectual gifts; he certainly aspired to an eminence only they could give him. But he has chosen a way of life certain to obliterate them—surrounding himself with sycophants; avoiding for decades any new idea or challenge; dealing always with minds he considers inferior to his; putting on display a learning whose credentials need never be renewed; condescending to his own followers; refusing to deal with those whose submission is not predictable. If Thieme "had the time" to read anybody but himself, he might with profit meditate on some lines of the greatest poet of the Protestant Reformation. In "Lycidas," Milton criticized ministers who do not feed their flocks intellectually:

> The hungry sheep look up, and are not fed,
> But swoln with wind, and the rank mist they draw,
> Rot inwardly. . . .

The problem with evangelical religion is not (so much) that it encroaches on politics, but that it has so carelessly neglected its own sources of wisdom. It cannot contribute what it no longer possesses.

PART FOUR

❖◆❖◆❖◆❖

"Postmil": Pat Robertson

⬦ F I F T E E N ⬦

Coffee=Cup Apocalypse

During the 1988 campaign, Jesse Jackson, moving through a crowd, was saying, "Vote for me! Vote for me!" One man said, as he was brushing by him: "I can't, I'm a Republican." Jackson stopped, put both hands on the top of his head, looked up at the heavens and said, "Heal!" The joke was partly on him. Faith healing is part of the tradition from which his ministry came. Shortly before this, Randall Terry, the antiabortion activist, saw a man in a restaurant cut his hand on an electric slicer; he began loudly praying for it to be healed. Political Left and Right had a common ancestry of faith as communal therapy.

"Premils" like Colonel Thieme believe the present age is ruled by diabolic power, the Lord of this World. Only a catastrophe can end this period, through battle and trial. The thousand-year reign will come as a calm after that storm. But other believers in the millennium think that Armageddon and Last Judgment will *succeed* the millennium. These "postmils" do not foresee a catastrophe intervening between the present age and history's fulfillment. The Spirit is already building the elements of the earthly kingdom.

It is easy to call the premils pessimists who have despaired of the world and simply await its ending. It is equally tempting to call the postmils optimists who think reform can change the worldly into a godly kingdom. In practice, many premils and postmils disappoint these neat distinctions, according to the niceties of their theology or their temperament.[1] Ronald Reagan, for instance, sometimes talked the language of premils, yet he is incurably optimistic. He wants the story to have a happy ending right away.

But it is true that some premils, like Colonel Thieme, think the Spirit of God no longer works openly on believers as in the New Testament era of miracles and revelations. (Thieme cordoned off these public manifestations of the supernatural by declaring Christ's lifetime a separate dispensation.) The revelation ended, so far as our era is concerned, with the last canonical texts of the New Testament. Now there are no miracles or open "signs," just the hidden "grace pipeline" for those who accept what the Bible says.

But others think that the Spirit that drove Jesus into the desert place "blows where it wills." The world is always permeable by its Creator. Signs and gifts reveal that Spirit's motion, just as churned waters in its wake show the passage of a great ship. America's most characteristic religious rite, the revival, is a continual manifestation of the Spirit, whose impact is registered in shouts, tears, sighs, swoons, tongues, and other physical agitations that accompany the arrival of peace in the soul. Calming the agitated is part of a large healing process that is always going on in the Christian ministry.

Revivals were "pentecostal"—that is, they repeated some of the experiences recorded in the Acts of the Apostles as occurring at the first Pentecost (Fifty Days). Fifty days after the Ascension of Jesus, during the Jewish feast of Harvest, the literally dispirited followers had fire fall on them. It struck their wits from them and they babbled so that bystanders thought them drunk; but Peter argued that this behavior signaled the entry of new energies into the course of history.

Saved people at American revivals struggle in the Spirit, their reluctant fallen nature being remade with a shudder—with "quakings" and "shakings" and holy "rollings." At the huge Cane Ridge revival of 1803, Barton Stone catalogued the various forms of trance and seizure—"the jerks," barking, ventriloquism ("belly-speaking" without lip movements), "the shouts." But one particular reaction, glossolalia, or "tongue-spieling," was made in the late nineteenth century a form of "second baptism" (one of fire, not water) for the sanctified. The Holiness Movement that produced the Nazarenes (Gary Hart's church) had laid a theological foundation for the importance of tongues, though Nazarenes later recoiled from the excesses of Pentecostalism.

The *ritual* use of tongues in gatherings was codified at a little church in Los Angeles—the Azusa Street mission—in 1906. An eschatological frenzy had seized California after the earthquake that shook the whole state and toppled much of San Francisco. Two black disciples of a disreputable Middle Western forerunner of the movement (Charles Fox Parham) made the little mission rock, and the world took (often mocking) note.[2]

The Pentecostal movement featured many *charismata*, "gifts" or graces, for example, prophecy and healing, along with tongues. It spread among the dispossessed, and was ecumenical as well as interracial. At this stage the movement was still premil. Those expecting earthquakes to end the world do not build churchly structures of their own. But when Pentecostalism moved up the social ladder, believers began to acquire the longer-term views of the world that come with institutionalization. (This is the paradox that often divides against itself any church founded on the expectation of dissolution, *begun* with a message of the *end*.)

Famous Pentecostals like Aimee Semple McPherson struck secular observers as bizarre; but she hid the wilder antics of her first followers in "tarrying places," apart from the tents or halls where she held mass meetings. In much the same way, socially aspiring black preachers sometimes hid their more demonstrative followers from the eyes of "respectable" preachers. Indeed, McPherson was only a representative of her movement in the way that Paul Whiteman was "king" of jazz—he dressed it up for more general consumption. Oral Roberts did the same thing at a later stage of Pentecostalism, ridding himself of extravagances like those of "Sister Aimee."

After World War II, Pentecostalism had become, for many, not the voice of apocalyptic deprivation but of a yearning to escape from middle-class anomie. This is best symbolized in the Full Gospel Businessmen's Fellowship, which by the 1950s had access to the Eisenhower White House.[3] The movement of Billy Graham's biblical fundamentalism into public acceptance made even more demonstrative forms of evangelical preaching look attractive too. Golf-course spirituality was, in the fifties, becoming restless and spiritually adventurous. The idea of people meeting to speak in tongues had some of the appeal that, in earlier days, attracted men to secret Masonic rites. There was also a sense of returning to the lower sources of energy in society. Itinerant Pentecostals titillated the comfortable with tales of their work on the Bowery, rescuing bums (as the Salvation Army had) but reporting the results back to curious advertising executives. The Full Gospel Businessmen's Fellowship got reports from the street, of the sort that were later written up in the best-selling *The Cross and the Switchblade* (1963), a book that helped launch a ministry to "Jesus People."

A new kind of Pentecostal preacher was appearing—not the mass evangelist like Oral Roberts or Kathryn Kuhlman, but a quiet emissary from other social worlds like Harold Bredeson, who scuttled back and forth between soup lines and penthouses. On one of his missions to the celebrities, in 1957, he took along a young assistant pastor from his Mount Vernon, New York, base of the moment, to tell Mrs. Norman Vincent Peale, wife of the popular 1950s evangelist, that the baptism of the Spirit (marked by one's first speaking in tongues) is needed to fill the spiritual void within people who had succeeded by her husband's methods.[4]

The young pastor with Bredeson was a tongue-speaking Bible student named Pat Robertson. Robertson, the son of a United States senator, was still shopping around among the spiritual stimulants of the strangely narcotized fifties. He would later tailor the story of his quest to an audience of succeeders, saying he had been like them until he realized that "the world" gives only hollow rewards to its devotees. But his career had not, in fact, been a successful one. Dubious service in the Marines during the Korean War, poor grades at Yale Law School, a marriage "beneath him" when he got a nurse pregnant, failure to pass the bar exam, a series of business ventures from which his father had to bail him out—that had been his career until he begged God for something more.

Robertson needed spiritual healing, and he sought it in study for the ministry. His parents, respectable Christian leaders in Virginia, tried to direct him to one of the established schools of theology, but Robertson—whose grades had never been good—chose a small Bible school in New York, known mainly for training men and women for the home and foreign missions. The classes were not demanding, and Robertson felt the need for more spiritual guidance. He found it in the catacombs of the new Pentecostals—in student meetings where the Korean widow of a "martyred" war chaplain spoke in tongues; at a White House prayer breakfast where he met Robert Walker, a founder of neo-Pentecostalism; at a slum mission called Christian Soldiers where he met Harold Bredeson. He prayed, fasted, spoke in tongues, and hoped to win the gift of healing.[5]

His wife, Dede, the Catholic nurse he had married secretly in law school, suffered through this time when he reeled from one inspiration to another. He was away on "retreat" when she had her second child. He sold all the furniture when she was off visiting her family. He took her to Brooklyn for a short-lived ministry to blacks. Finally he took her "home" to a small religious television station in Virginia. His father regretted this son's association with fringe religiosity among his own constituents, but Robertson meant to use television for healing in a more intimate way than Oral Roberts had. In his scramble for money, he fell for a weird con artist who claimed to be an intermediary for the Hunt millionaires of Texas, who led him on a fool's quest for extensive funding.[6]

But gradually Robertson worked out on his TV network a formula of prayer, therapy, and friendly talk that took faith healing away from the high drama of the mass meetings. Now, in the comparative privacy of one's own front room, loneliness could be assuaged (and hemorrhoids cured) by a soft-voiced, wheezily laughing friend who offered, for many adults, the calm reassurance that Mr. Rogers brought to children on the same front-room tube. Robertson even launched other stars on his program, Jim and Tammy Faye Bakker, who went off and set up their own television network in imitation of his. The Bakkers first worked with puppets, and even the dolls seemed to shed tears when fund appeals were made with increasing pathos and increasing results.

Robertson's voice had, by 1975, become the most considerable force among Pentecostals. When some other leaders tried to make Pentecostalism more responsible to local churches, Robertson in effect banned them from national gatherings.[7] The success of his own network, using satellite relays, gave him the money to establish his own university (like Oral Roberts and Jerry Falwell). Setting up universities was the last thing that would have occurred to the founding Pentecostalists of Azusa Street. Why train a new generation for tasks it will never live to perform?

But Robertson, by now, was averting world catastrophe, not waiting for it. He choreographed over his network the massed prayers that cushioned the East Coast from Hurricane Gloria's assault in 1985. In more quotidian ways, he was using gifts of the Spirit to bring his audience material things. The preacher of disaster on the morrow has trouble persuading his flock to donate on the installment plan. Robertson carried further the "dignifying" efforts of his predecessors. The term *Pentecostal* still had a lower-class feel to it; "mainstream" Christians who began to speak in tongues during the sixties preferred a fancier designation for the same thing, *charismatic*. Robertson had abandoned both terms by the end of the seventies, using the broader and more inclusive label for all "low-church" Protestants: He was now an *evangelical*.

His change of terms was appropriate. Pentecost had been a public event, a "witnessing." Its portents of wind and fire make it, to the Christian church's founding, what the deliverance of the Law from Mount Sinai (amid thunder and lightning) was to the Chosen People of Israel. Robertson was privatizing his religion even as he began to fashion a political program for believers. He would become a "business executive" when he ran for president. The cult of success he had criticized, when he was visiting Norman Vincent Peale's wife, he now embraced. Success was a credential that he used to validate his campaign. In that way, he represented less an intrusion of spiritual claims into the secular realm than an absorption of them by it. He was taking into its final stages the Americanization of Pentecost.

The seeds of this development were always there in Robertson's ministry. The Bible school he attended was a very American affair—one of the "small-business" efforts of entrepreneurial Protestantism. The Biblical Seminary was founded in 1900, as the rift was growing between liberal Protestantism and the forces that would soon be called "fundamentalist." Wilbert Webster White (1863–1949), a well-trained Episcopalian theologian, wanted to take a middle course between those factions, emphasizing the *practical* study and use of the Bible.[8]

White proposed what he called an "inductive" approach to Scripture— an experimental use of it to open one's soul to God and find ways for dealing with the world. Ironically, in the light of Robertson's later attack on John Dewey as the father of secular-humanist education, White was clearly influenced by Dewey's pragmatic approach to education, tying it closely to the student's experience and needs. This is the way White approached the Bible (at first with the help of some fine scholars who taught at his pioneering school, men like Marcus Dods). Robertson's own use of the Bible looks like the caricatures he would draw of Deweyite methods in the public schools. He tells us, for instance, how he penetrated the key text of his teaching, that "the kingdom of heaven is at hand": He would go into his front room every morning, with a steaming coffee cup, and stare at his hand, waiting for the inspiration he could carry to others. He learned his Bible by the look-say method. Bob Slosser, who was the coauthor of Robertson's most ambitious book, *The Secret Kingdom*, remembers how Robertson used his exegetical method in the composition process:

I always remember him coming out of the Omni Hotel in Norfolk one day with me and, looking at his hand, he said, "What did John the Baptist mean about the kingdom of heaven being at hand?" Every morning he would get out of bed and, after he had finished his prayer time, he would sit out on the porch of that old house in Portsmouth with a yellow legal pad and an open Bible. He would also have a cup of tea in a great big mug.[9]

Robertson puts himself at his own home, with coffee. His collaborator worked with him at a hotel, with the aid of tea. In any case, the message Robertson brought was by now less a matter of fire falling on the inspired babbler than of practical inspiration shared around the morning coffee at prayer breakfasts for the Full Gospel Businessmen's Fellowship.

Since Robertson's book divides the world into two kingdoms, a visible and an invisible one, I asked him how he related his scheme to the most famous theology of two kingdoms, that of Augustine's "two cities." He let me know that his thought was original, immediate, and concrete— good Deweyite values. His ideas grew from his own hand, not others' writings. The book was an example, if not of parthenogenesis, then of what may be called cheirogenesis:

I wasn't a particular student [of St. Augustine]—I was aware of some of his sayings, and his own personal conversion, but his writing as such was not particularly influential. *The Secret Kingdom* was, in my estimation, pretty much seminal, if you will. I came up with concepts there that I thought I never really had seen fully expanded before. I had hoped that I was writing something that would be a primary work in this particular field.

Robertson considers the book his most important and original statement. I asked why he had used another writer to help compose it. He assured me that he was too busy with his corporate activities to do more than the coffee-steam stages of the volume:

It was a question of time. What I did was I wrote the outlines of the book myself, the chapter headings were pretty much mine, the bulk of what was going into the book, and he [Slosser] went over the tapes of all of the thoughts that were there. I'd been working on the thoughts for years, for five years, and then I had to turn it over to somebody, because I just didn't have the time, as chief executive officer of a big company and a daily television personality, so I asked for the draft, and what we did, we read line by line. Now, the introduction, that's mine, about the sea gulls and the moonlight, and all that, those words are mine, and other parts of the book are my writing, but, in terms of editing, I did extensive editing. The second book I did, I wrote it, the *Answers to Two Hundred of Life's Most Probing Questions*, I did that on tapes and had the tapes transcribed, and then did all the editing on that, so that was one I did all by myself, with a little bit of help on a couple of chapters, but most of that is my words.

Robertson, so distant from Colonel Thieme in most of his attitudes toward the Bible, is as slow to credit anyone else with his insights. Entrepreneurial evangelicals are always edgy about the competition. But one clearly derivative aspect of Robertson's book is his view of "dominion," and that is an unambiguously *post*mil concept. "Dominion theologians," as they are called, lay great emphasis on Genesis 1.26–27, where God tells Adam to assume dominion over the animate and inanimate world. When man fell, his control over creation was forfeited; but the saved, who are restored by baptism, can claim again the rights given Adam. Thus the true inheritors and custodians of this world are Christians who can "name it and claim it" by divine right. The most thorough and consistent dominionists in America are the followers of Rousas John Rushdoony, who are called Christian Reconstructionists. They resume authority under a revived covenant, renewing "Old Testament" law for modern times.

Ideas of dominion, of "claiming it" for the Lord, are widespread in the Christian schools and home schools that have grown so rapidly since the desegregation decisions. It is a great mistake to think that this school movement is, any longer, a mere effort to keep white children from contact with blacks. The dedicated leaders, teachers, and organizers of this movement have embraced a large Christian program, and they are training an elite in it.[10] Dissatisfaction with poor standards in the public schools, with "secular humanism" in the teachers, with Christian timidity in demanding prayer for schoolchildren, has made of these schools, at their best, what Catholic parochial schools used to be—highly disciplined, and very good at teaching the basics of grammar, rhetoric, and other language skills.

Pat Robertson is a particular favorite of Christian-school supporters, who formed much of the core of his movement around the country, because his campaign against Deweyite "permissiveness" was translated into an ambitious and expensive literacy program teaching "phonics." One of his *secular* claims in the campaign was that he promoted literacy outside a church-school context; but his supporters rightly saw a religious motive behind this emphasis on rigor in instruction.

The fervor and effectiveness of small Robertson cadres astounded the observers of his "takeover" in early stages of the primary process, especially in Michigan, where the electorate has a strong "Dutch" Protestant segment—the segment that made Gerald Ford campaign as a born-again Christian in the region of Calvin College. If an active minority of Christians could seize leadership within the Republican party process, they hoped to carry less committed Republicans along with them, capitalize on disaffection with the Democrats, and reassert the Lord's dominion over the nation. They realized that Robertson would have to downplay his ministry in order to benefit from this party takeover. (Unlike Jesse Jackson, he resigned from the clergy when he entered the presidential campaign.) But the theology behind his watered-down Pentecostalism was still that of miraculous intervention in the affairs of man. If God could divert a hurricane in response to the prayers Robertson summoned, what might He not do, in the course of the campaign, to tip things Robertson's way? It was a long shot, but miracles always are. As Robertson put it: "[Stopping the hurricane] was extremely important because I felt, interestingly enough, that if I couldn't move a hurricane, I could hardly move a nation."[11] And so, with this odd new qualification for office, Robertson launched a campaign that did, for a while, look like a miracle of holy opportunism.

❖ S I X T E E N ❖

Campaigning

SECRET SERVICE PROTECTION OF PRESIDENTIAL CANDIDATES IS VERY GOOD and professional. But a chain is only as strong as its weakest link, and in January of 1988 one of those links was the volunteer staffer driving the Robertson press van in the District of Columbia. Her Texas accent showed she was not at home here. She was fiercely intent on her work, and good at it, but not a world-class driver. And here she was, being harried through the night from Dulles Airport to the Washington Sheraton, at or above speed limit, with hair-trigger Secret Service drivers before and behind her, and with their injunction clearly weighing on her mind, to keep the motorcade "tight." It is the kind of van where one sits over the front wheels, behind a fishbowl front window; our lights hit point-blank the face of the agent staring (according to the rule) straight out of the back of his car, like a B-29 rear gunner in *his* fishbowl.

When I talk to the journalists behind me in the van, I face into other headlights immediately upon our rear bumper. Thus floodlit in her high bucket seat, the driver is so focused on her task that she does not hear me, seated beside her, when I speak to her—a foolhardy thing I regret having done when I see the forward car's red lights brighten suddenly, her foot stab at the brake, the lights behind flare up in my mind as they come mere inches closer, then back off. It is like the tug at couplings between railway cars, only here there are no couplings but the poor young driver's nerves, which are clearly at a stretch.

At this stage of the campaign, there are only three journalists in the van (yesterday there were five), and four staff persons, including the two most important advisers to Robertson—the campaign manager R. Marc Nuttle, just behind me, and Constance (Connie) Snapp, behind him on the last (full-across) seat of this seven-person van.

We journalists had been wakened, that morning, at Robertson's Virginia Beach headquarters, where we expected to spend the day while Robertson prepared at leisure his address for the National Religious Broadcasters meeting—the very engagement we are racing toward, at nightfall, in this motorcade. We went to bed the night before, a Friday, with Patrick Caldwell's assurance that we could sleep late for a change. Caldwell is an ex–Secret Service man who became Pat Robertson's personal security agent at the Christian Broadcasting Network (CBN) before handling the logistics of his campaign appearances.

Caldwell was hoping his assurances would prove true, though Robertson gave us broad hints that he would like to be in Michigan on Saturday, where his delegates were hastily putting together an alternative state convention, arguing that it would be the authentic one.

As happens during a campaign, aides and press living on the same plane day after day, stop after stop, talk campaign strategy at several levels, the staff trying out or planting ideas with the press, the press speculating about future moves as a way of eliciting information about the present. "Do you think he should go?" Caldwell asked the journalists about Michigan. Two of the three said no—and so did Caldwell. If there was to be a bitter fight, let the delegates bear the brunt of it, and give Robertson a result he could make the best of before the press—that was the press's view, beforehand.

But everyone in the conversation admitted that such reasoning left Robertson's character out of consideration. He likes to be in the middle of things. "I am a high-stakes roller," he later admitted of this sudden dash into Michigan. Scheduling is one of the most important things campaign managers do with a candidate; but the contender's own moods are so important to his performance that all plans have to be reconsidered if the candidate does not feel right about them. A candidate is tunneling, exhilarated, through a period when all his time is valuable and everything is done to make each moment useful—calling donors, meeting voters, making ads, getting free coverage. For this, the Secret Service runs red lights, the airports wave him through with his entourage, the advance people have their cars and drivers lined up. But every now and then this purposeful run through obstacles seems confusing to the candidate, who wobbles momentarily in the groove cut out for him, and floats up above it all, wondering how he touched off the wild scurry below him. These moments are not the least cherished ones in retrospect; they help explain a candidate's willingness to undergo such an ordeal again, to have again all that heat of human effort fill his balloon and push him aloft for moments of pseudomeditation amidst the battle.

We heard about the Michigan trip at 8:00 A.M. when Caldwell telephoned each of us in our hotel rooms. Connie Snapp had been talking with him from Grand Rapids in the early hours; she told him to let us sleep and just bring the candidate. It was for such skills at communication that she—as Robertson liked to tell audiences, demonstrating his concern for women's issues—drew the highest salary in his campaign. (Nuttle's opinion of this repeated boast is not on record.)

Caldwell, who has taken it on himself to maintain decent relations with the press (always a touchy matter with Robertson, and even tenser with his enthusiasts, on or off the staff), simply ignored Snapp's directive. He gave us half an hour to get down to the lobby, be shuttled by van to the airport, then wait for the candidate to get off the phone to Michigan so he could get on the plane to Michigan.

Don Miracle, Robertson's pilot, had been out early checking over the plane for any contingency. He knows the candidate as well as the plane, and did not expect the man to give the machine much rest. Despite his name, Miracle is not an unbearably godly man; he invested in CBN for its returns in cash, not prayer, and leased the plane to CBN—then, later, to the campaign—only after he held stock in Robertson's enterprises. His relation to the candidate is that of a business partner; Miracle has a hired steward, who comes with the plane, to take on himself the more menial services to "Pat" (as everyone calls the candidate in this Southern Christian world of "Jimmy" Carter and "Jimmy" Swaggart and "Billy" Graham).

I ask Miracle about his BAC jet plane, which was built in 1963. "It's barely broken in, in terms of its cycles, its real life." (A cycle is a takeoff and landing.) "It's got about ten thousand cycles on it. Most planes that age would have eighty thousand." It has been in private service most of its life—legend has it as the singer Kenny Rogers's personal jet during *his* expansive days. Like other things, it needed a kind of breakdown before its conversion. When Miracle found it, it had been sitting on the ground for two years, drying out in the sun at Anaheim. "I had to completely redo the hydraulics," he said. Chastened so, the plane has the stamina to keep up with a candidate fueled by all the mysterious energies of ambition.

Robertson was the only candidate except the vice-president of the United States to enter the race with his own private plane. Those who rented Lear Jets for particular trips (like Dukakis) or took commercial flights (like Babbitt) did not, at the time, have that continuing interaction of candidate and aides and press that ensures national coverage. Gerald Austin, Jesse Jackson's campaign manager, beginning with the slimmest wallet, made his first major commitment of money to a large jet plane— rather than channeling it, for instance, into making advertisements. "The plane *is* an advertising expense," he rightly said. It provides the forum where national journalists can keep in touch with the campaign on a steady basis, where the candidate sits still long enough for leisurely interviews.

Campaigns afraid of the press (like Robertson's) do not know how to put this to their advantage. Shrewder veterans—like Lee Atwater on Bush's plane—know how campaign junkies on the staff and in the press create the mixture of friction and collusion that gives campaigns their special excitement, creating on each plane a different ethos. The advent of marathon debates in 1987 and 1988 made the postdebate "spin patrol" a common part of political awareness. But riding on a candidate's plane has always been a continual exercise in spin patrol, and professionals welcome the challenge. Every candidate picks up a certain number of "campaign people," those who endure the off-election years just to get back into harness for a national candidate. This campaign year had been cruel to many of these junkies, early recruited and early set adrift by the aborted candidacies of Gary Hart and Joe Biden. When they could not get aboard some other candidate's plane, they attended the election from the sidelines, talking about it endlessly on TV, like the political consultants Robert Squier and John Sears.

Robertson's staff lacked such campaign people. He was running as an outsider, promising to bring in new voters, an invisible army of them. But that lack made Patrick Caldwell more important than he would have been on most planes. He had been there before, knew some of the obstacles, could warn his man about certain dangers. In the past, as a Secret Service man, he was guarding the candidate, not promoting him, but he saw close up the minor things that can vex or sour the relationship of any contender with his audience. Sometimes he saw things more close up than he wanted. "At one crowded rally," he told me, "Teddy Kennedy grabbed my arm like this"—he grabs my arm and pulls me to the front of him, then ducks down behind me—"pushing me through the crowd. I know we're *supposed* to be body shields, but this was so, so, so . . ." He had no word, really, to say *what* it was.

The only other Robertson aide who was supposed to have campaign experience is "R. Marc Nuttle, Esquire," as he entitles his curriculum vitae. A precise little lawyerly man, Nuttle led the effort in Michigan, "shopping for judges" to say that the Republican party was changing its rules and invalidating its own actions when it tried to escape the consequences of early-round Robertson victories. Nuttle served the 1984 Reagan-Bush campaign as an adviser on campaign rules, peripheral to that effort but central to Robertson's. Like many campaign officials, he has acquired the power mutter (*You* come to *me* if you want the *real* information, lean your head my way, form a flower pattern around me with all the petals turning inward). This seems to give all his words the same weightiness as those he whispers in the candidate's ear just out of microphone range. Nuttle also has the authoritative throat-clearing reduced to a kind of verbal tic—it occurs so frequently that it does not become a real *gurgle*, more of a *gurg*, played constantly as a pedal motif: "As *I* (gurg) see it, *this* (gurg) is what will *happen* (gurg)." What happened in Michigan was that Nuttle got a one-vote majority on the Republican state committee to declare the combined Bush-Kemp delegates, an overwhelming majority, not duly authorized. The Robertson forces crowded into a hall underneath the one where the larger body was meeting and elected a complete slate of delegates to the convention in New Orleans.

Robertson took this as a great victory, and the staff conference on the flight back from Grand Rapids—Nuttle and Snapp conferring with the candidate—was punctuated by frequent laughter. They were easily observed up front, where Robertson sits with a big Bible by his seat, since the plane's forward section is separated from the rear by glass panels and a glass door in the aisle. Connie Snapp, no taller than Nuttle, has the flouncy figure of a Dolly Parton snicked in at the waist. She was an advertising executive who handled, for Young & Rubicam, accounts as different as Helene Curtis and CBS before setting up her own company (It's a Snapp Productions.). She was doing the advertising for CBN before she came onto the campaign. "Communications," for Snapp, is the pitching of an ad directly to its target audience. She is disturbed at having to go through an intermediary, the press. The only woman reporter on the campaign at this point said: "I don't mind that she hates me. I mind that she does not even try to hide the fact." In their separate, diminutive ways, Nuttle and Snapp are the Jim and Tammy Faye of this campaign, technicians to facilitate the miracles, shuffling numbers instead of shedding tears.

The post-Michigan schedule, improvised during the day, was to stop off at Norfolk and pick up Mrs. Robertson for the speech to the religious broadcasters. But Don Miracle tells Caldwell that he needs to refuel the plane, and the airport where he gets his gas at cut rate is Patrick Henry, near Williamsburg. A cycle (in this case, a landing and takeoff) costs a thousand dollars for the BAC, so Caldwell decides Mrs. Robertson will have to be driven over to Patrick Henry from Virginia Beach rather than have her own thousand-dollar pickup.

While we wait at Patrick Henry for Mrs. Robertson's car to catch up with Mr. Robertson's plane, the candidate is expansive about what he accomplished in Grand Rapids. By branding Kemp a deserter from the right-wing cause, one who caved in to Bush's party strength, Robertson thinks he has eliminated his principal challenger as the spokesperson for the Right: "He's through. He didn't understand the process in Michigan. I tried to explain it to him on the phone, but he never really did follow it."

Standing in the airport, rocking up onto his tiptoes and down again, his hands behind his back, Robertson remembers all the times he landed at this airport when he flew his own plane: "I would miss the airport, or come in at the wrong altitude. I got lost." Why? "A businessman should never be a pilot. You get up there, and your mind starts working, and you forget where you are." He was not lost in religious meditation, even back in the seventies, before politics opened up before him—it was his business ventures that absorbed him as he floated in the heavens.

Mrs. Robertson arrives, the Catholic nurse who came late and uncertain to her baptism in the Spirit. She has been campaigning on her own, though with a lighter schedule than her husband's (the norm for a candidate's wife). Even his youngest aides have trouble keeping up the pace, day by day, with a man on fire for the presidency. The campaigners' wives, being their coevals, make fewer appearances, and even then they tire more easily. Before the religious broadcasters, Robertson will invite his wife onto the platform and ask her publicly about her own campaign efforts. She is slow to pick up cues, slips into embarrassing pauses, and is manifestly relieved when he takes the microphone from her face. But she gamely gets onto the plane that will take her to this meeting.

From Patrick Henry to Dulles is a brief hop for Don Miracle. We arrive in the early dusk with the Saarinen airport streaming light as if to fly up toward us. On the ground there is confusion. We ask above the jet noises which car is which. Caldwell gets into one limousine, and Snapp tries to get into another. But the cars are too few, and she and Nuttle run over, at the last minute, to board our van. Inside, rolling out of the airport, two network journalists take out their miniature television sets and tune to their respective Saturday-night news shows. Marc Nuttle has his own tiny set, with earphones that look too big for the set, or for him, and he adjusts the phones before he sees that the set is too fuzzy and the sound too weak. His batteries have run out.

The staff is hoping the Michigan story will come early and be given heavy coverage on this slow news day. "I know the Middle East is important," Snapp says impatiently through the opening segment, "but so is Michigan." The story comes late in the show, and is played in a way that casts gloom on the staff. Both networks call it a Bush victory, though Robertson held a rump convention. Nuttle is bewildered: "They didn't use any of me." All those power mutters into all those microphones, and not a gurg survived.

Robertson is proud of the speech he gave in Grand Rapids, and he tells us journalists—what his staffers had already emphasized—that he wrote it himself during the short flight to Michigan. He could find time for that, though not for writing his major theological work. When I interview him on the plane, Robertson does not want to discuss theology. He talks a little about his role as "CEO" of a broadcasting network, with emphasis on the secular shows he runs on it (like *Gunsmoke* and *Wagon Train*). But he prefers to talk of his Virginia ancestry and hereditary patriotism. His followers "claim" America by a divine right of dominion. But he gives as his main credential for office the political heritage of his family: "I did have a very proud heritage. I'm descended from the Duke of Wellington. I have had ten years of higher education, two graduate degrees. I have had privileges not everybody has." His father was a respected senator. On his mother's side, he boasts—like Colonel Thieme—that he is descended from Benjamin Harrison. But in Robertson's case the boast is true. This haunter of the slums in his Spirit-driven days has become a landed gentleman, living in a big Georgian mansion and breeding horses. He presents this as a natural return to his Virginia patrimony: "I have the nobility of education, the nobility of religious understanding, the nobility of opportunity that puts upon me obligations. It was something that was stressed very much at Washington and Lee, where I went to school."

Whatever one thinks of his miracle-working apostolate, Robertson's secular background looks impressive. Awed biographers claim that Robertson is "a scion of a kingly heritage" (John B. Donovan),[1] "a true American blueblood" (Jeffrey K. Hadden and Anson Shupe),[2] possessed like John Kennedy of "the calm self-assurance that breeding brings" (David Edwin Harrell, Jr.).[3] But his Virginia heritage, when one looks into it, is more an indictment than a credential. He now invoked his father as an honorable model for him to follow, "a statesman, not a politician." But he had implicated his father in maneuvers neither could take pride in, and he did not for a long time forgive what he had provoked in him. Robertson grew up in Jefferson country, in Robert E. Lee's town, near George Marshall's school, surrounded by monuments. It was an atmosphere freighted with notions of honor, which never seeped in.

✧ S E V E N T E E N ✧

"Claiming"

WHILE HE WAS BUILDING HIS TELEVISION MINISTRY, PAT ROBERTSON CON-sidered politics beneath him. He had become popular enough with key parts of his father's constituency to be helpful to him when the senator ran for reelection in 1966. But the son was hindered by a divine pro-hibition:

> I yearned to get into the fray and start swinging, but the Lord refused to give me the liberty. "I have called you to my ministry," he spoke to my heart. "You cannot time my eternal purposes to the success of any political candidate . . . not even your own father."[1]

In refusing to help his father, Robertson did not rely on only one divine sign, the word spoken in his heart. He also turned to sortilege, and found biblical sanction for his behavior:

> I slipped from the bed and picked up my Bible and let it fall open. As in times past, God spoke to me through Scripture, and this time my eyes rested on I Samuel 16:1. "How long wilt thou mourn for Saul, seeing I have rejected him from reigning over Israel? Fill thine horn with oil, and go . . ." Instantly I had peace. I knew my father's defeat was of the Lord,

for his soul was far more important than his seniority in Washington. Lyndon Johnson's administration had already begun to taint the federal government with the easy morality and arrogance of the Texas wheeler-dealer. How easy for a powerful man in this environment to misuse his power. I praised God. "Thank you, Lord, for closing this door also."[2]

Robertson's action is overdetermined. To the word spoken in his heart, and to the Bible text, he adds a political calculation—that if Senator Robertson had won, he would have been corrupted by the Johnson regime.

Robertson relied on a single verse sorted out of its context. But the part of the David story he turned to that most resembled his refusal to campaign is 1 Samuel 29.4. There David, now part of the Philistine armies marching against Saul, is prohibited from fighting in the showdown campaign since "he may turn traitor in the battle." The earlier text Robertson cited does not apply to Saul's defeat, but to his loss of legitimacy; and the oil Samuel is told to take off in his horn is for anointing the young David as a rightful successor to Saul. Thus Robertson exactly reverses the meaning of his own divinely sorted-out phrase from the Bible. Saul has not fallen from power, in that passage, but from divine favor. Robertson argues that his father must fall from *power* in order to retain divine *favor*. The final irony is that Samuel is going off to anoint David so that David can replace Saul, but only after he has first ingratiated himself with Saul and then deserted him. Robertson has been led to a text that is deeply political, not—as he takes it—a renunciation of politics. And it is a text for replacing the father figure.

But after all his divine justification for staying out of his father's campaign, Robertson confesses that he *did* contribute to it after all. He did enough to show he could have made the difference if he had wanted to. "I felt I could have helped my father tremendously in the campaign, but the Lord steadfastly refused to let me. I did write one speech which the newspapers said was the hardest-hitting speech of the campaign, but most of my efforts on his behalf were very frustrating."[3] The senator lost by a mere six hundred votes—a margin Robertson claims he could have reversed.

This harsh mercy toward his father—to prevent him from being corrupted—stands in dramatic contrast to his father's assistance in trying to keep him out of combat during the Korean War. To gauge the full meaning of that intervention, one must look into the Virginia heritage Robertson appealed to in 1988. By birth and blood, and even by birth-

place, Robertson is an offspring of American military memories. He was rocked, as it were, in the cradle of Mars—in Lexington, Virginia.

That colonial village was named, at its establishment, for the Battle of Lexington, fought three years earlier. Jefferson, sitting in the state legislature that established Rockbridge County, and with a proprietary interest in the area, may have suggested the name. One of the original streets is Jefferson Street. The town attracted to its vicinity an academy that was also renamed after the Battle of Lexington. What is left of that academy, Liberty Hall—only its end walls and four corner chimneys—stands just outside the town. But the academy had received a donation from George Washington, and when a fire drove it from its old site onto a ledge above the town, it changed its name again, to Washington College. Its five later buildings, made of brick, stand neatly in a row, all wearing classical white pinafores in deference to Thomas Jefferson, acknowledging the force of his university's colonnades, built twenty years earlier on the other side of the Blue Ridge.

When the War of 1812 was concluded, the Virginia legislature chose three sites as arsenals for storing the munitions left over from that conflict. The sites were strategically scattered, for defense and distribution of the muskets; and were kept well guarded, from an abiding fear that the slaves would someday seize arms. The westernmost arsenal was perched on the same ledge as Washington College, and guards off their watch were encouraged to study military topics (like engineering) at the college. From this arrangement a military school developed in the 1830s, its founders determined to make it rival West Point. Since Northern professors were not hired at Virginia Military Institute, the rivalry with West Point prefigured, even from the 1830s, a war in which the weapons first kept from slaves would be wielded to keep them in bondage. A professor at VMI, Thomas "Stonewall" Jackson, consulted his Bible on the defense of slavery by arms, and found such warfare "providential." Thus assured, he led his older students off to battles neither he nor they would return from. But a general who did return from the war, Robert E. Lee, restored Washington College to prestige when he assumed its presidency. For him a new president's house was built, complete with attached stable, so his famous war-horse Traveler was under the same roof with him. He also built a new chapel, where his body lies under a recumbent life-size statue. After his death, the school, renamed a third time, became Washington and Lee.

A town so closely linked to the Revolution, to Jefferson and Washington, to the War of 1812, to Stonewall Jackson and Robert E. Lee, also provided a famous graduate to serve in World War I, George C. Marshall. And, in World War II, while West Point supplied commanders like Eisenhower, MacArthur, and Bradley, their boss was a VMI man, General Marshall, whose war memorabilia are housed in his special library on the military school's campus.

Such a town's local holiday was bound to be martial—New Market Day, which commemorates the time when the whole school went up the Shenandoah Valley to join General John C. Breckinridge in defeating the Yankees at New Market. All 247 cadets went out this time, in the tradition of their elders who had ridden off with Stonewall. Of those who left, 177 returned. The rest did not outlive their teens. In their honor VMI conducts an annual parade and service in May; and, in the valley, the battle is reenacted with the glad noises of feigned combat. Pat Robertson grew up with that annual "battle" on his childhood's calendar—along with the VMI parades and graduations (the latter ending in a shower of thrown caps, snatched up by local children, who wore them as mock cadets throughout the summer). Those who fought with Breckinridge are buried in the town's cemetery, along with Stonewall, and Lee's shrine is on the grounds where Robertson went to school. He has written: "One of my heroes then and now was Robert E. Lee." In the South, Lee is St. Robert.

As if this acculturation to martial values were not enough, Robertson attended two military schools—McDonough in Baltimore and McCallie in Chattanooga—before returning to Lexington as an ROTC student at Washington and Lee. When the Korean War came, Lexington had its fresh store of military graduates ready for war in Asia, as its sons had been ready for every battle since New Market. The South tends to go to war a step or two before the rest of the country. As if to emphasize the guiding hand of the war god in his young life, Robertson sailed for Korea on the U.S.S. *Breckinridge*, named for the man who led VMI's cadets at New Market. And one of his shipmates was also a classmate from Washington and Lee, Edwin Gaines, whose father was president of the university named for the two most revered military leaders in American history. Fate—or something very like it, Southern tradition—was piping Pat Robertson off to war.

But something interrupted what seemed a destined course toward battle and glory. Robertson was moved out of ranks, and took several steps *back* from his fellow Marines, who went on to combat while he stayed in Japan. Was this an accident, one fluke running counter to all the social forces pushing him the other way? Sons of senators, admittedly, get preferential treatment in the military, even when they do not ask for it—especially the son of a prominent member of the military appropriations committee. But more than ordinary care was taken for Robertson. Senator A. Willis Robertson was a friend of his son's commanding officer, Lemuel Shepherd. Senator Robertson drew Shepherd's attention to his son from the earliest possible occasion. When Pat graduated from Washington and Lee, with military duty in his future, the senator wrote the general:

> Pat told his mother that he did not do himself justice on his final examination but in any event I am happy that he got by. I hope in the years to come he can continue his military training and develop for you into a satisfactory officer.[4]

On August 8, 1950, Robertson senior wrote to Shepherd that Pat had been recalled by the Marines from his graduation trip to England. On September 14 of the same year, he told the general that Pat was at Quantico. On December 22, he wrote that his son was moving to Camp Pendleton:

> Pat finished his preliminary training at Quantico today and I understand will proceed to Camp Pendleton shortly after the first of the year. While I think that Pat is serving in the best of all military units, I am, frankly, thankful that he did not have to go through the Korean ordeal. Of course, there may be others that will turn out to be just as tough but, in any event, those who face a new crisis will be better prepared to face it than many who were hastily thrown into battle in Korea simply because there was not adequate time to fully prepare them for the ordeal.

The senator planted the idea that Pat needed further training before exposure to battle—for which he was able to thank the general five weeks later:

> Thank you so much for your nice letter of the third [February] and for your encouraging message concerning Pat. I think he is going to make you a good officer and naturally I am happy that he will get some more training before engaging in combat duty in Korea.

While the senator was maintaining this correspondence, trying to delay his son's introduction into Korea past the time of heaviest casualties, he was writing to Francis Gaines, the president of William and Mary, for whom he had earlier done military favors, about Gaines's son Edwin, who was sharing Pat's good luck in 1950 and 1951. On April 4, 1950, even before the two men graduated, the senator was estimating the chances of their surviving in the military:

It naturally pleases me that Edwin and Pat have made satisfactory grades at Washington and Lee and upon graduation will receive their reserve commissions in the Marine Corps. I hope we will not have another war but if we do they will be called upon to serve and based on my two years service in the First World War I am satisfied it is preferable to serve as an officer than as a private. While the casualties of Marine Corps in the last war were the heaviest of any Branch of the service, if we should have a war with Russia I do not figure that it will be the type of island-hopping war we had in the Pacific with Japan which was so costly of Marine personnel. In any event, the esprit de corps of the Marine Corps is the highest of all units, its training system the very best and its personnel based solely on voluntary enlistments the finest. So I don't think Edwin and Pat made any mistake in choosing the Branch.

But once the two sons were being moved (it seemed inexorably) toward the bloody Korean War, the senator pulled what strings he could to exempt them from the esprit de corps. Writing "Dear Frank" on February 7, 1951, he said:

Three years ago I was able to help Senator Knowland and Mayor Knox of San Francisco on a ten million dollar water project there left unfinished by the Navy. When Pat went out to Camp Pendleton Knowland notified Knox that he was there. I enclose a copy of the letter I received today from Knox. Yesterday I received a letter from General Shepherd stating that Pat and Edwin were going to an interesting and historical part of Japan, where they would be given some valuable training before proceeding to Korea.

Dr. Gaines replied to this letter on February 9: "Shall always be grateful *for everything you have done*" (italics in original). Senator Robertson explained what he had done to another friend:

Pat and a few others in his category [one of them Ed Gaines] will be dropped off in Japan for further training, and naturally Gladys and I hope that before that is complete the issue in Korea will either have been settled or the united lines so stabilized that there will be no excessive casualties as in the marine retreat from the Reservoir area.

It is one thing, clearly, to have an annual celebration for the seventy young men who died at New Market. It is another thing entirely for the senator's son to join them in such early martyrdom. Pat did eventually go to Korea, but not into combat duty. Gaines was later assigned to combat and was wounded. If Pat Robertson got no special privileges, delaying his entry into Korea and keeping him from active combat, then his father and mother were misled in their relief. And if he got no such privileges, it was not for lack of trying on his father's part. A senator, a mayor, and a general were all told to take care of him and reminded of past favors the senator had done them.

Such a break with the Southern code of battle is the more surprising in this particular father. A. Willis Robertson came from a line of Southern preachers—the A. stood for Absalom. He was a famous hunter (Sportsman of the Year in 1926, according to *Field and Stream*), proud of his familiarity with guns, as well as a fervent patriot. He had served in World War I, and delighted all the rest of his life in being called "the Major." He, too, revered Robert E. Lee—he would later call it auspicious that Pat was taking his law exams at Yale on Lee's birthday. He was corresponding with "Frank" Gaines, a man living in the Lee residence, where the great general retired with his war-horse. Senator Robertson would himself be buried from the chapel at VMI.

The senator had political ambitions for both his sons, A. Willis junior ("Taddy") and the younger Pat, and those ambitions depended, in the 1950s, on honorable military service. It is interesting to contrast Pat Robertson's record with the response of Tennessee's Albert Gore, Jr., to the Vietnam War, in which he served though he opposed it, upholding his father's political reputation as a senator with the Tennessee electorate. The young Gore was more protective of his father's good name than was Robertson *père* of his son's.

Perhaps that was because Senator Robertson had low expectations for Pat. Born when his father was already forty-two, Pat never became a drinking and hunting pal with his father, as did Taddy. In fact, during Pat Robertson's adolescence, the senator lived alone in Washington for most of the year, while the boys stayed in Lexington with their mother, who, detached from her husband and his career, filled her life with prayer and the Bible, neither of which decreased a pride in her own family. Though Pat's parents were first cousins, the great names in the family came from her side—the Churchills and the Harrisons.

While his birthplace provided Pat Robertson with constant reminders of the Revolution, the War of 1812, and the Civil War, his own family traditions tied him even more intimately to all three conflicts. Benjamin Harrison the Signer (called that to distinguish him from his many illustrious namesakes) not only helped declare war for the new country by signing the Declaration of Independence, but served on the Board of War and Ordnance that kept Washington's armies in the field. William Henry Harrison, though he won early military fame from an indecisive battle fought against Indians at Tippecanoe, made his real contribution to the nation's safety by his service in the field throughout the War of 1812. Benjamin Harrison the President, a lawyer with no military training at the beginning of the Civil War, raised and led the Seventieth Indiana Infantry, ending up a brigadier general after service in many bloody fights. Each of these ancestors had entered the pantheon Gladys Robertson honored and hoped to see her own son enter.

But the head of the family into which she had married was not, it seems, eager to renew its military glories. Absalom Willis Robertson was an Isaac in reverse, looking for a substitute in less favored sons before he would put flesh of his flesh on the block. One need not admire the Southern code to know there are less shameful ways of breaking it. While paying lip service to the glories of his tradition, Senator Robertson abandoned the one thing worth keeping in that historical medley of trash and the odd treasure—the region's partly exculpatory if hypertrophic sense of honor.

Senator Robertson's son was not, after all, entirely without reason for surmising in public that his father might be corruptible. He had not only observed but occasioned actions not very commendable in the senator. That made it grimly appropriate that, having rebuffed his father's request for help while he lived, he should make the dead senator a model of his own "statesmanship." The quality of that statesmanship became clear after the Iowa primary in 1988. Robertson stunned the Republican establishment by coming in second there, ahead of George Bush. But Robertson's attempt to reach beyond his own core of organized early starters failed. He made claims he could not back up about Russian missiles in Cuba. He accused Lee Atwater, Bush's campaign aide, of engineering the exposure of Jimmy Swaggart's voyeurism in order to taint all evangelical leaders. Actually, Atwater had done something far more damaging to Robertson. He had arranged the early wooing of Southern religious leaders by Bush, which led to the massive rejection of Robertson in his own region. After "Super Tuesday," the cluster of Southern primaries, Robertson had to cut back his campaign, give up Don Miracle's airplane, and bargain for a token appearance at the national convention. The fact that Virginia and its sister states disappointed Robertson most seriously was entirely fitting. He was falsest, always, as a Southern gentleman.

PART FIVE

Politics and Black Religion

⟡ E I G H T E E N ⟡

African=American Miliasm

Jon Butler has argued that there was a "spiritual holocaust" in colonial America—the obliteration of African religious systems as the slaves arrived here.[1] This was "the most dramatic religious change in any period of American history before 1815"—more important, according to Butler, than "the evolution of Puritanism or the emergence of American evangelicalism" in shaping America's religious experience.[2]

Butler does not treat the Indian wars as a specifically religious event, though they, too, had a crusading aspect: They were meant, among other things, to stop the devil-worship that threatened Christian communities. The Indians' external spells were felt to be far more threatening than the internal outbreaks of witchcraft among European women.

Butler sees mainly secular apprehension in the crushing of African religion in America: "Throughout the colonial period planters worried about collective slave activity of any kind." This suggests that repression of "false" religions was of a kind with the discouraging of gossip circles. But to people who believed in the devil, and in the diabolic nature of "heathen" worship (whether among Native Americans or Africans), there was a more pressing motive for extinguishing evil rites: Those rituals menaced the people trying to stamp them out. The first, instinctive response to foreign religion was not merely "prejudice" or a wish to convert. It was self-defense. African religion was quashed so reflexively that there is little evidence of the process. It was too obvious to those enacting it for them to articulate a rationale for discussion. It literally "went without saying" that diabolic religions must be opposed and defeated.

Once the slaves' religion was extirpated, their conversion posed the problem of treating one's property as one's brother or sister in Christ. That had been a difficulty even in Christianity's earliest days, when the impending fate of the world made it unnecessary to plan long social reforms like the ending of slavery. Even in the brief interval St. Paul felt he was living through, he hoped that a Christian like Philemon would free the runaway slave Onesimus ("Useful"), whom he had converted:

> I, Paul, ambassador as I am of Christ Jesus—and now his prisoner—appeal to you about my child, whose father I have become in this prison.
>
> I mean Onesimus, once so little use to you, but now useful indeed, both to you and to me. I am sending him back to you, and in doing so I am sending a part of myself. I should have liked to keep him with me, to look after me as you would wish, here in prison for the Gospel. But I would rather do nothing without your consent, so that your kindness may be a matter not of compulsion, but of your own free will. For perhaps this is why you lost him for a time, that you might have him back for good, no longer as a slave, but as more than a slave—as a dear brother, very dear indeed to me and how much dearer to you, both as man and as Christian.
>
> If, then, you count me partner in the faith, welcome him as you would welcome me. (Epistle to Philemon, 9–17)

This genuine letter of Paul was not a favorite with American slaveholders. They preferred the pseudo-Pauline exhortation that slaves obey their masters in the Epistle to Titus (2.9).[3] Some American Christians were afraid of the idea that they might meet their slaves in heaven.[4] Paul, for whom there was neither slave nor master in Christ (1 Corinthians 12.13), would have others greet Onesimus as "part of myself."

Most American slave owners did not mean, by baptism, to make their slaves part of themselves. They would, in fact, prefer to see them as alien. After all, so long as Indians were subjects of the devil they could be killed with a good conscience (given the conscience of the day). Slaves, if in thrall to evil, could be mistreated at will. But it was impossible to let a strong adverse religion exist in a people kept within the owners' domain (as opposed to the Indian culture, driven off from that domain). And if false religion were crushed among the Africans, it was hard to oppose those Christian preachers who said the true religion must replace it. A spiritual vacuum had been created, which must be filled. Better an in-conveniencing true religion than the outright subversions of any false cult of the devil.

Still, Christianity could be used as an instrument of control, so long as the passages on slave obedience were taught as central to it. This went against the use Puritans and others made of the gospel as a political charter of freedom; the Christian religion could be made to mean different things. Yet, precisely *because* of this variety in the forms of faith, how could the masters be sure the religion they preached would continue to be the religion slaves observed?

The price of monitoring the slaves' religion would be a high one. If free whites were to preach a single faith, that would demand a single observance—with blacks and whites at the same communion table. Better to let the slaves have their own meeting places, even their own preachers, so long as they were kept separate from white worshipers—which meant that blacks might organize their own leadership. The difficulty Jon Butler saw in African ritual applied equally to Christian meetings, if the problem were simply that of organized slave gatherings. What distinguished the two situations was the basic belief of the owners that Christianity was the true religion and African religion was devil-worship.

Truth is a dangerous thing to entrust to others. Christianity, meant as an instrument of control from above, could be seen as a vehicle for rebellion from below. That is just how certain black miliasts saw it. In the same period when William Miller was preparing white evangelicals for the end of the world, the black Baptist preacher Nat Turner heard the Lord tell him His kingdom was at hand, and he took up the sword of Armageddon.[5] That was in 1831. Nine years earlier, a Methodist Episcopal church in Charleston had become a revolutionary cell prepared to follow Denmark Vesey in rebellion.[6]

But miliasm did not normally—and could not—take this form in the black community. If not a religion of entire compliance, Christianity had to be, at the most, a form of quiet resistance so long as the weapons of violence were in the control of the owners. And, prior to that, the religion had to be one of comfort in suffering, of dignity in conditions that dehumanized. It used to be said that the literature of the white South had, after the Civil War, a resonance no other region's could claim, one forged in loss and suffering, since no other part of America has experi-enced defeat on its own soil. But the sufferings of the Confederacy were a mere surface scratch compared with the lot of those who suffered an almost total cultural deprivation when they were transferred to America. They, too, made art out of their pain, and their principal cultural artifact was their religion. This was designed for them as an instrument of subordination; but they refashioned it as a form of lament and consolation. In the process, they regained possession of themselves as a people, as a spiritual entity. The entire Christian legacy had to be remade in their minds in order to accomplish this act of recovery. As Donald Mathews puts it: "The religious ethos which southern blacks projected into society was rich and powerful precisely because it was something which blacks had fashioned for themselves and in doing so had revealed a new way of expressing Christianity."[7] They would in time give back a purified religion to those who had imposed it on them in a debased form—a gift Abraham Lincoln had the genius to recognize and accept.

White miliasm in the founding period was aggressive. It brought the saints into the New World, where they expected to meet the Antichrist and bring on the millennium. But for blacks, dragged to the New World, mastery of their environment was indefinitely postponed. The parts of Scripture that came to vivid life in their experience were ancient Israel's Egyptian captivity and Babylonian exile. As slaves of Pharaoh, blacks could yearn for their own Moses, to take them across the "deep river" (Red Sea) into "campground" (the Promised Land).

When Israel was in Egypt's land
    (Let my people go),
Oppressed so hard they could not stand
    (Let my people go).

As fellow exiles, blacks could claim the great songs of consolation as their own:

Comfort, comfort my people;
    —it is the voice of your God;
speak tenderly to Jerusalem
    and tell her this,
that she has fulfilled her term of bondage,
    that her penalty is paid. (Isaiah 40.1–2)

"Comfort my *people*." Under the almost cooing phrases of Deutero-Isaiah, the slaves became a people. Torn from different tribes and governments, betrayed by their own countrymen or African captors, bought and brutalized by alien lords, the blacks found a corporate identity in the biblical image of God's favored captives. Offered a new promise of deliverance, they did not think of the isolated soul but of the suffering totality. Calvinist individualism led preachers like Jonathan Edwards to an accusing homiletic: The sinner should see himself in the hands of an angry God. But Deutero-Isaiah describes the exiles all held together "safe under the shelter of my hand" (Isaiah 51.16)—He's got the whole world in His hands.

The first requisite of the slaves was a new sense of community, the mutual support of those with a common bond of suffering. They could not afford to be as judgmental as the white Christians, to launch jeremiads at each other. In 1790, a white preacher, William McKendee, was indignant that two mothers should bring their babies to be baptized and produce the same man as father of the two. McKendee says he told them "to repent or they would all go to hell together, and sent them away shocked."[8]

The censorious preacher could not understand that the most important theological insight of black America was God's faithfulness to *all* his people in bondage. A white preacher noticed in 1842 that black "members of the same church are sacredly bound by their religion not to reveal each other's sins, for that would be backbiting and injuring the brotherhood." Another minister said of the South Carolina slaves: "It was a rule among the members of those societies, rigidly enforced, never to divulge the secret of stealing; to do so brought dire punishment upon the informer."[9]

This responsibility to and for each other's safety was seen precisely as a *religious* duty. When a slave was suspected of being an informer, others would pointedly sing when he approached them:

O Judyas he was a 'ceitful man,
    He went an' betray a mos' innocen' man.
Fo' thirty pieces o' silver it was done,
    He went in th' woods an' isself he hung.[10]

The God of Deutero-Isaiah cannot find terms of endearment great enough to reassure His people in their time of anguish. Even past punishments are made the occasion of fond expression now:

These days recall for me the days of Noah:
as I swore that the waters of Noah's flood
should never again pour over the earth,
    so now I swear to you
never again to be angry with you or reproach you.
    Though the mountains move and the hills shake,

> my love shall be immovable and never fail,
>   and my covenant of peace shall not be shaken.
> So says the Lord who takes pity on you. (Isaiah 54.9–10)

Even the Ark became a symbol of refuge from the surrounding turmoil for those who had survived the Middle Passage. Now they gathered in their meetinghouse, bound close to each other and to God. Rocked with song and prayer, the building seemed to detach itself from its moorings and bear its passengers off already to the land of deliverance:

> Oh, de ole ark a-moverin',
>   a-moverin',
>   a-moverin',
> De ole ark a-moverin',
>   a-moverin' along.[11]

They would all arrive together who had traveled together in the vessel of God's promise:

> That awful rain she stopped at last,
>   the waters they subsided,
> An' that old Ark with *all on board*
>   on Ararat she rided.

The people were fastened to God through their hold on each other. As Jacob would not cease wrestling with God or God's angel, so they would "hold on":

> O wrestlin' Jacob, Jacob day's a-breakin',
>   I will not let thee go!
> O wrestlin' Jacob, Jacob day's a-breakin',
>   He will not let me go!
> O, I hold my brudder wid a tremblin' hand,
>   I would not let him go!
> I hold my sister wid a tremblin' hand,
>   I would not let her go![12]

The "rainbow" sign showed that the people's ordeal would not last forever:

> God gave Noah the rainbow sign,
> Not by water, the fire next time.[13]

Black eschatology has largely been the orthodox premilism of the Rapture: God will come in the clouds, and his saints will meet him in the air—

O little did I think he was so nigh,
Looks like my Lord a-comin' in de sky.
He spoke an' he made me laugh and cry,
Looks like my Lord a-comin' in de sky.[14]

The sense of release as one breaks the bonds of earth is celebrated—
freedom at last.

What kind o' shoes is dem-a you wear,
Dat you can walk upon de air?
Dem shoes I wear am gospel shoes,
An' you can wear dem ef-a you choose.[15]

When all God's children have their gospel shoes, they can walk all over
God's heaven.[16] They have the freedom of the skies.

Some-a dese mornin's bright an' fair,
I'm goin' to lay down my heavy load;
Goin' to spread my wings an' cleave de air.[17]

Did you ever
Stan' on mountain,
Wash yo hans
In a cloud?[18]

The black church prays to escape the *Peirasmos* by its Rapture with Christ:

When this world is all on fiyuh,
Hide-a-me. . . .
When the stars in heaven are fallin',
Hide-a-me.[19]

Being "hidden away in Christ" (Colossians 3.3) had a special meaning
for blacks, so much of whose intercommunity life had to be kept hidden
from their masters. Covering up for each other drew the veil over their
spiritual activity, as well as over the resistance to their owners' control.
Their preacher was their leader and source of pride; but he, too, was
close to them in his frailty and had to be protected. He was not distant
in learning and ascetical conventions, like a New England minister. The
Spirit's gifts were on him, in his eloquence, but he had to be supported—
as when Moses' arms would have fallen from weariness if his disciples
had not held them up. The leader must be carried by the community:

Come along, Moses,
    don't get lost
    don't get lost.[20]

Moses was a fellow captive; he led his people by having suffered with them:

> I see brudder Moses yonder,
>   And I think I ought to know him,
> For I know him by his garment,
>   He's a blessing here tonight.[21]

Jesus himself is a fellow sufferer, whipped and spat on:

> De blood came twinklin' down
>   An' He never said a mumblin' word.
> De blood came twinklin' down,
>   An' he never said a mumblin' word,
> Not a word—not a word—not a word.[22]

Yet he was strong enough for others to "lean on." And when one of his sheep was lost, he sought the one, leaving the ninety-and-nine safe ones:

> Ef you fin' him, bring him back,
> Cross de shoulders, cross yo' back.[23]

This Jesus is the Suffering Servant of the Deutero-Isaiah text, whose beatings turn to blessings:

> the chastisement he bore is health for us
>   and by his scourging we are healed.
> We had all strayed like sheep,
> each of us had gone his own way;
> but the Lord laid upon him
>   the guilt of us all.
> He was afflicted, he submitted to be struck down
>   and did not open his mouth. . . .(Isaiah 53.5–7)

He did not open his mouth, even in mumblin' words. Endurance was sanctified in Jesus; an experience of the Spirit became a necessity for survival. Without the sense of communal blessing in pain, life would have been unendurable.

Black Christianity was strong on forgiveness. Other forms of American Protestantism flirted with antinomianism; but in the salon of an Anne Hutchinson this took the form of censoriousness toward the unsaved. Among African Americans, the gospel texts on judging-not led to a permissiveness that included, dangerously, forgiving even one's masters. (Psychologically, forgiving was perhaps the only realistic alternative to killing them.) It is an ethic still being preached, and still being criticized. I heard Jesse Jackson tell an Iowa audience early in 1988: "Grievance is too heavy a burden to bear. You have to turn around and look back to pick it up. And then, when you carrying it, you can't go forward." Some wrongs are so enormous that to contemplate them is to risk paralysis. The secular equivalent of this "hardening one's heart with hope" shows up in the blues: "Got th' blues, an' too damn mean to cry. . . ."

In the same place, Jackson said: "Jesus told us to love our enemies. One reason to love them is that if you love someone you keep your eyes on them." For all the accommodations made by black preachers over the years to white oppression, there have always been black preachers and believers ready to use the Christian professions of the masters against them—preachers like John Jasper or Vernon Johns; or believers like the faithful slave who, given the privilege of burial in the owner's family vault, said: "I don't know—when the Devil come, he might mistake me for the master."[24] Among the weapons of the weak, even prayer can be mobilized. When a black cadet was driven out of the Citadel, a military school in South Carolina, by his white-robed fellow students, Jesse Jackson went to speak on the campus. While he was standing on the grounds with some students around him, a school official came up and said he could not speak there. Not even softly? Cannot speak at all. Cannot pray? The official, caught off guard, was not used to interdicting prayer. Jackson grabbed the man's hand and prayed out loud with his brother for justice to come to the Citadel.

Millennial hope has been so strong in the black churches as to be called an escapist form of optimism. If so, it is an optimism forged in the harshest imaginable places. G. K. Chesterton wondered at the so-called optimism of Dickens, whose worst period as a child was spent bottling boot polish: "If he learnt to whitewash the universe, it was in a blacking factory he learnt it."[25]

Martin Luther King was mocked by black militants during his lifetime as "De Lawd," the God of Marc Connelly's play *Green Pastures*, who presides over a heaven that is a glorified fish fry. But the psalm of the play's title ("He makes me lie down in green pastures") was always used in the Christian literature to describe an eschatological feast where Jesus will preside, a last supper that never ends (Matthew 26.29). When King had a dream, it was of the millennium, when Isaiah's lion shall be at peace with Isaiah's lamb, and a little child shall lead them, just as in any *Peaceable Kingdom* painted by Edward Hicks:

> I have a dream that one day on the red hills of Georgia the sons of former slaves and the sons of former slaveowners will be able to sit down together at the table of brotherhood. . . .
>
> I have a dream that one day the state of Alabama, whose governor's lips are presently dripping with the words of interposition and nullification, will be transformed into a situation where little black boys and black girls will be able to join hands with little white boys and white girls and walk together as sisters and brothers. . . .
>
> I have a dream that one day every valley shall be exalted, every hill and mountain shall be made low, the rough places will be made plains, and the crooked places will be made straight, and the glory of the Lord shall be revealed, and all flesh shall see it together.

The millennial hope of American history has never been made more explicit or compelling.

The millennial dream has been astonishingly durable, and even practical, in African-American life. In the 1930s, it was embodied in Father Divine's rural settlements, appropriately called the Promised Land, which were more successful than most utopian communities in America—as were Divine's urban missions during the Depression. Robert Weisbrot, contrasting Divine with other social critics of his time (religious ones like Father Coughlin and Gerald L. K. Smith, secular ones like Huey Long and Francis Townsend), finds him more successful precisely where he was more optimistic, even forging interracial support for his programs at a time when this was almost unheard of.[26]

A Father Divine—or a Dr. King—may seem infuriatingly serene in his forgiveness. A more realistic assessment of white guilt can be heard in the recriminations of an Eldridge Cleaver, Rap Brown, Stokely Carmichael, Huey Newton, Bobby Seale, George Jackson, or Angela Davis. They did give up the anodyne, the opiate, of Christian optimism. But the immensity of the wrongs they had suffered tended to consume them. They were *too* realistic to exist in the reality they saw. The secular apocalypse of fire in the cities burned the blacks' own ghettos. Their very assault on whites tore blacks apart. The Christian millennium, by contrast, is almost Machiavellian in its practicality. Jesse Jackson likes to say, "If it is morally right, it is politically right." That may be true nowhere else; but it has been uncannily true in black America.

Hope welling up from the darkest places remains the miracle of African-American Christianity. Dr. King was on a secular mission—to help garbagemen with their strike for better working conditions—when he was killed in Memphis. But the strikers' hall was turned into a rocking, wailing church where Christians spoke words of comfort to each other on the day after the murder. I heard preacher after preacher. The fourteenth sermon was the best. James Bevel told the crowd, responsive to him as he challenged it with his defiant belief:

> There's a false rumor around that our leader's dead. *Our* leader is not dead. Martin Luther King is not our leader. [Some hesitation, here, on the *"Talk it!"* cries.] Our leader is the man who led Moses out of Israel. (*"Thass the man!"*) Our leader is the man who went with Daniel into the lion's den. (*"Same* man!") Our leader is the man who walked out of the grave on Easter morning. Our leader never sleeps nor slumbers. He cannot be put in jail. He has never lost a war yet. *Our* leader is still on the case. Our leader is not dead. One of his prophets died. We will not stop because of that. Our staff is not a funeral staff. We have friends who are undertakers.

"Let the dead bury their dead," Jesus said (Matthew 8.22). Bevel's sermon was a midrash on that text, an example of continuing creativity in the African-American homiletic.

Yet Bevel, like the rest of the Southern Christian Leadership Conference staff, flew out from Memphis the next day for the funeral of Dr. King in Atlanta. The garbage strikers who had signed up to go to Atlanta were left stranded in a church, waiting for buses, unable to go look for them because of the curfew. When three buses showed up, too few and too late, those able to fit in put folding chairs down the aisles. They can just make it by a ten-hour nighttime drive through feared territory (Mississippi and Alabama), worried that a bus might break down, leaving them alone, stranded on alien turf. (I am the only white person on the three buses.) Yet the talk is not disconsolate. A kind of sleepy chorus is maintained, hour after hour, of scattered reminiscences—how *young* King was, how he had come to them, how the mayor of Memphis was intimidated, how lucky the strikers were to have heard King's last speech. "He was *for* us." Despite all the obstacles—the tense stops made for relieving themselves (all the chairs in the aisles taken out and put back in)—the strikers made it. There was no time or place to put on the good clothes they had carried with them. But they had arrived, their old arks a-moverin all night long.

Abraham Lincoln was haunted by a scene he had witnessed going down the Ohio River in 1841. There were twelve slaves being taken down South, chained to each other and to the boat ("strung together precisely like so many fish upon a trot-line"). He said, fourteen years later, that the image had been "a continual torment to me"; yet he wondered, at the time, how the pinioned human beings could sing and laugh in their plight.[27] These were people traveling to a land beyond the place others thought they were taking them. All around them was a storm, and Lincoln would be part of it. But these people would stay linked to each other and to God till on Ararat they rided.

◇ N I N E T E E N ◇

Lincoln's Black Theology

*See, see, where Christ's blood streams in the fir-
mament!*

MARLOWE, *Doctor Faustus*

DESPITE HIS FLICKERING AWARENESS OF DIRER ARMAGEDDON PROPHECIES,
Ronald Reagan's favorite millennial phrase was "city on a hill." That
description of America's exemplary role came from the famous sermon
preached by John Winthrop on the *Arbella* as it made its way to the New
World. The words are often used to indicate America's sense of its own
exceptionalism. But Winthrop was speaking the language of Puritanism
on both sides of the Atlantic. John Milton wrote of his England as the
country that was (under Cromwell)

> the first that should set up a standard for the recovery of lost truth and
> blow the first evangelic trumpet to the nations, holding up, as from a hill,
> the new lamp of saving light to all Christendom.[1]

For Milton, the Puritans' armed camps were cleared spaces in enemy
territory. Reagan's citations of Winthrop leave out this military aspect of
the millennium. But we must put the "city on a hill" back in its context
to see what it meant to its first audience. Here is what Winthrop said:

> We shall find that the God of Israel is among us when ten of us shall be
> able to resist a thousand of our enemies, when He shall make us a praise
> and glory, that men shall say of succeeding plantations: "The Lord make

it like that of New England." For we must consider that we shall be as a city upon a hill, the eyes of all people are upon us.[2]

The millennial nature of God's kingdom in America was the binding vision of Cotton Mather's work:

> Look upon [our] towns and fields, look upon [our] habitations and shops and ships, and behold [our] numerous posterity, and great increase in the blessings of the land and sea. . . . Indeed, if we cast up the account and lay all things together, God hath been doing the same thing here that is prophesied of Jacob's remnant. . . . He that hath said, "I will make the wilderness a pool of water, and [in] the dry lands I will plant a cedar," hath fulfilled that word before our eyes. And we may conclude that he intended some great thing when he planted these [American] heavens, and laid the foundations of this [American] earth. And what should that be if not a *scripture-pattern that shall in due time be accomplished the whole world throughout?* [Italics added.][3]

Since the saints came to establish one definitive way of life, to serve as a template against which all future communities could be measured, Perry Miller is justified in saying: "To allow no dissent from the truth was exactly the reason they had come to America."[4]

The idea that America should serve as God's pattern for the rest of the world has been given less overtly theological expression in later versions of America's mission. But when wartime calls for sacrifice, American duty becomes again a divine imperative. The military note returns. That was true even of the Revolution in the skeptical eighteenth century. It would be more fiercely evident in the Civil War.

Romanticism and transcendentalism helped create, in mid-nineteenth-century America, what Jon Butler calls an "antebellum spiritual hot-house." Abraham Lincoln was interested in necromancy, and his wife held seances in the White House (outdistancing Nancy Reagan's later consultation of an astrologer).[5] The heating of the spiritual atmosphere reignited millennial yearnings. John Brown accepted the mantle of Nat Turner, calling whites to a millennial showdown with slavery's evil empire. The American landscape itself took on a doomsday appearance in paintings like Frederic Edwin Church's *Twilight in the Wilderness* (1860). Earlier American landscapes had emphasized the untouched treasures of the continent, but here was a wilderness already ravaged before humans reached it—a weird red sky, ruined trees, and the eagle stranded on a bare branch. The next year war began, and Church painted a small

picture in which the apocalyptic clouds of *Twilight* were rent by a blue
patch of sky with night stars in it—the heavens themselves forming a
blurred flag. *Our Banner in the Sky* became a popular chromolithograph,
its proceeds going to the Union cause.[6] The land was pictured as groaning
with cosmic strife.

As the crisis over slavery raveled out normal party politics, Abraham
Lincoln, who regularly used biblical language, turned to Revelation.
That book speaks, in one of its psychedelic images, of robes washed white
in the blood of the Lamb (7.14). Lincoln, in 1854, told an audience in
Springfield:

> Our republican robe is soiled, and trailed in the dust. Let us repurify it.
> Let us turn and wash it white, in the spirit, if not the blood, of the
> Revolution.[7]

Lincoln was already disposed to see the nation's ordeal as a purification
rite. Earlier yet, in 1838, he had written:

> Let it [federal law] become the *political religion* of the nation; and let the
> old and the young, the rich and the poor, the grave and the gay, of all
> sexes and tongues, and colors and conditions, sacrifice unceasingly upon
> its altars.[8]

When war actually began, there was an outburst of apocalyptic imagery
that gave Union rhetoric the accents of John Brown. The best-known
example of this eruption is Julia Ward Howe's biblical paean, written
hastily in an army encampment, that actually used the tune of "John
Brown's Body," but set it to verses drawn from Revelation. Though Mrs.
Howe was descended from Cromwellian warriors, her evangelical background had not mattered to her much until war renewed her childhood
memories of biblical crisis:

> Mine eyes have seen the glory of the coming of the Lord;
> He is trampling out the vintage where the grapes of wrath are stored. . . .

The coming of the Lord is the second Advent. "Mine eyes have seen"
recalls the eyewitness vouchings for each vision called up by John of
Patmos in Revelation: "After this I looked and saw . . ." (7.9); "Then I
saw . . ." (10.1). "Then I saw . . ." The second line comes from Revelation 14.19–20:

> So the angel put his sickle to the earth and gathered in its grapes, and
> threw them into the great winepress of God's wrath. The winepress was

trodden outside the city, and for two hundred miles around blood flowed from the press to the height of the horses' bridles.[9]

"He has loosed the fateful lightning of his terrible swift sword" recalls the sworded horseman who comes in judgment, another passage associated with the winepress:

> Then I saw heaven wide open, and there before me was a white horse; and its rider's name was Faithful and True, for he is just in judgement and just in war. . . . He was called the Word of God, and the armies of heaven followed him on white horses, clothed in fine linen, clean and shining. From his mouth there went a sharp sword with which to smite the nations; for he it is who shall rule them with an iron rod, and tread the winepress of the wrath and retribution of God. (Revelation 19.11, 13–15)

In Howe's second stanza, her vision continues ("I have seen Him") amid the campfires:

> They have builded Him an altar in the evening dews and damps;
> I can read His righteous sentence by the dim and flaring lamps.

In his first vision, John "saw seven standing lamps of gold" (1.12), which fume in an altar arrangement in Dürer's famous engraving of this passage. At Revelation 2.1, the Lord of the Vision "walks among the seven lamps" like the bearer of the fiery gospel of the camp. "Before the throne" at Revelation 4.5 there are "seven flaming torches."

In the third stanza, Revelation's version of the *lex talionis* is recalled: "Hear, you who have ears to hear [a gospel is preached]: Whoever is to be made prisoner, a prisoner he shall be. Whoever takes the sword to kill, by the sword he is bound to be killed" (13.9–10), in "the time to destroy those who destroy the earth" (11.18):

> I have heard a fiery gospel writ in burnished rows of steel.
> As ye deal with my contemners, so with you my grace shall deal.
> Let the Hero, born of woman, crush the serpent with His heel.

The last line refers to the apocalyptic woman who stands on the moon at Revelation 12.1 and delivers a son menaced by the dragon. Her offspring, as was promised at Genesis 3.15, treads the serpent under heel.

The fourth stanza begins with the "last trump," to which other trumpet calls have marked stages on the way:

He has sounded forth the trumpet that shall never call retreat.

"When the times comes for the seventh [concluding] angel to sound his trumpet, the hidden purpose of God will have been fulfilled, as he promised to his servants the prophets" (Revelation 10.7). Then comes judgment from the throne:

He is sifting out the hearts of men before the judgment seat.

The Lord of the visions sifts hearts because "I know all your ways" (Revelation 3.7).

The fifth stanza has no direct quotes from Revelation, though the visionary Lord glows with transfiguring fire at 1.13, making John of Patmos swoon and be restored, so that he can see the changed (robed) saints "walk with me in white" (3.4). Then the bearers of the Word give witness unto death, "for they did not hold their lives too dear to lay them down" (12.11). That complex of ideas lies behind Howe's concluding lines:

In the beauty of the lilies Christ was born across the sea,
With a glory in His bosom that transfigures you and me;
As He died to make men holy, let us die to make men free.

The doxology to the hymn ("Glory, glory, halleluia") comes from the "glory, glory" of Revelation 4.8 and the four "Halleluia" refrains of chapter 19. Mrs. Howe's hymn is an uncompromising call to wage the ultimate battle. It was appropriately set to John Brown's song. I wonder what contemporary congregations make of it when they sing it on Sunday morning.

War fever encourages such absolutism, and Lincoln needed to use the enthusiasms of the North to support his war. But he had no stomach for the rhetoric of Mrs. Howe. Even when he invoked the violence of Revelation, he hoped people would be washed in its *spirit* rather than its blood. In fact, his view of the American idea was something he tried to extricate from physical transactions. Being American, he emphasized, did not require blood descent from the original founders. Those who entered the country after its founding were, in their way, better witnesses to the essential American idea: They were incorporated into the citizenry by their acceptance of the doctrine that all men are created equal. Speaking to an audience just before the Fourth of July in 1857, he reminded them that "quite half of you are not even descendants of those who are referred to at that day."[10] The next year he elaborated the thought:

> We have, besides these men descended by blood from our ancestors, among
> us perhaps half our people who are not descendants at all of these men;
> they are men who have come from Europe—German, Irish, French and
> Scandinavian—men that have come from Europe themselves, or whose
> ancestors have come hither and settled here, finding themselves our equals
> in all things. If they look back through this history to trace their connection
> with those days by blood, they find they have none, they cannot carry
> themselves back into that glorious epoch and make themselves feel that
> they are part of us, but when they look through that old Declaration of
> Independence they find that those old men say that "We hold these truths
> to be self-evident, that all men are created equal," and then they feel that
> that moral sentiment taught in that day evidences their relation to those
> men, that it is the father of all moral principle in them, and that they
> have a right to claim it as though they were blood of the blood, and flesh
> of the flesh of the men who wrote that Declaration, and so they are. That
> is the electric cord in that Declaration that links the hearts of patriotic and
> liberty-loving men together.[11]

"Moral sentiment" is the "father of all moral principle" in Americans,
replacing physical generation in the spread of a self-choosing people. The
bloodline carries mere physical resemblances. The "electric cord," the
still-wondrous telegraph wire, carries entire *messages* intact. This intellectual transmission of a pure original doctrine is what sets Americans
apart. Lincoln's constant invocation of "our fathers" referred to the enu-
merators of that doctrine, "fathers of all moral principle," not mere
physical begetters.

    Lincoln talked of Americans in his day as morally begotten. But even
the fathers brought forth their country from America's virgin land by the
impregnation of an idea. By the speaking of the Declaration's word—as
at the angel's annunciation to Mary—the country's parthenogenesis took
place. This is the basic image behind the Gettysburg Address.

> Fourscore and seven years ago our fathers brought forth on this continent
> a new nation, conceived in liberty, and dedicated to the proposition that
> all men are created equal.

Once Jesus was born he was dedicated in the temple (Luke 2.22–24), as
the new nation was dedicated to its proposition. But the idea itself could
no longer be purified, only retained in its original form: "It is rather for
us to be here dedicated," to "take increased devotion to that cause for
which they [the dead at Gettysburg] gave the last full measure of devotion . . . that this nation, under God, shall have a new birth. . . ."

If the Union is saved on that basis, Lincoln said in 1864, "the succeeding millions of free happy people, the world over, shall rise up and call us blessed to the latest generation"—as Mary sang in her Magnificat, after the virgin birth, that "all generations will count me blessed" (Luke 1.48).[12] This is the same song in which, according to the translation Lincoln used, Mary says her child is the fulfillment of what was spoken "to *our fathers*, to Abraham, and to his seed" (Luke 1.55). Lincoln's favorite term for America's founders was "our fathers."[13]

Lincoln's imagery of the American mission was as biblical as Julia Howe's, though he preferred the Gospel of Luke to the Book of Revelation. Most of his references are implicit, but when he made the Bible an explicit guide to constitutional interpretation, he enforced the same moral. The American task is to preserve an originally given doctrine. In most hands, this view would lead to a "fundamentalist" concept of American law given in its entirety beforehand. But Lincoln escaped literalism in his constitutional interpretation by subordinating the Constitution, the Supreme Court's decisions, and history itself to the one "proposition" of human equality contained in the Declaration of Independence. Alexander Stephens had quoted to Lincoln the maxim of Proverbs 25.11 in the Authorized Version, "A word fitly spoken is like apples of gold in pictures of silver." Lincoln wrote an answering note for his own guidance:

The expression of that principle [all men are created equal] in our Declaration of Independence was the word "fitly spoken" which has proved an "apple of gold" to us. The Union and the Constitution are the picture of silver subsequently framed around it. The picture was made not to conceal or destroy the apple; but to adorn and preserve it. The picture was made for the apple, not the apple for the picture. So let us act, that neither picture nor apple shall ever be blurred, bruised or broken.[14]

For Lincoln, the original dogma was not only perfect in itself but intended for *all* people's eventual subscription. In 1857, he wrote, "I had thought the Declaration contemplated the progressive improvement of all men everywhere."[15] He saw the Declaration's ideal as "constantly looked to, constantly labored for, and, even though never perfectly attained, constantly approximated, and thereby constantly spreading and deepening its influence, and augmenting the happiness and value of life to all people of all colors everywhere."[16] Thus it would serve, like Paul's preaching of the Cross (Galatians 5.11), as "a stumbling-block to those who in after times might seek to turn a free people back into the hateful paths of despotism."[17]

This was certainly a vision of America that could be fit into the millennial mainstream. It presented the United States as a light unto the nations, the city placed upon a hill. But Lincoln was famously reluctant to adopt a triumphal righteousness during the war. He wanted a return to the original "covenant" of the Declaration, but he would not denounce the foe as was customary in such self-purifications. New England's covenant renewals were meant to distinguish the saints from diabolic forces (Indians, French Catholics, Laudian imperialists). Julia Howe marshaled "burnished rows of steel" against God's "contemners." But Lincoln mourned for the South, instead of denouncing it. And mourned, as well, for the North, instead of celebrating it. The lack of partisan spirit is what gives the Gettysburg Address its nobility. Lincoln seemed to shy from moral pretensions. He spoke of slavery as a national sin, and expressly recalled Northern complicity in the trade that brought Africans to America. He called for a national day of fast and humiliation in which all were to confess their "own faults and crimes." There is nothing more astonishing in the history of war than this attempt to wage it without being partisan, to forgive while killing, and to ask for forgiveness from those one kills.

What produced this extraordinary magnanimity in Lincoln, his constant forswearing of malice or petty hates as he directed the first modern war of mechanical destruction? A number of factors contributed to his attitude, none perhaps strong enough in itself to produce exactly the tone and autumnal music of Lincoln's public addresses. The political situation, his personal temperament, the rhetoric of mid-nineteenth-century religion—all had to converge on, reinforce, and redirect each other.

The problem given Lincoln by the political situation was easier to state than to grapple with. While placing the highest value on union, Lincoln could do nothing to disrupt that ideal, even while at war. He had to treat the South as still part of the nation, misled for a time but not permanently severed from the concerns (or privileges) of other citizens. He would condemn the sin of slavery, but he spent little energy on the sinners, the slaveholders. He granted that "the fathers" had recognized the rights of slaveholders within their original bounds; and he would not offend filial piety by claiming that their descendants could have done—even could do now—better than "the fathers" had.

To me it seems that if we were to form a government anew, in view of the actual presence of Slavery we should find it necessary to frame just such a government as our fathers did; giving to the slaveholder the entire control where the system was established, while we possessed the power to restrain it from going outside these limits. From the necessity of the case we should be compelled to form just such a government as our blessed fathers gave us.[18]

He had little patience with those who tried to use religion to justify slavery. He answered a Baptist Home Mission Society's good wishes this way:

To read in the Bible, as the word of God himself, that "In the sweat of *thy* face shalt thou eat bread," and to preach therefrom that, "In the sweat of other mans [sic] faces thou shalt eat bread," to my mind can scarcely be reconciled with honest sincerity. When brought to my final reckoning, may I have to answer for robbing no man of his goods; yet more tolerable [would be] even this, than for robbing one of himself, and all that was his. When, a year or two ago, those professedly holy men of the South, met in the semblance of prayer and devotion, and, in the name of Him who said, "As ye would all men should do unto you, do ye even so unto them" appealed to the Christian world to aid them in doing to a whole race of men, as they would have no man do unto themselves, to my thinking, they contemned and insulted God and his church, far more than did Satan when he tempted the Saviour with the Kingdoms of the earth. The devil's attempt was no more false, and far less hypocritical. But let me forbear, remembering it is also written, "Judge not, lest ye be judged."[19]

That final sentence was more typical of Lincoln's approach to slave owners than were the preceding sentences. He did not ordinarily try to answer on their own grounds those Southerners who cited the Bible in defense of slavery. He relied, for this subject, on the political religion of "the fathers," and on their sacred document, the Declaration. He had, as we shall see, other uses for biblical religion.

Aside from his attempt to combine an irenic politics with a destructive war, there was something in Lincoln that hated personal conflict. He is still known for his far-reaching leniency, his efforts to find every excuse to stay executions or to commute the harshest penalties—or, sometimes, his willingness to do without excuses:

The case of Andrews is really a very bad one, as appears from the record already before me. Yet before receiving this I had ordered his punishment commuted to imprisonment for during the war at hard labor, and had so telegraphed. I did this, not on any merit in the business, but because I am trying to evade the butchering business lately.[20]

Lincoln was readier to pardon than punish; and when he punished it was with an oddly consolatory air toward the victim. He seemed to know, from his own melancholy, how easily spirits are broken, and he lifted up men with his words even when denying them rank or requests or pardon. It was almost better to be refused a place of honor, with his accompanying letter of encouragement, than to get the post.[21] He spared the dignity of those he must rebuke; gave room for saving face to those he quarreled with.[22] He comforted those who had failed in a mission.[23] His thoughtfulness was evident in the way he corrected subordinates without being censorious. A typical regard for the feelings of those in trouble appears in this letter to an officer—the brother-in-law of Lincoln's rival, Stephen A. Douglas—who had been disgraced by Peeping-Tom and brawling charges. Lincoln pardoned him, with this emollient reprimand:

Capt. James M. Cutts.

Although what I am now to say is to be, in form, a reprimand, it is not intended to add a pang to what you have already suffered upon the subject to which it relates. You have too much of life yet before you, and have shown too much of promise as an officer, for your future to be lightly surrendered. You were convicted of two offenses. One of them, not of great enormity, and yet greatly to be avoided, I feel sure you are in no danger of repeating. The other you are not so well assured against. The advice of a father to his son, "Beware of entrance to a quarrel, but being in, bear it that the opposed may beware thee," is good, and yet not the best. Quarrel not at all. No man resolved to make the most of himself, can spare time for personal contention. Still less can he afford to take all the consequences, including the vitiating of his temper, and loss of self-control. Yield larger things to which you can show no more than equal right, and yield lesser ones, though clearly your own. Better give your path to a dog, than be bitten by him in contesting for the right. Even killing the dog would not cure the bite.

In the mood indicated deal henceforth with your fellow men, and especially with your fellow officers; and even the unpleasant event you are passing from will not have been profitless to you.[24]

This letter is important not merely for the sensitivity it shows to another's embarrassment, but for a statement of the code Lincoln himself lived by for avoiding personal contention. Lincoln did not crow over victories, take credit even where due, add salt to the wounds of others. Inflicting pain, even and especially psychic pain, seemed to give him pain. As he said when called on to reject the appointment of a friend's son, a rejection that would cruelly affect the father: "I cannot be the instrument to crush his heart."[25]

Lincoln's attempt to rise above gloating resounds in the response to his own reelection:

> While I am deeply sensible to the high compliment of a re-election, and deeply grateful, as I trust, to Almighty God for having directed my countrymen to a right conclusion, as I think, for their own good, it adds nothing to my satisfaction that any other man may be disappointed or pained by the result. May I ask those who have not differed with me, to join with me in this same spirit towards those who have?[26]

Lincoln's rare ability to enter into others' feelings—especially the feelings of loss, hurt, and guilt—was partly debilitating in his own life, reflecting his own vague sense of guilt and acute bouts of depression; but he was able to put this trait to good political use. Brooding over the common sufferings of all participants in the war, he forged a bond of pain transcending partisan gains and losses. Given the political rhetoric of the time, this position had to find a religious form of expression, just as Julia Howe's triumphalism did.

The religious meaning Lincoln gave to the war was one of expiatory suffering. His lenient temper inclined him, anyway, to the course marked out for the Suffering Servant in Deutero-Isaiah:

> He will not break a bruised reed,
> or snuff out a smouldering wick. (Isaiah 42.3)

When, in his second inaugural address, Lincoln says that the nation must, "with charity for all," strive on to "finish the work we are in," he does not list first in that work the effort toward battle and victory but "to bind up the nation's wounds" (a phrase from Psalms 147.3).[27] Even prior to that task was the *recognition* of a whole nation's wounds. In the 1863 proclamation of Thanksgiving, Lincoln asks that Americans pray that God may "heal the wounds of the nation," but only after urging everyone to confess "with humble penitence for our national perverseness and disobedience." All alike must ask pardon from God's "remembered mercy" (a phrase from Psalm 25.6).[28] The next year's proclamation urged the people to "humble themselves in the dust."[29] These are the same points made by Lincoln in his proclamation of a day of fast and humiliation at the beginning of the war. He asked for an acknowledgment that "all people, at all times," need "to confess and deplore their sins and transgressions," to "recognize the hand of God in this terrible visitation," to remember their "own faults and crime as a nation and as individuals," and beg to be "spared further punishment, though most justly deserved."[30]

The *great* sin to be remembered among all others is slavery, which is not to be imputed only to one region. After all, "our fathers" had condoned it. The nation had commerced in it, profited by it, built on it, drawn its tainted profits:

> The Almighty has his own purposes. "Woe unto the world because of offences! for it must needs be that offences come; but woe to that man by whom the offense cometh!" [Matthew 18.7]. If we shall suppose that American Slavery is one of those offences which, in the providence of God, must needs come, but which, having continued through His appointed time, He now wills to remove, and that he gives to *both* [italics added] North and South, this terrible war, as the woe due to those by whom the offence came, shall we discern therein any departure from those divine attributes which the believers in a Loving God always ascribe to Him? Fondly do we hope—fervently do we pray—that this mighty scourge of war may speedily pass away. Yet, if God will that it continue, until all the wealth piled by the bond-man's two hundred and fifty years of unrequited toil shall be sunk, and until every drop of blood drawn with the lash, shall be paid by another drawn with the sword, as was said three thousand years ago, so still it must be said, "the judgments of the Lord, are true and righteous altogether [Psalm 19.9]."[31]

The people are working out God's will together by their suffering, in Lincoln's vision, and yet that very ordeal is a sign of God's superintendence, bringing good out of evil. The task is to endure, and trust. It was more fitting, probably, than Lincoln realized that his religious views should so closely approximate those of the slaves who were at the center of the moral struggle. The distinctive features of African-American theology, considered in the previous chapter, are all repeated in Lincoln's thought—the solidarity of the people; their nonjudgmental and forgiving bent within that solid community; a trust that God is working out his will in the people's affliction; an acceptance of mystery but not of cruelty; an affinity for the comfort literature of the Jewish Bible, and especially for Deutero-Isaiah's treatment of exile. There is an even snugger fit between the slaves' belief that "deliverance" would free all slaves and the view that Lincoln gradually came to, that abolition—though never a war aim or conscious policy on his part—was God's purpose being revealed in events after they had occurred.

At the outset, Lincoln was skeptical about reading God's clear purpose in the war. When a delegation from Chicago assured him that God was calling the nation to abolish slavery, he was agnostic:

> I hope it will not be irreverent for me to say that if it is probable that God would reveal his will to others, on a point so connected with my duty, it might be supposed he would reveal it directly to me.[32]

But two years later, after being forced to partial emancipation measures as a "military necessity," Lincoln could say:

> When the war began, three years ago, neither party, nor any man, expected it would last till now. Each looked for the end, in some way, long ere today. Neither did any anticipate that domestic slavery would be much affected by the war. But here we are; the war has not ended, and slavery has been much affected—how much needs not now to be recounted. So true is it that man proposes, but God disposes.[33]

Lincoln still has not received a revelation; but he thinks, now, that events have formed a pattern that can be discerned in retrospect, though he did not foresee or plan it in advance.[34] The sheer scale, the long course, of the war indicate some larger result than its participants first conceived: "Surely He intends some great good to follow this mighty convulsion, which no mortal could make, and no mortal could stay."[35] History itself is saying "Let my people go."

> In telling this tale, I attempt no compliment to my own sagacity. I claim not to have controlled events, but confess plainly that events have controlled me. Now, at the end of three years' struggle the nation's condition is not what either party, or any man devised, or expected. God alone can claim it. Whither it is tending seems plain. If God now wills the removal of a great wrong, and wills also that we of the North as well as you of the South, shall pay fairly for our complicity in that wrong, impartial history will find therein new cause to attest and revere the justice and goodness of God.[36]

Atonement is the theme of Lincoln's meditations on the war as it prolonged itself, to his horror, beyond any merely politic goal he would have used to justify it. And all must atone. In the words of the Servant Song:

> We had all strayed like sheep,
> each of us had gone his own way. . . . (Isaiah 53.6)

The four Songs of the Suffering Servant, edited into the text of Deutero-Isaiah, state in the most radical way the concept of redemptive suffering.[37]

Scholars identify the Servant in various ways; but all admit that, at some level, the people share in the agony of their representative. If Lincoln thought of himself as personifying the people in their agony, that is not unusual. The conflation of their personal trials with the captivity and exile of Israel, and then with the passion of Jesus, was normal among slaves. The *corporate* affliction and its *personal* consequences allowed them to think at several levels, as the text of the Songs invites one to.

Lincoln presented himself as "the representative man of the nation" even when speaking to those who had not voted for him.[38] In Philadelphia, on his way to be inaugurated, he spoke extemporaneously about "the Declaration principle" of equality: "If this country cannot be saved without giving up that principle—I was about to say I would rather be assassinated on this spot than to surrender it."[39] A day earlier he had said he would give his testimony at his inauguration "if ever."[40] He was haunted by the image of a pilotless bark that informed Whitman's poem of lament for him four years later. "I trust I may have their assistance in piloting the Ship of State through this voyage, surrounded by perils as it is; for, if it should suffer attack now, there will be no pilot ever needed for another voyage."[41] And: "If all do not join now to save the good old ship of the Union this voyage, nobody will have a choice to pilot her on another voyage."[42]

Lincoln's dreams and meditations on death have led some to find in him a "Messiah complex." One could as well say that the slaves expressing their theology in the spirituals had a Messiah complex. They were at one with their suffering people. They did not imagine pain as contained within themselves, but shared it with the suffering God in everyone around them. That is Lincoln's state of mind as well. His emphases on union heightened his language, made this controlled politician an emotional artist. He even went so far, in identifying himself with blacks, as to use "the Saviour" in thanking the Baltimore freedmen who presented him with a Bible—a locution common to them, but not to him.[43]

The Servant Songs imagine the union of God with his people as a *marriage* covenant: "The Lord has acknowledged you a wife again. . . . With tender affection I will bring you home" (Isaiah 54.6–7). Lincoln thought in those terms when contemplating the very idea of "divorce" between North and South.

> In their view, the Union, as a family relation, would not be anything like a regular marriage at all, but only as a sort of free-love arrangement. A husband and wife may be divorced, and go out of the presence and beyond

the reach of each other; but the different parts of our country cannot do this.[44]

And if North and South are bound in wedlock, so are slave and free. North and South were enslaved in a common guilt; they must be freed by a common deliverance. That was Lincoln's millennial vision. It was the same, in essence, as Dr. King's would be.

> Oh, I hold my brudder wid a tremblin' hand,
>   I would not let him go!
> I hold my sister wid a tremblin' hand,
>   I would not let her go!

❖ T W E N T Y ❖

Marginal Man

In a Christmas sermon delivered during World War II, a black preacher said:

> You see, there's some question about *all* our ancestry. Jesus knows how we feel. When he was born, there was some question about *his* ancestry. He shares with the lowest men and races in our society the stigma of questionable parentage![1]

In James Baldwin's novel of black life *Go Tell It on the Mountain*, the young hero is living with his mother's husband, who himself had sons by two different women. The confused relationship of black young men with their fathers gives special meaning to Scripture passages on Isaac's sons by different women: "Only the son of the bondman stood where the rightful heir should stand," Baldwin writes.[2]

"Sometimes I feel like a motherless child," goes one of the more forlorn spirituals. But even in later verses of that song, which ring changes on the sad theme ("Sometimes I feel like I'm almos' gone"), one does not hear the singer feel like "a fatherless child"—that is too common a situation to be treated as an extremity of suffering.

Jesse Jackson would in time use his illegitimacy as a credential, a sign that he can sympathize with social outsiders. He has even compared his plight to that of Jesus—shocking some, though the identification is common in black churches. His situation was not unusual in a world that has done so much to batter the black family. As Joe Mathis, his high school football coach in Greenville, South Carolina, told me: "I was brought up like Jesse, no daddy, momma working, back door or no door to anything better. I knew that if I left Benedict College, the mill where I had been working would defeat me, the way it did others, who ended up dead or addicted to alcohol." Mathis had just completed a term on the Greenville city council when I interviewed him.

In some respects, Jackson was better off than he might have been. He knew who his father was—Noah Robinson, who gave him his father's name, Jesse, and his own middle name, Louis. Robinson wanted a son, and thought his wife could not give him one (though later she did). He had his son by a neighbor girl, who later married Charles Henry Jackson. Jesse was adopted by Jackson, and grew up calling him father. But the fascinating side of his family was represented by his natural father. Noah Robinson's father had been a preacher, part of a famous team of twin-brother evangelists. Robinson told me, in 1983, the family legend of the twins' preaching debut at age fourteen. One led off: "I *am* the *way*." The other responded, "*And* the truth *and* the *life*." The jazzy responsorial rhythms are those of Jackson's own trademark chant: "I *am* some*body*." He had heard the story of his grandfather and great-uncle from childhood on. Soon Jackson was saying that he would be a preacher too. Robinson did not take him seriously at first. But when he went to visit him in college, "He told me again. I didn't believe it. But he told me he had a dream that he was called. 'I can do it. I dreamed I was a preacher, leading people through the rivers of the waters.' " Noah Robinson was impressed by that. Dreams are an important matter in his family. After his own father died, he was tending the sickbed of his uncle, the other twin, who told him: "Tonight I'm going to see blessed Buddy [his brother]. Blessed Buddy came to me in a dream and told me I would be seeing him tonight." He died that night.

I asked Jackson if he could remember any intense prayer experience. He thought a moment and said it was when he arrived at Chicago Theological Seminary to begin his studies for the ministry. He had just moved his own and his wife's few things into their rented room. "I sat on the bed and just cried." Why? "I knew I was where I was meant to be."

He had moved partway in from the margin. Good as his real father and his adopted father were to him, Jackson moved enviously around the periphery of the Robinson house, outside looking in, watching his half-brother Noah live in a home he could only visit. When he ran for president, people said he was seeking "recognition." He claimed that he wanted recognition for blacks in general, who have been treated as "the party concubines—they [the Democrats] get the fun with us, then they marry other people. We want to be full partners."[3] The imagery is revealing. It is also, as we have seen, biblical, the claim of a whole people whose marriage has been sealed by covenant.

Jackson's path to the seminary (which he entered in 1964) involved the normal tests of manhood for one growing up in the pre-civil-rights black South. He was a football star on a team that instilled pride under Joe Mathis, one that specialized in surprise and psychological warfare. "They called us a cocky team, but I wanted them to feel they could handle anybody. We would just ease onto the field, no rah-rah, and do our calisthenics without a word. Then we'd *explode* on the first play." Even more than physical quickness, one needed deft verbal powers to be a leader in the black ghetto. "Dozening," the ritual insult game, was a daily test of one's survival skills. Dick Gregory described the daily obstacle course: "Before they could get going, I'd knock it out first, *fast, knock* out those jokes so they wouldn't have time to set and climb all over me." Black militants would dozen "whiteys" in the sixties, Rap Brown boasting, "I'm peeter jeeter the womb beater, the baby maker, the cradle shaker."

In Greenville, dozening was called "signifying," and Jackson was a master at it. A friend from that time, LeRoy Greggs, remembers: "He would stick that needle in." Did Greggs ever feel the needle? "No, we had a neighborhood concept. We stuck by each other and signified against rivals." Jackson's rhyme-responses would be mocked in later years, and could get him in trouble. When accused of not following up on projects he had launched, he replied, "I'm a tree shaker, not a jelly maker." That would come back to haunt him when he asked for positions of responsibility, including the presidency. So would his boast to fellow Greenville outsiders that he and other waiters at Greenville's Poinsetta Hotel spit in the white folks' food before serving it to them. He tried to shrug that off by saying, "They lynched us, we played tricks on them."

On his graduation from high school, Jackson was offered a contract to play professional baseball, but he knew he would need an education to reach the ministry, to have the kind of influence he wanted. A football scholarship took him, briefly, to the University of Illinois, but he found his path to stardom blocked by another black quarterback already on the scene. (Later he would say he left because blacks were discriminated against.) He went where he *could* star—near home, at North Carolina Agricultural and Technical College. Lunch counter sit-ins had begun in the South, and in 1963 he led some students in one. He was arrested for organizing this protest ("inciting to riot" in the quaint language of the region) and spent a night in jail.

In 1964 he won a Rockefeller scholarship to Chicago Theological Seminary, one of the respected cluster of divinity schools on the campus of the University of Chicago. There he studied the basic curriculum— Old Testament, New Testament, modern theology. "He was serious about what he wanted to learn," says Perry Lefevre, a former dean of the school who taught him the basic theology course. Jackson talked his way through classes that did not interest him, avoiding written assignments whenever possible. His natural gift is entirely oral. He is vigorous and eloquent when he can speak his mind. When his grammar gets bent, it gains by the experience. At debate after debate in the 1988 campaign, Jackson asked those in the audience who had a television set or stereo to raise their hands; then he asked those who owned their own interconti- nental missile to hold up *their* hands. When none were raised, he said: "We makin' what ain't nobody buyin'." That is the pretense-shattering language of the spirituals: "Ever'body talkin' 'bout heaven ain't goin' there." Reduced to print, such a passage loses the ease of Jackson's per- fectly placed "ain't." In fact, most of those who quoted the comment tried to tidy it up, and just destroyed its rhythm.

But the colloquial mode should not mislead people. Jackson's mind is creative, and creativity involves the extraordinary ingestion of materials to be remade. He is a quick learner and shrewd analyst. At Chicago Theological Seminary, he was drawn to activist teachers in an academic setting—it was the sixties, and all of higher education had to cope with a world wrenched free of its moorings. In Jackson's case, that made two of his teachers special mentors, the kind who like a student with the curiosity and drive Jackson showed. One of these, Ross Snyder, had established an exchange program with South African theologians and their students. This gave an international basis to Jackson's thinking, at a time when the African heritage of blacks was being recaptured. Jackson would wear a mushroom-cloud Afro in the years ahead, and a stylish range of dashikis; but he was fortunate in making his first acquaintance with the continent in terms of common *Christian* efforts against oppres- sion at home and abroad. Jackson never thought that re-Africanization meant de-Christianization. The religion of the slaves in America was not, of necessity, a slave religion in his eyes. He stayed on the side of Dr. King in this respect.

The other teacher who influenced Jackson, and gave him influence, taught at the University of Chicago Divinity School, but attracted activist students from all the affiliated theological schools. Alvin Pitcher was a white participant in the community organizing that gave many blacks their voice in Chicago, where the black establishment had been indebted to the machine. Pitcher introduced Jackson to fellow members of Al Raby's Coordinating Council of Community Organizations and to black pastors like Clay Evans (who would later ordain Jackson).

By his second year at the seminary, when he led a group of fellow students down to the 1965 Selma march, Jackson could tell Dr. King that he might prove useful if King heeded the people asking him to go north into Chicago's different world of segregation. The Selma situation was tense, following as it did on the murder of Jimmie Lee Jackson and the march to Montgomery aborted at Edmund Pettus Bridge on "bloody Sunday," March 7, 1965. Organizing a new march was proving difficult. Dr. King's SCLC was being criticized as not radical enough by the leaders of the Student Nonviolent Coordinating Committee. SNCC's attempts to create a new policy were "marked by repeated shouting matches with SCLC's Jim Bevel."[4] Bevel and Andrew Young tried to keep Malcolm X out of the explosive situation.[5]

Jesse Jackson intruded on this scene with typical assurance, giving out speeches and advice. King's advisers, young in absolute terms (King was only thirty-six himself), had lived through beatings, hoses, dogs, and jails—whole generations, as it were, of white weapons systems—and they did not want to listen to a latecoming loudmouthed kid.[6] Yet Jackson found one ally in the King circle, and at its very center. Ralph Abernathy, King's contemporary and friend, had trouble keeping the leader's ear in the press of younger men around him. Perhaps another young voice, added to the clamor, would dilute the influence of the aging "kids" who pushed at each other and at Abernathy. In this way, the man who would later have most to resent in Jackson's rise helped gain him entry.

Jackson went back to Chicago after the Selma march, ready to beat the drum for King's intercession in that city. When King arrived in Chicago the next year, Jackson dropped out of the seminary to be helpful to him—he was driving the car that picked him up at O'Hare Airport. Though Jackson was himself a newcomer to Chicago, his marginal status could be put to use. Since he was not ordained, he did not look like a rival to the established preachers of the area, each of whom had his own church. When Jackson began services for his own SCLC activity (Operation Breadbasket), he held them on Saturday morning, avoiding any conflict with the Sunday-morning sermons of his elders.

Operation Breadbasket, which SCLC had developed in Philadelphia, involved "covenants" between black buyers and businesses that would commit themselves to black hiring, especially at management levels. The opposite of covenant favors to any business was a withdrawal from buying—boycott. Jackson would be accused of blackmailing businessmen by his critics on the right, and of capitalist deal-making by his critics on the left. Meanwhile, Jackson marched around Chicago with Dr. King, part of King's ineffectual search for a confrontation with Mayor Daley. Daley could blur the talk about schools, housing, and police behavior with double-talk about administrative difficulties. He eluded King's attempts at a moral showdown. With a sense, almost, of relief, King turned back south to the Memphis garbage strike.

Jackson was not involved in the garbage strike, but he was carping at King's other plan for shifting the focus from Chicago—a poor people's march on Washington. When militants broke up one march in Memphis, King called in his organizers from Atlanta, Chicago, and elsewhere to keep the peace at a new march. Jackson was still arguing with a harassed King about the wisdom of going to Washington. At an afternoon meeting at the Lorraine Motel, where all the aides were shouting at each other, King told Jackson to go start his own movement if the SCLC's did not satisfy him.

Later, when King went out onto the balcony to talk with those driving him to dinner, he patched things up with Jackson, who stood in the parking area under the balcony with Rev. Samuel (Billy) Kyles, at whose house the SCLC group meant to eat. King's last words were spoken to the two men, since the assassin's bullet shot away his jaw on one side and part of his neck. Jackson, whose area of responsibility was in Chicago, with Operation Breadbasket, flew back there and went on television to plead for peace as riots broke out and Mayor Daley ordered police to shoot looters. Jackson also, to the disgust of other SCLC leaders, went on national television the next morning from Chicago. His colleagues later claimed that he left Memphis only to grab the limelight—which would have shown an odd sense of self-promotion. I know, from my own luck in getting a last seat out of Baltimore, that there was a rush of journalists and cameras toward Memphis, where the very people later critical of Jackson were aggressively courting attention. When these people left Memphis, it was to the even better-covered funeral in Atlanta, and then they left so abruptly that the garbage strikers had to find their own buses. The story, at the outset, was in Memphis, and anyone concerned exclusively with exposure would have done better to stay there.

But what most offended the younger echelon of SCLC leaders—an offense relayed in Barbara Reynolds's influential first biography of Jackson—was his claim when he appeared in Chicago to be wearing a turtleneck shirt stained with Dr. King's blood. People like Hosea Williams swear he never got near Dr. King's body. He was standing below the balcony when his conversation with King was cut off. Like the others, he crouched down, waiting for more shots. But Billy Kyles, beside him, had rushed up to the body. The body was pumping blood from its neck artery, not stanched by the towel put on it. "There was blood everywhere," Kyles says. When he put a motel bedspread over King's body, he got blood on his hands, and wiped it off on a handkerchief—he still had the handkerchief when I talked to him in 1983. It is a natural instinct to save the blood of martyrs. When Jesuit priests were hanged, drawn, and quartered in Elizabethan England, Catholics used to press around the scaffold to dip handkerchiefs in the spattered blood (the actual butchered limbs were kept from them by the authorities, to deny them "first-class relics"). Shakespeare recalls that scene when Decius, in *Julius Caesar* (2.2.90), predicts that great men shall push each other around the "fountain" of Caesar's blood to acquire "tinctures, stains, relics, and cognizance [emblem]." Responsive to that instinct, Jacqueline Kennedy would not remove the suit stained with her husband's blood while she was returning from Dallas to Washington.

Billy Kyles does not doubt what was on Jackson's turtleneck: "Of course he got blood on him—we all did." It was inevitable that Jackson would go up the stairs to get a last glimpse of his fallen leader. Even car accidents draw the curious to look, and Jackson is not shy about such things. And if he got anywhere near the body, he got near the blood. It is odd that those who accuse Jackson of shouldering his way too close to King at his first meeting in Selma think he would keep an unnatural distance that night in Memphis. Even if we take the most unfavorable view of Jackson, as a calculating fellow who wanted to have something that looked like King's blood on his shirt, the most readily available thing that would *look* like the blood *was* the blood. The charge that he would go away from the obvious source and contrive some substitute for the tragically available original stuff is a measure of the anger Jackson inspired in other followers of King when this latecomer got so much attention. He will always be, in some measure, illegitimate in his claims—of ambiguous paternity where King is concerned, just as with his first two fathers.

But there can be no doubt that Jackson planned to *make* himself King's heir, in the most conscious way. He schemed with Chicago political manager Don Rose to do just that in the aftermath of King's death. By using Chicago as his base, rather than Atlanta, he put himself outside King's last orbit, where "legitimate" successors would scramble with each other, over the years, united only in their conviction that whoever wore the mantle in the long run, Jesse Jackson should not even make a *bid* to assume it.

There were special problems, having nothing to do with internal SCLC tensions, in the choice of Chicago as a base. This was the city that had defeated King. It was Mayor Daley's fiefdom, a place where even black politicians rose only with the help of Daley's machine. Later in the year of Dr. King's death, Daley became infamous for beating white middle-class youths who came to his city for the Democratic convention. But one of the most interesting (if least noticed) aspects of that August riot in the streets is that resident blacks took no part in it. Daley had given Lyndon Johnson his word that black neighborhoods would be sedated by the end of the summer—all of them set afloat in the gush of new swimming facilities and loose cash that washed around black precinct workers' circles. In Chicago, succeeding to Dr. King's position was putting oneself in line for humiliation.

Jackson tried to fight back in symbolic ways, as Dr. King had done, putting himself up for ridicule when he tried to mount an independent race against Daley for mayor. Jackson tried to enter the Democratic party as he had the civil rights movement, in a slanting arrival through a side door, ignoring the long flight of steps one had to climb toward the front door. He watched in 1971 as another outsider in the civil rights "family"— Shirley Chisholm—mounted a maverick campaign for president from her independent New York base. The black "elders" tried to head her off, then had to give her grudging support as a matter of black solidarity, in a first small version of what would happen with Jackson twelve years later.

The full measure of Jackson's illegitimacy in the Democratic party came out in 1972. That was the year he helped William Singer run a slate of delegates to supplant Mayor Daley's at the Miami Democratic convention—but under withering questions from the Illinois credentials committee it emerged that Jackson had not even voted in the primary he was challenging, or in any other Illinois election. As Mike Royko put it, in a mocking column: "Jesse the Jetstream didn't make it to his local polling place. He's being hailed as a new political powerhouse, and he couldn't deliver his own vote."[7] Jackson's dubiously assembled slate prevailed over Daley's in Miami—more from Larry O'Brien's autocratic rulings, and from Daley's refusal to bargain with the reformers, than from any skills at party maneuver on Jackson's part. His prominence in Miami would become another count against him back in Chicago, where he had earned more enemies than friends among Democrats of all degree. Even his successes at achieving "covenants" with local corporations hurt him with the wider audience in Chicago, where he was seen as hustling for black interests rather than creating community ideals. When his annual "Black Expo" became successful, he detached it from the SCLC, which was foundering under Ralph Abernathy's uncertain leadership. Abernathy suspended Jackson, and Jackson resigned from the SCLC.[8] He was on his own for the first time.

The reform Democrats Jackson had worked with in 1971 helped him during the Carter years. Joseph Califano, Carter's secretary of health, education, and welfare, proposed a grant to Jackson's Operation PUSH (People United to Save Humanity, later amended to *Serve* Humanity) after hearing how Jackson preached discipline and study to black students.[9] The federal moneys that went to the resulting PUSH/Excel program were poorly accounted for, and Jackson's program was never very good apart from Jackson's own performances in the schools. Ernest R. House, who was given a federal contract to evaluate the government's own evaluation of PUSH/Excel, concluded that the program was run like "the Baptist church, historically the strongest institution in the black social order."[10] That was also the way SCLC's finances had been managed—to Andrew Young's continuing exasperation.[11] But the PUSH/Excel program did keep Jackson on the road, forming a national constituency among the young at a time when other civil rights leaders disappeared into local politics or private misery. During the 1970s Jackson was the only black spokesman still addressing a national audience. He kept up his ties to Africa and—through the Black Muslims—with Arab countries. These latter ties were useful when Jackson negotiated with Syria for the release of the downed American flyer Robert Goodman in 1984. They would become a hindrance when Black Muslim Louis Farrakhan's anti-Semitism became an issue.

When Jackson decided to run for president, he used a typical preacher's device to include others in the decision-making process. Pat Robertson would do the same thing four years later—asking supportive congregations if they wanted this to happen and were willing to back it. That is the way televangelists raise money for ambitious new churches, broadcast facilities, or universities. Jackson varied the formula by making the "Run, Jesse, Run" rallies an appeal for *many* minority candidates to run—blacks, women, Asian Americans, and others. The "Rainbow Coalition" would unite all the dispossessed or underrepresented in another "covenant"—Noah's rainbow sign was a covenant with humanity.

The civil rights "family" was even unhappier with Jackson's bid than with Shirley Chisholm's in the seventies.[12] They had not yet come to terms with his leverage in the black generation that had come of age since Dr. King's death. An ABC poll in 1983 showed that Jackson was considered by 51 percent of blacks as their most important leader. The runner-up, Andrew Young, got only 8 percent. The rest went down, toward invisibility, from there.

Jackson hoped for liberal support of his coalition, definitely including Jewish support. Black militants had forsworn white contributions to their cause by the end of the sixties, arguing that Jews, in particular, spoke more for service providers than service receivers.[13] This was the source of conflict in the Ocean Hill–Brownsville school dispute in New York and the affirmative-action debates around the *Bakke* case. But Jackson, whose "covenanting" strategy was always negotiatory and inclusive, tried to keep the Jewish-black alliance alive. He had formed the anti-Daley delegation in 1972 with William Singer, a Jewish liberal Democrat. He and his family marched with Jews protesting a Ku Klux Klan rally in Skokie, and he sent a letter of protest when General George Brown, chairman of the Joint Chiefs of Staff, said that Jews control America's banks and newspapers.[14]

But Jackson was suspect among Jews for his support of Palestinian rights, a support given vivid expression when he was photographed in his travels embracing Yasir Arafat. Thus when it became known that he had referred to Jews as "Hymies" in private conversation, and that his Black Muslim supporters called the Jewish religion "dirty," Jackson was accused of anti-Semitism. For a week he tried to deny or shrug off the "Hymie" issue—a bad mistake, since it gave time for emotions to become indurated on either side. Some Jews were ready to admit that *schvartzes* was used as readily in their circles as *Hymies* had been in Greenville when Jackson was growing up. But the man who had rebuked General Brown for insensitivity should have acknowledged his own lapse the minute it was drawn to his attention. By the time he brought himself to apologize, the firestorm of criticism around him was taken by many blacks as a form of

Jewish racism. Adolph Reed, in an otherwise scholarly book, denounces it as "caterwauling."[15] Some made it a point of principle, by then, that Jackson *not* apologize. (His wife was in their number.) When Jackson apologized a *second* time, there was anger among his followers—and even more when he apologized still again in his speech at the Democratic convention. But his own rhetoric of reconciliation among the afflicted made apology mandatory.

The same dynamic was observable when Louis Farrakhan became an issue. The Black Muslims were widely respected in black communities for their success against drugs, their discipline, their restoration of proud black manhood in convicts and reformed criminals. I first heard of Farrakhan when I called Barbara Reynolds in 1983 to ask if she had altered any of the harsh views she expressed about Jackson in her 1975 book. She said no, that she found more representative leadership, now, in the sermons of Minister Farrakhan.

Farrakhan had gone to Syria with Jackson, providing him bodyguards for that and other trips. He considered all white religions, and white people, "dirty"—he had a biblical/physiological explanation of the racial degeneration of whites, one as clever and complicated as Colonel Thieme's explanation of the virgin birth.[16] Farrakhan, an ally of Malcolm X, had supplanted the Muslim leaders responsible for Malcolm X's death; but he had not taken part in politics until Jackson enrolled him in Harold Washington's campaign to become mayor of Chicago. The ethos of black solidarity forbids any renunciation of a "brother" who has come under white criticism—but Jackson professed to be speaking, now, for a larger coalition. Though the closed code of one strand in the "rainbow" was incompatible with other strands in it, Jackson was driven by the "Hymie" controversy back on his narrower base in the black churches, to restore his own confidence and the larger campaign's finances. The rainbow that was to be brown, yellow, red, white, and black was restricted to the original black by the time Jackson distanced himself (too late) from Farrakhan.

Even his contracted band of followers went to the 1984 convention bitterly divided among themselves and hostile to the party's organizers. His own followers said Jackson was making insufficient demands on the platform committee—and even those reforms were being rejected. When the Mondale forces chose Andrew Young to present the platform committee's rejection of Jackson's plank against runoff elections, they thought they would placate Jackson supporters. Instead, the use of Young was considered a further provocation. Even a moderate Jackson delegate, who later published his journal of the campaign, said he was "shocked and surprised that Andrew Young would choose to oppose Jackson's key plank openly on national TV."[17] This, too, broke the code of black solidarity. When Young appeared on Tuesday, he was booed by black delegates.

Jackson's troops were seething that Tuesday, when Jackson was scheduled to address the convention. The delegate's diary continues:

> Believe that Mondale had made critical misjudgment as to impact of defeat of Jackson's minority planks—not necessarily in defeat of specific planks but in the way in which Mondale people wanted to show their control of the convention, particularly to show how badly he could beat Jackson and generally how he could show other interests that he was not giving in to yet another interest. Along with many other Jackson delegates, I personally resented deeply this kind of treatment. Wounds deep and won't heal easily.[18]

It was against this background that Jackson rose to speak. He had kept his message secret from the Mondale people (who were asking for his support) and his own delegates (who were encouraging him to defiance). The apology he offered in the speech came as an unpleasant surprise to his own wife—and it infuriated people like Victor McTeer, who had worked on his platform proposals: "When he said to the Jewish community, forgive me—my reaction was: for what? . . . There were a lot of supporters who'd been upset with a conciliatory speech at that moment." But after saying that to a friend, McTeer began to notice the response of others in his own Mississippi delegation: "White people around me are crying. I mean the men. I'm not talking about no lightweight little white girls. I'm talking about we're-going-to-fight-you-nigger-till-you're-gone white folks. . . . I'm standing there next to this white lady from Mississippi who's there in tears on my shoulder. I realized, 'My God, I'm part of something important.' "[19] Jackson had asked forgiveness for any "error of temper, taste, or tone" in his campaign, and he went on to plead:

> We must turn from finger-pointing to clasped hands. We must share our burdens and our joys with each other once again. We must turn to each other and not on each other and choose higher ground. . . . All of us count and all of us fit somewhere. We have proven that we can survive without each other. But we have not proven that we can win and progress without each other. We must come together.

Jackson, driven back to the margin of politics, was only legitimate as the voice of the dispossessed. And it was religion that, in his case as in King's, let him reach people with an authentic voice for common suffering. As Victor McTeer said, with wonder: "Jesse Jackson held church in the Democratic National Convention." For some, that was a disqualifying consideration. "A religious metaphor dominated the [Jackson] campaign," according to Yale political scientist Adolph Reed, Jr.; and Reed thinks that was its greatest failing. [20]

Preacher Jesse

STANDING OVER MY SEAT IN HIS OWN CHARTERED AIRPLANE, JACKSON shadowboxes with the empty aisle just darkened for takeoff. It is February, deep into the primary campaigns of 1988, and he is explaining the cold war. "It's like a fighter who's got his guard up high, looking over at the Bear"—his head periscopes around his hands—"and you expose yourself to these terrible body blows. Drugs!" His midsection hardens at the imagined blow, but the hands stay up. "Debt!" He buckles. "The purchasing of America!" A grunt. "Energy!" Another. "I start my policy toward Russia from here, from the hurt"—he spreads his fingers on his ribs—"and move on out to others. We've been leading with our left, with our left"—he jabs automatically. "Always military first, not economic, not diplomatic."

Still standing up during takeoff, Jackson says, above the engines' roar: "Reagan said something that should have got more attention from the press. He said the last forty years have not been good for the West. These last forty years have been the most exciting and liberating for the world. Whole empires have fallen, new nations been created, people taking charge of their own lives. What Reagan meant is that all those little shits in the UN have been beating up on us for forty years—*us*, Somoza; *us*, Batista; *us*, Marcos. We've got to redefine *us*."

One of Jackson's skills as a preacher is his ability to put complex ideas in vivid form, or to give them concrete applications. I went with him, once, on one of his high school tours. He was teaching constantly. Standing with students in an airport, he continued his lesson on the need to learn. "Go get a ticket. If you can't count, you get the wrong change. If you can't read, you go to the wrong gate. If you can't handle numbers, you get the wrong flight at the wrong time." Arguing about the arms race, the drive for ever bigger weapons, he says—as five of us crowd into a little car—"We make elephant weapons for Toyota wars." Sitting next to the driver, he makes the same point by stabbing repeatedly at the dashboard: "Since we can't find the right place and put the key in, we just keep making bigger keys."

In the string of 1988 debates among Democratic candidates, Jackson's vivid formulations of the problems—problems of corporate responsibility, of drug interdiction, of trade imbalance—were echoed, sometimes verbatim, by other candidates as the series progressed, prompting Michael Dukakis to say, "That's Jesse's line!" Columnist George Will, who seemed to think Jackson became vivid only by oversimplifying, undertook the role of intellectual disqualifier on the ABC Sunday-morning show *This Week with David Brinkley*. Like an old Southern cracker giving a literacy test at the polls, he asked: "As president, would you support measures such as the G-7 measures [*sic*] and the Louvre Accords [*sic*]?" Like the redneck quizzers, Will got the trick question slightly wrong—the Louvre Accord *was* a G-7 measure for the international market.

What was surprising about Jackson's debating was his ability to explain himself *without* falling into the usual oversimplifications. While Richard Gephardt was Japan-bashing, Jackson criticized American firms for seeking cheap labor abroad. He argued that tax incentives as well as penalties should keep those jobs home. Jackson's populism did not feed on the hatreds that are populism's ordinary and disheartening fuel. His plea that all the outsiders should unite to confront their problems went counter to the claim that Jackson was acting only for black interests. He said that corporate barracudas "swim very deep, where it's very dark; they can't even tell whether they are swallowing white fish or black fish."

Jackson's didactic flair drew on the preacher's use of parable and Scripture tales. No other candidate was so open in his religiosity. When discussing homelessness, he said that Jesus was homeless, born in a stable. When discussing health insurance, he said Jesus did not ask the woman with a hemorrhage if she could pay before he healed her. This religious note embarrassed some secular blacks almost as much as if he had reverted to minstrel-show stereotypes. Yale political scientist Adolph L. Reed, Jr., found it debilitating that blacks should still depend on "the principle of clerical political spokesmanship." He points out that church activism on civil rights must be measured against church acquiescence in the power arrangements of the past. Reliance on preachers revealed, in the early stages of black activism, "several factors that retarded political development." When genuine (i.e., secular) political organization takes place, it renders the church matrix "a politically redundant entity." And in the process the authoritarian, nonaccountable model of leadership by preachers is submitted to democratic pressures. Politics and religion are at enmity by their very nature, since "the realm of politics by definition is temporal intervention."[1]

Reed admits that some preachers—Andrew Young, Walter Fauntroy, William Gray—have entered electoral politics. But that gives them an entirely new kind of validation. Electoral discrimination replaces the emotional acclamation of the preacher's audience. By entering local races, these valid spokespersons for their constituents "meet the requirements of more formally articulated legitimating rules." They move from symbolic politics to real politics. By election they are cleansed of their suspect clerical antecedents:

> Elected officials are the only claimants to black political leadership status who are held accountable for their actions by the presence of unambiguous mechanisms for popular ratification within the Afro-American community. . . . The rise of elected officialdom has regularized black political participation, and provided a set of concrete, systematic avenues for expression and realization of *black* interests . . . [so that] elected officials should be seen as the principal bearers of *black* political interests.[2]

I italicize *black* in that last quote because, in Reed's model of pluralism, an authentic voice must speak for *particular* interests in the push and shove of the total society. Jackson, by pretending to embody a "rainbow" of varying interests, did not attend to the one and only interest he might have represented. Claiming to promote everyone, he ends up nobody's real champion, as one could see by the grab bag of proposals he made to the 1984 platform committee. His opposition to nuclear "first strike," for instance, "cannot be considered a distinctively black concern."[3] Reed thinks elected black officials were right to oppose Jackson's intrusion on their turf, and he finds it a sign of maturing in the black political community that Jackson was treated as an outsider when he tried to mediate for blacks in Miami after a civil disturbance there.[4]

That Miami incident brings to mind what was in some ways the most dramatic episode of Jackson's 1984 campaign. Reed does not mention it—neither, surprisingly, do Bob Faw and Nancy Skelton in their book on that campaign. After Andrew Young had been booed by black delegates for proposing the Mondale platform, a black caucus was called for the next day. It was a very emotional session, with angry cries at Young when he appeared. Coretta Scott King, as the widow of the sainted leader, rose to bring back peace—and *she* was booed. When she tried to mention Young's services in the civil rights cause, Jackson delegates shouted, "That was yesterday!" and "What have you done recently?" Dr. Reed would, presumably, answer that Young had got elected, first to Congress, then to the mayor's office in Atlanta. That did not seem to satisfy the delegates. Young skipped out a door behind the congregation. Finally, when the emotions seemed to be reaching a crescendo, Jackson arrived, went onto the platform, hugged Mrs. King, and rebuked those who had booed her: "When I think about the roads I've walked with Andy, and the leadership of Mrs. King—her home bombed, her husband assassinated, her children raised by a widow—she deserves to be heard." Jackson soon had all the leaders present up on the stage, linked hand to hand, swaying back and forth as they sang "We Shall Overcome." The angers turned to emotional reconciliation and tears. It was a more virtuoso performance than Jackson's speech to the convention the day before; and he was the only one in America who could have brought it off.

Admittedly, these were Jackson delegates, activated and brought into the political process by his campaign. But by Reed's norms they were illegitimate voices of their community. They had been interested and sophisticated enough to get themselves elected to their party's national convention, but they had done so in response to a symbolic preacher, not a real power broker, according to Reed's analysis.

Still, here at the heart of the national convention of a major party, even Andrew Young, an elected mayor, had to rely on memories of church leadership past—on Dr. King's widow—to reconcile him with a new generation of black politicians; and even that had not worked until the most "retardative" leader stepped in. That is a sequence that should give Dr. Reed pause.

For one thing Reed seems to do, in his attack on Jackson, is validate Jackson's claim to be the heir of Martin Luther King. Everything Reed criticizes—symbolic leadership, lack of electoral validation, concern for larger issues than black welfare, moral appeals to a broad spectrum of clashing interests—marked King's life and work. And if Jackson continued along the course marked out by King, it was not by any conscious *defiance* of King's values, as some have claimed. Nor was there anything wrong, on the face of it, in aspiring to continue that legacy. Others certainly attempted it—Ralph Abernathy, for instance, and Hosea Williams, and James Bevel (all later critics of Jackson).

James Bevel, who delivered the greatest speech I have ever heard in my life (see chapter 18), was expelled from the SCLC, like Jackson; his demagogic bent was at least as great as Jackson's, but less disciplined. Bevel set up Making a Nation (MAN) in Baltimore, and tried to recruit me as a celebrant of his one-man march on the UN, where he would demand separate representation for the black nation in America. Williams, less erratic than Bevel but also undisciplined, ended up with similar promotional efforts in Atlanta. Abernathy, jealous of King while King lived, was prickly in wanting the same kind of adulation after King's death. Abernathy's need for attention would finally make him support even Ronald Reagan, when Republicans were among the few still courting him.

The strains within the civil rights movement are glossed over by those who take testimony from its veterans against Jesse Jackson. Danger, persecutions, exhilarating victories, and soul-draining defeats took a devastating toll on those who bought our freedoms with their pain. If Jackson kept up a national vision of black pride throughout the seventies, it was by a *refusal* to succumb to the temptations that faced so many activists when the heady times of suffering and witnessing seemed to have faded entirely. The seventies was a period of hangover for many former leaders. Jackson's campaign against drugs and alcohol in the high schools was a witness that—like the Muslims'—had a special appeal for blacks in that "decompressing" aftermath to the movement.

Some, of course, did go into electoral politics, with success. But they were not all free from the excesses of the church structure that Reed thinks electoral politics must supplant. Authoritarian rule was still possible, *especially* when based on the kind of sheer *black* interest Reed calls for. Jackson ran PUSH/Excel as a church organization; but Marion Barry and Coleman Young also ran their respective city halls that way. Their critics found they were as immune from blame among their "congregations" as any black preacher of the old days. Even Andrew Young, a man of entirely different disciplines, was seen by Atlantans—especially, as we shall be noticing, by blacks—as "too much the preacher" rather than an ordinary politician.

There were other temptations facing those who took the route recommended by Reed, practicing black-interest electoral politics. Ivanhoe Donaldson is a good example of one faced with those temptations. Donaldson, a handsome young hero of the sit-in movement, was as talented as any black leader I met in the sixties. His poise, his articulate intelligence, his fierce commitment arrived too late on the scene to have their full impact during the protest days. When I met him, he was taking stock of the situation blacks were left in after passage of the civil rights bill. He was reading and writing at the Institute for Policy Studies, organizing African support groups.

He went into electoral politics with spectacular success, as Marion Barry's one-man brain trust and as the most desired outside consultant for campaigns like that of Harold Washington in Chicago. But he took with him the us-against-them attitude of one who was committed solely to black issues. I saw an example of this when I stayed with him in Washington while writing about him. On the way back to his apartment, we stopped at a cocktail party thrown by an ex-leader of the civil rights movement. The only other white there was a young woman from South Africa, strong in her opposition to apartheid. Since I had already had my session of white-baiting for the day, Donaldson began twitting her on her political guilt-assuagement. She took a certain amount of this before calling him a racist, at which he slapped her, hard.

In the Marion Barry administration, where he was the moving force at the outset, Donaldson began taking and giving out favors that led him, in time, to a jail sentence. Given his ideological sincerity, I am sure he considered the luxuries he commandeered as spoils of war—compensation wrested from the system that had deprived him and his in their hard times. Like some other veterans of the civil rights movement, he took into local politics the guerrilla mentality of his besieged days.

On the other hand, politicians like Andrew Young have not followed Reed's program of speaking only for black interests. They consider themselves representative of their entire city, or district, or whatever electoral unit chose them. Nor do they deprive themselves of support from religious and other communal groups. Why should they? This would be to disarm themselves, as Michael Dukakis did, in opposing candidates who very successfully combine political and religious appeal. Reed's approach would deprive not only Jesse Jackson of political legitimacy, but Ronald

Reagan and George Bush as well—indeed, it would disqualify a public moralizer like Abraham Lincoln, who used theological categories (of providence, of divine will, of redemptive suffering, of a people's solidarity with its God) to address as fundamental a political issue as war.

In trying to put limits on the influence of the black church, Reed argues that there is an antipathy between religion and politics. He recommends a secular religious test, for Jackson, of the sort that we saw people trying to impose on the Jesuit priest Timothy Healy (see chapter 7). Another Jesuit, Robert Drinan, from Dukakis's own state of Massachusetts, proved that religion does not have to be a reactionary force in American politics. When Father Drinan served in Congress, his liberal positions on matters like the Vietnam War were clearly connected with his theological training in the morality of just wars. This did not preclude his cooperation with constituents and colleagues who did not share his theological tenets; but a moral opposition to the war was seen as compatible with religion in his case. And the moral passion he shared with others of a different faith (or no faith) was more easily grasped by the electorate, even in liberal Massachusetts, than was the morally tepid (barely discernible) dislike of the war professed, in the sixties, by Michael Dukakis.

Father Drinan was ordered to resign political office by Pope John Paul II, who decided that New World priests should not be involved in politics (though he allowed great political activity by the clergy in his native Poland). Whatever the pope's motives in this matter, which Father Drinan honored, there can be no reason for Americans to bar the clergy from political activity, since the Constitution recognizes them only as citizens. There was no constitutional bar to Father Drinan's service in Congress. Indeed, one might argue that Drinan, trained as he was in moral distinctions, brought a valuable set of views to the public debate. He demonstrated, among other things, that a more traditional morality could be opposed to the radical, deliberately extraelectoral activism of his fellow Jesuit, Father Daniel Berrigan, who is a pacifist rather than a believer in just-war theory.

If Father Drinan could contribute certain skills in moral debate and distinction-drawing, Jesse Jackson can draw on a similarly rich background of moral discourse—one so rich, as we have seen, that when Abraham Lincoln voiced the most profound theological insights into political life, he was just echoing the black religious tradition. Dr. King brought that tradition to the moral debates of the 1960s—the debates over the Vietnam War and other issues of nonviolence, as well as matters like civil rights bills and poverty programs, which more directly affected African Americans.

Many people in the 1960s claimed that Dr. King had no right to speak out on the war. They wanted to confine him to "his" concerns—to put limits around his citizen activity. Others, in the South, had earlier denied that he could speak legitimately even on civil rights: As a clergyman, they said, he should have confined himself to matters of private morality, not issues of public policy. Ironically, Adolph Reed is updating this kind of restriction in the critique he makes of Jackson.

Jackson's clerical background was not something that resonated only in the depths of blacks who heard him. Many whites gave him a readier hearing because he is a preacher. This was one of the least-noticed aspects of the campaign. In Iowa, when Jackson, the urban black activist, first talked to white farmers, he was somehow less menacing, less alien, because he shared their language on Sundays. Staying overnight in voters' homes, he said prayers before meals. He appeared in local pulpits. Was this taking unfair advantage of people? Only if one thinks political issues can be debated in a kind of isolation from personal values and historical ties. It is hard to invent an entirely new moral language for each situation, as the 1988 campaign of Gary Hart demonstrated.

But even if the Democrats could, in the name of "value-free" discussion of public policy, divorce their politics from religious values, they could not enforce a similar self-denying ordinance on the Republicans, who profit from appeals to the evangelical Right. Democrats of the Dukakis persuasion will themselves into a tongue-tied state. No wonder Jackson seemed so comparatively free, grounded, and eloquent in the debates. He was reaching toward a larger audience, using traditional appeals, just as Ronald Reagan had in his 1980 debates.

Jackson's religious references did not seem to disturb his secular supporters, any more than Father Drinan's clerical collar bothered *his* allies in the opposition to Vietnam. Many of those allies had been at civil rights and peace demonstrations where Roman collars were frequently in evidence. But white evangelicals like Bert Lance did have a special affinity with Jackson, who did not yield any tactical advantage to the president in his 1984 convention speech: As Jackson had taken the hand of the security man at the Citadel and joined with him in prayer, so he answered Ronald Reagan's calls for prayer.

Mr. Reagan will ask us to pray, and I believe in prayer. I have come this way by the power of prayer. But then, we must watch false prophecy. He cuts energy assistance to the poor, cuts breakfast programs from children, cuts lunch programs from children, cuts job training from children, and then says to an empty table, "Let us pray." Apparently he is not familiar with the structure of prayer. You thank the Lord for the food that you are about to receive, not the food that just left. I think we should pray, but don't pray for the food that left. Pray for the man that took the food—to leave.

Jackson not only preached and campaigned in churches white and black, he also raised campaign funds in (mainly) black church gatherings. That does seem to violate the separation of church and state—though even so ardent a proponent of separation as Nat Hentoff sees nothing wrong with it. He argues, in fact, that it is the right of any group of citizens to support the views and people they want in a democracy. Some churches have partially surrendered that right to protect their tax-exempt status. That presents no problem to Hentoff, who does not believe that churches should be tax-exempt. What separation of church and state *does* involve is a large question I shall be taking up later. But in terms of actual political support, what Jackson was taking from the churches did not essentially differ from the support sought by Ronald Reagan, George Bush, and Dan Quayle at the annual meetings of the National Religious Broadcasters or the national prayer breakfasts.

In the past, a candidate's religion clearly was taken into account in voters' assessment of his representative character. That is why it took so long to put a Catholic into the White House. And even when John Kennedy was elected, it was not on the grounds that his religion was irrelevant. He surely profited as much from the importance of Catholic city machines in the Democratic party as he was hurt by Protestant misgivings. Anyone who saw nuns turn out to cheer Kennedy could not really believe his Catholicism was electorally irrelevant.

I saw the equivalent of those nuns in Atlanta, on the day when Jackson's campaign bus pulled into Piedmont Park for the 1988 convention, after a barnstorming tour down from Chicago. Asked why he took the bus to town, Jackson told the cheering crowd: "We took the bus north. We just came back on the other side of the highway." Jackson was coming to town on the vehicle blacks have traveled in for years. He reminded the crowd that he is a part of them. "Weren't no cameras at the door when I was born. My momma could not serve us turkey dinner at three o'clock on Thanksgiving Day. She was busy making another family's turkey. That's my testimony [the church term for public witnessing]. But when my name goes in nomination for president, my momma's prayers are confirmed." The young black woman standing next to me was almost in tears at this point. She was well attired in a professional-looking suit, but she had sung and clapped along with the hymn to the Holy Spirit that the crowd bellowed just before Jackson's bus arrived.

The mayor of Atlanta, Andrew Young, was not at Piedmont Park when Jackson arrived. Atlanta has a broader-based, longer-lived black establishment than any other city—the woman beside me was probably part of it. But Jackson did not differ from Young as a preacher compared to a "legitimate" politician. They are both preachers, but of two very different kinds.

Preacher Andy

THOUGH MAYOR YOUNG OF ATLANTA IS A JACKSON, HE WAS NOT NAMED— like Jesse Jackson—for a black preacher. He got his name, like his father before him and his son after, from a white political leader: He is *Andrew Jackson* Young, reflecting his place of birth (New Orleans) and his father's aspiration for acceptance. Young was criticized for his emphasis on white acceptance in his days with Dr. King. He even had to punch it out with Hosea Williams after Williams claimed, once too often, that he was a CIA plant.[1]

But Young *is* a black preacher, by an act more deliberately willed than Dr. King's choice of vocation ever was. King succeeded to his father's Atlanta congregation, in a place where middle-class black preachers were the natural leaders of society. Young grew up in a prosperous dentist's home, where the "advance" into secularity that Adolph Reed recommends had already been accomplished. Though Louis Armstrong was his father's dental patient, and Young himself took trumpet lessons in his youth, he did not grow up in the New Orleans of jazz and "gospel" and the blues. "We were not allowed to go to places where that was played," he told me. "We went to the symphony. My parents wanted to escape black culture. That was when you talked about how Indian you were." (Like Jesse Jackson and Julian Bond, Young has Native American ancestors.) Young says his family "lived in a transplanted New England culture. My father played *The Messiah* at home. The closest we came to gospel music was the Fisk Jubilee Choir." He was taken to hear black artists if they were classical singers—Roland Hayes, Marian Anderson, Todd Duncan, Paul Robeson—"and I had no idea of Robeson's politics the two or three times I heard him sing."

Even if Young had grown up in the broader culture of New Orleans, that was not the "real" South he would contend with in the 1960s. "We always thought of New Orleans as civilized," he says now. Southerners who think Atlanta is no better than a Northern town think New Orleans is no better than a European town. And even there the Youngs were set apart. Though Young was born in the Depression, in the very year Roosevelt was elected, both his parents were college graduates (from Congregationalist Dillard University). His father had white patients as well as black. Most of Young's childhood friends were white, but "poor white"—when they played it was with *his* ball. I asked if these friendships endured. "No, they ended at puberty." Does that mean he had played with white girls before that? "Oh no. We pretended white girls didn't exist, even when we were good friends of their brothers."

Young first entered a fully segregated world in public grade school, where he was the victim of *black* prejudice: "It was a class resentment at me, for being middle-class." That was not the only problem Young had to contend with. His parents could afford, in the Depression, to send their precocious child to a nursery school; by the time he went there he was already reading. When he entered public school, he was skipped directly to the third grade. "I always regretted that," he says. There was an age gap between him and his schoolmates, one that showed in sports. "I never did well in school because I was busy making social adjustments." Young is a master ingratiator, and part of his accommodating style must date from this time when he was the "rich kid" placating poorer, older schoolmates.

On the other hand, being one of the boys meant cheeking the teachers, something that came easily since he was bright and bored, restless in an unchallenging situation. He thinks of that now as an education in unproductive kinds of conflict, and regrets the lack of serious study. When I asked if any teacher influenced him, he said he had a crush on his fourth-grade penmanship teacher, with the result that "when I went to New York and tried to open a bank account, I was turned down because my signature was too studied to look real. 'You've got to develop a

signature,' they said." When he writes out some names and phone numbers for me, they still look like a calligraphic exercise.

Young's delayed adolescence came when he was at Howard University:
"I did the growing up in college that I should have done in high school."
But even then—despite an initial year spent at his parents' college, Dillard—he was the kid in an older world. World War II veterans were
returning. Young was on the track team, but "my running buddies were
in their late twenties, or early thirties." Young had graduated from high
school at fifteen. And, once again, he ran into an odd kind of black
prejudice: "Howard was the center for the achieving black bourgeoisie,
interested in degrees and material things. They looked down on blacks
from the South." A neat twist—in grade school, he was resented for
being too middle-class; in college it was assumed that nobody from the
"deep South" could be middle-class enough. Without ever being really
rich or really Southern, he had been discriminated against for being
both—and in each case by his fellow blacks.

This was, among other things, a signal that his parents' dream of escape
into "respectability" was not worth further pursuing. Young had gone to
Howard with the idea of becoming a dentist like his father (the course
his brother did pursue), but more serious things began to nag at his
attention during his college years. When a white missionary from Yale,
preparing to go to Africa, stayed with his family in New Orleans, Young
was intrigued by two things—the ministry, and Africa. Each had an
ambiguous allure. They drew him farther off from his first base; but they
also returned him to it. Even the Congregationalist presence in New
Orleans could be traced back to African influence. The Yale ministers
who came south after the Civil War to open schools derived their inspiration from the case of the *Amistad*—the ship of mutinous African
slaves who reached Connecticut in 1839, where New England divines
found them wonderfully quick to learn. Like Jesse Jackson responding to
Snyder's South African ministry, Young was drawn to Africa by specifically Christian concerns.

Young went to the Hartford (Connecticut) Seminary Foundation in
1951, acquiring a Northern Congregationalist style of theology far removed from that of the Southern Baptists he would work with later.
There he met another missionary: "Dr. McDowell talked to us about his
work in Angola. He was in his seventies, but he couldn't retire since
there was no one to replace him. Jean and I decided to go." He had met
Jean Childs while doing his own missionary work "back South" during
a summer vacation from Hartford. He was assigned to her hometown,

in Marion County, Alabama, another Congregationalist mission area. "It [the county] has the reputation," Young says, "of producing more black Ph.D.s than any other place in the South." Jean was home on vacation from her college, Lincoln Normal, an old pacifist school. "I was studying Gandhi and nonviolence—it was exciting to find Jean already familiar with those ideas," Young says. He had not yet heard the name of Martin Luther King, who was pursuing his own theological studies in New England. Nor had Young spent any time in King's native city of Atlanta. Yet the farther away he traveled, intellectually, from the little Baptist churches of the South, the more he was being carried, insensibly, back to those cockpits of social struggle in the sixties.

He still had several detours to make on his way to that goal. He and Jean had not been allowed to go to Angola, since they were not yet married—they were waiting for her to finish college. By the time they married, the Portuguese government was opposing the entry of Americans—especially black American missionaries—so Young took the more orthodox missionary route for a Congregationalist minister trained in New England, back to one of the churches in that network of Southern parishes founded during Reconstruction. Young went to Thomasville, Georgia, near what would be the bloody and notorious site of Albany in the coming days of conflict. But this was 1955, and Young ran the prim kind of church he had grown up in. His parishioners were astounded when he went to the front door of white people's homes, instead of the back door; but he was such a polite and earnest minister that this "effrontery" was not rebuked. Young easily crosses social boundaries as well as geographical and political ones.

By 1957, Young was back in the North, as an ecclesiastical bureaucrat living in Queens and going to work in the large headquarters of the National Council of Churches. "Of over three hundred executives, only two or three of us were black"—though Young would have said "Negro" at the time, as Dr. King did till his death. Still, pride in black culture was growing, and for the first time Young steeped himself in jazz and blues: "I had heard the blues, but not the words. I became an avid collector. I had never consciously put together a sense of the heritage that was always there." He even forced himself to read Richard Wright's *Native Son*. Every time he had picked it up before, he had been forced to lay it aside as too debilitating. "I don't like to entertain unproductive angers. That's why I don't like much of black literature. It is too depressing." Like Jackson, Young says that remembering wrongs can prevent one from moving beyond them. In fact, he now claims he has learned more about racial hatred from the Holocaust literature than from black literature—it is just distant enough for him to handle the shock and outrage. Once again, he travels far off to arrive at his spiritual home.

Young learned of the civil rights movement the way most of us did, from his television set. He went south to run nonviolence training centers, and met that period's master at muting unproductive hatreds, Martin King. King's broad sense of strategy can be seen from the way he used Young's talents. Young is not a great preacher in the Southern style. He does not naturally elicit, and then play to, the "A*mens*" and "*Tell* its" and "*Preach* somes" that make preacher and congregation breathe together. This was the opposite of his first relation to the blues—here he knew the words but not the tune. On the other hand, he was the best of King's associates at disarming white opposition, at bargaining coolly while everyone else's emotions ran high. He could even put himself in the white sheriff's shoes, telling him why it would serve his own interest to prevent violence. Those who accused King of deliberately inciting violence neglect Young's efforts, undertaken at King's bidding, to head off all the trouble that he could—"I sent telegrams to the FBI telling them just what we were going to do, so there would be no surprises or misunderstandings."

When King went to jail, he took Ralph Abernathy with him, and Hosea Williams. Young was asked to be the outside man, explaining and negotiating. He went to jail only three times (one more than Jesse Jackson). I asked if he felt left out because of this. "No. The civil rights movement was no romantic thing for me. I treated it like a business. I was no adolescent, after all; I was married, with three children." Young was only three years younger than King—an elder statesman to those who left college in order to join the sit-ins and the marches.

Yet if the civil rights movement had to be managed like a business, it was a business in which, Young says, "we all expected to die." I asked how he could do that with a young family of three children. "You believe in heaven," he answered straightforwardly, as if glancing toward the bottom of a ledger. "I've never thought death was the end. And Martin prepared us. He used to joke about it, telling me not to worry—if they killed me first, he'd preach me the best eulogy ever." King prepared his own children: "I talked to them the day after Martin was killed, and they had no bitterness toward his killer. They just said, 'He could not have known Daddy.' The very day he was killed we held a meeting to carry on the nonviolent movement, making plans for the Poor People's Campaign." Young partly blames the press for the explosion of nonproductive anger that followed King's assassination. People were not prepared, he thinks, to suffer without hatred. "There is a masochism in some whites. After every outrage they would come to us and say, 'Now are you ready to give up on nonviolence?' We were never going to give up on it."

Young would finally leave the SCLC, along with John Lewis, when it expelled James Bevel. "His [Bevel's] behavior was admittedly bizarre; but you don't give up on a brother who has risked his life with you over and over." (Young expressed no such concern when Jackson was suspended from the SCLC.)

It was as a United States congressman that Young campaigned for Jimmy Carter, and he became the principal architect of what will be seen, in retrospect, as Carter's major achievement: Carter was the first American president to take seriously the entire postcolonial era that has remade the globe since World War II. Inheriting the diplomacy of Kissinger, who saw all things in terms of the superpowers and referred to "the so-called third world," Carter recognized that it would be impossible to address developing nations so long as the United States possessed its own colonial outpost in the Panama Canal Zone. Young worked on the diplomacy leading to passage of the Panama treaties—but worked more visibly, as our UN ambassador, opening contacts with African and Arab nations, and with the whole third world.

Young and Jackson, who differ in so many ways, are agreed on one matter that will be of growing importance in the future—that the United States government's attitudes toward domestic minorities and toward the deprived areas of the globe are linked in multiple (if subtle) ways. A nation unconcerned about its own slums is unlikely to feel social responsibility for the third world, and vice versa. Some Americans feel threatened by the idea of an alliance between a black minority at home and a nonwhite majority of the earth's inhabitants. But a fellowship of the oppressed is bound to exist, especially in a country that offers itself as an embodiment of the proposition that all men are created equal. That was the nexus that Young's Congregationalist forebears perceived in their work with the *Amistad* Africans and the United States "missions" down south. In an age of television and other forms of instantaneous communications, freedom is infectious—as the Communist-bloc countries learned in the 1980s. We cannot talk one language, in this small world, for human dignity abroad and a different one for life in the inner cities of America. Young points out the meeting of domestic and foreign policy concerns in a very concrete instance: "It was impossible for us to wage war in favor of South Africa, given the number of blacks in our army."

Some would resent this as an inhibition on our government's freedom to make foreign policy. Young thinks of it, rather, as a reality control on what we can (or should) attempt. The presence of a black subclass whose needs are clamorous is an *opportunity* for coming to grips with a larger world in which *whites* are the minority.

Young sees no conflict—quite the opposite—between his advocacy of black rights in the 1960s and his diplomatic activities in the 1970s. Like Jackson, he ran into opposition from Israeli's supporters who think Palestinian longings for their own homeland are illegitimate. And, like Jackson, he would become especially objectionable when he dealt, even through intermediaries, with PLO leader Yasir Arafat. Jackson's embrace of Arafat, on meeting him, left behind a more vivid single image than did Young's informal meeting with PLO spokesmen. But Young's action set off even more alarm signals in the Jewish community, because of his position as ambassador to the UN. In fact, resentment against Young was so great in some quarters that he put off indefinitely any strong defense of his act.

That, of course, did not help assuage misgivings on the other side, among blacks. When Jackson created his 1984 troubles with "Hymietown" and Farrakhan, some blacks were quick to compare his treatment with Young's five years earlier. Both Jackson and Joseph Lowery, Ralph Abernathy's replacement at the head of the SCLC, had toured the Middle East shortly after Young's resignation, trying to talk with both sides, but rebuffed by Israelis *because* they were talking with Arabs. All this history was on the mind of Jackson's delegates in 1984:

> I was very pleased with Jackson's strong defense of Andrew Young. I thought that President Carter should have given Young more support. At bottom, I suppose, I abhor any policy that precludes talking with anyone, even your enemies. . . . Moreover, I was surprised and affronted when Israeli officials refused to meet with Jackson and other black civil rights leaders on their Middle East trip after Young's ouster. Whether they liked Jackson or not, he and the other black leaders did indeed represent a significant segment of the views of Black America and others as well. To me, Jackson was not just any person; he was one who commanded more respect and decency than Israeli officials accorded.[2]

Young had established, at his confirmation hearings, that he took his office as an opportunity for creative diplomacy. When Senator Dick Clark of Iowa asked if, as ambassador to the UN, he would "avoid a veto by working out with other countries issues in advance of the vote," he said:

"I think one of the most valuable opportunities that the United Nations affords is the opportunity to communicate informally with a large number of the nations of the world on a moment's notice." Young says he was thinking, at that time, about representatives of Vietnam, unrecognized by America, though Secretary of State Cyrus Vance was encouraging further contacts. But when it came time to do exactly what Senator Clark had encouraged—prevent an unproductive American veto by informal talks beforehand—Young was arguing a procedural matter, delaying a vote, with a recognized (if nonvoting) PLO delegation to the UN *during the month when Young was acting president of the Security Council.* It is absurd to be the president of a body without the power to communicate with delegates to that body. Because Young did not meet the PLO representative by direct appointment or in secret—nor, as Jimmy Carter's memoirs have it, in his own suite—but in a contrived accident set up by representatives of other countries, news of the meeting was soon in those countries' cable traffic. When Young realized that, he went to Israel's UN ambassador to explain that the delay was in Israel's interest—without it, America could have been maneuvered into the veto of a proposal that included PLO recognition of UN Resolution 242. He now says, "The Israelis misinterpreted what I did, because they read it in conjunction with other meetings that I was unaware of—they thought the State Department was trying to signal a change in policy."

The popular memory is that Young had to leave because he lied about this meeting to the State Department—but the truth is almost exactly the opposite of that. The State Department pretended it did not know what was in the cable traffic, and tried to get Young to back an evasive statement of that pretense. Young refused. As Wolf Blitzer, the Washington correspondent for the *Jerusalem Post*, wrote at the time:

> Young told Assistant Secretary of State for International Organizations, William Maynes, the truth about the exact nature of the meeting when first questioned about it on August 11. But the State Department decided to cover up. . . . The entire matter probably would have blown over if Young—having told his bosses the truth—had gone along with the State Department's lie. Instead, for whatever reason, Young confided to the Israeli ambassador at the UN, Yehuda Blum, that the "official" version was not true. . . .[3]

When I read Young that and other excerpts from Blitzer's article, he confirmed them.

If Young had not left office, President Carter might have been saved from the major mistake of his presidency, the admission of the Shah of Iran to the United States. Young was well acquainted with the sensibilities of Arab and other nations to our meddling in the government of Iran, and he was perfectly willing to stand up to Zbigniew Brzezinski and others who wanted to admit the Shah. Nor was he as condescending toward medicine in the third world as those who thought the Shah could not be treated in Mexico.

Even after the American hostages were taken, in retaliation for Carter's insensitive act, Young's first instinct was to prevent a hysterical preoccupation with the hostages—a reaction fed by television networks and by President Carter. Carter said he could not campaign for reelection because of full-time engagement with the hostage problem—which was, for a while, the best way of campaigning, though not of governing. I talked with Young during that period, and asked what he would advise Carter if he were still in the administration. "When Iran demanded an apology from the United States, we should have printed up thousands of copies of the Church Committee's report [on the CIA's overthrow of Mossadegh in 1953], to show we do not have to wait for others to point out our errors." If the president had taken that attitude, he could have made a case that the Shah's contacts with America were the result of humanitarian concern rather than political plotting. The real Iranian fear—that we were preparing the Shah for return to Iran—would have been undercut. But Carter created a political atmosphere in which—as Senator Kennedy learned during the 1980 primaries—no one could say anything against the Shah without being accused of "giving in" to Khomeini. Carter's highlighting of the captives' plight backfired when the crisis he was nurturing dragged on for a year, and forced him toward his desperate rescue raid, which foundered at its desert relay point.

Young is philosophical about criticisms of his UN days. He thinks it is a good thing that Jewish advocacy at home engages Americans in foreign policy—that is precisely what Young hopes for from black identification with third world countries. When I suggest that Jewish lobbying for Israel is more effective than black efforts for the poor, either here or abroad, he shrugs: "The Jews' influence in foreign affairs is highly visible because concentrated [on Israel]. If black interest centered on just one country in Africa, it would be clear that we have power, even now." When Young went on to election as the mayor of Atlanta in 1981, he used municipal office to encourage international trade, spending so much time abroad that his critics called him an absentee official. Yet his travels produced enough business contracts to justify the efforts he obviously found congenial. He is as deep a believer in capitalist answers to poverty as Jesse Jackson is. And neither sees blacks as limited to a client status in America.

Young refused so adamantly to be represented as a spokesman for black interests alone that some blacks in Atlanta thought he was insufficiently protective of them. In fact, when I went to interview Young in the early eighties, a black cabman histrionically shuddered when I gave him the address of city hall: "I don't like that place. Too many preachers there." I asked if everyone in the administration was a preacher. "Just about. Or lay deacons, just as bad."

"Tough preachers, though: They went to jail a lot."

"That's the trouble. They're trying to put everyone else in jail just because they went."

Inside the preachers' den, I repeated this conversation to Young. "Yeah," he says, "but we went to jail for doing right." When I ask about the driver's hostility, he frowns: "We had to discipline the taxi industry. It used to be made up of Atlantans, but when it became big business, with a lot of strangers ignorant of the city, we had to crack down." He is being diplomatic about *drivers'* ignorance of the city. They counted too much on their passengers' ignorance, driving them by such round-about routes from the airport that a fixed rate had to be imposed on them.

Some Atlantans claimed that theirs was a city where outsiders drive outsiders around. For those Southerners who think in generations, even their mayor was an outsider. Atlanta was becoming an international city, a fate Southerners lamented even as they totaled their profits. Atlanta is itself a latecomer to the South, incorporated a mere seventeen years before Sherman burnt it to the ground, giving it an instant history. Natives have been simultaneously exploiting and erasing the past ever since.

One of the first things an international city must worry about is safe streets. Muggings are all right, among friends, but rich visitors have to be protected. Andrew Young, who for years conducted campaigns to break the law, became a law-and-order mayor. On his first day in office, he met with every police officer on the downtown beat and promised his support. There were complaints, as he took office, of sexual harassment on the city streets. Within a week of his inauguration, undercover female officers arrested fifty-four people in two days for lascivious overtures. Young made inner-city cops more mobile by putting them on motor scooters. During his first year in office the crime rate fell six percentage points, the murder rate fell sixteen points, though the crack epidemic shot up violent crime statistics by the end of the eighties.

Young, his days of civil disobedience long behind him, is as insistent on law and order as Jackson when he campaigns against drugs and alcohol in the high schools. Both men call for black discipline even as they try to extend black influence on American policy. New England's Congregationalist tradition and the South's Baptist tradition unite to offer Americans another chance at forging a single nation of America, at realizing the Union for which Lincoln said the entire community undertook its expiatory labors in the Civil War.

What Did Jesse Want?

THOMAS JEFFERSON CONTRASTED HIS EXUBERANT SOUTH WITH THE CAL-
culating North of his contemporaries. July 4, 1988, was a night for
reversing those stereotypes, at least so far as the candidates' wives were
concerned. Kitty Dukakis, the hostess of the evening, is an impulsive
person, brittle but with a show-biz brashness. Kitty Carlisle Hart was her
godmother, part of the theater scene she grew up in as the daughter of
a musician.

Jacqueline (Jackie) Jackson, by contrast, is a Southerner of great restraint, style, and dignity. She exudes a certain formality, like the preacher's wife she is. She brought her five children up with the manners of
the South (saying "Yes, ma'am" and "No, ma'am"), in a home where
parental authority was emphasized. The Dukakis home was unconventional, Kitty acting almost as a pal to her children while her husband
did the shopping, cooking, and counseling of his two daughters and his
adopted son (by Kitty's former marriage).

Relations between these two families had been strained throughout the
primary season, as Jackson refused to concede defeat though running
behind Dukakis on Tuesday after Tuesday. Some claimed this gave Du-

kakis an advantage, since the New England liberal was made to look moderate by comparison with Jackson, and interest was sustained on the Democrats' side long after Bush had the Republican nomination sewed up.

But Jackson was considered a potential troublemaker by old-line Democrats, who thought he had made unacceptable demands on Mondale in 1984, keeping people in suspense before his conciliatory speech at the convention. The more delegates Jackson picked up in the 1988 primaries, the greater his capacity for making mischief in Atlanta. Dukakis wanted a clear promise that Jackson would accept the results of the nominating process, and he did not want to make reciprocal pledges, which would be represented as "caving in" on his part. He held Jackson at arm's length—and even then Lee Atwater tried to say Jackson would be the silent partner in the White House if Dukakis won. Jackson was not quite Willie Horton in Atwater's view, but close enough to be used as a brush for tarring the Democrats.

So Jackson's aides thought Dukakis was making a concession when—in the interval between the primaries and the convention, at a time when jockeying for the vice-presidential choice was at its height—Dukakis invited the Jacksons to have dinner with him and Kitty at their home. This was considered a breakthrough on the personal level, where the two men had not communicated through all the backstage joshing of the early debates. Dukakis tends to freeze when personal banter is being exchanged, and Jackson had to check his impulse to tease his robotic opponent. Dukakis's staff did not even like to see their man stand close to Jackson since he was dwarfed by Jackson's height. The Dukakis people were always touchy on the question of their leader's stature. They slipped little platforms under him when he went to the podium. During a debate before the Congressional Black Caucus in Washington they told Congressman Gus Savage to pull this platform out whenever Dukakis came to the microphone. Once, when Savage forgot to move the platform after Dukakis sat down, Jackson followed him to the podium, looked quizzically at the riser, stood up on it for a moment (towering above the microphone), and cracked: "I've waited years for equal standing."

Moments like that did not endear Jackson to a man who, according to his *Boston Globe* observers, "had trouble in his career forging relationships with black people who weren't lawyers or doctors or college professors."[1] This general difficulty was sharpened, in Jackson's case, by the clash between Dukakis's narrowly secular background and Jackson's easy use of preacher talk. If ever the two could make contact, it would be in a private meeting of the sort Dukakis had set up, with no press or staff present, just the two couples.

Yet things went wrong from the outset. The Jacksons were expecting to be met at the airport with transportation, and they arrived late at the Dukakises' Brookline home. That put scheduling pressure on the meal, since the hosts wanted to take their guests to hear the Boston Pops and see holiday fireworks. Jackson thought his staff had alerted the Dukakis people that he does not eat milk products; but, by a weird happenstance, almost everything served had a milk base—New England clam chowder, poached salmon with cream sauce and peas, chocolate tart and ice cream.

Jackson wanted to engage in serious talk about political strategy, about the vice-presidency and the campaign ahead. When he broached the matter, a Dukakis daughter joined the conversation over dessert. The Dukakises thought they were doing their duty if they invited the Jacksons for a social evening. The Jacksons took this as patronizing. Mrs. Jackson, a short woman, can be quite lofty in manner when she thinks her husband is not being taken seriously. Kitty's hot informality further chilled responses from Jackie. The symbolic gestures of the evening were all too clearly lacking in substance.

Jackson is a shrewd political maneuverer; yet the Mondale campaign never seriously sought his advice in 1984. He was treated as an outsider. He was not included among those publicly considered for the vice-presidency (some of whom were included just to please certain constituencies). Then, to make it obvious that he was an outsider, Jackson learned—in the presence of the press—about the selection of Geraldine Ferraro only when the public announcement was made. That galled Jackson, and he let Paul Brountas of the Dukakis staff know that he did not want it to happen again. Brountas warmly assured him it would not—and then it did. The staffer who was supposed to call Jackson about the Lloyd Bentsen choice, Susan Estrich, claims the neglect was accidental; but she did not seem displeased at the accident. She was one of those who advised against "caving in" to any Jackson demands.

Democratic party pros tend to talk of their "Jackson problem," seeing nothing but menace in a candidate feared by centrists, people Dukakis hoped to woo with a nonideological pitch based on "competence." But Jackson had proved, just as the presidential campaign was beginning in 1987, that he could function well in a coalition. He helped lobby Southern senators on the battle over confirmation of President Reagan's nominee for the Supreme Court, Robert H. Bork, in a political victory for liberals that was unexpected and should have set a pattern for the Democrats' campaign the next year.

The very possibility of defeating Bork arose in part from Jackson's voter registration drive in the 1984 campaign. He had taken blacks direct from his rallies to the registrar—often, direct from a church service. Over a million new black voters were added in Southern states alone. It was said that black registration would just lead to countervailing increases among whites. Andrew Young, who praised Jackson's registration drive, said: "I hope it will. Most of the white middle class is already registered, so the bulk of new voters will be poor people, and they will not be Reagan supporters. The trickle-down never trickled down to them." In fact, black registration of new voters exceeded that of whites in eleven Southern states. In nine of those, blacks registered twice as many new voters as whites did:

> NBC News found that in the Georgia and Florida primaries [of 1984], 20 percent of the black voters had registered within the previous six months. And a CBS News/New York *Times* survey found that from 4 to 11 percent of all black voters were voting for the first time.[2]

These were the voters who showed up again in 1986, even though new voters tend not to participate a second time, and even though 1986 was a presidential off year. Young blacks actually voted in greater percentages than young whites in the key Southern states, where five Democratic seats were gained in the Senate, restoring control of that chamber to Democrats. Jackson deserves some credit for the fact that Democrats would be chairing the confirmation process for Judge Bork. As he says: "We did it [blocked Bork] under the chairmanship of Senator Biden. We couldn't have done it under the chairmanship of Senator Thurmond." So Jackson helped set the stage for the Bork confirmation struggle. As Senator Howell Heflin told Jackson: "We don't want to do anything to discourage the new votuhs [i.e., newly registered blacks]."

The Bork defeat was a pivotal event in recent political history, for the reason that Bork gives in his book on the transaction: "This nomination became the focal point of the war within our culture."[3] Bork presents himself as the target of "a left-liberal culture in near despair" because its members "dislike this society," in which a George Bush can prevail "on the symbolic cultural and class issues of the pledge of allegiance and the Governor's [Dukakis's] pride in being a 'card-carrying member of the ACLU.' "[4] Bork was not able to prevail, as Bush did over Dukakis, because the liberal Left, which he describes as a minority despairing of electoral influence, was somehow able to mount "an enormous coalition" of people willing and able to distort his record, to advance their program of "sexual permissiveness," nihilism, and "subversion of the law's foundations."[5]

Though Bork refers throughout his book to the cultural war being waged over his head, he offers himself as an innocent victim strayed onto the battlefield, a nonpolitical legal technician caught in the ideological crossfire. As he writes of his nomination to the United States Court of Appeals in 1981:

> President Reagan has been accused of appointing judges with a political agenda, but that was most certainly not the case. He was committed to the idea that judges should not make up law but should interpret law. [Attorney General] William French Smith barely knew me and had no idea of my personal views on most of the divisive issues of the time, but he knew that my idea of judging corresponded to his and Reagan's.[6]

If the attorney general knew little of Judge Bork's views, he was more drastically ill informed than even his critics could know. Bork had been a hero to the right wing ever since he gave Barry Goldwater arguments against the civil rights bill in the 1964 campaign.[7] It was very late in the day for Bork and his followers to present him as a moderate, "in the mainstream," an appropriate follower to Justice Lewis Powell in the swing position *between* Court factions.[8] Bork had cultivated a reputation as a gadfly, one who would *defy* the mainstream. In 1971, defending the Court's older decisions against free speech, he said his argument would have "at least the charm of complete novelty," since he was taking a view "completely undercut, or at least abandoned" by the Court.[9] Ronald Dworkin rightly said that Bork was not a conservative, in his views on the judiciary, but a radical, and he had become more, not less radical, in his views over time.[10]

When Bork came into public view as a critic of the Warren Court, it was on fairly limited grounds—that Warren was hurting the Court's reputation by his partisanship, that his Court advanced no general principle for its actions, that it did even the right thing (e.g., the school desegregation decision) less for the wrong reason than for no reason. In those days, as Bork confesses, he did not limit his views to an "original intent" view of the Constitution. In fact, he wrote, in a *New Republic* attack on civil rights decisions: "Heretical though it may sound to the constitutional sages, neither the Constitution nor the Supreme Court qualifies as a first principle."[11] He proposed, instead, a presumption in favor of citizen autonomy.

Five years later, and again three years after that, Bork had a new rationale for attacking the Warren Court, one he also abandoned in time—that Court's failure to find a neutral principle for its decisions. He was still maintaining that "we cannot solve our problems simply by reference to the text or to its history."[12] Sometime after 1971 Bork took up his third (and lasting) norm for disagreeing with the Warren Court. Yet under these shifting criteria the stable thing was his criticism of "liberal" decisions. What happened, however, as Bork kept looking for better weapons against these outcomes was that he called into question more and more of the Court's decisions, reaching farther and farther back, until his 1990 book argues, essentially, that the Supreme Court has been a "runaway institution" from the time of John Marshall. The "subversion" of the Court does not date from the Warren years, or even from the New Deal time.

Marshall is partly excused for laying "an intellectual foundation for judicial supremacy," since the nation was young and may have needed a strong central institution, but Marshall "argued, quite incorrectly," for his views, in moves "none of [which] made much sense."[13] Later in the nineteenth century, Chief Justice Roger Taney invented substantive due process, one of the most destructive instruments of the modern Court: "Substantive due process, wherever it appears, is never more than a pretense that the judge's views are in the Constitution. That has been true from *Dred Scott* to today."[14]

In 1874, in the *Loan Association* decision, the Court adopted views that (Bork claims)

> would convert the government into a "judicial despotism"; in some degree, it has. The despotism is selective; it does not operate on all subjects of life all of the time. But it is there, ready to hand, when judges feel strongly enough.[15]

Marshall's judicial supremacy of 1803 had become judicial despotism by 1874. There seemed nowhere to go but down; and that happened, in a plunge. The *Allgeyer* decision in 1897 gave us official "lawlessness," and the 1905 *Lochner* case amounted to "judicial usurpation." The Court then erred, not only in defending the minimum wage, but in striking down state laws that forbade teaching foreign languages, where it used standards "wholly without limits, as well as without legitimacy."[16] New Deal measures, when at last defended by the Court, meant that "due process protection of economic liberties has never returned."[17]

And so, at last, Bork reaches the symbol of perfidy with which he began, the Warren Court, the desegregating Court. But even the Burger and Rehnquist Courts continue the "runaway" course of history. In fact, the Burger Court was guilty of *Roe* v. *Wade*, "the greatest example and symbol of the judicial usurpation of democratic prerogatives in this century."[18] The Rehnquist Court has proved that "the drive of judicial revisionism has by no means ended" in its defense of flag burners and dial-a-porn.[19]

Why would Bork want to join such a corrupted and corrupting institution, whose erroneous decisions he disagreed with in so many areas— free speech, abortion, women's rights, desegregation, civil rights, pornography, one-man-one-vote, affirmative action, and others? He gave his right-wing supporters the obvious motive—to *end* the judicial distortion, usurpation, and despotism. To the Philadelphia Society he said, just three months before his nomination:

> It may take ten years, it may take twenty years, for the second wave to crest, but crest it will and it will sweep the elegant, erudite, pretentious, and toxic detritus of non-originalism out to sea.[20]

Shortly before that he told the Federalist Society:

> An originalist judge would have no problem whatever in overhauling a non-originalist precedent because that *precedent*, by the very basis of his judicial philosophy, *has no legitimacy.* [Italics added.][21]

When a tape of Bork was played at his nomination hearing, the Senate Judiciary Committee heard him tell a college audience in 1985:

> I don't think that in the field of constitutional law precedent is all that important. . . . If you become convinced that a prior court has misread the Constitution, I think it's your *duty* to go back and correct it. . . . I don't think precedent is all that important. I think the importance is what the framers were driving at, and to *go back* to that. [Italics added.][22]

Bork claimed this was an ill-considered extempore remark, not representing what he really thought. But then what does one make of his 1987 remarks, saying the same thing, to the Philadelphia Society and Federalist Society? He was lying to someone—to the conservatives who believed he would overthrow "judicial despotism," or to the Senate committee when he said he would not overthrow precedent. Right-wingers at the time thought he was lying to them, that they were knocking themselves out to elect a moderate. "Why go to the mat for him?" asked Pat Robertson. "Who cares about moderates?" said Richard Viguerie of *The Conservative Digest*. What happened to the message that the Court was astray? asked Bruce Fein of the Heritage Foundation.[23]

But his subsequent book proved that Bork was lying to the senators when he denied any intent to reform the Court. In the book he is free to speak his mind again, as he would have been on the Court. His brief unnatural time of moderation passed, as quickly as it had arisen, when he had no more occasion for it. In the culture war he refers to in his book, he was a major figure on one side, promoted by his allies to blunt or reverse all the decisions that had offended them, every one of which he had criticized somewhere.

The service Bork performed for his enemies was to draw up, around him, all those who had reason to fear the overthrow of decisions he had attacked. Women were concerned with his refusal to think of discrimination against them as unconstitutional. Blacks and other minorities feared his civil rights and affirmative action stands. Believers in the separation of church and state knew what he thought about prayer in schools and other religious expressions by official bodies.[24] Union leaders knew of his comments against business regulation, going back to the New Deal measures. Free speech advocates feared his view that only expressly political speech is constitutionally protected. Those concerned with abortion, privacy, and gay rights came forward. The resulting coalition was, in Bork's own words, "enormous." Four members of the American Bar Association rating panel pronounced him "not qualified." Two thousand law professors and thirty-two law school deans wrote against his confirmation. The ACLU and Common Cause voted to abandon their historical neutrality on specific nominees.[25] The National Council of Churches opposed Bork, as did black church groups, consumer groups, environmentalists. He had set up a magnetic field in which all kinds of disparate interests arranged themselves like metal filings in a dense hedge around him. They formed a counterpattern to what was called the "moral majority"—only they made up, in the polls, a plurality greater than the so-called majority could muster. After Bork's appearance at the hearings, "all polls were decisively against confirmation."[26]

The people who worked together against Bork were just those elements that were supposed to pull against and defeat each other in the Democratic party's makeup. Ann Lewis, the party official and lobbyist who worked in the anti-Bork movement, noted that the judge was done in by Jesse Jackson's "rainbow coalition." As Jackson had said three years earlier in San Francisco:

If blacks vote in great numbers, progressive whites win. It is the only way progressive whites win. If blacks vote in great numbers, Hispanics win. When blacks, Hispanics and progressive whites vote, women win. When women win, children win. When women and children win, workers win. We must all come together.

The communities that formed ranks against Bork were the real moral majority in America. They made up what George Will contemptuously but accurately called a "compassion industry," and by the end they included even most evangelicals.[27] They discerned Bork's coarseness toward minorities and the disadvantaged. This came out in his 1963 article against forcing barbers or chiropodists to deal with blacks, on what Bork called "a principle of unsurpassed ugliness." Bork attacked the sit-ins as undertaken by "a mob coercing and disturbing other private individuals in the exercise of their freedom." At his hearing, he claimed he had repented of this article; but in his subsequent book he defends it with new arguments, saying blacks unhappy with segregation in the South could have moved to the North rather than break the law.[28] This concept of immigration as a remedy for unjust law was demolished, two centuries ago, by David Hume:

Can we seriously say that a poor peasant or artisan has a free choice to leave his country when he knows no foreign language or manners and lives from day to day, by the small wages he acquires? We may as well assert that a man, by remaining on a vessel, freely consents to the dominion of the master, though he was carried on board while asleep and must leap into the ocean and must perish the moment he leaves her.[29]

Bork's unconcern about blacks was equaled by his callousness toward the sterilization of women as a work condition: "I suppose that they were glad to have the choice."[30]

The moral bond of those opposing Bork was just what Jackson said could unite people: Recognizing the justice of other people's claims, the disparate groups validated their own and made a common impact possible.

Farmers, you seek fair prices and you are right, but you cannot stand alone. Your patch is not big enough. Workers, you fight for fair wages. You are right. But your patch, labor, is not big enough. Women, you seek comparable worth and pay equity. You are right. But your patch is not big enough. Women, mothers, who seek Head Start and day care and prenatal care on the front side of life, rather than welfare and jail care on the back side of life, you're right, but your patch is not big enough. Students, you seek scholarships. You are right. But your patch is not big enough. African Americans and Hispanics, when we fight for civil rights, we are right, but our patch is not big enough. Gays and lesbians, when you fight against discrimination and for a cure for AIDS, you are right, but your patch is not big enough. Conservatives and progressives, when you fight for what you believe, right-wing, left-wing, hawk, dove—you are right from your point of view, but your point of view is not enough. But don't despair. Be as wise as my grandmama. Pool the patches and the pieces together, bound by a common thread. When we form a great quilt of unity and common ground, we'll have the power to bring about health care and housing and jobs and education and hope to our nation.[31]

Ann Lewis became a consultant to Jackson in 1988. As a Jew, she overcame misgivings about the Farrakhan tie, feeling it was less important, by that year, than the appeal to a large coalition of exactly the sort that had defeated Judge Bork. She could not fully anticipate (though she came from Massachusetts) the discomfort Michael Dukakis felt with moral appeals. He shied by temperament from "ideological" groups like those in the rainbow of concerns arrayed against Bork. He would campaign on "competence." The man who could not get heated when asked to contemplate his wife's hypothetical rape and murder was not liable to borrow rhetorical fire from a preacher. His personal discomfort with Jackson was backed by the advice of party pros, who think of minorities, causes, and liberal interest groups as embarrassments to the Democrats, not as potential advantages. In appealing to the middle, they decided to show their unhappiness at Jackson's theatrical ways. They thought they could play down their party's dependence on blacks—as if no one would notice it. Given the role blacks have to play in Democratic victories—and that they *did* play in the 1986 election of five Southern senators—the wiser course would be to assure people that concern for minorities does not threaten the majority. Jackson was able to do that, in his own person and campaign, for only 10 percent of whites, the number who voted for him in the 1988 primaries. But others, working with Jackson in the general campaign, had a better chance of making that case than of convincing people that blacks could be ignored if Democrats won—which was the message Dukakis forces tried to convey. One cannot build a moral majority on the insensitive attitudes Susan Estrich gloried in, trying to show how tough she could be with Jackson.

The party leaders need to have some of the creativity, in dealing with potentially dissident elements, that Jackson showed when he called for black support of a ticket that included Lloyd Bentsen. Speaking to his own restless delegates after the 1988 convention, he said:

I've had to learn the science of politics. I've watched it from its many angles. I'm often asked, what does the Lloyd Bentsen wing of the ticket mean to me? I tell you what it means. It represents a wing. We represent a wing. It takes two wings to fly. When all is said and done, hawks and doves are just birds. As long as they fly the same air, they cannot afford to have their air poisoned by pollution. What does Bentsen being on the ticket mean to me in practical terms? It means that the contras have lost a vote [in the Senate]. It means D.C. statehood has gained a vote. It means Mandela has gained an ally. And so, my friends, in this process we're transformed. We've become bigger people, better people. [32]

Though Jackson won only 10 percent of the white vote for himself in 1988, that was an achievement won against many disadvantages. As he said, his was the poorest campaign in terms of money. In Iowa, he won only 9 percent of the white vote statewide; but he won 18 percent in the caucuses where he had organizers. He won 60 percent in the Greenfield area where he made his headquarters and spent most time.

Blacks in general are only 10 percent of the voting population, but in certain urban and regional areas they are a majority. Taken overall, Democrats need them in ways that far outweigh their mere number. Democrats must combine white majorities and black minorities in some areas, black majorities and white minorities in others. As Jackson likes to say, "everybody counts." The Democratic party has the burden of the less privileged among its constituency. If the party treats them as a burden, it is hampered by self-fulfilling prophecies. But if it means truly to represent the disadvantaged, it will find that most groups in America think of themselves as disadvantaged in one way or another. This feeling issues in grievance, in a politics of resentment, on the Republican side, where it is felt that minorities are getting more than their share of society's goods—an unreal complaint from the comparatively privileged, but a powerful one. The answer to this challenge is not to debate comparative grievances but to see where they overlap instead of conflicting. They overlapped in visible ways for those opposing Bork. They overlap less obviously, but just as really, in the electoral marketplace of our time. One can find unity in suffering, as Lincoln did, rather than disunity, as Lee Atwater did.

Jesse Jackson is able to make groups look less menacing to each other. He has spent years walking on picket lines, going to farm closings, AIDS hospices, churches, schools. Most politicians are uneasy when they have to put on campaign headgear, and take it off as soon as possible—Dukakis backers bristled when Marion Barry put a farm hat on their man at the

Dukakis-Jackson press conference in Atlanta. But Jackson, given a cap early in the day, wore it the rest of the day. "This is not a campaign hat for me," he said. "This is my regular hat."

At a time when whole segments of our country are marked off as dead zones, battle scenes of crime and lost souls, Jackson was the only politician who could not only enter such sites but stay there, talk there, make sense. What will happen to this country if no one can do that? Keeping hope alive is a matter of the whole society's health. Jackson cannot do it by himself. The Dukakis campaign needlessly hampered itself when it thought it could do so without Jackson.[33] Over and over skeptical observers asked of Jackson, "What does he want?" His followers saw that as implicitly racist: What is a *black* doing running for president? It never seemed to occur to them that he was doing exactly what white politicians were doing. As Rev. Billy Kyles said in 1983: "People did not keep asking why John Kennedy ran." Jackson wants what all politicians do—he wants up, he wants attention and the limelight, he wants fame and flattery. But his way up is from the margins, with the help of marginal people, the "embarrassment" to other Democrats, the problem constituencies. Still, the Democrats' "problems" can be worse trouble for other people. Ask Judge Bork.

PART SIX

Politics and Pornography

◇ T W E N T Y = F O U R ◇

"With Ladies Present"

NO LEGAL THEORIST HAS BEEN SUCH A FRIEND TO CENSORSHIP AS ROBERT Bork. Outside the confirmation hearing room he has been characteristically blunt: "Moral outrage is a sufficient ground for prohibitory legislation."[1] The First Amendment does not enter into the question for Bork:

> Constitutional protection should be accorded only to speech that is explicitly political. There is no basis for judicial intervention to protect any other form of expression, be it scientific, literary, or that variety of expression we call obscene or pornographic. Moreover, within that category of speech we ordinarily call political, there should be no constitutional obstruction to laws making criminal any speech that advocates forcible overthrow of the government or the violation of any law.[2]

Bork backed partway off from that position, but only in a grudging way. It would be hard to enforce, he admitted, if "almost any speech could be made protected by simply adding a policy proposal at the end."[3] He still thinks scientific and literary speech is not covered by the First Amendment; but the Court would be helpless against any modern Galileo willing to append, to any cosmological treatise, an attack on imperialism. Of course, if the Galileo in question neglects or refuses to do that little dance at the end, he remains fair game for the ban imposers, so far as Bork is concerned.

Another of Judge Bork's views, repeatedly argued in connection with the *Griswold* (contraception) case, is very useful to modern opponents of pornography. These censors have tried for years to prove that pornography incites to crime—that it creates two victims, first (directly) the inflamed audience of the pornographic depictions, and then (indirectly) the objects of these ignited people's depredations. Defenders of pornography have denied the link between viewing sexual acts and committing them. The evidence is so far inconclusive; and since the burden of proof lies with those alleging the tie, this part of the war on pornography has not been very successful.

Bork has an ingenious solution to this problem—the victim of pornography, in his argument, is the person who never sees or wants to see it:

> No activity that society thinks immoral is victimless. Knowledge that an activity is taking place is a harm to those who find it profoundly immoral.[4]

How am I "harmed" by knowing that, somewhere or other, someone or other (I cannot know who) is allowed to view pornography? I am being denied something I want (namely to prevent others from acting in ways I disapprove of); the pain inflicted on me is my loss of "moral gratification." The desire of others to do a thing, and my desire that they not do it, are treated with surreal equity once Bork is allowed to structure the matter this way:

> Every clash between a minority claiming freedom and a majority claiming power to regulate involves a choice between the gratification of the two groups . . . [and] why is sexual gratification more worthy than moral gratification?[5]

Common sense would suggest that a person has a greater claim over his or her own act than over those of others. But Bork makes the pornographer's act somehow *belong* to the person who would *ban* it, by a kind of imperial gaze—I *annex* the activity as part of my gratification (or the denial thereof). This tortuous argument suggests that Ronald Dworkin and Philip Kurland were right when they suggested that Bork lacks a real legal theory, that his views are simply configured to right-wing preoccupations.[6] His treatment of baffled censors as victims was perfectly responsive to the anguish many feel over modern society's permissiveness.

This anguish was, at one level, a concern for children brought up as no others have been—exposed from birth to the libidinous solicitings of modern advertisements, sitting for hours before a TV screen convulsed with violence, sealed off from their elders behind a wall of blaring sound. It was not only the Jerry Falwells who lamented this form of socialization. Professor Allan Bloom's 1987 best-seller, *The Closing of the American Mind,* convinced many people that a whole generation had been conditioned to "nonstop, commercially prepackaged masturbational fantasy."[7] Pornography, having "slipped its leash," was now the dominant form of the youth culture.[8] As a result of this drenching in the sensual, society was coming unstuck. Its basic elements were undergoing a meltdown: "The women's movement is not founded on nature. . . . Its crucial contention is that biology should not be destiny, and biology is surely natural."[9] Phyllis Schlafly and others were able to defeat the Equal Rights Amendment by convincing people that it meant to erase all difference between the sexes.[10] Sexual differences, these people argue, are being erased by a coalition of feminists and gays, by what Midge Decter has called the "propaganda of homosexuals" built into modern cultural comment, by celebrations of "the joys of buggery" (as Hilton Kramer puts it).[11] The whole nation is committing what George Gilder calls "sexual suicide."[12] When AIDS appeared in the gay community, Jerry Falwell and Pat Buchanan were not the only ones pronouncing it a doom upon sinners. Norman Podhoretz thought that extra funds devoted to the disease by government would be "a kind of AIDS in the moral and spiritual realm," signaling the society's willingness to "allow them [homosexual men] to resume buggering each other with complete medical impunity."[13]

Judge Bork, too, has been concerned for a long time that government, by its tolerance, might express some approval for homosexuality. He first became actively involved in campus politics at Yale when discrimination against homosexuals became an issue in 1978. In a memo he circulated to the faculty, he argued that "societies can have very small or very great amounts of homosexual behavior, depending upon the degrees of moral disapproval or tolerance shown."[14] He was anxious that failure to retain antisodomy laws would signal some "right to homosexual conduct."[15] He repeats this concern in his 1990 book.[16] And then he adds: "It has never been thought, until the rampant individualism of the modern era, that all individuals are entitled, as a matter of constitutional right, to engage in any form of sexual activity that appealed to them."[17]

Though Bork wants to use the law to signal social disapproval, he objects when others try to remove the opprobrium of a law against conduct they approve of. For the private-use-of-contraceptives case (*Griswold* v. *Connecticut*, 1965), Bork not only invented his "moral gratification" theory; he denied that the plaintiffs were justified in challenging the law. Since "there was, of course, no prospect that it would ever be enforced," those who brought a test case were just making a statement about "cultural values," and "the upshot was a new constitutional doctrine [privacy] perfectly suited, and later used, to enlist the Court on the side of moral relativism in sexual matters."[18]

Bork uses the same argument against those who challenged the anti-sodomy law of Georgia (*Bowers* v. *Hardwick*, 1986). This, again, was "one more sortie in our cultural war," since "Hardwick was in no greater danger of prosecution than any heterosexual."[19] Gays have no real grievance if laws against them exist but are not enforced. But in his Yale memorandum, one of the justifications he gave for discrimination against gays was the existence of state laws against their activities.[20]

Though Bork admits that there are arguments against retaining unenforced laws on the books, he thinks it is useful to retain them, nonetheless, as expressions of moral opprobrium, as a proclamation of "the right of society to impose moral standards."[21] He would not entirely return to the religious basis of America's first antisodomy laws, the death penalty in Leviticus 20.13, as enforced in the Massachusetts Bay Colony:

He was this year [1642] detected of buggery, and indicted for the same, with a mare, a cow, two goats, five sheep, two calves and a turkey. Horrible it is to mention, but the truth of the history requires it. He was first discovered by one that accidentally saw his lewd practice toward the mare. (I forbear particulars.) Being upon it examined and committed, in the end he not only confessed the fact with that beast at that time, but sundry times before and at several times with all the rest of the forenamed in his indictment. And this his free confession was not only in private to the magistrates (though at first he strived to deny it) but to sundry, both ministers and others; and afterwards, upon his indictment to the whole Court and jury; and confirmed it at his execution. And whereas some of the sheep could not so well be known by his description of them, others with them were brought before him and he declared which were they and which were not. And accordingly he was cast by the jury and condemned, and after executed about the 8th of September, 1642. A very sad spectacle it was. For first the mare and then the cow and the rest of the lesser cattle were killed before his face, according to the law, Leviticus XX.15; and then he himself was executed. The cattle were all cast into a great and large pit that was digged of purpose for them, and no use made of any part of them.[22]

Even the Bork supporters who want America to retain its religious heritage do not want to go back quite so far as that.

But others, the critics of attempts to police private sexuality, do think that our laws reflect, however distantly, the nation's Puritan origins. That misstates the case. For one thing, the account of the Massachusetts trial discredits the conception of "puritans" as squeamish and reticent, as practicers of what D. H. Lawrence called "the puritan hush! hush! which produces the sexual moron."[23] The Puritans of New England were brutally frank, in ways that would shock people misnamed for them in later ages.[24] Theirs was an open, scriptural morality enforced by literal investigations that would be hard to cover in family newspapers even now.[25] It was a society of trained male ministers and magistrates, with explicit theological arguments for its judgments.

What we think of as culturally "puritan" arose, with great rapidity, early in the nineteenth century. A cultural reticence began to inhibit open discussion. It was promoted largely in the name of women, who were considered inappropriate voices of the sexually specific. By 1831, when Alexis de Tocqueville came to America, matters of sex, morality, and the family were entrusted primarily to women, and to pastors who had themselves withdrawn from the making of public policy. Sexual morality was a private matter, extrapolitical, though enforced by social sanctions backed by the state:

> I do not question that the great austerity of manners that is observable in the United States arises, in the first instance, from religious faith. Religion is often unable to restrain man from the numberless temptations which chance offers; nor can it check that passion for gain which everything contributes to arouse; but its influence over the mind of women is supreme, and women are the protectors of morals. There is certainly no country in the world where the tie of marriage is more respected than in America or where conjugal happiness is more highly and worthily appreciated.[26]

There we can see, taking shape, the later division of nineteenth-century life into a feminine sphere (culture, morality, the family) and a masculine one (business, public affairs, government). What caused this rapid alignment? Ann Douglas argues that American culture was "feminized," in this period, by the change from a rugged New England orthodoxy to the softer views of what Henry James, Sr., called "a feeble Unitarian sentimentality."[27] But this change in elite views explains less than does the surge of democratic religiosity described by Nathan Hatch.[28] The censoring impulse is often populist, and connected with the anti-intellectual aspect of democracy.[29] These strands were manifest in revivalist and Holiness movements.

Tocqueville shrewdly analyzes the "female" domain of religion in Jacksonian democracy. It controls what is properly said "before the children" or "with ladies present." When men go outside the home, they retain their formal deference to the woman's "superior" values wherever the two domains touch. It does not matter that this deference is often feigned, since it is socially useful—as a cohesive force, working counter to individualism, a curb on the experimental and improvising drives of democracy.[30] There is a gentle satire playing underneath the worldly Frenchman's praise of American religiosity, as one can see in the deadpan connectives of a passage like this:

> One can assume that some proportion of the American population maintains its forms of worship more from convention than conviction. Yet religion, even taking that into account [d'ailleurs], is the highest value in the United States; and thus it follows [par conséquent] that hypocrisy is widespread; yet this is all the more reason [mais . . . pourtant encore] why the Christian religion has retained a greater hold on the spirit here than anywhere in the world, giving the best proof that religion is both useful and suitable to human nature, since [puisque] the country most enthralled by it is also the freest and most liberal.[31]

The ironies of that passage imply the later costs that could be paid for any "widespread hypocrisy" involved in male deference to a "female" religiosity.

These costs became apparent after the Civil War—which, like most wars, loosened morals. Social dislocation and temporary living arrangements, along with the previously unthinkable acts and expedients of a society organized to kill, call into question the settled mores of a society. Pornography first circulated widely during the war, and Anthony Comstock began his incredibly successful campaign against it in the postwar restoration of discipline. From his base in the Young Men's Christian Association, Comstock set up volunteer "vice societies" and became a bounty hunter for the post office. His efforts led to the banning not only of pornographic but educational publications dealing with contraception and abortion. In a grisly example of the "hold of religion on the spirit" described by Tocqueville, Comstock hounded a famous free-love advocate (Ida Craddock), pornographer (William Haynes), and abortionist (Madame Restell) to their suicides.[32]

Implicit in the situation described by Tocqueville was the claim that women, as custodians of morals, were too cloistered (i.e., too little experienced *and* too "good") for full participation in politics. This ideal of a useful class not fully active as citizens is hard to maintain in the twentieth century, when more intrusive education has taken children from the home's semimonopoly over their lives, and when women themselves have moved higher and higher in that educational process.

The right wing sees clearly the challenge of the women's movement to the whole social configuration praised (somewhat condescendingly) by Tocqueville. A vast structure of social inhibitions has been crumbling since World War I, and doing so with increased speed during the cold war. College education as the norm (rather than high school) makes it hard to treat women and children as a separate part of the community. The pervasiveness of new communications techniques—movies, radio, television, computers, FAX machines, videocassettes—brings the adult community of war, politics, and social problems (race, weaponry, disease) into the home as well as onto the old "male" marketplace.

Movies were policeable for a while, by the traditional guardians— especially by the Catholic church, whose disciplined schools, run by celibate priests and nuns, improbably maintained the cloister values of the nineteenth-century home in twentieth-century classrooms.[33] But after the 1960s, maintaining the isolated convents (a precondition to staffing Catholic schools) became impossible. Even nuns and priests had entered the wider world of educated professionalism.

The added costs of higher education for all children, including females, had the circular effect of requiring married women to *work* with the education they had received in order to educate their daughters. This integration into the economic market made it impossible to keep women segregated from the political market. The vote, campaigning, holding office breached the essential division at the heart of Tocqueville's two spheres. (He repeatedly insisted that what kept religion pure was the inability of priests to run for or hold office.) With women no longer presiding, along with their ministers, over their "own" realm of religion, morality, and higher culture, religion faces a difficult choice: It must try to maintain the old sphere without its principal ally and patron, or it must follow those patrons (mothers and culture consumers) into the secular world. Evangelical religion has tried to maintain the former position. "Mainline" religions have been venturing on the latter course— responding to Dietrich Bonhoeffer's claim that it is time for religion to emerge from its service to infantile piety and act as a force "come of age." When religion does this, it takes on the older "male" concerns of business and political morality, leaving the traditional sexual concerns less policed. Catholic authorities, for instance, despite their continued hard line on abortion, have at least gone out of the movie-censoring business. More and more thay have turned their attention to matters like the American bishops' letters on nuclear weapons and economic justice.

Thus, at the very time when a technology of total exposure floods the home with salacious material, old barriers against erotica have been weakened or removed. This has caused tremendous concern about the morally dizzying effect of hedonism in a culture of market individualism. All the forces Tocqueville feared, and relied on religion to contain, now seem rampant: immediate gratification, weakened social discipline, individual preferences opposed to social consensus. We are told that a country cannot compete with cultures of delayed gratification (e.g., the hardworking and saving countries of the Far East) once it has given up the family restraints of the past.

Such fears explain the popularity of social laments like Allan Bloom's, Norman Podhoretz's, and Robert Bork's. Even those who call for a social discipline from the Left have misgivings about the consumer-oriented sexuality of recent times. Herbert Marcuse criticized the "repressive tolerance" of such a distracted populace.[34] Jean Baudrillard argues that a society of such diffuse sexuality lacks the discipline even to enjoy its own hedonism.[35] Feminists say that women have been moved from a protected state to one preyed on, going "from reverence to rape."[36]

There seems to be no effective way to return to "the puritan hush! hush!" on sexual matters. Even criticism of pornography contributes to that talk of sex Michel Foucault thought characteristic of modernity.[37] The censors collecting evidence to make their case begin to resemble pornographers—Senator Jesse Helms carrying dirty pictures around Capitol Hill to show his colleagues, the Meese Commission producing a report that had to be kept under cover because of its own salacious material.[38] A measure of the censors' desperation is their attempt to recruit science to their cause, relying on experiments to indicate some causal relation between viewing erotica and committing crime. This merely promotes the sex analysis that was first denounced when Alfred Kinsey tried to put it on an empirical basis. The laboratory demystifies sexuality, and is at an extreme of articulation removed from any "hush! hush!" It is feckless to support a taboo, whose point is to repress analysis, by scientific *analysis*. And, to make things even more disappointing to the censors, tests like those cited by the Meese Commission have not reached the conclusions censors hope for.[39]

In this situation, one must ask if the "female" task of cloistering the young away from sexual knowledge can be performed, any longer, by the churches in our society. Margaret Atwood, in her novel *The Handmaid's Tale*, suggests that only totalitarian means could return women from their status as citizens and professionals to the sequestered role of breeders and religious models. In that story, the Tocqueville family virtues return as a nightmare revenge on the world of untrammeled freedom.[40] Is that the only way we can look at religion in our time, as the apocalyptic scourge of modern decadence? The question makes us wonder how valid the Tocqueville scheme ever was. Why did the churches assume such a guardian role over sex?

In the Christian tradition, at least, that attitude is derived in part from responses to the teaching of St. Augustine, responses very powerful though not always well informed. The Augustinian tradition deserves another look.

❖ T W E N T Y ᴥ F I V E ❖

In Praise of Censure

SOME OPPONENTS OF PORNOGRAPHY SEEM TO BELIEVE IN A KIND OF EATING eye—you are what you see, as well as what you eat. In Catholic grade schools, "holy cards" (pictures of saints) were given out to make people good, just as "dirty pictures" were supposed to make them bad.

Earlier it was believed that what one saw at the time of conception determined what one's offspring looked like. So Jacob gets brindled lambs by showing striped rods to mating sheep (Genesis 30.31–43).[1] Dionysius the Tyrant kept beautiful pictures in front of his wife during intercourse, to achieve handsome offspring.[2] More generally, depictions of an activity were used to induce it—for example, pictures of a sleeping person were put in bedrooms as a soporific.[3]

Plutarch, who believed that descriptions of lives *could* affect the soul, protested that the process was not as simple as a determinist like Democritus claimed. The depicted life is raw material, to be shaped by the action of one's mind on it, not something that *does* the shaping all by itself:

> I took up the writing of biography for others, but continued and made it my own for personal use, treating what I write as a mirror before which

to compose myself, making my features clash less with the good points of the men reflected there. For we receive each subject of biography as a visitor from some other land, welcomed and entertained here so that by intimate communing with him we may inspect "the hero's very mass and moves [*Iliad* 24.630]," weighing what is best and most adaptable for our own purposes. [As Sophocles says,] "Ah, what can more enchant" than this—or lead to more strenuous remakings of ourselves? Yet Democritus slipped into philosophy a false view of this matter, promoting superstition in the inexperienced, when he said we must pray to encounter *only* worthy images, usefully accordant types wafted around our senses, instead of any base or perverting types. Rather, we exercise ourselves in this discipline of biography, faithfully pursued in writing, to work the memory of great and imitable men deep into the mind, so we can be impervious to vicious or ignoble patterns brushed up against us, fixing our thoughts on a calm and focused regard for better models.[4]

For Democritus, the flux of atoms shaped character by mere impingement. Plutarch wanted a more active role for the mind, which goes out to appropriate models, incorporating them by a reflective effort (comparing this and that trait, as in a mirror that shows the model and oneself). Otherwise, all one would have to do is bombard young people with the images of heroes (or saints) in order to turn out predictable hero-copies at the end of the educational process.

Still, if holy cards and saints on the wall are unlikely, of themselves, to propagate virtue, the *erotic* image is different in effect from other depictions of imitable things. We do not get angry just by looking at Hercules in a rage, any more than we get chaste by looking at a statue of the Virgin. But we unquestionably get horny when looking at erotica— tests of the Masters and Johnson sort have established that for a wide range of women as well as men.[5] The bodily impact of such material is immediate and, often, unwilled—far more so than with any comparable image. Some might vomit at the sight of blood, but not as predictably as most people tumesce at the sight of their preferred sexual images.

So, what is wrong with that? There is nothing evil about sexual arousal as such. But there are inappropriate times for it—when teaching a child, for instance. Society imposes taboos, among other things, to cope with the unpredictability of sexual arousal. One of the functions of clothes is to veil both provoking and responding bodily changes, to channel them in socially desirable directions.

The uncontrolled aspect of sexual arousal—or flaccidity—was the thing St. Augustine took as the most intimate reminder of original sin, of the human being's loss of control over body responses. Augustine did not, as many have claimed, present this as the greatest or most destructive result of Adam's fall. Death, murder, war, the lust for domination, are far more serious consequences of sin. But we all die only once, and most of us murder infrequently; while sexual uneasinesses are always with us. As Georges Bataille says: "Man goes constantly in fear of himself. His erotic urges terrify him."[6] Carrying such explosive material within themselves, human beings feel an internal division and estrangement from some "original" self—the condition Diderot described in Rameau's nephew: "Nothing was less like himself than himself."[7] And this *internal* division is connected somehow with the separateness of the sexes, the wound of some aboriginal rending from each other. In the version of the fall given by Plato in the *Symposium*, Aristophanes tells how Zeus sliced a bisexual being into two partial natures (drawing the excess skin up, as by a purse string, at the navel). Now each feels the absence of the other like the ache in an absent limb.[8] As Diderot says through the mouth of Mademoiselle de L'Espinasse, "Man is just a freak woman, woman a freak man."[9] Versions of the fall attempt to explain this loss of psychic integrity. As Pascal said, "It is unthinkable that there should have been an original sin, and unthinkable that there should not have been."[10]

This being-at-odds-with-oneself is explained, by St. Augustine, as the sign of a chosen estrangement from God. By the loss of the controlling love in their lives, Adam and Eve were "giddied about" in storms.[11] Adam "willed what he could not do" (become God), so that now he does what he has not willed.[12] In the great sins, those of pride and hatred, the soul is defeated by its own forces. Lust is a lesser thing, but it is "especially embarrassing" *(maxime prudet)*, since here the soul is overcome not by itself but by the body. Urges come and go unbidden, the body's tumescence clouding the soul's vision, or leaving the body unable to respond when the soul is prepared for lust: "At times the desire arises awkwardly, when not summoned; at other times it ignores desperate calls, so that concupiscence, burning in the soul, becomes ice in the body."[13] The soul in this case is like a horseless rider.

What intrigues Augustine about sex is its dramatization of the human being's internal disjunctions. He dwells more on the body's impotence than its importunacy, since the former shows a kind of ultimate rebellion, when the soul cannot get the body to go along even with its *sinful* plans. Here "desire will no longer serve desire" *(libidini libido non servit)*.[14] The great revolutionary of Eden, grasping at godhead, cannot even find a willing recruit to little rebellions of the flesh. It is the unpredictability of the organs' response that makes the genitals embarrassing *(pudenda)*. In Eden, where they were under control, they were not an embarrassment. But now humans seek privacy for their trysts, even in brothels. They cover their genitals in public because they do not want them seen aroused—or limp—when that is inappropriate. Even the Cynic philosophers, who try to shock people by copulating in public, carry their traditional cloak and club so they can "fake it" if nervousness over their performance makes them impotent.[15] St. Augustine would have understood perfectly the difference between live sex on a stage and sex enacted for a camera in comparative seclusion, where the photographers can wait to shoot the penetration scenes.

For Augustine, sex is an appropriately comic punishment for human pride. Since he is thinking primarily of the male, his deflationary view makes of the penis a clown's "bauble," that clumsy stick-and-bladder getting in the way or collapsing in indecorous ways, as it does in Shakespeare's plays: "For this drivelling love is like a great natural [idiot] that runs lolling up and down to hide his bauble in a hole."[16] When he talks about the integrity of desire and performance in Eden, Augustine says traces of such control of the body can be found even in humanity's fallen condition. Some people can wiggle their ears at will, so obedient is their body to their whim. Others are ventriloquists. And "some can from their bottom produce odorless notes so deliberately timed *(numerosos pro arbitrio sonitus)* that they seem to be singing from that end of all places" *(ex illa etiam parte)*.[17] Jazz musicians used to say of the cornetist Bix Beiderbecke that "Bix even farted in tune." St. Augustine would have found in that fact a memory of paradise—and would have added, no doubt truthfully, that even men who can fart to a score cannot have repeated erections at will. Adam *could*.

So the instinct of privacy around the sex act is not merely a matter of "the puritan hush! hush!" It is a protection of human vulnerability, a cloak for the lack of self-command. Bataille notes that those who would degrade people usually strip them.[18] This not only takes away all social badges or indications of rank; it deprives the victim of the means for presenting himself or herself in a chosen way. It is brutally reductive, an indication that one is completely under the jailer's control—"Nakedness offers a contrast to self-possession."[19]

Clothing is necessary in our culture to the protection of things like the incest taboo—which, Bataille claims, "makes humans of us all," buttressing the minimal self-command that allows humans to make social choices.[20] Constant nakedness would provoke and reveal, in intimate quarters and by constant exposure, arousal of children by parents or vice versa. It would show arousal by others in the presence of one's children or spouse. It would undermine the murder taboo by jealousy, possessiveness or impulse. It could unsettle the claims to legitimate succession of family property. At this very basic level the state has a duty to contain sexual expression—to ban public nudity, or "flashers," or exposure to minors. [21]

Religion has an even more obvious stake in matters that concern human aspirations and vulnerability, the sacred and taboo aspects of family life, the linked mysteries surrounding birth, reproduction, and death. The general vulnerability surrounding sexual performance, the quirkiness of its appeal, the connection with higher longings, are accentuated in the dissolution effect of orgasm, what folk culture often calls a "little death." St. Augustine saw a dying away from Eden in this bleared moment. Mystics, looking forward instead of backward, treat such a forecast of death as a glimpse of the moment when one will meet (and melt into) God—the orgasmic seizure of Bernini's St. Theresa. [22]

The momentary dysphasia of orgasm, an evidence of human displacement to Augustine, was as important, in a different way, to the Marquis de Sade. According to one of the two people who could testify about Sade's own sexual performance, he shrieked as if crazed in orgasm. [23] His resemblance to his own whinnying character, the Duke of Blangis, has led many to conclude, with Simone de Beauvoir, that "he experienced orgasm as if it were an epileptic seizure, something aggressive and murderous, like a fit of rage." [24] Rather than yield to this dissolution, in which "freedom and consciousness would be lost in the rapture of the flesh," Sade imposed on the experience a rationality that delights in the reduction of *others* to disorder while the libertine retains clarity of mind and the logic of deliberate assault. Paroxysms are linked in a scheme that critics have compared to production lines, conveyor belts, Busby Berkeley choreography, monastic scheduling, and death camps.

The common note in all of this hyperrational arrangement of desire is the need to dominate the experience of the flesh, to submit it to outside imperatives, to wear it down. So Sade finds worn and used flesh more appealing than fresh bodies: He is that much closer to a final victory that progresses through torture, dismemberment, and—as the final separation of consciousness from the body—murder. Murder is the ultimate sexual act in Sade, the complete subordination of the flesh. The ascetic nature of his sexuality is shown in the rigors of his utopia at the Château de Silling in *The 120 Days of Sodom*. The division of labor, the use of prescriptive space, the bookkeeping of the rituals is a mad inversion of life in a monastery. Sex is contained and codified in a denial of spontaneity that is absolute. [25]

Normal society will not accept the regimen of the monk or of Sade. But these two extremes show the tendency of sexual passion to throw up frameworks of restraint around itself in social contexts. "Convention" is another code, one at odds with the celibate and the libertine regimens— and *necessarily* at odds with them. The convent code denies the family; the brothel code attacks individual dignity. Here there is no question, merely, of tolerance over restraint, but of one rigor meeting another. If Sade's code is allowed to prevail, humane standards cannot be maintained.

For Sade, it is the *duty* of any woman to submit to any man's sexual desire at any time and in any form that attention takes:

> I have no right to the ownership of the fountain that lies in my path, but I certainly have the right to make use of it; I have a right to enjoy the limpid water offered up to my thirst. In the same way, I have no actual claim to the possession of such and such a woman [the marriage claim as Sade defines it], but I have an incontestable one to the enjoyment of her; and I have the right to force her to this enjoyment if she refuses me for any motive whatsoever. . . . Has not nature proved to us that we have this right, by allotting us the strength necessary to force them to our desire? [26]

Not only all women but all girls of any age are under the same natural compulsion to submit. "Whoever has the right to eat the fruit off a tree may assuredly pluck it either ripe or green according to his taste." [27] Against such claims society enacts laws forbidding rape, child molestation, obscene phone calls, sexual harassment.

Sade, by the logic of sex's imperious claim, must oppose the taboos on murder and incest. It is at nature's urging that one *conquers* nature, and that is done by imposing sex on others while remaining in command of it oneself. Denial of this imperative is Sade's version of the "fall" of man into the "perversion" of self-denial. As Simone de Beauvoir notes, even Sade imagines an original Eden from which the human race has been driven: "Society manifests its original perversion by the very way in which it contradicts Nature." [28]

Society punishes those who act on Sade's views, though a country that includes free speech among its humane values cannot ban the expression of those views. Yet one can censure views that are not censored, stigmatize them, mobilize social opprobrium against them. That is what has been done, for instance, to people who use terms like *kike* or *nigger*. Saying such things is not against the law, but many are aware that some social cost will be exacted for using the terms in circles (widening circles) that disapprove of them. And distributors of information are rightly disturbed if anyone employs those terms in the conduits they offer for commercial use. Thus baseball executive Al Campanis and sports commentator Jimmy "the Greek" Snyder lost their jobs when they endorsed disparaging myths about blacks.

One way censure expresses itself is the boycott. Liberals approve of that when it is a question of staying off buses with Dr. King or refusing to buy lettuce with Cesar Chavez. Some organizations refused to hold conventions in states that rejected the Equal Rights Amendment. In 1990, feminists threatened not to buy Idaho potatoes if that state's governor did not veto a bill restricting abortion.

But liberals cry censorship when Tipper Gore, the Tennessee senator's wife, asks people not to buy records from companies that refuse to label the brutal contents of some rock songs—for example, "I kill children, I love to see them die," by a group called the Dead Kennedys.[29] The impression conveyed is that liberals are indifferent to verbal aggression— though who has a better right than liberals to deplore the use of the Kennedy name to make ghoulish jokes for money?

Labeling materials that might offend is a way of preventing a kind of verbal "flashing," intruding unwanted explicitness on people who would prefer to choose their moral environment. It does not prevent adults who choose to hear from hearing, any more than movie ratings prevent people from seeing X- or R-rated movies. If the access of children is limited, that simply works on the principle that limits, for a while, their ability to drive cars, buy liquor, marry, or do other things for which society does not yet hold them entirely responsible, morally, financially, or politically.

Much of the Left is so chary of disagreement with views covered by the First Amendment that Tipper Gore had to make an apologetic appearance before Hollywood representatives when her husband ran for president. When another woman (Terry Rakolta) complained to sponsors about the contents of a TV comedy, an editor at *Penthouse* claimed that her complaint was not protected by the First Amendment (so she should shut up); and the musician Frank Zappa accused Tipper Gore of marital "insider trading" since she is the wife of a senator.[30] (Some tried to silence Eleanor Roosevelt on the grounds that a president's wife should not be expressing her own opinions.) Some defenders of free speech think anyone should be allowed to express an opinion except those who have harsh opinions about verbal thuggery. They seem to like all consumer advocates except those who study the consumption of commercially packaged sex and violence.

The Left in America has been trapped, at times, in a position of implicit support for the *content* of protected speech because it upholds the *right* to it. This leaves it at a great remove from the general public which, feeling inundated by "the media," favors some restriction on the lurid.[31] We see this gap in public reaction to the ACLU's self-manacling position on "kiddy porn." The problem is not with the basic legal argument of the union—that sexual acts with minors are illegal even if they do not occur before cameras, so there is no need to legislate especially for the latter circumstance. The problem is that, like Dukakis in the 1988 campaign, the union so rarely goes beyond legalism, failing even to deplore the titillating (even if legal) offer of minors' pictures for sale.

It is ironic that liberals should be so paralyzed in this respect, since they have been critical of commercialism and shady consumer practices in other respects. It was the Left that stigmatized the "vast wasteland" of television in the sixties and tried to promote "healthy" programs like *Sesame Street* and *The Electric Company*. Jesse Jackson has for years told parents to get more involved in what the children are doing—to turn off the TV and monitor their homework. The mindless violence of TV has been attacked by critics of the macho ethic; but the infantile sexuality that so often goes with it is exempted from the same critique.

When *Penthouse* paid the prostitute who posed for Jimmy Swaggart's voyeuristic pleasure, it shot her pictures in an insulting black-and-white griminess, in the squalid setting of a motel. This attempt to distance her activities from the essentially similar poses of its beautifully lit and colored "Pets," who are imagined in health spas and ski resorts, was a way of saying that the whore's failing, and Swaggart's sin, was an economic offense. It paid the woman for an act of class voyeurism more despicable than Swaggart's act by far. *Playboy*, too, suggested that Jessica Hahn's sin, in her coupling with evangelist Jim Bakker, was a lack of sufficient grooming at the courtier school where Hugh Hefner later improved Hahn's bustline, wardrobe, and party manners. The Left said little on such moral issues. It gets tongue-tied when sex enters into the predatory commercialism of our culture.

The ability of sex to mute people's censure is seen when cruelty and torture—otherwise deplored by the humane—are made matters of "individual preference" as soon as whips are taken into the bedroom. There is nothing in sex that ennobles suffering deliberately inflicted on another.

The argument that people want the suffering does not make inflicting it any more humane. Suicides want Saturday night specials. Boxers want to be punched, as the price for punching others—yet professional boxing is brutal and degrading, worse than bearbaiting or cockfights, which our society has put behind it.[32]

The argument for censuring the infliction of pain applies equally to heterosexual and homosexual sadism, and undercuts the claim that criticism of sadomasochistic studies like Robert Mapplethorpe's must be "homophobic." The exhibit of Mapplethorpe's work that caused so much controversy in 1989 and 1990 included a self-portrait with the thick end of a bullwhip inserted in his scarified, well-trafficked anus. Another gay activist, John Rechy, shows that there is no reason to privilege such brutality just because it occurs between consenting adults:

> A thousand Anita Bryants cannot do the devastation we are committing upon ourselves by substituting the fist, which is the most powerful symbol of aggression we have, for the penis. The act is a symbolic assault. There are no sexual sensations in that and there is no sexual response. With fist-fucking there is always a soft cock. There are very few hard cocks in the orgy room. There are mind experiences and experiences of degradation. In fact, I've often said that in a homosexual S&M ritual, there is only one sadist—the invisible heterosexual whose hatred we're ritualistically duplicating.[33]

Because of pictures like Mapplethorpe's self-portrait, and that of one man urinating in another's mouth, the question of federal support for his exhibit was raised (at first somewhat irrelevantly, since his show at the Corcoran Gallery of Art was canceled even though no federal money had been assigned for it). The denial of a subsidy is not censorship. Federal moneys, collected by force of law, will not be expended by politicians in ways that a majority of their constituents consider inimical to their own values—nor should they be. Governmental projects are conservative because they are based on representative government. Avant-garde art by definition is out of the mainstream of society. It deliberately shocks and offends. It is absurd to expect main-guard support for avant-garde activities. Only rather tame rebels can say they are silenced unless they get the government's approval and support for everything they do.

The other censorship issue raised around the Mapplethorpe show was the Tipper Gore approach to labeling. In some places, the exhibit was mounted without incident because the challenged images were put in a separate room with warnings about the nature of the pictures inside. The

Cincinnati gallery at which the exhibit appeared, going beyond this internal segregation, excluded all patrons under eighteen from the entire exhibit. This latter arrangement was excessively restrictive (though it did not prevent indictment for obscenity by a repressive local government). Warning labels protect the concept of choice (whose value the Left respects where abortion is concerned) and prevents the obtrusion of unexpected or unwanted images on people who expect more decorous fare from a museum. All these censures can be made of a Mapplethorpe without getting into *legally* insoluble questions about the merit of his art. Those who wish to see it are free to do so, and those who criticize it are equally free.

It should be noticed that the problem with Mapplethorpe's images is not titillation or arousal. Few who do not already share his taste will be lured to it by his brutal candor. In fact, the problem with Sade and his imitators is that they may cause disgust at sex, especially to those exposed to it before they have experienced gentler forms of sexuality. Even those with a strong stomach often flinch at Sade. Camille Paglia, in a generally praising treatment of him, still cautions the reader: "Don't read Sade before lunch!"[34] The argument against uncritical acceptance of such images is not that they cause people to commit sexual acts, any more than the sight of swastikas of itself prompts fascist feelings in people. If we discourage the honoring of swastikas, it is because we consider them symbolic affronts to our concept of civilization.

The argument of the Meese Commission that pornography causes sex crimes fails, on many grounds; but it is not needed for mounting social resistance to brutal pornography. The trouble with attempts to prove a link between pornography and crime is that both may be symptoms of a third thing rather than causes of each other. We *do* have evidence that people's values are affected by their family setting and the larger context in which views are rewarded or discouraged. In that setting, the criticism of commercial hedonism, exploitation of humans, and images degrading to human dignity takes place, not because they *cause* evil but because they are symbols unworthy of our own aspirations. Not wanting degrading images of any sort to be honored in the home is like not wanting swastikas on the wall.

The Meese Commission takes the Democritus approach to images—a mere exposure to them directly shapes the character of the beholder. Plutarch's criticisms of Democritus lay the foundation of a saner regard for the cultural environment. We should choose the images we want to live with, and we should have some freedom to do so. We should honor, and work down into our considered layers of consciousness, the preferred images, and slough off those we consider unworthy of social regard, honored retention, or mutual celebration. These standards can be upheld without censoring by legal bans the free expression of values we disagree with, discourage, or dishonor. If the churches direct their efforts at this kind of education to humanity, rather than the mere avoidance of sexual explicitness, there is no reason pornography should be any more favored in our society than are racist comments or fascist emblems. They will continue to exist, but under civilized opprobrium.

❖ T W E N T Y = S I X ❖

A Theology of Erotica

THERE WAS A STORY, TOO GOOD TO BE TRUE, TOLD IN VARIOUS FORMS IN the 1960s. A policeman tells a protester to come back after she has removed the obscenity from her placard, FUCK THE WAR, and she quickly returns with the sign reading FUCK THE ———. The story illustrates the problem of treating any word as evil apart from its usage. Right-wing censors have spent years laboriously extracting J. D. Salinger's *Catcher in the Rye* from school and public libraries, largely because it uses the word *fuck*—ignoring the fact that the narrator is shocked at the graffito "Fuck You," and tries to remove it as an affront to his sister's innocence. He is on the censors' side, but they are too lathered up to notice it.

The French word *merde* was considered unprintable when Victor Hugo published *Les Misérables* in 1862. But Hugo rhapsodizes for two pages on this "most splendid word any Frenchman ever used" when Cambronne speaks it to the English who ask for his surrender after Waterloo. The word "perfects Leonidas with a touch of Rabelais."[1]

The treatment of any word—or act, or attitude—as ineligible for public representation is a doomed effort. Feminist critics of pornography should have found that out when the Indianapolis antipornography statute they championed was knocked down by the courts. It seems sensible to argue that no work of art should dwell on the degradation of women—but what, then, does one make of Shakespeare's *Titus Andronicus*, where the heroine is traduced, raped, mutilated, and killed in a sequence Sade could hardly improve on? Much as one may deplore incest, few will try to ban Sophocles' *Oedipus*.

Hollywood's Motion Picture Production Code of 1931, written by a Catholic layman and a priest, took the view that certain things should never be seen or heard at all—words like *damn* and people like prostitutes; it insisted that "*white-slavery* shall not be treated."[2] Nothing that might upset the audience was to be admitted: "*Miscegenation* (sex relationships between the white and black races) is forbidden." There should be no cruelty, or even "apparent cruelty," to children or animals—a ban much like the Indianapolis one forbidding cruel treatment of women.

Because of the Hollywood code, moral ambiguity, challenge, and struggle were officially excluded from the cinema. No cruelty to children? Much of Dickens's most harrowing work was not transferable to the screen. No prostitutes? One of Dostoyevski's most spiritually moving scenes could not go before the camera. Not even a *damn?* The most famous line in Margaret Mitchell's *Gone With the Wind* had to struggle its way past the code onto the screen. Actually, Joseph Breen, the keeper of the code, was more intent on removing the word *nigger* from David Selznick's movie, and he used a concession on the movie's famous line to get his way on the racial slur. Is *nigger*, then, the one word we can all agree to do without?[3] Only if we mean to cut and distort Mark Twain's masterpiece.

The code forbade all nudity—a ban that would empty museums around the world. In America, museums had sometimes kept women from viewing nude works of art, and for a long time the force of public opinion prevented women from painting nude works or posing for them.[4]

There is a religious argument for public modesty, based on the doctrine of original sin—the involuntary response to exposed physical beauty that St. Augustine described so eloquently. But some religious censors have gone far beyond what Augustine intended, encouraging a hatred of the body, or of its attractive powers. Augustine, firm in the rejection of Manichean belief in any kind of evil existence, argued that the lowliest body has a depth of beauty. The minute anything edges across the boundary between nonbeing and being, it immediately reflects the creative power that holds it in existence. It has unity insofar as it is *a* thing, and variety insofar as it is not *the* Platonic One; and there is endless shifting interplay between the diversity and unity. As Augustine says, taking the lowliest form of body as a basis for praise of every other (higher) kind:

> I could descant in all candor on the worm, when I look at its glancing color, its perfect corporal rotundity, its meshing of end with middle, middle with end, each contributing something to a thrust toward oneness in this lowliest thing, so there is no part that does not answer to each other part in the proper measure. And what of the principle of life pervading it—its rhythmic activation of the whole, its turn toward that which serves life, its triumph over or aversion from whatever menaces it, its reference of all things to a normative center of self-preservation, bearing a witness to the creative unity behind all natural life, more striking than the mere body itself?[5]

Augustine says the same evidences of beauty can be found in fleas, ashes, excrement, rotting flesh, and functioning bowels.[6]

When Augustine moves up to more exquisitely organized bodies, he is more and more reverent. Monkeys are called ugly by comparison with humans, but they have their own functional beauty, which makes human bodies all the more (a fortiori) stunning.[7] The exhaustless variety of human faces, so instantly distinguishable despite the limited number of elements to be arranged, is a miracle of God's artistry.[8] Asked the function of (milkless) male nipples, St. Augustine says they are used to articulate the space of the chest, and they prove that beauty is a value in itself, not tied inevitably to utility in the human body.[9]

Church people who show hostility to the human body are theologically aligned against its creator in St. Augustine's view. And representation of that body involves another filtration, as it were, of flesh through spirit. Imitation of the real is not, in Christian theology, what it was in Plato's scheme—a diminishing of the real by paler imitation of a thing that is already an imitation of a Form. This approach made for religious icon-oclasm, which the Christian church had to respond to with a defense of holy images. Representation of a saint's life, or any other life, is what Kierkegaard calls "repetition," an appropriation of the real by a human act of assessment and continuing regard. As St. Augustine says: "Better is a body's image in the mind than that body's corporeal self, to the extent that it has entered a higher nature."[10] The imitation transcends the par-ticular thing appropriated—thus pictures of a thing can outlast it, and always carry the evidence of what the imitating artist held in regard. The body has passed through a soul and escaped in some measure its bodily fate of dissolution.

One might ask, then, how one can condemn *any* image of a thing good in itself (as all beings are), created by a process that is ennobling, not debasing. The intent can be evil—as when the artist makes a whip or chain for use on humans. Here the materials, good in themselves, show by their very design an evil intent. It is only the soul that can sin, in Augustine's view, never the body. Pornography shows evil intent if it exploits the involuntary responses of the body in ways that mock freedom. As Simone de Beauvoir puts it: "Even a child is aware that crude drawings are more obscene than the organs and gestures which they represent, because the intention to defile is present in all its [paradoxical] purity."[11] The spiritual purpose of using the body to deny higher spiritual purpose in man is what can be condemned in pornography—and only that.

Thus, though representation is an act that of itself tends to transcend the bodily particulars imitated through the spiritual vision of the re-creator, the pornographer tries to baffle this motion toward transcendence. Sade is the perfect example of this. He tries to plug all the human bodies present into each other's sockets to form a closed system with no aspiration out. He sets up a process circling back and back on itself with increasingly destructive fury. He would seal in the human spirit by scribbling dirty words all around the walls that enclose it. The chemist in *The New Justine* plots to blow up surrounding villages, a sight he means to watch while copulating with a goat, showing a kind of mad magic that by *desecrating* nature will destroy it.[12] Another character aspires "to attack the sun, to deprive the universe of it, or to use it to set the world ablaze."[13] The aim is "to cultivate everything that irritates nature—in a word, to insult all her works."[14] As Edmund Wilson notes of that passage: "To encourage this impulse is the ultimate blasphemy—far more terrible than the Voltairean jeering at theology or the Byronic defiance of law—and it is Sade's queer unique distinction to have declared it with the ultimate audacity."[15]

The real hatred of sex is not found in Puritans or monkish ascetics but in the mad design to use body parts as ordnance to bomb the world apart at its most intimate jointures. This use of sex is crazily defiling. It must degrade the act to use it in defiling everything else. Some see in Sade's plodding campaign, to keep doing this in insanely literal detail, a kind of comic overstatement. But those who take Sade seriously, as he intended, soon begin to feel suffocated—as he intended. The instinct is to throw open windows, reach a wider air, cleanse the shut-up brain. Edmund Wilson, not a prude, could only respond by saying, "Let us hope his moment [after the horrors of World War II] is passing"—and add that "no one can blame Sade's family for locking him up."[16]

One effect of reading Sade is to find a kind of winning innocence in pornography that merely tries to entice rather than disgust. In fact, the transcendent notion of representation leads most pornographers to escape their narrow program (of provocation and physical engagement) with "gratuitous" efforts at good lighting for its own sake, or interesting stories, or some other aspect of beauty in representation. To bared breasts the artist, on no matter how small a grade, is tempted to add the "male nipples" of what Augustine called beauty for its own sake. There is a kind of artistry in any genre that engages professional instincts and pride, as Linda Williams demonstrates in her book on copulation films, *Hard Core: Power, Pleasure, and the "Frenzy of the Visible"* (University of California, 1989).

Those who censure should be able to discriminate the degrading (sadistic, brutalizing) from the merely titillating. But that calls for an adult approach to censure, not a ban on anything that would have been excluded from the infantile and "feminine" world of "genteel culture" in the nineteenth century—or under the Hollywood Production Code.

To talk seductively about seduction is not, necessarily, to degrade human auditors—as Kierkegaard proves spectacularly in *The Diary of a Seducer*. It is possible to treat this simply as a piece of erotica, as Jean Baudrillard does—prompting criticism of both Kierkegaard and Baudrillard for an essentially predatory attitude toward women.[17] But those who read the book in conjunction with Kierkegaard's other works of the time—and especially with *Fear and Trembling*—are bound to notice the seducer's resemblance to Kierkegaard's riddling and demanding God. The seducer is careful to respect the victim's freedom—she must choose to fall: "She moves to the melody of her own soul; I am merely the occasion for her moving. . . . In me she is seeking her freedom, and the more firmly I encircle her, the better she will find it. . . . And the more tightly this ring encircles us, the more inseparably it knits us together, the greater the freedom, for your freedom consists in being mine, as my freedom consists in being yours."[18]

The seduction of the young woman is a parable of the fall from innocence, the *felix culpa* of Christian theology: "Her development—that was my work."[19] In his elusiveness the seducer resembles that imperative but ambiguous sender of signals who commanded Abraham to sacrifice Isaac: "Everything is a metaphor; I myself am a myth about myself, for is it not as a myth that I hasten to this tryst?"[20] Thus the "girl" of the *Diary* is not woman in a sociological sense, but the human soul, as in much of the mystical literature, where God is interpreted as a wooer.

Sade uses erotica to seal up the universe, like some crypt in a Poe story. Kierkegaard uses it to open the world to its creator, who beats at its outworks like the lover shaking the lattice in the Song of Songs: "The eternal in erotic love is that in its moment individuals first come into existence for each other."[21] It is not surprising that those who see God basically as a lover are more liberal in their attitudes than those who see him primarily as a judge—though it is useful to have this commonsense conclusion quantified by a clever new series of polls.[22] An adult censure of degrading erotica is more to be expected from those who see the spiritual possibilities of erotica. But infantile censoring of the nineteenth-century sort is the kind still associated with religious crusaders against pornography.

These latter troops cannot recognize allies when they encounter them. One of the targets of censorship in the 1950s was *Lolita*, Vladimir Nabokov's tale of sin and damnation. All the censors could see was the subject matter, love of a child-woman ("nymphet"). They considered this child molestation (as did Nabokov) without noticing that the subject lay at the heart of Dickens's *Oliver Twist* and Fritz Lang's movie *M*—which is not to deny the evil of gratuitous child torture of the sort displayed in Peter Greenaway's film *The Cook, the Thief, His Wife, and Her Lover* (1990).[23]

Nabokov does describe his hero's fascination with nymphets. But Humbert Humbert seduces Lolita in the last moment before she emerges from her chrysalis of pubescence. During the four years the novel covers, Lolita is no longer a nymphet. Humbert sees her, finally, splayed in a cowlike pregnancy, and he has never loved her more. By his own fastidious measure, cultivated half a useless lifetime, she represents a fall from aesthetic grace; he must die into time to follow her, linked to her sagging flesh as his own body returns to earth. Having flirted with her in the Eden of his mind, he loves her outside the fiery gates.

This is a love story, and a tale of sin repented. Humbert is tortured by the innocence he destroyed. Listening from a hill to the play of children, he muses:

> One could hear now and then, as if released, an almost inarticulate spurt of vivid laughter, or the crack of a bat, or the clatter of a toy wagon, but it was all really too far for the eye to distinguish any movement in the

lightly etched streets. I stood listening to that musical vibration from my lofty slope, to those flashes of separate cries with a kind of demure murmur for background, and then I knew that the hopelessly poignant thing was not Lolita's absence from my side, but the absence of her voice from that concord.

The realization of his sin informs Humbert's literary exercise in prison:

Unless it can be proven to me—to me as I am now, today, with my heart and my beard, and my putrefaction—that in the infinite run it does not matter a jot that a North American girl named Dolores has been deprived of her childhood by a maniac, unless that can be proven (and if it can, then life is a joke), I see nothing for the treatment of my misery, but the melancholy and very local palliative of articulate art.

Driving toward his final destination Humbert feels an urgency to express his discord with the universe. As Sade's hero couples with goats while cursing the world, Humbert drives toward his private hell in a fittingly transgressive way:

The road stretched across open country, and it occurred to me—not by way of protest, not as a symbol, or anything like that, but merely as a novel experience—that since I had disregarded all laws of humanity, I might as well disregard the rules of traffic. So I crossed to the left side of the highway and checked the feeling, and the feeling was good. It was a pleasant diaphragmal melting, with elements of diffused tactility, all this enhanced by the thought that nothing could be nearer to the elimination of basic physical laws than deliberately driving on the wrong side of the road. In a way, it was a very spiritual itch. Gently, dreamily, not exceeding twenty miles an hour, I drove on that queer mirror side.

The one service Humbert can do for Lolita is to kill that mirror-self that still treats her as an exploitable nymphet, the replicative Humbert's doppelgänger, Clare Quilty. Quilty is the last believable devil in our literature, the evil Humbert sees when he looks in the mirror. He appears with the traditional "equivocations of the fiend," with an acrid scratch of a match on the darkened hotel porch:

"Where the devil did you get her?"
"I beg your pardon?"
"I said: the weather is getting better."
"Seems so."
"Who's that lassie?"
"My daughter."
"You lie—she's not."

"I beg your pardon?"
"I said: July was hot. Where's her mother?"
"Dead."

Quilty calls Humbert back to the decadent connoisseur he has ceased to be—as when he offers Humbert "a young lady with three breasts, one a dandy." This element of Sade in himself is what Humbert must destroy, or be destroyed by it. The final struggle is a reverse orgy of the Sade kind, all bodily extensions lost in mere coagulation: "I rolled over him. He rolled over me. They rolled over him. We rolled over us."

At a time when 37 percent of Americans believe in the devil, and Christians read the many scriptural texts dealing with that dark personage, how can adult believers silence such important testimony to the person-ification of evil as *Lolita*?[24] Scholars can read René Girard or Jean Staro-binski in the attempt to make sense in modern terms of the scriptural treatment of devils.[25] But a living debate in the larger adult audience will never occur unless the "repetition" of art regains the experience of ex-orcism in a story like Nabokov's. The censors who banned *Lolita* were excluding whole areas of the human spirit that religion should be the first to explore and keep open. Religious leaders have an itch to censor serious treatment of diabolic themes, occurring amid sex and violence in a novel like Robert Stone's *Hall of Mirrors*, while praising shabby popular shockers like the book and movie *The Exorcist*.[26]

One area where we might hope for clerical expertise is that of blas-phemy. But even here the censors are their own worst enemies. For one thing, they rarely reflect that Job is probably the world's most blasphemous book. Nor do they see the ambiguous nature of blasphemy itself. One cannot attack the sacred without a concept of the sacred, as G. K. Ches-terton realized when he challenged modern people to think blasphemous thoughts about Osiris. The romantic model of defiance was Milton's Satan, whose courage of resistance evaporates if there is no God to fight. Swinburne's "raptures of vice" have become as faded, now, as any dead lilies of virtue. The one thing that still animates his best verse is the picking up of Job's complaint, not as a lover, but as a foe:

Yea, but albeit he slay me, hating me . . .
Of me the high God hath not all his will.[27]

Blasphemy is not a secular category.

Yet some censors try to maintain a childish standard of blasphemy, the untouchability of holy things. Certain themes cannot be handled at all. So pope and bishops inveighed against Jean-Luc Godard's 1985 *Hail*,

Mary (Je vous salue, Marie), which tried—pathetically—to restore a mythic force to the virgin birth. Nothing in the movie, including intense efforts at an innocent nudity, was as offensive as the leering commercialism of Cecil B. DeMille's biblical epics—for which DeMille had the Jesuit author of the Production Code say Mass on location (as a Jesuit was called in to bless the set of *The Exorcist*). Clerical endorsement has a bad track record with regard to religious art—the Jesuits were Rubens's patrons at a time when Dürer was remaking theology with his woodcuts.

The most famous recent object of clerical harassment in the field of art was Martin Scorsese's 1988 film, *The Last Temptation of Christ*. A coalition of evangelicals tried to prevent its being made. Because of their pressures, Gulf + Western withdrew its original backing of the film. When Scorsese sought French funding for his work, the archbishop of Paris, Cardinal Lustiger, warned President Mitterrand not to let Jack Lang, the minister of culture, support such a project.[28] When Scorsese did get American funding, it was minimal because of the risk that opposition would prevent distribution. The actors worked for union-scale wages, as a way of subsidizing a project they believed in.

Threats were made against distribution. The film was released ahead of schedule, to give demonstrators less time to organize. Prints were guarded, and viewers entering the first run in New York were searched. The great scandal of this film was not anything contained in it, but the threat of violence against it, and the ugly anti-Semitism expressed by those who demonstrated against Lew Wasserman, chairman of the company responsible for the film's release. The protesters, led by the Reverend R. L. Hymers, chanted "Bankrolled by Jewish money"—though the film's director and writer are Christians (one a Catholic and the other a Protestant) who both studied for the ministry, and they had planned the project long before Wasserman's company became involved with it.

Pat Robertson and Bill Bright (of Campus Crusade for Christ) urged Christians to prevent the movie's release. Donald Wildmon, the Methodist leader of the American Family Association, sent out 2.5 million mailings and scheduled counteradvertisements on seven hundred Christian radio stations and fifty television stations. Erwin Lutzer, the pastor of the historic Moody Church in Chicago, published a booklet calling for continued agitation against everything the movie stood for.[29]

Many of the film's most vociferous critics did not see it. Some relied on an early draft of the screenplay that was smuggled out to evangelicals. Others were content with the report that Jesus is shown in sexual intercourse (as part of a sequence showing the life that Jesus *rejected*). Any linking of sex and Jesus—except surreptitiously in the DeMille manner—is considered unthinkable.

I suppose there are things one can reject *a priori*, without ever viewing them. Snuff movies (in which a person is murdered on camera) are a modern myth; but if there were such things, one could condemn them by their very nature—as one could condemn the filming of real torture, rape, mutilation, child molestation, if it were enacted just to be filmed (as opposed, say, to war documentaries). But what made Scorsese's film so unacceptable that it could be condemned without a viewing?

Pat Buchanan, the former Nixon aide new to theology but not to the defense of persecutors, wrote that Christians should "drive the pornographer who produced it back under the rock whence he came." Quoting from the script (since he refused to see the film), he found it particularly offensive that Jesus should say, "Lucifer is inside me." Yet entirely orthodox authors have stressed the identification of Jesus not only with sinners but with sin itself, whose entire burden he took on himself. Indeed, Cardinal Newman thought it was less the foresight of physical pain—which Jesus shared with other martyrs—than the assumption of this load of sin, including all its shame and guilt, that tortured blood from his body in the Garden of Olives:

> There He knelt, motionless and still, while the vile and horrible fiend clad His spirit in a robe steeped in all that is hateful and heinous in human crime, which clung close around His heart, and filled His conscience and found its way into every sense and pore of His mind, and spread over Him a moral leprosy, till He almost felt himself to be that which He never could be, and which His foe would fain have made Him. Oh, the horror, when He looked, and did not know Himself, and felt as a foul and loathsome sinner, from His vivid perception of that mass of corruption which poured over His head and ran down even to the skirts of His garments: Oh, the distraction, when He found His eyes, and hands, and feet, and lips and heart, as if the members of the Evil One, and not of God! . . . Such heart-rending, revolting, detestable, maddening scenes; nay, the haggard faces, the convulsed lips, the flushed cheeks, the dark brows of the willing victims of rebellion, they are all before Him now; they are upon Him and in Him.[30]

In short, he felt as if Lucifer were in him.

Other critics of the film, or of its script, have taken offense at the friendship between Jesus and Judas, and at Jesus' insistence that Judas betray him in order to fulfill the divine plan. The film seems to misrepresent the role Judas plays in the Gospels. Yet that role is in itself mysterious, as reflected in Jesus' imperative, "Do swiftly what you do" (John 13.27). Even more enigmatic is the incomplete sentence in Matthew (26.50), as Judas is about to kiss Jesus: "Friend [*Hetaire*, "comrade"], what you are here for . . ." Most modern translations supply an understood imperative here, too: "[Do] what you are here for," though one might as well take the phrase to mean, "[This is] what you are here for." Jesus seems complicitous in Judas' sin, if not provoking it.

Indeed, there is an odd intimacy in the exchanges of the two men at the final supper and in the moment before Jesus' arrest. Only these two know what is really happening. They seem to fence over the heads of the uncomprehending followers. Each knows he is the other's doom. Both will soon be dead, hanging from a new Tree of Life and Tree of Death. Each wills his own death while causing the other's. They have the eternal bond of the betrayer and the betrayed—and if Jesus is luring Judas to his damnation, he is the greater betrayer. It is this feeling that makes the priest in Shusaku Endo's novel *Silence* feel tempted to believe that "Judas was no more than the unfortunate puppet for the glory of that drama which was the life and death of Christ."[31] Later, the Catholic writer Endo, in his *Life of Jesus*, argued that Jesus used Judas to save Judas—that redemption was won for sinners, and the supreme prize was the supreme sinner.[32]

It is the orthodox teaching that Jesus was killed by human sin, every sin, those sins that flooded into Jesus' consciousness in Cardinal Newman's Garden of Olives scene. In that sense, every sinning Christian must accept responsibility for betraying Jesus, and Judas is merely our representative—far more than Pilate or the Sanhedrin, or the disciples who did not know what they were doing. The believer's only hope to be saved is that of Judas, by the inversion of the cross, which makes the death-dealer a life-receiver.

This is sounder theology than that of Rev. Wildmon, who makes Jews the killers of Christ and Lou Wasserman the representative of those Jews. The serious attempt to rethink Jesus' relation to sin and sinners makes Scorsese's film far closer to modern theologians' insights than to its cinema predecessors (or its silly literary source, Nikos Kazantzakis's novel *The Last Temptation of Christ*). At a time when the understanding of Jesus among theologians has diverged from that among the laity, nothing could advance dialogue better than use of this movie by Christian teachers. When was the last time you heard people leave a theater discussing the double nature of Christ?

The use of adult censure will not be credible unless genuinely spiritual questions are recognized when they are raised in art. Unfortunately, clerical guidance entirely lacks credibility now, especially where the depiction of anything sexual is concerned. Evangelical and Catholic attitudes on women are still bound by a biblical fundamentalism that makes them the guardians of a separate sphere for women.

Tocqueville included priests with women in the protection of a moral realm apart from politics—priests, like women, were not fully citizens, but something different from (and useful to) the male participants in full civic life. This concept, of different areas of competence, was congenial to Tocqueville as a Catholic, since much of Catholic history has made a similar distinction in church matters. As males in Tocqueville's America guided the state, leaving private morality to women, so priests in Catholic ecclesiology conducted the public life of theology and the liturgy, while nuns and the laity cultivated a purely private sanctity. Only priests could be taught theology—in separate all-male institutions, using a special professional language (Latin). Others could not read proscribed books or pronounce on dogma.

But the condition of modern life means that women and priests can participate in public life *only* as citizens, with no special preserve of their own to make people fall silent "before the ladies" or "before the good father." If they want to influence public life, it must be with argument and persuasion; and certainly better arguments are needed than Cardinal O'Connor or Reverend Wildmon could supply on *Hail Mary* or *The Last Temptation of Christ*. If there is to be censure of sexually offensive material on religious grounds, that will call for a theology of erotica, which is the last thing we can expect from evangelical or Catholic teachers. Their record on the subject of abortion proves that.

PART SEVEN

Politics and Abortion

❖ T W E N T Y = S E V E N ❖

Catholics: Mario Cuomo

CATHOLICS, 28 PERCENT OF THE POPULATION, AND JEWS, ONLY 2 percent, have had a powerful influence on America's Protestant majority. Both groups have a highly developed tradition, strongly inculcated, that was brought to America. Each resisted for a long time the dilution of its community by intermarriage. American Protestantism, individualist and improvisational, diffuses its impact in sectarian rivalries. It lives by revivals, starting over from scratch. The strength of Catholicism and Judaism lies, by contrast, in their continuity.

Of these two groups, Catholics have the stronger structure of authority, prompting Lenny Bruce to call Catholicism the only *the* church. This church influences American politics in two ways, on separate tracks. It addresses outsiders, "men [*sic*] of goodwill," with well-formulated arguments from a long natural-law tradition, while delivering doctrinal fiats to its own members, who are expected to act from them in the public arena. Thus arguments are used against contraception in public debate, while those arguments *and* church tradition are held to bind Catholics.

This double approach has been taken even when the strict teaching authority of the church (its magisterium) is not involved. Thus Catholic bishops argued in the public realm, mainly through lay people, for the

Hollywood Production Code, as a matter of civil decency, and, at the same time, they enlisted Catholics in the Legion of Decency, condemning movies with moral authority.[1]

In the same way, the Catholic bishops in America say that abortion is not a religious issue when addressing the public at large. In that forum, they rely on natural law, common sense, and probabilist arguments (even if the fetus is only *probably* human, one should not kill what *might* be alive). But Catholics are told they must hold to the church's position out of loyalty to their ecclesiastical rulers. The two tracks were clearly marked in 1990 when the hierarchy paid millions of dollars to a public-relations firm to make its public case, while bishops in New York State said that the Catholic governor of New York, Mario Cuomo, was endangering his soul and could not speak in diocesan institutions because he did not support a legal ban on abortion.

In earlier presidential campaigns, Edward Kennedy's in 1980 and Geraldine Ferraro's as the running mate for Walter Mondale in 1984, Catholics were particularly punitive to their own on the abortion issue. Kennedy's position, for instance, did not differ from Jimmy Carter's during the Democratic primaries of 1980; nor, obviously, did Geraldine Ferraro's differ from Walter Mondale's in 1984. But Catholics picketed and appealed to their bishops against Kennedy and Ferraro while largely ignoring the stands of Carter and Mondale. Partly, of course, this was just a matter of striking where one could have the most impact. But the situation that made that impact possible was the double standard by which Catholics are reachable—not only by the arguments made to all political candidates but by a special bond that is supposed to limit Catholics in what they can do while claiming membership in good standing with their fellow believers.

Mario Cuomo was not new to these pressures when, in 1990, Bishop Austin Vaughan publicly opined that he might be on his way to hell. Cardinal John O'Connor, Vaughan's superior in the archdiocese of New York, had entertained and not rejected a public call for excommunicating Cuomo in 1984, at the time when pressures were being brought to bear on Congresswoman Ferraro. Cuomo was watching O'Connor on television when this occurred. So was his fourteen-year-old son Christopher, who asked if his father was about to be dischurched. Mario Cuomo is a very sincere Catholic, an intensely devoted family man, proud, competitive, and thin-skinned. His wife said, after watching him react to this public challenge: "Boy, did he [the cardinal] pick on the wrong person."[2] Three months later, at a widely publicized event at the University of

Notre Dame, Cuomo delivered his answer to the cardinal, a speech he crafted very carefully. His biographer calls this "a brilliantly argued answer."[3] When, four years later, the Catholic former governor of Arizona ran for president, he was able to answer questions about abortion by subscribing to "the Cuomo position." Bruce Babbitt told reporters: "Geraldine [Ferraro] got into trouble on the issue because she didn't have her facts straight. Mario got it right." Cuomo had cleared the way for other Catholics.

Some compared Cuomo's Notre Dame speech with John Kennedy's 1960 address to Protestant ministers in Houston. But in some ways Cuomo was in a tighter bind. Kennedy was addressing non-Catholics, who might be opposed to him but would observe certain restraints of our pluralist code. He had the Catholic community rallying behind him, even if he went farther than some bishops would have preferred. He granted the existence of the two different claims on Catholic loyalty but said that, if the private exertion of authority conflicted with the public appeal to natural reason, he would resign before putting the purely Catholic appeal above public arguments from the common good. The clearinghouse, in any case, was his conscience. The only hold the church had on him was his own free acceptance of church authority. That was enough for most critics in 1960.

More was demanded of Cuomo in 1984, though he did not really deliver more. The surface difference lay in his exposed position as a Catholic arguing not only with other Catholics but with his ecclesiastical superiors. Columnist Mary McGrory wrote at the time: "Cuomo is the first Catholic politician to pick a fight with a prelate. Not so long ago, such an initiative on the part of a Catholic politician would have been nothing less than suicide."[4]

It was a close call, even so. Cuomo's speech, kept under careful embargo and worked on to the last minute, was rushed ahead for Father Theodore Hesburgh, the Notre Dame president, to read before he would risk introducing the governor. Then the president played a characteristically careful game by welcoming Cuomo to the campus in the name of free exchange yet rushing a criticism of the speech out through a specially syndicated column given national release. Some conservatives on the Notre Dame campus grilled Cuomo at the press conference before his talk. He had arrived late, after a harrowing flight through storms in his small governor's airplane. (Jokes about divine disfavor were bounced about the cabin.) Orange juice jostled onto the one corrected copy of his speech made its pages stick as he delivered his talk, prying at the edges of the next page as he read the one just uncaked from its fellows. In moving from the press conference to the site of the speech, he was bumped by picketers, one of whom called him a murderer. It was a severe test of the combative man's equanimity.

Yet he was irenic in the tone of his address. He stood his ground; but he made no advance on the Kennedy position of 1960. He, too, admitted there are separate claims on his conscience. As a Catholic, he accepts "church doctrine" on abortion (i.e., that it is impermissible). Yet, as a public official, he accepts the political sense of the community, as articulated in the law. If the law allows abortion, and he is elected to uphold the law, he is not himself committing abortions—this preserves his conscience on the matter; but he is also not overriding the majority vote of the authorized legislators—not, that is, forcing his conscience on others, who do not have his reason for submission to his church. If he fills a double role, it is because the church itself distinguishes between its two "tracks."

Why was that position, satisfactory in 1960, felt to be inadequate in 1984? Some objected that, for one who recognizes the evil of abortion, Cuomo was doing very little to persuade others of that view—as he would do, say, if slavery were the issue. He might, like Lincoln in 1860, have to administer a political entity with slavery legally in place; but he could speak out against slavery, express a hope to see its abolition, lobby and argue and maneuver toward that—none of which Cuomo was doing for the abolition of abortion.[5]

But, more important, a vast change had occurred in Catholic attitudes toward authority, especially on sexual matters, since John Kennedy spoke in Houston. The Second Vatican Council redefined the church in public ways as a "people of God" rather than a government of prelates, and, at the same time, Pope John XXIII set up a commission of that people (clerical and lay) to reconsider the traditional position on birth control. When the commission reported *against* the old ban on artificial means of contraception, the persuasive track was clearly moving apart from the authoritative track, even within the church's own councils. The commission was made up of responsible Catholics, all raised under the old norms, all professing belief in the natural-law premises on which the old teaching was supposedly based. Paul VI, after he succeeded to the Papacy in 1963, expanded the commission, adding bishops and theologians (who should have made it a more predictable body). Yet a majority of the commission—three to one in the case of the bishops involved, four to one of the theologians—rejected the "natural law" argument against contraception.

It was at this point that Pope Paul VI, after much soul-searching, took a momentous step: He overruled the commission with his 1968 encyclical *Humanae Vitae*, saying this was a question to be settled "by Ourself" (*per Nosmetipsos*). It is important to see just why this action mattered so much. It was a resort to *sheer* church authority where persuasion had failed—and this in an area not of direct revelation but of natural reason. Contraception is never mentioned in Scripture. Church authorities had differed on the subject in the past. This was not a matter that belonged to "the deposit of faith" as preserved in ancient creeds or the purely theological conclusions of doctrine-shaping councils. Those matters— the nature of the Incarnation, the Trinity, saving grace, and so on—are intimately involved with the Christian revelation. By the logic of the church's two forms of address in American politics, those matters should be the principal concern of authoritative pronouncement, for Catholics to observe as part of their recognition of church authority. Matters of natural ethics are better suited to the "track" of open discourse with all people concerned about morality. For the pope to use church authority (though not infallible "defining" authority) to maintain church discipline on an ethical issue, while confessing that he could not *convince* Catholics, undermined the very powers invoked.

It is quite wrong to say the laity "rebelled" against a clerical ban on contraception contained in Pope Paul VI's encyclical, *Humanae Vitae*. Fertility studies had shown widespread use of contraceptives by Catholics as early as the fifties, and in 1963, five years before the pope's encyclical, 50 percent of Catholics told pollsters that contraceptives were not immoral.[6] Even in the Depression of the 1930s, Catholic birthrates had indicated a turn to contraceptives (though observant Catholics may still have been confessing that as a sin).

What changed in 1968 was not the observance of the ban but the attitude toward authority expressed in it: Priests and seminarians, no more convinced than other Catholics by the papal arguments, were forced to teach what they did not believe. They had to accept external compliance as a condition of ordination, maintaining a system of mutual pretense with their bishops—all to satisfy Roman edicts on seminary training and the discipline of the confessional.

This system bred a skepticism about church authority that manifests itself in ways going far beyond the issue of contraception itself. Some seminarians refused to dissemble as the price of being ordained. Others went through the motions in a way that destroyed respect for the process. The need for outer compliance is one of the many things that has destroyed morale in the priesthood, leading to unprecedented defections and low levels of recruiting.[7] It also helped destroy the credibility of the nun's life as a submission to church discipline, draining away the teaching pool at Catholic schools. The sudden unpredicted falloff of Catholic regard for and use of the confessional was affected by the rules priests were supposed to impose and uphold there. Either they observed these rules or they refused to—in either case, the moral authority of this intimate tribunal was damaged.

The Papacy had tried to use doctrinal authority for an essentially ascetical purpose—the rhetoric of Roman prelates held that contraception was a yielding to modern hedonism and sensuality. This argument has great force for people whose celibate vocation calls for resistance to even normal sexual solicitings. It is out of place in married and secular life. The ban on contraception was part of a whole constellation of rulings that show clerical preoccupation with sexual matters—the maintenance of a celibate and all-male priesthood; the policing of reproductive processes (not only as regards contraception and abortion but in bans on sterilization and artificial insemination); the nonlegitimacy of any sexual pleasure not "open to" reproduction (not only masturbation, indulgence in pornography, fornication, and adultery, but even intercourse in marriage that is interrupted, blocked by contraception, or conducted after deliberate sterilization); and the censorship of explicitly depicted sex.

Most Catholics have concluded that their clerical leaders are unhinged on the subject of sex. Thus a stand taken to defy the world's permissiveness has backfired and *introduced* a whole new sexual ethic among Catholics. Until the 1960s, Catholics were measurably more ascetical in their sexual attitudes than other Americans. Since then, they have become more tolerant than the national average—accepting premarital sex, for instance, in twice the numbers reported for Protestants.[8] This tolerance has undermined teachings that even liberal priests once thought unchangeable (e.g., the bans on divorce and homosexuality). And on abortion, Catholics are no longer very different from most of their fellow Americans, either in belief or in practice.[9] Cuomo was able to use this datum in his Notre Dame speech, noting that the bishops were calling for a law that would forbid abortion not only for those non-Catholics who find nothing wrong with it, but for Catholics as well. Where their own teaching has failed with their own people, they would resort to state coercion, just as they tried to use papal coercion to forbid contraception.

As Cuomo said in his Notre Dame speech:

> Despite the teaching in our homes and schools and pulpits, despite the sermons and pleadings of parents and priests and prelates, despite all the effort at defining our opposition to the sin of abortion, collectively we Catholics apparently believe—and perhaps act—little differently from those who don't share our commitment.
>
> Are we asking government to make criminal what we believe to be sinful because we ourselves can't stop committing the sin?

Yet Cuomo reasserted his sincere belief that abortion *is* sin. He still accepted "church doctrine" as his own personal discipline, even on a matter not directly revealed. He spoke of the *church's* teaching as if "the people of God" were not the church but only the teaching authorities *in* that church. He spoke like John Kennedy, though the contraception dispute had changed Catholic attitudes toward "church teaching" on sexual matters.

In fact, as a ploy against the bishops, he stressed the *similarity* of the ban on contraception and that on abortion, and reminded the bishops that they have given up their effort to change the law for everyone on the sale and use of contraceptives:

> On divorce and birth control, without changing its moral teaching, the Church [by which he means leaders of the church] abides by the civil law as it now stands, thereby accepting—without making much of a point of it—that in our pluralistic society we are not required to insist that all our religious values be the law of the land.

Cuomo was not challenging the "church doctrine" on contraception or divorce, just pointing out that the application of one's beliefs to political debate—what he called the job of prudentially "translating Catholic teachings into public policy"—varies according to circumstance.

Cuomo's position was bound to be unsatisfactory. By accepting a "church teaching" valid for him as a Catholic, he makes some wonder why he does not show enthusiasm for that teaching in public debate. He merely *receives* it passively in his own case—despite the fact that this particular teaching indicates that murder is being committed. (Abortion is like genocide to those who think human persons are being killed—not something one can witness *without* moral protest.)

On the other hand, for those who question the credibility of clerical decrees on ethics, Cuomo's docility is the frustrating aspect of his speech. Why should he accept "doctrine" in this case (or in that of contraception, the parallel he invokes)? After all, popes have no special expertise for telling when life begins. *They* are not "applying" the Bible or some theological truth. If they have a good case to make, it must be one that convinces even Catholics in the *public* discourse that failed on contraception. If they have a better case on abortion, they must *make* it, and Cuomo should lend these arguments his eloquence. But he does not argue the matter; he merely accepts (privately) and sets aside (in public) the datum that a fetus is a human life from conception. This is very different from his eloquence and enthusiasm in opposing the death penalty, on which he has strong personal convictions.

What this means, of course, is that Cuomo claims to believe the church's teaching on abortion, but *acts* as if he does not. Pro-choice critics are infuriated by his belief; pro-life believers are just as indignant at his actions (or lack of them). Since most of the public is not simply classifiable as pro-life or pro-choice, this may be a shrewd political position; but it damages Cuomo in his claim to be a Catholic intellectual who reaches his conclusions from a well-trained conscience and not as a matter of political expediency.

If popes have no sure answer to the question When does life begin, neither does modern science. It depends on what one means by human life. Christian theologians have long said what *they* mean by that term— they mean the soul that is saved by Jesus' redemption; but that gets one no nearer an answer to the question of when that soul comes into existence. In fact, it was precisely because of St. Augustine's theology of the soul that he confessed repeatedly, in his period of episcopal teaching, that he did not know when or how the soul was joined to the body.

St. Augustine's theological concerns made him ask most urgently not when *life* begins but when *guilt* does. He was certain of two revealed truths: that the sacrifice of Jesus redeems the baptized soul, and that original sin made that redemption necessary. But when and how does the soul join the human race in its communal experience of historical guilt? If God creates each soul directly, can He be blamed for producing defective goods (the soul flawed by original sin)? If the soul is one with Adam, does that mean it descends from his soul as well as his body? But *how*? Aristotle said animal souls were carried in male semen, but in the Christian scheme, this would mean souls are somehow lost when semen does not impregnate.[10] Did God create a kind of bank *(thesaurus)* of soul stuff, from which he could draw in supplying later bodies?[11] If so, then the soul stuff in that treasure house must have sinned in solidarity with the two embodied human souls (Adam and Eve). Baffled by these difficulties, Augustine kept flirting with the suspect view of Origen that the individual soul had sinned before being consigned to the death-prone bodies derived from Adam.[12] In agonies of ingenuity, Augustine even made up his own heretical-sounding hypothesis—that the soul of an unbaptized child might return to God while the body goes out of existence forever ("I have not heard of this opinion or read it elsewhere").[13] After listing the only four hypotheses he could support, Augustine was careful not to favor or exclude any of them (even one approximating Origen's) because

> I have not been able to discover in the accepted books of Scripture anything at all certain on the origin of the soul. . . . And when a thing obscure in itself defeats our capacity, and nothing else in Scripture comes to our help, it is not safe for humans to presume they can pronounce on it.[14]

When St. Thomas Aquinas addressed the problem of the fetus's humanity, he followed Aristotle in thinking there are successive animations (ensoulments) of a fetus—a vital soul *(anima)* when the embryo grows like a plant in the woman's body (the umbilicus is the "root" planted in the woman's body), an animal soul when the fetus initiates its own moves, a rational soul when it reflects on what it does.[15] Evidence of rationality occurs only after birth, so Aquinas was not sure when God infuses the immortal soul. But it is clearly not in the early stages of vital and animal ensoulment—that is why St. Thomas opposed the doctrine of the Virgin Mary's "immaculate conception." Her sinless soul would not have been infused at conception.[16]

The evidence of church belief derivable from its baptismal practices shows a similar lack of certitude about when there is a soul to baptize. St. Thomas was against baptizing the fetus while it is still in the womb, where "it cannot be subject to the operation of the ministers of the church, or it is not known to men" (or, presumably, capable of knowing response).[17] There was a wide variety of beliefs and practice on baptizing aborted fetuses, and baptism after birth was sometimes delayed to wait for clear signs of rationality.

Church authorities have more recently argued that the rational soul is infused at the moment of conception. They were influenced in part by the doctrine of the Immaculate Conception. This is the hodgepodge of considerations Mario Cuomo is bowing to when he accepts without question the "doctrine of the church" on abortion. He does not advance arguments of his own to repeat, enforce, or explain that doctrine. He simply deposits it in his own little *thesaurus* of faith, not to be expended outside his home.

There are elements in this theological history that are suggestive. St. Augustine thought of the beginning of life as the entry into the *social* nexus with history called original sin. You become an individual by becoming Adam's child, one of the people destined to inhabit the City of God or the Earthly City. St. Thomas's stress on the lack of interaction with other humans in the enwombed fetus points in the same direction. St. Augustine argued in *The Trinity* that persons exist only in interaction with other persons, even in the triune divinity. Modern theorists treat the human as coming to expression when it acquires a historically specific language system—including the gestures and body language Augustine observed in his baby son Adeodatus and described with such empathy in book one of the *Confessions*.

To say this is not to declare the fetus outside the human community. We humanize each other by our willingness to *include* others within that basic fellowship—the sick, the deformed, the retarded, the old. We have not become fully human unless we recognize their humanity. It is a mark of the humane to extend its own obligations—even to a kindness toward animals. The theologian Cuomo likes to cite, Teilhard de Chardin, thought that all of evolution was working toward a general "personalization" of the universe.

A stress on human community would contrast not only with the biological-mechanical approach that some Catholics think of as "natural law," but with the extreme pro-choice position that says a woman can do anything with the body she "owns." This view of private property as giving the owner laissez-faire rights is at odds with leftist positions on property as entailing social responsibility—as something held within a community, part of a nexus of mutual commitments.

William Buckley, in his early defenses of an absolutely private right in property, used to say that he could, with perfect morality, build a great palace on a mountaintop and blow it up. If it was his, he could do anything he wanted with it. That was Ronald Reagan's attitude toward the Panama Canal in the 1970s: "We bought it, we paid for it, it's ours."[18] We can keep it, do what we want with it—blow it up, presumably, if that is how we mean to dispose of the thing we bought absolutely.

John Locke treated the self as a "first property" (*proprium*), but even he said it was given in trust by God—which means one cannot reject the gift unilaterally by suicide.[19] When society condemns suicide, it says that even the right to one's body is not absolute. Disposal of that item affects others—parents, spouses, friends, children, the political community—for whom a person, so long as he or she remains responsible, must have regard. Even the apparently lone person must not be encouraged to give up hopes or claims on the community, as if his or her loss were to be considered of no wider concern. Among other things, this would foster a callousness of society toward its members.

Those who treat the fetus simply as property sometimes take a proprietary air toward the very *discussion* of abortion. They say only a woman can decide not only in the specific case of her own action but on the general values to be upheld. Logically, this should mean that only women who are or have been pregnant can form the moral discourse on this topic. In their own way, such feminists re-create the separate "woman's sphere" that Tocqueville described in nineteenth-century America. Both forms of this separatism are at odds with the citizen values of republicanism, wherein everyone in the community is invited to ponder together all moral issues. We do not say, in a republic, that only the military can decide on the role of the military in public life, that only the academy can frame educational issues, that only believers can frame religious issues, and so forth. Cuomo seems to be taking an enlightened stand when he apologizes, as a man, for speaking on abortion, but it is a nonrepublican position.[20]

Yet, *because* the community has its claims, the fetus should have no more absolute a right to life than the woman has an absolute right to her "property." Pro-life champions who treat (and act for) the fetus as a full person, with all the rights of one, have their own form of possessive individualism: The putative baby's rights are equal to the mother's, sealed off within it, to be played off against the mother's—hardly a communal arrangement. This, if logically pursued, would mean the state must give full protection to the fetus, even against the mother, by sheltering it from damaging "aggressions" like maternal smoking, drinking, drug use, and poor health practices. It would mean mothers must be forced to deliver fetuses whose humanity they and their most trusted associates doubt or firmly deny. Anti-abortion activists take the enforcement of this right into their own hands when, in the name of the fetus, they mount assaults on the fetus's mother in her attempt to reach an abortion clinic.

If the pregnant woman has social responsibility, it is asymmetrical to give the fetus all of the formed person's human rights and no responsibilities. The woman is called on to be self-sacrificing in certain social circumstances—for example, to protect her family or country. The fetus, if given human rights, does not (cannot) balance those with responsibilities. The mother can deny herself for the fetus's sake. The fetus cannot reciprocate. If we could imagine for a moment, *per impossible*, the fetus as having any moral claims against it as a responsible person, it would have to recognize that *its* right to itself is no more absolute than the mother's, that it would have to sacrifice itself for others, for the common good, for the country.

Trying to pit the rights of the fetus against those of its own mother and her helpers raises problems not only of enforceability—Cuomo says it would be like trying to enforce Prohibition—but of communal morality. Where there is disagreement on whether an object has entered the language-system of recognized mutual responsibilities, and that language-system of debate and exhortation is not so evil as to justify overthrow—as the slave system or the Nazi regime was—then attempts to coerce rather than persuade violate the humane concerns of the community. That is why pro-life comparisons of abortion to slavery or the Holocaust are misguided.

It is true that some religious extremists *do* think modern society is basically evil and corrupt—Godless in its government, pagan in its sensuality, morally unresponsive to divine signals. For them, overthrowing the communal arrangements is desirable, though few would use force. But their focus on abortion as merely one symptom of the perversive evil should have no influence on those who, however uncertain themselves on the abortion issue, do not doubt the good faith of those debating it. It also shows bad faith for the religious extremists to try to use a corrupt government to suppress one practice. They are resorting to tactics meant to undermine the regime itself and not the single practice.

This is not an argument for the disposability of a human life. But, precisely because we do not know—any more than the pope does, or science, or St. Augustine—when the person begins, to treat the questionable human as having *more than* normal human immunities and exemptions is morally absurd. It is especially dubious to assume a full contractual partnership between the "individuum" in the womb and that part of the human community, the mother, that is its mode of passage into partnership with others.

If Cuomo were to take a communal approach to abortion, little in his practical recommendations would have to change (counseling, adoption, support of mothers and their babies, better social services after birth)—though some things would be different because "church doctrine" would not be deferred to: Better education on contraception would be a Cuomo cause, and wider distribution of free condoms. The real difference would be a consonance between his practice and his profession. That would free him to use argument and rhetoric with a passion and consistency that he has stored in the deposit box with that "church doctrine" he claims to be preserving.

There is nothing in the approach I have recommended that conflicts with Catholic faith, so far as I am aware. It may even be more consonant with Augustine's theology of the person—a theology that made it impossible for him to find a single demarcation point for the joining of the human community. It certainly does conflict with the discipline the pope and bishops would like to impose on the subject of abortion. But this is the same discipline they have tried to impose on the subject of contraception, and most Catholics, clerical and lay, now recognize that discipline as an elaborate sham. The church "line" on abortion is also obsolete. It is a useful fiction for the bishops. For Mario Cuomo, it is more like a political dodge. I know it is unrealistic to expect a Catholic politician to defy the bishops, but I am not considering the man's career, just his argument. Those who think, with Bruce Babbitt, that "Mario got it right" are probably too sanguine.

Evangelicals:
Francis Schaeffer

ST. AUGUSTINE FELT THAT HE COULD NOT MAINTAIN HIS POSTURE OF suspended judgment *(cunctatio)* about the soul's origin unless he made a systematic search for enlightenment on the subject from Scripture. But he could not turn up a text with anything definitive *(certum)* in it. He was galled when his critics said he (of all people) had given up on the quest for knowledge. He responded with a testy counteraccusation: If Scripture does not settle this kind of problem, perhaps it is sinful to aspire after knowledge denied to man. But even in making this response Augustine continued to test every verse of Scripture brought up by critics for its relevance to the subject.[1]

Evangelicals have recently come up with a biblical passage that, they claim, solves the problem. In the San Diego Museum of Creation there is a large image of a fetus; under it, blown up to poster-size lettering, is verse 13 of Psalm 139. This says, in the New English Bible version: "Thou it was who didst fashion my inward parts; thou didst knit me together in my mother's womb."[2] One wonders why St. Augustine never took this verse as conclusive since he liked to meditate on the fact that God knew him, in childhood, even before he knew himself—a fact that lay at the heart of Augustine's epistemological claim that God is a party to one's knowledge even more intimately than is the knower: He is "more immediate to me than I am to myself" *(intimior intimo meo)*.[3]

But Psalm 139 turns out to be less useful to the evangelical case when we read beyond verse 13. The entire passage runs:

> Thou it was who didst fashion my inward parts;
>> thou didst knit me together in my mother's womb.
> I will praise thee,
>> for thou dost fill me with awe;
> wonderful thou art, and wonderful thy works.
> Thou knowest me through and through:
>> my body is no mystery to thee,
> how I was secretly kneaded into shape
>> and patterned in the depths of the earth.
> Thou didst see my limbs unformed in the womb,
>> and in thy book they are all recorded;
>> day by day they were fashioned,
>> not one of them was late in growing.

This has some useful references to God fashioning a person in the womb; but it goes too far in tracing his superintendence back into the roots of time. How was the soul "patterned in the depths of the earth"?[4] This suggests God's providence over all the elements that might someday be drawn into the physical stuff of a human being—and one cannot show "reverence to life" by treating every molecule as, potentially, part of a future fetus. The same difficulty obtrudes if the pro-life theologian cites the second half of the distich at Jeremiah 1.5: "before you were born I consecrated you." The line preceding says, *"Before I formed you in the womb* I knew you for my own" (italics added). Again, God's foreknowledge is prefetal.

Another passage of the Jewish Scripture is cited by fundamentalists as decisive for the abortion issue: that one who accidentally strikes a pregnant woman, causing either premature birth or stillbirth, must pay the penalty—even to life for life—demanded by the husband (Exodus 21.22–25).[5] But in the tribal world of ancient Israel, damaging another's seed was taking away an investment in a certain family line. That is what makes the sin of Onan, not masturbation (as moralists used to say), but the denial of his seed to a woman with a right to an heir from his family. The same word is used three times in two verses of Genesis (38.8–9), to suggest the comprehensive claim of the woman's family over what might be called seed-rights: Onan was bound to maintain his brethren's seed

*(zera*c*)* by not spilling his own seed *(zera*c*)* on the ground but giving it
to his brother's wife as offspring *(zera*c*).*[6]

It is Abraham's *seed* that will be blessed, and the lodging of that seed
in a woman is a time to be celebrated, as the hope for offspring becomes
concrete. So the Psalmist dates life from the womb (Psalms 22.10, 51.5,
58.3), just as the Spirit blesses the Virgin Mary's womb (Luke 1.42)—
another verse the evangelicals use is Luke 1.41, where John the Baptist
quickens in the womb at Mary's approach.

None of these patriarchal texts, celebrating the fertility of endangered
family lines (much as marriage celebrates the commitment to that hope)
is a convincing marker of when life begins—as St. Augustine recognized.
In fact, this whole biblical approach to abortion is a novelty even in
fundamentalist circles. These are new readings, not accepted parts of
Protestantism's biblical heritage (like, say, the virgin birth or other fundamentals from the first decades of this century). Evangelicals admit as
much when they say they came late to this issue, that they are zealous
now out of penance for earlier neglect.[7] Abortion has now become a
more galvanizing issue for them than for Catholics, from whom they
have taken away the leadership so far as pro-life activism is concerned.[8]

What led to this development? One man deserves more credit than
anyone else—Francis Schaeffer (1912–1984), the American social critic
whose Swiss chalet became the shrine of a new oracle in the 1970s.
Schaeffer was a product of the breakup of Presbyterianism in the 1920s.
When theological liberalism finally took over the stronghold of biblical
literalism, the Princeton Theological Seminary, J. Gresham Machen led
the last literalists out into the desert to found a pure new community in
Philadelphia—the Westminster School of Theology, established in 1929.
But the quest for purity is never-ending, and in 1937 a charismatic young
man trained at Westminster, Carl McIntire, took disciples away from
Machen, to be fundamentalister-than-thou at Faith Theological Seminary.[9] Schaeffer, who had begun his studies with Machen in 1935,
continued them with McIntire, in whose network of separatist mission
activities Schaeffer achieved his first prominence.

Sent to Europe in 1947, to size up mission possibilities there, Schaeffer
decided to approach the postwar culture of European existentialism as if
he were a preacher in the South Sea Islands dealing with "native" gods.
When he moved to Switzerland in 1949 he dealt with the use of Søren
Kierkegaard by modern non-Christians as if he had come across the traces
of a jungle missionary whose teachings had been turned into a travesty

of the gospel. As he pursued this idea, he decided that the earlier preacher (Kierkegaard) had misunderstood the gospel himself, betraying it in ways that invited infidelity. In fact, Kierkegaard became for Schaeffer the initiator of a despair that could be discerned in all of modern culture, its philosophy, its art, and even its theology.

Kierkegaard, according to Schaeffer, had given up the integrated world of grace and nature bequeathed by the Reformation. Unable to make sense of the "lower story" of natural knowledge, he made a leap of faith into the "upper story" of grace and revelation.[10] As these two aspects of life were separated, the "lower story" fell apart, with no higher principle for integrating its constituents, and the "upper story" became a floating place of desperate hopes and dreams. A failure of reason below led to increasingly hallucinatory mysticisms above (like Teilhard de Chardin's).[11] The jostling of these incompatible worlds inched Western culture across a "line of despair" into panicky modernity.

Different parts of Western culture crossed the line of despair at different moments—Europe as a whole getting most of its thought and art over the line by 1890, America lagging behind (it crossed the line in 1935, a date suspiciously close to that of the schism at Westminster Theological Seminary). Artists first dissolved the "lower" world (Impressionists), then fragmented it (Cubists), then dismantled it (Duchamp), then dabbled in the ruins (Pollock). Music took the same course, but with a slight lag, going from Debussy to Schönberg to John Cage to the Beatles.[12]

Though nonevangelicals would consider Schaeffer's art criticism philistine, it was a refreshing *initiation* into cultural criticism for those who had been encouraged to neglect secular concerns. Schaeffer found theological statements in literature and music, praising "Reformation artists" like Bach and Rembrandt. And though Schaeffer made Kierkegaard's supposedly Christian existentialism the dynamite that had started the whole landslide of modern collapse, he invented an "apologetics" that pushed non-Christians deeper into their despair for therapeutic purposes.

Conversion, according to Schaeffer, depends on bringing a person to a "point of pressure" where the (upper story) aspirations of false mysticism pull one against the residue of order and reality in the (lower story) world of God's created nature. Such a person tries to mask the tensions, and the evangelist then rips off this cover. "Taking the roof off," Schaeffer called it, and he admitted this process risked becoming a form of benign torture, or human experimentation, unless one prayed that the Spirit remain in control of the process:

We ought not to try first to move a man away from the logical conclusion of his [false] position but towards it. . . . As I seek to do this, I need to remind myself constantly that this is not a game I am playing. If I begin to enjoy it as a kind of intellectual exercise, then I am cruel and can expect no real spiritual results. As I push the man off his false balance, he must be able to feel that I care for him. . . . It is unpleasant to be submerged by an avalanche, but we must allow the person to undergo this experience so that he may realize his system has no answer to the crucial questions of life. . . . The hardest thing of all is that when we have exposed modern man to this tension, he still may not be willing for the true solution. . . . We confront men with reality; we remove their protection and their escapes; we allow the avalanches to fall. If they do not become Christians, then indeed they are in a worse state than before we spoke to them.[13]

Schaeffer justified this form of preaching in terms of "presupposition-alism," the apologetic method taught him, at Westminster Theological Seminary, by Cornelius Van Til.[14] Van Til claimed that one cannot reach other people with the gospel so long as worldly presuppositions block access. One must break down the presuppositions; and Schaeffer felt the best way to do this is by throwing the person's whole weight on them, to see if they will bear it. Ironically, this made his attack on existentialism take the form of deeper plunges into it, an attempt at a homeopathic cure. He was surprisingly like the postwar Catholic existentialists—Jacques Maritain's followers—who were encouraging a Sartrean anguish for Christian purposes.

Adolescent moodiness was the most promising field for Schaeffer's dabblings in benign despair. His ministry in America had begun in the Child Evangelism Fellowship, from which he broke to form the McIntire-inspired Children for Christ ministry. This meant that he had good contacts with youth ministries in Europe. As enterprising young people discovered the novelty of his approach, they began to treat journeys to his first chalet in Champéry as an existentialist adventure. Schaeffer was driven out of Champéry in 1954—by Catholics, he says, who resented his conversion of one of their young people to evangelicalism. He settled in Huénoz and purchased the chalet he called L'Abri (The Refuge) through what his followers call "a series of miraculous circumstances."[15]

As the youth culture of the sixties grew, "Jesus people" and drug addicts became harder to distinguish. Some pious attendants at L'Abri felt that, like the holy bishop in Les Misérables, Schaeffer entertained people possessed by devils.[16] His counseling became more shrewd and worldly, and his cultural pronouncements more grand. Elaborating a history of God's work in taped Saturday-night bull sessions, Schaeffer came up with a theory of pre-Reformation fall to match his post-Reformation theory of Kierkegaard's ravages. The villain of earlier time was St. Thomas Aquinas. Kierkegaard had abandoned the "lower story" of reasoning and nature; but Aquinas had concentrated too much effort there, convinced he could explain everything with Aristotle's help. He gave short shrift to grace and the "upper story" of the mystical. Kierkegaard's impact on art was disintegrative, but Aquinas made the physical world *too* solid and stable; too self-sufficient, thick; no longer lit through with the supernatural. The Kierkegaardian "fall" went from Renoir to Pollock by way of Picasso, shredding reality. The Thomistic fall went from Cimabue to Michelangelo by way of Masaccio, compacting reality into the dense and inert physical.[17] By 1977 Schaeffer was ready to present his version of Western history in a ten-part television series hailed by American evangelicals as the "answer" to the humanist Kenneth Clark's *Civilisation* series. This film, *How Then Shall We Live?*, gave Schaeffer his reputation as an American C. S. Lewis, a devout litterateur, using seminars instead of revivals to bring people to Christ.

There was a torrent of books and articles by and about Francis Schaeffer in the 1970s, as he emptied his taped talks into two dozen different volumes. His revised *Complete Works* were published in five volumes in 1982. Young evangelicals were inspired to academic careers by his pronouncements on philosophy; and many young academicians became serious evangelicals.

In 1973, the *Roe* v. *Wade* decision convinced Schaeffer that he could no longer encourage modern despair in the hope that it would self-destruct. The legalization of murder showed that modern society had entered a demonic new phase that called for resistance, even to the breaking of the law. With the help of C. Everett Koop, the brilliant pediatric surgeon who later became United States surgeon general, he made a new film series attacking abortion *(Whatever Happened to the Human Race?)* in 1979, and he issued *A Christian Manifesto* in 1981. The latter work expanded his version of the Reformation and modernity's fall from it. According to Schaeffer, the intellectual source of the American Revolution was the Scottish theologian Samuel Rutherford, whose views on ordered freedom under God were disseminated to our founding fathers by Princeton's president, John Witherspoon. Rutherford's form of legitimate government began breaking down in the 1840s (under the flood of Catholic immigration) and reached the point, in 1973, where

Christians accepted the authority of a "baby-killing" regime, a modern Moloch.[18]

When I first met Randall Terry, the activist leader of Operation Rescue, as he was about to close some abortion clinics in California, he asked if I had read Francis Schaeffer. I had to confess that I had not. "You have to read Schaeffer's *Christian Manifesto* if you want to understand Operation Rescue." Terry had been assigned several books by Schaeffer in his classes at Elim Bible Institute in Lima, New York, and had a whole new world of insights opened to him. Convinced that Schaeffer was "the greatest modern Christian philosopher," Terry began his self-education in history, interpreting America's past in Rutherfordian terms. When I mentioned St. Augustine to him, Terry dismissed him by saying he was the forerunner of the Renaissance—a confusion of Augustine with Schaeffer's villain, Aquinas. "I hate the Renaissance," he explained.

By the time he attracted national attention at the 1988 Democratic Convention in Atlanta, where mass arrests of his followers took place, Terry had gathered around him a cadre of dedicated young evangelicals who were responding to Schaeffer's call for civil disobedience. Schaeffer had traveled the country showing his films against abortion while dying of cancer—a proof, for his cultists, that he "gave his life" for unborn babies.

By the 1980s, evangelists like Jerry Falwell and Pat Robertson were quoting and praising Francis Schaeffer; but Terry's group considered the lucrative preachers' careers corrupting. They felt toward the electronic church rather as Dorothy Day's *Catholic Worker* staff felt about the television priest Fulton Sheen in the 1950s. The quiet witness of the resister had become a model for radical Christians on the Protestant side, who were repeating some of the activities that led Dorothy Day's followers into the civil rights and antiwar movements.

There was even a direct tie. Some Catholic leftists, adopting Cardinal Bernardin's "seamless garment" approach to the sacredness of life, combined opposition to abortion with stands against capital punishment, nuclear weapons, and exploitation of the poor. They brought the nonviolent tactics of civil disobedience to their protests at abortion clinics. This early activism by Catholics produced the most respected martyr of the movement—Joan Andrews, a pacifist opponent of the Vietnam War who served two and a half years in a Florida jail for attempting to disengage a suction machine used in abortions. She practiced "loving noncooperation" with her jailers and was put in solitary confinement. After her release, she traveled abroad, especially in Catholic countries (Spain, Italy, and Latin America), continuing her protests. Others in this movement included John Kavenaugh-O'Keefe, a Harvard graduate inspired to pacifism by the writings of the Trappist Thomas Merton, and Juli Loesch Wiley, who dropped out of college to organize workers for Cesar Chavez in the California lettuce fields—she became an early press representative for Operation Rescue. Daniel Berrigan, the Jesuit war protester, also joined anti-abortion actions.

These nonviolent activists were at odds with two other groups of their fellow Catholics—the National Right to Life Committee (derived from an early organization founded by the nation's bishops, which discouraged breaking the law and depended on letter writing and Washington marches), and frankly harassing organizations that indulged in kamikaze activities like bombing clinics and threatening doctors. Terry, who went to several national gatherings of anti-abortionists in the 1980s, wisely chose the nonviolent Catholic activists as his model, and worked to impose discipline on the thousands of protesters he was able to turn out by the end of the 1980s.

During Holy Week of 1989, I met Terry in Pittsburgh to fly with him to California for a series of rescues in the Los Angeles area. He went over with his traveling staff the plans for the next few days. Rescues involve surprising the staffs at abortion clinics—an early warning would make them either close the clinic (preventing a confrontation) or bring in counterdemonstrators to keep the doors open. Alternate targets, "feints," last-minute changes, radioed messages to bypass clinics too well prepared—all these are part of the elaborate jockeyings that take place even before the rescuers reach their goals (sometimes one, sometimes several on a day, depending on the number of rescuers available, the state of their transportation, the geographical spread of the clinics). Each side—pro-life and pro-choice—tries to infiltrate the other's intelligence system, to spread confusing rumors and false claims there while picking up sound information for itself.

News of Terry's arrival has reached his foes, though he switched planes on his way to Los Angeles, coming in at the San Diego airport. A member of the crew comes back to say that airport security men, wanting to avoid trouble, will bring the van meeting Terry onto the tarmac and spirit his party out a side way. Terry frets that he will look like a "wimp'" for ducking this opportunity to confront his foes; but the staff dissuades him from driving around to the front of the airport to surprise his surprisers.

The motel where Terry meant to stay has canceled his reservation, since it too fears trouble. His team scrambles to nearby fleabags where his name will not be recognized. Terry has to go to a night rally, held across from Disneyland in Anaheim, where songs and sermons lead up to instructions on the nonviolent closing of clinics. Terry is everywhere at the rally, greeting people while others talk, playing soft-rock hymns on an electronic organ, delivering an emotional harangue in the style of a younger Billy Graham.

It is still dark when the cars start arriving the next morning. Rescuers have been warned to go easy on the morning coffee since there will be no breaks to go to the bathroom once they are wedged in at the doorways. Some middle-aged middle-class people look uncomfortable in the old clothes they have put on for lying on the sidewalk and wearing in the prison. The younger leaders bustle around, nervous with their last-minute choices of targets, ready to switch even now. They have alternate maps and Polaroid photos of each relevant clinic's layout. They will pass out the routes for the cars only as each car leaves the parking lot.

Even while they confer, deciding that enough of their troops have gathered to move out, panicky aides with walkie-talkies bring news that pro-choice opponents have blocked all exits from the lot with their own cars. Terry wants to gather some of the heftier men and go lift the locked cars out of the exitways; but Jeff White, the California leader in nominal charge today, calms him down by circling nearby leaders for a prayer session. Better news arrives when the prayer is ending—police have started clearing the cars, since their orders are to keep open access no matter who is doing the blocking. The pro-choice people return to their cars, and ride alongside the file of rescuers' vehicles, radioing each change of route to indicate where they will strike.

At this day's site, in Cypress, the first arrivers sprint to the clinic's front door, where thirty people are prepared to counter their efforts. The rescuers use superior numbers to crowd the pro-choice people back on the doors, making them part of the dense wedge ("They are helping us save the babies"). Others, as they arrive, jam themselves around the six other ways into the clinic.

Conveniently, the small Cypress police station is just across the street from the clinic. Negotiations on procedures could be opened immediately. Joseph Foreman, thirty-four, is the Operation Rescue man delegated to police relations this day. He informs the police of the group's intention to block the doors and asks what charges will be brought against them. The rescuers normally go limp, so that it takes four police officers to carry off one demonstrator, but the means of entry into arrest vans is always negotiable. Foreman agrees to have his people walk onto the buses:

"I hate to have them carried onto the buses. Someone always gets hurt." But when Foreman tells Terry of the arrangements, Terry sends him back to get assurances that the police will not arrest at too great a speed, in exchange for the walk-on. It is the kind of change in terms that makes the police distrustful of Operation Rescue, and Foreman is clearly unhappy at this infringement of his on-site authority.

Some seven hundred pro-lifers at the clinic are divided into three main groups—the rescuers, jammed in the doorways; authorized "sidewalk counselors," who tell any arriving patient that she can discuss a way to keep her baby at a nearby "crisis pregnancy center"; and "prayer supporters," who are asked to sing hymns and observe the police. Each group has its own marshal instructing it, and no one in the three groups is supposed to talk to any outsider—police, press, or hecklers. Most observe the discipline, but the prayer supporters are the least predictable—sympathizers who do not mean to go to jail, they often get carried away because of the hecklers, or at sight of their friends being arrested. At every rally they are urged not to get into arguments. Mike McMonagle, the only Roman Catholic in the leadership of Operation Rescue, told them the night before: "If you shout even something as unthreatening as 'We will help you' to an arriving mother, the sound of thirty voices shouting that does not say what you mean it to say. Leave it to the sidewalk counselors, who are trained at persuasion." Prayer supporters would be more of a nuisance than a help if so many of them did not decide, on seeing their comrades arrested, to fill in the emptied places in front of the doors. In almost every case, more people go to jail than had intended to.

Pro-choice protesters ring the pro-lifers, trying to cover them up with placards, so that the TV cameras register support for the clinics. The pro-choicers chant and demand the arrest of the pro-lifers: "Read 'em their rights, and take 'em away." Each group has its grisly signs—aborted fetuses on one side, women's corpses bloody from illegal abortions on the other. It is a noisy scene, hymns versus chanted slogans, with both sides resorting to bullhorns to be heard above the din (police finally adding their own loudspeakers). The task of the police is first to detach the two groups, ordering those who do not wish to be arrested to move away. That brings all but the most embedded pro-choicers out of the milling near the doors. Then the arrests begin—373 of them in Cypress on the Thursday before Easter.

On the Friday before Easter, the rescuers showed up in Long Beach, where the police are under a shadow of alleged brutality. Officers were especially polite, clearing some paths but making no arrests. The clinic closed down. On the day before Easter, in Los Angeles, 725 arrests were made in a pelting rain that turned the rescuers into sodden clumps. Most of those arrested remained in jail over Easter, refusing to give their names or be released until felony charges were dropped against four of their leaders (including Terry).

These experiences have "radicalized" many staid churchgoers who never expected to see the inside of a jail. Dr. King has become the improbable hero for people who opposed him during his lifetime. A few more literate leaders are busy rediscovering an evangelical heritage of civil disobedience—including the Oberlin College stop on the underground railway that helped slaves escape from the South.[19] Terry likes to cite the case of Dietrich Bonhoeffer, the Lutheran minister who resisted Hitler. The young corps of Operation Rescue leaders have sold homes and divested themselves of attachable properties to live immune from confiscations. Terry and others are in and out of jail. Though critics doubt their sincerity, the level of dedication seems as high as that of the civil rights and antiwar protesters, whom they have come increasingly to resemble. If one *does* think that abortion is the taking of innocent life, surely their response makes more sense than does Mario Cuomo's.

Feminists and Fundamentalism

ONE DOES NOT NEED A SPECIFICALLY RELIGIOUS MOTIVE TO CONCLUDE that the human fetus has a life that is worth preserving, but statistics show that it helps. The two groups most supportive of full human rights for the fetus are also the two which deny women full access to church office. In the case of Catholic authorities, this second-place role for women is derived from a fundamentalism about tradition—the tradition of the celibate male priest. Among evangelicals who lean toward biblical fundamentalism, the role is determined by passages in the Pauline writings— and especially from a fatal verse (11.8) in the First Epistle to the Corinthians.

Both Catholics and evangelicals say they are not denying the dignity of women when they emphasize the vital role of motherhood and the completion of all (wanted or unwanted) pregnancies. But if they are so concerned with women, why do they deny them clerical status in their churches? Both claim they want to protect women—by the suppression of pornography, by the rejection of any alternative to heterosexual and monogamous marriage except celibacy. But this protection often looks like sequestration, so that a prominent Catholic like Phyllis Schlafly and a prominent evangelical like Beverly LaHaye oppose feminism as a challenge to the home, where a woman should be enshrined (or imprisoned, according to one's view).[1] The two fundamentalisms converge in their opposition to things like the Equal Rights Amendment.

Though St. Paul has become the target of feminist critics of the Bible, his early communities differed from their Jewish matrices by a *lack* of female sequestration. Women were involved in the wide range of leadership functions named in the authentic letters of Paul. They make up a third of the forty-eight individuals named.[2] The Phoebe of Romans 16.1–2 is deacon to the church of Cenchreae.[3] Prisca is named before her husband at Romans 16.3—as at Acts 18.18 and 18.26.[4] (Paul lived at Prisca's household when he was in Corinth.) Even the verse that has caused so much trouble for women's rights occurs at the point where Paul is *defending* women's right to prophesy in the gathering (1 Corinthians).

The trouble does not arise because Paul says that women prophets should wear veils, but in the hortatory reason he adds for maintaining that custom: "A man has no need to cover his head, because man is the image of God, and the mirror of his glory, whereas woman reflects the glory of man" (1 Corinthians 11.7). That passage is now offensive to women, though it simply reflects Jewish commonplaces of the time— and Paul goes on, shortly, to deprive it of its invidiousness: "And yet, in Christ's fellowship woman is as essential to man as man to woman. If woman was made out of man, it is through woman that man now comes to be; and God is the source of all" (1 Corinthians 11.11–12). In the creation myth, woman's extraction from the side of man reflects the solidarity of the human race, which is reciprocally expressed every time a male is extracted from the woman's womb. The cycle had to begin somewhere, but its meaning is fully expressed only when the cycle is completed. This is in accord with Paul's teaching that in Christ "there is neither male nor female" (Galatians 3.28).[5]

The problem for fundamentalists arises from the concessive clause in Paul's final argument: "If woman was made out of man . . ." The basis for that assumption was stated bluntly in the intervening verse (1 Corinthians 11.8): "For man did not originally spring from woman, but woman was made out of man." Here Paul seems to treat the Genesis account of creation as ordinary history, and the fundamentalists become triumphant: "You see? This is a case of inerrancy redoubled. The inspired author of one part of the Bible gives us proper guidance for reading another part of the Bible." The real importance of the passage has, for them, less to do with Corinth than with disputes over creationism.

Francis Schaeffer made this verse the crucial one for defending the whole of Scripture:

> What is involved here (as in this whole discussion) is not just the first chapters of Genesis, but the authoritativeness of the New Testament as well, and especially the writings of Paul. If Paul is wrong in the factual statement about Eve's coming from Adam, there is no reason to have certainty in the authority of any New Testament factual statement, including the factual statement that Christ rose physically from the dead.[6]

Other evangelicals have welcomed the chance to pack multiple issues of inerrancy into this single verse, making creationism, the status of women, and the self-confirming authority of the Bible reinforce each other. So heavily was this one verse freighted with significance that challenge to it from an evangelical scholar set off hysterical reaction in the 1970s, in what came to be known as the Battle for the Bible.

Fuller Theological Seminary, set up in 1947 by the "new evangelical" Billy Graham and the "old evangelical" Charles Fuller, was supposed to show that people could be true to an inerrant Bible yet welcome the insights of modernity. The guardians of inerrancy were dubious about the project from the beginning and kept the school under close doctrinal scrutiny. Other disputes had been bitter, but one of the harshest grew out of a professor's argument that inerrancy should yield to women's rights. Paul Jewett, who had begun his scholarly life as a literalist, asserted in *Man as Male and Female* (1975) that the very verse on which Francis Schaeffer pinned so much was simply wrong. George Marsden, who wrote the history of this controversy, describes Jewett's offense:

> Now Jewett had quite frankly changed his position. Since he had arrived at Fuller, other faculty had been noticing this transition. Its full extent, however, now becomes dramatically (and for some disconcertingly) apparent in his efforts to reconcile what he saw as the dominant biblical teaching of equality of the sexes with the apostle Paul's statements apparently to the contrary. Jewett's way of revealing this conundrum was, in the evangelical context, startling. Rather than claiming that the apostle was saying something other than what he seemed to be saying or that Paul's statements about the subordination of women had only local or temporal application, Jewett argued that the apostle was simply mistaken.[7]

Harold Lindsell, a founder and ex-vice-president of Fuller who had edited the leading evangelical journal *Christianity Today*, mounted an attack on his old institution. Associating himself with Schaeffer's defense of the key verse in Corinthians, he wrote *The Battle for the Bible* (1976) and

The Bible in the Balance (1979). Others, accepting his definition of the terms of combat, wrote books like *The Battle for Creation* and *The Battle for the Resurrection*. The seminary was rocked by public controversy. Fearing for its funds, it had to issue placatory statements in an attempt to hold the different factions together. Founders and alumni of the school took sides and vilified each other. One founder, Charles Woodbridge, denounced his own son for not denouncing the school with sufficient vehemence.[8] It was what Marsden calls "evangelical civil war," fought over the single verse by which Schaeffer would have the entire Bible stand or fall.

Paul Jewett stood his ground, and went on to publish *The Ordination of Women: An Essay on the Office of Christian Ministry* (1980). But he was clearly at odds with the history of his own institution, where women had been discouraged from studying theology—they could not, after all, be ministers and should not be encouraged to defy that ban.[9] Some people bravely try to favor women's rights while staying true to an inerrant Bible, but a work like Ronald and Beverly Allen's *Liberated Traditionalism* (1985) shows how tortuous is the process. The authors try to convince themselves that the unveiled women "prophets" in 1 Corinthians 11 were former prostitutes with shaved heads.[10]

The Bible is used by less sophisticated fundamentalists to justify a patriarchal family, with wife and children obeying the man as God's representative. In Christian schools, for instance—which have been opening at a rate of two per day since 1960—the subordination of women is demanded along with the sacred right of paddling children.[11] The Genesis account of creation is also used to mobilize people against gay rights. In the creationist slogan, "God created Adam and Eve, not Adam and Steve"—as if one cannot be male or female unless one is ordinated to heterosexual intercourse.[12]

Thus the fundamentalist view of creation is not simply a doctrinal nicety, or even a protest against social Darwinism in accord with Bryan's position of the 1920s. It is also the basis of a social agenda deeply opposed to liberation from the patriarchal family. That is the context that makes it easier for evangelicals to see women's duty as preservation of the male seed in all cases. There is a clear parallel with the way biblical fundamentalism shored up the institution of slavery in the nineteenth century—a connection Forrest G. Wood has recently made.[13] Thus it is important for the good of civil society that believers should persuade other Christians not to use the Bible against people's rights.

For Catholics, biblical literalism does not impede the recognition of women's rights. Their problem is with literalism about traditional rites. Catholics used to be taught that church life revolves around the sacraments validly administered—and especially around the Eucharist. Consecration of the sacred bread and wine, the central sacrifice of the church, was something only a priest could do—but he could do it anywhere, even if he was alone, unworthy, stranded like a "whiskey priest" in a Graham Greene tale. The consecration acted like magic.

The impression was created that this had always been the church's activity and attitude. But no apostle or leader of the early church—in all the rich welter of titles given—is ever called a priest *(hiereus)*.[14] Paul never calls himself or his colleagues that—and he never mentions his or their presiding at the Eucharist.[15] In all the controversies surrounding the Eucharist—especially at Corinth—there is no mention of the person who presides over it. Indeed, the disputes over eucharistic meals presuppose that there was no central officer in charge, other than an arbiter chosen for some special occasion. The host or hostess at whose house the Eucharist was offered was the closest thing to a "celebrant" in the modern sense. That is because the whole community "concelebrated" (to use a modern term). The people of God shared in the one priesthood—of Jesus.[16]

The idea of a priest as the officiator, and of the Eucharist as a sacrifice that is efficacious if correctly performed, came in after the destruction of the Temple in 70 CE, when the Christians ceased to be a Jewish sect and began to think of themselves as replacing the old rite (or testament) with a new, "fulfilled" order of religion. At this time the Christian priest took on some of the characteristics of Jewish priesthood—including the need for ritual purity to offer the sacrifice. Since the early apostles and their followers were married, this meant abstinence from intercourse (or seminal discharge of any kind) on the night before celebration of the Eucharist. By the fourth century, when daily celebration of the Mass had become the norm in the Western church, perpetual abstinence was legislated.[17]

The need for ritual purity disqualified women from the Christian (as from the Jewish) priesthood. A woman was unclean during and after menstruation, childbirth (forty days for a male child, eighty for a female), miscarriage, or any other vaginal discharge (of the sort Jesus cured at Matthew 9.20–22).[18] Even virgins consecrated to God could not be unveiled in the third-century church of Tertullian, as if they had escaped the essential uncleanness of menstruation.[19] As the cult of virginity grew around certain female martyrs, the challenge to priestly holiness became acute, leading to conflicts between virgins' factions and a laxer clergy. St. Jerome fired sallies at the corrupt Roman priesthood from the sanctuary given by his chaste female patrons.[20] Eastern bishops late in the fourth century had again to drive unveiled women, and those with shaved heads, from the churches as a threat to their authority.[21]

In the ritual-purity contest of Christian asceticism, some women threatened to overcome their natural disadvantage over men, since they were consecrated virgins for life while married priests were just abstinent before the celebration of Mass.[22] The growth of male monasteries with their own form of celibacy also undermined the standing of a married clergy.[23] Where ministry in Paul's time had been service in and for the community, celibacy was now used to distinguish even further the clergy from the laity: "Masses said by married priests and those living with a woman were boycotted." The laity began to preach.[24] In order to regain status, ordinary priests had to borrow some of the prestige of the religious orders—a program systemized by the reforming monk-pope, Gregory VII, in the eleventh century. This led, finally, to the legislation that required celibacy of Western priests in 1139.[25]

When Luther and other reformers charged that medieval models of priesthood—the monks and religious orders—had grown corrupt, they returned to the married ministry of the early church. This hardened Catholic emphasis on sacramental purity: The Protestant minister could preach, but only the priest can consecrate. On the subject of corruption, it was said that unworthy intermediaries cannot pollute the graces moved through authorized channels. The sacrament works by virtue of the rite performed (ex opere operato), not by virtue of the one performing it (ex opere operantis). The magical quality of this procedure was ensured by the preservation of sacred formulas in a sacral language not spoken by the laity. Even the laity had to practice abstinence—from food—to be worthy of receiving Communion.

Only against this background of a separate and hieratic ceremonialism can one understand the shock of certain modern reforms in the Catholic church—the use of vernacular in the liturgy instead of Latin, the removal of nuns' veils (floating convent walls), the thought of women presiding at the Eucharist, the idea of married priests.

In America at least, lay Catholics and priests have been far readier to accept these returns to earlier Christian traditions than has the hierarchy. Priests themselves favor making celibacy optional—if for no other reason, to make recruiting other priests feasible again.[26] Even bishops have not been reliable enough—which has led to a papal "stacking" of the dioceses with appointments docile to Rome.[27]

In Rome itself, resistance is dogged on the triad of interconnected issues related to sacramental mystery—an all-male priesthood, a celibate priesthood, and women's acceptance of this monopoly on the sacramental. Early in Pope John Paul II's reign, I interviewed in Rome Father Vincent O'Keefe, an American assistant to the general of the Jesuit order, Pedro Arrupe. We talked about the new pope's reversal of Pope Paul VI's policy for priests who wanted to leave the priestly caste (ordo in Roman law). Pope Paul had "laicized" these men, to allow them to remain on good terms with the church. Pope John Paul refused to do this. Laicizing Jesuits around the world had been one of Father O'Keefe's duties, and he was dismayed by the human waste and bitterness involved in forcing men to be rebels against their church as well as resigners from the priesthood. "For the only time in my life, I told a pope I knew more than he did, on this one issue." But O'Keefe made no headway. In fact, when the Jesuits made O'Keefe acting general during Arrupe's final illness, the pope intervened to appoint his own man as the leader of the Jesuits, blocking the probable election of O'Keefe as Arrupe's successor.

I asked a monsignor in the Roman curia what good it does to force disaffection from the church on men who no longer wish to be priests. "At least," he answered grimly, "now we don't have to pretend that we believe Father So-and-so when he tells us he found Christ by screwing Sister Mary Something." A certain stratum of the clergy obviously sees its moral investment in celibacy becoming devalued, and it means to punish those who devalue it. This is a bitter and futile endeavor, unfortunately endorsed by the pope. It stands in marked contrast to St. Paul's attitude toward his own celibacy, expressed in the First Letter to the Corinthians. He does not claim that it made him better than Peter, James, or the other married apostles (9.5). By contrast with the unmarried Corinthians, who claim to be above the baser concerns of others, he says that "each one must order his life according to the gift the Lord has granted him" (7.17). His advice is pragmatic, nonprescriptive, hedged about with qualifiers:

> All this I say by way of concession, not command (7.6).
> Everyone has the gift God has granted him, one this gift and another that (7.7).
> I say this, as my own word, not as the Lord's (7.12).
> On the question of celibacy, I have no instruction from the Lord (7.25).

It is my opinion (7.26).
In saying this I have no wish to keep you on a tight rein (7.35).
That is my opinion (7.40).

Pope John Paul certainly *does* want to keep ex-priests on a tight and punitive rein, and the monsignor I talked with is hardly exemplifying the charity Paul puts over *all* gifts, including celibacy, in this very letter.

The attempt to punish others is self-penalizing. The church rulers lose the talents of the men they will not compromise with. The priests left behind are demoralized by their inability to fill the emptying ranks, to recruit with conviction, to convince superiors that *they* are not vindictive. Trying to protect those who stay, the Roman curia cripples them, so that polls show "the occupational satisfaction of associate pastors is no higher than that of semi-skilled workers."[28] In order to appoint "safe" bishops, the Roman leadership does not draw on all the talents in its shrinking pool of candidates: Incompetence is permitted, so long as conservatism is assured—another factor in the demoralization of all but the most docile.[29]

Women, of course, are excluded even more ruthlessly. Told to expect no change on ordination, the contraception teaching, abortion, they have little incentive to become closely associated with a church whose rulers discourage, if they do not penalize, any challenge to the legacy of treating women as unclean. It insults the intelligence to say that Jesus chose male apostles, so no women can be priests—though he appointed married apostles, and the authorities were happy enough to change *that* matter.

Teenage Catholic women are three times as likely to consider church service as teenage men, but many are shrewd enough not to place themselves at the disposal of the hierarchy in religious orders.[30] The falloff in the number of nuns is even more dramatic than that of priests; and a combination of demographics and economics makes any reversal of this trend unlikely. The median age of nuns now is in the high fifties. The work product of the orders has shrunk, and their liability for health care has soared. Any young people who join convents will be working to care for the survivors of large convents that can no longer be maintained. Even outside the convent, Catholic scholars like Rosemary Radford Ruether are freer to work in non-Catholic schools of theology than under the Catholic system that disciplines teachers like Father Charles Curran, the moral theologian removed from his teaching position.

Refusal to abandon the celibate male priesthood has the same impact on Catholic reaction to women's rights as does the biblical fundamentalism about Paul's words to the Corinthians. Individuals can edge away from institutional restraints—Paul Jewett easing off from inerrancy, Catholics simply ignoring their bishops when they pontificate on sex. But this involves both groups in great friction within their own body and with their fellow citizens who take a different view of women's rights.

Paul was dealing with fundamentalists as well as with perfectionists in his complex negotiatory message sent to Corinth, to that place Peter Brown calls "a sociological beargarden."[31] To the perfectionists, he said—with irony, sarcasm, and heartfelt pleading—"Join the rest of us weaker sorts." To the fundamentalists he said—with a similar virtuosity of rhetorical devices—"Do not trust yourself to fixed words or ritual." He begged each side to free itself by lowering its guard against the other, denying no one's gift, admitting all to the table of concelebration that makes up the community.[32] Not a bad political lesson—and the one women's liberation has been teaching us.

PART EIGHT

Church and State

❖ T H I R T Y ❖

Religious Separatism

THE SEVENTEENTH-CENTURY CHURCHES SET UP IN PURITAN MASSACHU-
setts were surprisingly like the communities St. Paul wrote to in the 50s
CE, fractious, spirit-filled, divided on points of doctrine and practice, and
maintaining an uneasy peace with the secular authorities—for it is wrong
to think of those settlements as theocratic. Leaders like John Winthrop
tried to protect the churches by keeping the secular authorities separate
from them, a pattern that would develop into America's more far-reaching
attempts at separation in the eighteenth century. Winthrop's strategy can
be seen in his treatment of the two most famous religious troublemakers
of seventeenth-century New England, Anne Hutchinson and Roger Williams.

Feminists are giving new kinds of attention to Anne Hutchinson, the
spiritual teacher driven out of Boston in 1638.[1] This is appropriate. Mrs.
Hutchinson's foes used against her the very lines, from St. Paul to the
Corinthians, that modern fundamentalists like Francis Schaeffer marshal
against women's rights. On the other hand, Mrs. Hutchinson was herself
a close student of that Pauline letter, which gave her some ideas for her
own kind of perfectionism, even though Paul was arguing *against* the
perfectionists.[2]

The perfectionist party at Corinth—which St. Paul called with irony the "strong ones"—was listening to "super apostles" (2 Corinthians 11.5, 12.11).[3] If ever anyone believed in super apostles it was Anne Hutchinson. Her own special preacher, John Cotton, had drawn her to America in the first place, where she hoped to escape the disappointing mediocrities of her Lincolnshire church.

But she could not instantly join the Boston church which the newly arrived Cotton served as teacher. Boston was not Lincolnshire, where any baptized person joined a parish just by residing in it. Those who sailed for Massachusetts in the 1630s were not all saved. Some were servants or craftsmen brought over for their skills, others were sincere Christians not yet visited by the Spirit in a "born-again" conversion experience. To join a Congregationalist church—organized not by the state or by an overarching established church—one had to testify to the Spirit's working, convince the saints of the particular community that one's experience was authentic.

Mrs. Hutchinson had no problem making her experiences vivid to the listeners. Her problem was doctrinal. If one held "popish" or other false views, the Holy Spirit could not be prompting one's soul. Only the devil uses falsehood. A fellow passenger heard Mrs. Hutchinson express views of questionable orthodoxy on the trip across the Atlantic. Besides, her evident devotion to the learned teacher John Cotton was enough to provoke suspicion in the pastor of the church, John Wilson, who felt threatened by Cotton's learning and popularity.

For two years Anne Hutchinson was part of the civil community in Boston but not of the church—which should give pause to those who talk about any union of church and state in New England. There was an established church in New England, but it was the church of Old England, from which the Massachusetts Bay Company was careful not to separate itself. This relationship was one of the many anomalies in colonial law. A convenient fuzziness was cultivated in the early days, when the Bay Company feared for its patent. In 1630, the "Romanizing" Archbishop Laud had become King Charles's lord commissioner of plantations. He would not look kindly on any attempt of the company to sever its ties with the church.

The Bay Colony gave tax money to the private organizations (actually, those set up by the Holy Spirit) called churches; but it did not appoint the ministers (chosen, with the Spirit's help, by each congregation for itself), establish the rules of their conduct, or admit any of the clergy into its civil offices (a far cry from the state in England, where Laud was archbishop of Canterbury *and* what we would call the secretary of state for foreign affairs).

Thus the Church of England was formally established in New England but practically ignored; while the Congregationalist bodies were formally nonestablished but practically all-important to the community's life. This situation offended logic, and Puritans were very logical; but it served many, purposes. The state (company) was a buffer between the local church communities and the formal but distant church officially recognized.

Still, the true purists in New England felt contaminated by *any* ties with the "High Church" regime of Laud. The pragmatic governor John Winthrop fought a never-ending battle against outbreaks of zeal that would repudiate Anglicanism and, very probably, end the "holy experiment" of the Massachusetts Bay.[4] In the very year of Anne Hutchinson's arrival (1634), John Endecott had risked treason proceedings by publicly cutting the red cross out of the English flag, since it had been added, in the past, with the pope's permission. Similar trouble was brewing with William Staughton in Dorchester and Roger Williams in several towns. It is against this background that Anne Hutchinson's challenge to the compromises of the Massachusetts situation must be read.

Mrs. Hutchinson, finally admitted to the church, began to attract a circle of women to discuss the previous Sunday's sermon. As a mystic and student of Scripture, she soon departed from the lackluster preaching of John Wilson. She found rich pickings in Paul's First Letter to the Corinthians, especially verses 44 and 45 of the fifteenth chapter:

> If there is such a thing as an animal body, there is also a spiritual body. It is in this sense that Scripture says, "The first man, Adam, became an animate being," whereas the last Adam [Christ] has become a life-giving spirit.

This explained her experience of a total new creation in Christ. It made her think her existence prior to that was shadowy and evaporating. Her church trial would turn almost entirely on the theological consequences of this insight.[5]

Mrs. Hutchinson found few preachers able to breathe the high mystic air with her. She suggested that the others in Massachusetts were not fully saved, that they still preached a gospel of meritorious human works rather than that of the wholly unmerited and totally transforming grace of God. She attracted an awed following, made up of the well-to-do and influential.[6] Her favored preachers were joined by the handsome young

Henry Vane, briefly in Boston on his way to glory and the scaffold in the later days of Cromwell. Vane was elected governor (at age twenty-three) in 1636. It looked as if the whole city of Boston had become Hutchinsonian—and the whole province could follow suit. John Winthrop set out to prevent that by maneuver and repression. He saw here a repetition of Roger Williams's progress, the year before, from criticism of the Church of England to criticism of the Massachusetts churches. If the government itself could be brought to repudiate the clergy of New England, as well as that of Old England, the colony would offer an affront to Laud far weightier than Endecott's desecration of the flag.

Was Hutchinson's offense political or theological? It was both—but not for the reason Charles Francis Adams gave in his pioneering study of this controversy. He said that she challenged the union of church and state represented by Winthrop and others.[7] That gets things exactly backward. By carrying her perfectionist theology into the election of Vane, the Hutchinsonians were merging the churches with the state in a way that would have removed the state's buffer status *between* the local congregation and the "mother church."

Hutchinson was given two separate trials—as a disturber of the peace by the state, and as a heretic by her church. Winthrop had trouble making his secular case against the clever theologian until, in an urge to bear witness to the Spirit within her, Mrs. Hutchinson lost her last defenders by claiming a special mission that would indict all her accusers. It is often said that her most damaging admission was that her views came to her by a direct revelation. But for those who knew their Bible as the Puritans did, the most dumbfounding moment must have come when she said:

> This place in Daniel [Daniel 6] was brought unto me and did show me that though I should meet with affliction, yet "I am the same God that delivered Daniel out of the lion's den, I will also deliver thee." Therefore I desire you to look to it, for you see this scripture fulfilled today.[8]

The scene is that of Jesus reading the prophecy of Isaiah in the synagogue, then informing his listeners: "This day is this Scripture fulfilled in your ears" (Luke 4.21). When she said that by their treatment of her "you will bring a curse upon you and your posterity," few could doubt that she was a troubler of the peace. Winthrop destroyed her in order to protect the partial separation of church and state.

At the heresy trial, she was questioned on her novel meanings for *soul*, *life*, and *the new Adam*. She recanted some views and claimed to have held others only since her arrest. This last contention was a lie, in the view of her former "super apostle" John Cotton, who adduced the punishment of Ananias by the early church as a precedent for dealing with her: "You have lied not to men but to God" (Acts of the Apostles 5.5).[9]

Anne Hutchinson and her husband withdrew into the territory that would become Rhode Island, where Roger Williams had preceded them and established good relations with the resident Indians. (Mrs. Hutchinson was not so fortunate; she was killed by Indians in 1643.) Had Laud retained his power in England, Williams would probably have fared as ill in his new place as he had in Massachusetts. He could not, by his own principles of noncontact with the corrupt Church of England, have sought a patent for his territory. But the Civil War overthrew King Charles and his archbishop; Henry Vane was high in the councils of Cromwell, who treated Williams graciously; and Williams turned his own religious separation into a paradoxical program of civil inclusiveness.

Make no mistake, though—Williams never abandoned his exclusionist theology. No one could have differed more from Dr. Johnson, who said of the crazed poet Christopher Smart, "I'd as lief pray with Kit Smart as with anyone else."[10] Williams always had trouble finding people pure enough to pray with—his enemies could never make out whether that meant he prayed only with his wife or not even with her. They were certain it precluded him from grace before meals except when he dined alone.[11] Williams had prepared himself with great discipline to be an apostle to the Indians, learning their languages for the purpose, only to throw the whole project up when he decided he could not find a church pure enough to bring them into. What was the point of leading people "from one false worship to another"?[12]

He was harshest in his opposition to Quakers, whom he called "Foxians" so he could pun endlessly on the name of their founder, George Fox. Fox's writings were his "brutish barkings." He did the work of Jesuits: "Their faces look divers, but they both carry firebrands in their tails to burn up the holy Scripture" (a reference to the foxes in Judges 15.3–4).[13] Everything about the Quakers irritated him—their long hair, their handshakes (instead of the Puritans' kiss of peace), their uncoordinated singing, their silent meetings ("what spirits are their dumb spirits in their dumb meetings but those foul dumb spirits mentioned in that gospel, which the Lord Jesus will cast out and tumble down to Hell, whence they came, in his holy season"), their disorderly outbursts when they did speak, their ignorance of Scripture's original languages, their ungrammatical *thees* and *thous*, their informality ("cheek by jowl with all their betters"), their lack of respect for superiors in age and dignity, their letting women preach.[14]

As for the agitation that gave them the name they accepted, boasting of their quaking, that was the work of the devil: "Which extraordinary motions I judged to come upon them, not from the holy Spirit and power of God, but from the spirit and power of Satan."[15] He would not persecute even these diabolical meddlers, but he gave them fair warning that the civil power reached, as its name implies, to incivility, "as that is a duty and command of God unto all mankind."[16] Thus he protested with great eloquence the whipping of Baptists in Massachusetts, but not that of the Quaker women who walked naked down the streets of Salem or into the town meeting at Newberry.[17]

Some early Quakers took to themselves the command that Isaiah "go naked for a sign" (Isaiah 20.2–3)—and in Massachusetts, of all places. This was the proof, for Williams, that the devil had subverted nature itself in the Quakers, overcoming women's innate modesty.[18] He had a vision of Quakers calling on all women to strip down in the meetinghouse:

> I demanded of them how it should be known that it was the voice and command of God, the God of holiness, and not the command of the unclean Spirit? For I told them that, under that cover that one of them might be so commanded and sent in such a posture and behavior amongst men, why might not ten or twenty, yea, all the women in this present assembly be so stirred up as it were by the Spirit of God, to the horror and amazement of the whole country, yea of the whole world?[19]

As one can gauge from his reaction to Quaker behavior, Williams was a stickler for Puritan practices, and he castigated others for their unwillingness to maintain his own high standards within the churches. If Massachusetts expelled him it was only as Coriolanus was exiled from Rome: "I banish you." He had been telling the Bay authorities that they were still in the embrace of the pope. He declared that they must sever that tie, by rejecting all association with the Church of England, before he would accept them. When the community in Salem refused to join him in this view, "he refused communion with his own church," as Winthrop put it.

If Puritans in general feared Rome, Williams outdid them. While liberals of the 1950s were extolling Roger Williams, they criticized people who found Communists under every bed. But Williams was able to find the pope lurking everywhere, even in Luther's incompletely reformed church.[20] While Massachusetts was in communion with the church of

Charles I, that king was "committing fornication with the Whore" of Rome.[21] "Who sees not, then, but by the links of this mystical chain New England churches are still fastened to the Pope himself?"[22] Calling John Winthrop of Boston a willing handmaid of the pope was roughly like saying, in the 1950s, that General MacArthur was a secret agent for Joseph Stalin.

Naturally, the ultimate charge Williams had to bring against the Quakers was their convergence with Catholicism. To Williams, the Foxists were "the new Papists"—in fact, the new Jesuits.[23] George Fox aspired to be a Protestant pope, supreme among those with the "Foxian itch of being called Masters."[24] Surface differences should not distract people from the fact that "the Papists' and Quakers' tongues are both spitting and belching out fire from one fire of Hell."[25] The more Williams thought about the Quakers, the more he seemed to find even the Catholics preferable to this new assault from hell. "The Papists come nearer the truth" on the meaning of justification, and as for destroying the peace of souls, "the Papists [do it] not so much as the Quakers."[26]

How did a man who was ecumenical only in his impartiality of attack become the American symbol for tolerance? Paradoxically, his theological intolerance is the key to his political permissiveness. The most abominable thing he could do in the eyes of his fellow New Englanders was to admit Roman Catholics to his province of Rhode Island. But we have to remember that almost everyone, even his admiring opponent John Winthrop, was a Roman Catholic to him—either the pope's agent or the pope's dupe, allied to Rome by intent or by effect, a collaborator in the larger campaign being orchestrated by Satan. So letting an actual Jesuit into Rhode Island would not be much different from admitting a benighted Quaker. (When two Quaker women came to convert him, saying they were sent on the mission of the prophet Joel, his wry answer was: "That is not everyday work.")[27] He was lax, by New England standards, in legislating even against witches, since he felt that most of his neighbors were in some measure compacting with the devil. Clearly the Quakers were—why else did they quake? So if he started hanging witches, he would be forced to proceed thence to Quakers and afterward, by degrees, through almost the whole of the population. Once he had resigned himself to the prospect that Rhode Island would fill up with consorts of the Whore of Babylon, wearing almost every guise imaginable, there was not much he could do but get along with them, day by day, as he had with the devil-worshiping Indians.

Getting along with sin in the world was not simply the outcome of his practical situation. It came from his deepest theological insight, which repeated that of St. Augustine in *The City of God*. Like Augustine, Williams was oppressed with the vision of a world doomed by original sin. All positions of authority, even those in the Christian churches, were tainted by ambition and avarice. What better performance could the political order promise? The only way people could strip the state of its pretensions was by lowering their expectations of what it might deliver.

The reduction of political claims took place in the political terms each man was given. For Augustine that meant challenging the Greek definition of a polity as the arbiter of justice. In a famous argument, he removed justice from Cicero's definition of the state, and said that only a more modest agreement on loved things held in common could unite people on earth, while they moved mysteriously toward their ultimate communities—the eternal City of God and the equally eternal Earthly City (hell). [28]

Williams, by contrast, accepted the seventeenth-century belief that all sovereignty is derived from the people, but added that it was a people darkened in mind and will by sin. It is one thing for a government to rule *legitimately* at the will of a people so blinded. It is quite another to say that such a government, or even the people constituting it, have any right to speak for God through His church. It is only because Williams gives full scope to popular authority, in the first paragraph here, that his denial of its claims on the church is so powerful in the next paragraph:

> The sovereign, original, and foundation of civil power lies in the people, whom they [Williams's critics] must needs mean by the civil power, distinct from the government set up [by the people]; and, if so, then a people may erect and establish what form of government seems to them most meet for their civil condition. It is evident that such governments as are by them erected and established have no more power, nor for no longer time, than the civil power or people, consenting and agreeing, shall betrust them with. This is clear, not only in reason, but in the experience of all commonwealths, where the people are not deprived of their natural freedom by the power of tyrants.
>
> And if [it be] so that the magistrates receive their power of governing the church from the people, undeniably it follows that a people as a people naturally considered—of what nature or nation so ever in Europe, Asia, Africa or America—have fundamentally and originally, as men, a power to govern the church, to see her do her duty, to correct her, to redress, reform, establish, et cetera. And if this be not to pull God and Christ and Spirit out of heaven and subject them unto natural, sinful, inconstant

men, and so consequently to Satan himself by whom all peoples naturally are guided, let heaven and earth judge. [29]

So, precisely *because* he was a democrat in politics, Williams would not let politicians preside over the church. He believed men are too depraved to be given such a divine trust. As in Augustine's scheme, humankind is too contrary to agree on an ultimate justice, which will be perceptible only in the City of God.

The radical insight of Augustine and Williams extended not just to the state but to the visible church on earth. For neither man was this coterminous with the City of God. People enter and leave the visible church (Williams mainly leaving); some are destined to be saved who are not yet even in it (as Augustine was not for so many years); some now in it will not continue there. Only God knows who his real saints are, and he will manifest them only at the Last Judgment. No doctrine could have been more unwelcome to the Puritans of New England, who hoped to form a community of visible saints on earth, a new and better Israel, one as certainly under divine guidance as the old one, but with a superior order of grace won by the First Coming of Christ. For such saints, salvation meant little if "perseverance" in the church were not included among its gifts.

Perry Miller contrasts Williams's Augustinian "typology" with Luther's approach to Scripture. [30] For Williams the figures in Jewish Scripture were "types" to be fulfilled in Christ. They lost their independent meaning after that fulfillment. [31] With this stand Williams struck at the "federal" theology of New England, which had modeled a covenant *(foedus)* on Israel's ancient contract with God. Williams stood apart from the Protestants of his day (and later) for a reason Martin Marty suggests in this comment: "American Christians always did get more of their civil views from the Hebrew Scriptures—which they call the Old Testament—than from the New." [32] That was never true of Williams.

For Augustine, there was no manifest providence outside the special circumstances of prophecies fulfilled in Christ. [33] He belonged, after all, to a *Christian* Roman Empire that was falling apart. The burden of his argument was that this did not show any special judgment against Rome, as opposed to the general tendency of "the world" to fall apart. He mocked Christian superstition as well as Christians' lingering fondness for pagan auguries and astrology. [34] He dismissed the scheme of readable prophecies in Revelation, removing that book from active influence on orthodox Christianity for most of the Middle Ages. [35]

Both Augustine and Williams relied heavily on the New Testament parable of the wheat and the tares (Matthew 13.36–40), which must grow together until God separates them at the harvest (the Last Judgment), when the tares will be burnt.[36] For Williams, this meant that God's punishment of the crimes against Him—the so-called "First Table" (tablet), the first four commandments of God (those carried in Moses' right arm in the Charlton Heston scene)—were reserved for God alone to punish. The state can punish only civil disturbances. That was the logic of Augustine's later position as well, though he had earlier violated it to call Donatist unrest a *civil* matter.[37]

It is not surprising, perhaps, to find the learned Williams, trained at Cambridge University in an age when theology was the queen of the sciences, agreeing with the basic argument of Augustine, the great father of the church from the fifth century. But people are justifiably startled when they see passages of Williams chiming so well with things written a century later by a secular hero of the Enlightenment, Thomas Jefferson. Jefferson is thought of as the one who added to the Constitution's simple ban against federal establishment the image of a *wall* of separation between church and state. He did this in his letter of 1802 to the Baptists of Danbury, Connecticut:

> I contemplate with sovereign reverence that act of the whole American people which declared that their legislature should "make no law respecting an establishment of religion or prohibiting the free exercise thereof," thus building a wall of separation between church and State.[38]

But Williams had advocated a wall of separation in his treatise of 1644, *Mr. Cotton's Letter Lately Printed, Examined and Answered*:

> The faithful labors of many witnesses of Jesus Christ, extant to the world, abundantly proving that the church of the Jews under the Old Testament in the *type*, and the church of the Christians under the New Testament in the *antitype*, were both separate from the world, and that when they have opened a gap in the hedge or *wall of separation* between the garden of the church and the wilderness of the world, God has ever removed the candlestick, et cetera, and made his garden a wilderness, as at this day. [Italics added.][39]

In his practical comments on the futility of persecution, Williams also sounded Jeffersonian. Williams, for instance, wrote: "A false religion and worship will not hurt the civil state in case the worshiper break no civil law."[40] Jefferson put the same thought more vividly: "It does me no injury for my neighbor to say there are twenty gods, or no god. It neither picks my pocket nor breaks my leg."[41]

Most of those who note the resemblance between Williams's words and Jefferson's have treated it as accidental. The two men were speaking from different sets of values, we are told. Jefferson was trying to save a secular republic from the superstitions of the past, Williams trying to sequester religion from the interference of earthly rulers. This division may be too neat, as we shall see; but there certainly is an a priori case for thinking that Williams's views on toleration, though interesting to a historian, had no powerful effect on the course of history. Certainly that is the judgment of Perry Miller, whose views are never to be treated lightly:

> Roger Williams, if viewed in a strictly historical perspective, is a relatively minor character. He furnishes an episode in the history of Massachusetts. He is the chief pioneer of Rhode Island, but only one among the obstreperous band who finally created the colony, more by good luck than by good management. As for any direct influence of his thought on the ultimate achievement of religious liberty in America, he had none.[42]

He could not be more blunt than that. Nor does anyone separate Williams more drastically from Jefferson's influence on religious liberty:

> Only after the spread of the Enlightenment, after the teachings of Jefferson, the First Amendment, and the sheer multiplication of denominations had made the "voluntary principle" the only possible mode of religious activity, would liberals, including reluctant ones, look back with pleasure upon Roger Williams and salute in him an almost forgotten prophet of themselves. This secular interpretation of Roger Williams is a misreading of his real thought.[43]

One could argue with the specifics of Miller's description. Admittedly, others settled in the area that was to become Rhode Island—Anne Hutchinson's followers in Portsmouth, William Coddington's at Newport, Samuel Gorton's at Warwick. But none of them could have settled or developed their claims without the peace Williams had made with the Narragansett Indians. Was this, as Miller claims, more a matter of luck than of management? Certainly the Indians were using Williams: "It was convenient to have friendly white settlements between them and the more aggressive Puritan colonies."[44] But it took the particular virtues and knowledge of Williams to capitalize on this situation, and in doing so Williams may have saved not only his fellow pioneers in Rhode Island but the mother colony of Massachusetts itself. He provided a buffer not only between Indians and Europeans, but between competing tribes of Indians, whose combined force could have swept the Massachusetts Bay area clean of its Europeans.[45] Thus he inadvertently did the native Americans a disservice and their exploiters a favor.

There is something inadvertent about much of Williams's achievement. He cared most about leading a reformed church, and could never form such a thing. He cared comparatively little about a secular power, yet that is what he set up. The tolerating state was only a means, in his mind, to serve the end of true religion. Toleration, instead, became an end in itself for many in Rhode Island, and ushered in the very errors he most opposed. Quakers had become a majority within the Rhode Island Assembly by the 1670s, when Williams thundered against them so tirelessly.

Rhode Island was never considered a model by the other colonies. On the contrary, it seemed a pattern of all the things to be avoided by a responsible polity. Quaker opposition to taxes, oaths, and service in the militia, coupled with a free-enterprise spirit that encouraged smuggling and the slave trade, led others to call the place Rogue Island.

Because of its constant friction with the Board of Navigation, Rhode Island was quick to throw off British government—a year before Massachusetts destroyed the tea shipment, Rhode Island forces had burned the British ship *Gaspée*. But the state was as unwilling to be controlled by the Continental Congress as by Parliament. It fought congressional taxes, refused to send delegates to the constitutional drafting convention of 1788, and rejected the Constitution thirteen times over a period of two years before joining the Union—late, reluctantly, and by the closest of votes—after Washington had already been sworn in as president. The state even lapsed at times from the one great virtue of its government, banning some Catholics and Jews.

But these lapses should not distract us from the extraordinary accomplishment of Williams's Patent of 1644, the Assembly's Civil Code of 1647, and John Clarke's Charter of 1663. In the middle of the seventeenth century, Rhode Island had given greater protection to freedom of religion than any other government in what was then known as Christendom. Nor was this an aberration. The process by which those zealous for religion separated it from government presented in microcosm the process that would be worked out in America over the next centuries. The secular state came from the zeal of religion itself. The Rhode Island Civil Code accomplished this, as the Constitution would later do, by a restriction of the secular power's sphere. As G. B. Warden puts it, the Rhode Island code

> did not establish religious freedom, religious rights, or religious toleration by any explicit, positive means. Instead, such toleration was accomplished by the omission of the regulatory provisions contained in other codes and English statutes. By that indirect means alone was it possible to maintain some semblance of accommodation with strict Biblicists in Newport, with Antinomians in Portsmouth, with separating Congregationalists in Providence, and with crypto-Anglicans in Warwick.[46]

It was the most religious community that produced the most religiously neutral state, just as—a century later—it would be a very religious nation that produced the first secular state. This latter development did not occur because Americans had ceased to be religious, or even become less religious, by the eighteenth century, but because they were following the logic of the position that Roger Williams, with his genius, had arrived at by way of Augustinian reflection on the world, the gospel, and government. Those reflections were not as distant from the later arguments of Jefferson and Madison as scholars have made them. But even if they were, the actual motive of people in ratifying the First Amendment was closer to the desire to protect the purity of religion than to protect the prerogatives of the state. As Mark DeWolfe Howe wrote in his provocative book on church and state: "In making the wall of separation a constitutional barrier, the faith of Roger Williams played a more important part than the doubts of Jefferson."[47] The partial separation of church and state that Winthrop had contrived, for the protection of his congregations, Williams turned into an entire separation. In the process he purified American churches in ways that his distant ally, Oliver Cromwell, never succeeded in doing for England.

❖ T H I R T Y ꞏ O N E ❖

Jefferson:
The Uses of Religion

JEFFERSON'S WORDS ARE PUT TO MANY USES IN DEBATE OVER THE RELA-
tionship of church to state in America. We know more about his personal
views on religion than we know about any other person's at the origin of
our state. But our knowledge is drawn from sources denied to his contemporaries, who speculated widely about his "atheism" or made un-
founded charges about his hostility to organized religion of all kinds.
Echoes of those charges have haunted his reputation, even to this day.
Fundamentalists have denounced his deism—or, with compensatory
zeal, have co-opted him to the cause of a "Christian nation." A faculty
member at Pat Robertson's CBN University even made Jefferson a conduit
for the Christian views of Samuel Rutherford, the myth of whose influence is derived from Francis Schaeffer.[1]

Jefferson's views were sufficiently unorthodox for him to take care that
they not become generally known. He refused to be drawn into a public
defense of them, and he was chary about letting even the most trustworthy
people see his private writings on Jesus, Christianity, and the churches.
As he wrote to Benjamin Rush, when sending him his "Syllabus" on the
ethics of Jesus:

In confiding it to you, I know it will not be exposed to the malignant perversions of those who make every word from me a text for new mis-representations and calumnies. I am moreover averse to the communi-cation of my religious tenets to the public; because it would countenance the presumption of those who have endeavored to draw them before that tribunal, and to seduce public opinion to erect itself into that inquisition over the rights of conscience, which the laws have so justly proscribed [in America]. It behoves every man who values liberty of conscience for him-self, to resist invasions of it in the case of others; or their case may, by change of circumstances, become his own. It behoves him, too, in his own case, to give no example of concession, betraying the common right of independent opinion, by answering questions of faith, which the laws have left between God and himself.[2]

Jefferson kept his library at Monticello locked; he opened it only to conduct favored guests through. His most compromising materials he carried with him. These texts were kept by his family throughout the nineteenth century, and were not published until this century—his Ex-tracts from the Gospels in 1902, his Literary Commonplace Book in 1928, his (reconstructed) "Philosophy of Jesus" in 1983. Only with the help of these three works can Jefferson's views be adequately measured.

Jefferson kept his Literary Commonplace Book close to him throughout his life, and his family cherished it for this intimate association. He began to compile it as a teenager. It was with him when his first library was destroyed by fire at his mother's plantation house, Shadwell. Jefferson was twenty-seven years old. He sifted and rearranged its contents for a dozen or so years after that, and put it in its final binding before he left for Europe in 1784, where he used it in composing his treatise on poetic meters. The Library of Congress bought it from his descendants in 1918, and Gilbert Chinard first published it ten years later. Biographers made heavy use of it after that, but without knowing how to date the various entries. It was not till 1989 that Douglas Wilson's model edition made such dating possible.[3]

Wilson used the evidence of handwriting, binding, papers used, and the editions cited to show how carefully Jefferson preserved and rearranged the extracts he continued to value—principally the long passages copied out from Henry St. John, Viscount Bolingbroke. (Originally, there were even more than the ten thousand words of Bolingbroke retained in Jef-ferson's final binding of his collection.) Bolingbroke is important here because he was considered a scandalously irreligious author in his day.

He did not publish his religious views in his own lifetime, and after his death (1751) pressure was brought on his executor to leave his "blasphemies" unpublished. Dr. Johnson denounced the five-volume edition of his work that appeared in 1754, when Jefferson was eleven. By 1765, when Jefferson was twenty-two, he had read all the five volumes and lovingly copied long passages from them, with special emphasis on philosophical materialism (which Jefferson held ever after), the denial of miracles and the supernatural, the absurdity of Jewish Scriptures, the arbitrariness of the Christian canon of "inspired" works. That Jefferson was entertaining dangerous thoughts we can see from the one place where he breaks into his copyings from Bolingbroke: He puts a confirming passage from David Hume right after Bolingbroke's argument that incest is not against natural law.[4]

Jefferson's general views on religion were formed by Bolingbroke, and he retained the major tenets copied into his book. This makes all the more startling the major departure from his mentor's views. Bolingbroke claimed, in words Jefferson wrote over again, that the ethical teachings of Jesus were less formed and systematic than those of pagan moralists. He said this could be proved if one collected the moral sayings from all four Gospels for comparison with similar collections from the sages:

> Were all the precepts of this [ethical] kind, that are scattered about in the whole New Testament, collected, like the short sentences of ancient sages in the memorials we have of them, and put together in the very words of the sacred writers, they would compose a very short, as well as unconnected system of ethics. A system thus collected from the writings of ancient heathen moralists, of Tully [Cicero], of Seneca, of Epictetus and others, would be more full, more entire, more coherent, more clearly deduced from unquestionable principles of knowledge.[5]

This passage helps explain the honor Jefferson gave to Cicero, Seneca, and Epictetus among moral teachers he continued to consult. But, more than that, this paragraph gave Jefferson an assignment he carried out, years later, in two of his major efforts at ethical reflection: He made precisely the kind of collection from the Gospels that Bolingbroke had suggested (the "Philosophy" and "Extracts"), and he made a comparison of that collection with the teachings of the pagan moralists (the "Syllabus"). But Jefferson came to an exactly opposite conclusion from Bolingbroke's: He found that Jesus offered the better, more extensive, more systematic program of virtue. Bolingbroke claimed that a thorough investigation would show that Jesus offered no "unerring rule" of moral duty; Jefferson concluded that Jesus was "a master workman" at forging an ethical teaching and

> that his system of morality was the most benevolent and sublime probably that has been ever taught, and consequently more perfect [sic] than those of any of the ancient philosophers.[6]

Jefferson did not always hold this view of Jesus. He could still describe him as the dupe of his own followers in 1787: "a man of illegitimate birth, of a benevolent heart, enthusiastic mind, who set out without pretensions to divinity, ended in believing them, and was punished capitally for sedition."[7]

What made Jefferson change his mind about Jesus? Eugene Sheridan argues that it was the convergence of a number of things affecting Jefferson in his first term as president.[8] The works of Joseph Priestley had convinced him that Jesus was misrepresented by Christians after his death, and Priestley's "harmonies" of the various Gospel accounts set a model to Jefferson for making his own extracts of the "authentic" teachings of Jesus from the corrupt accounts of his life. But, more than that, the fierce divisions of the 1790s, and the vicious personal attacks on Jefferson, had driven him to seek hope from an ethics of positive charity. He found this in Jesus, and not in the classical self-improvers. As he wrote, midway through his first term as president, of the pagan moralists:

> Their philosophy went chiefly to the government of our passions, so far as respected ourselves, and the procuring our own tranquility. On our duties to others they were short and deficient. They extended their cares scarcely beyond our kindred and friends individually, and our country in the abstract. Jesus embraced, with charity and philanthropy, our neighbors, our countrymen, and the whole family of mankind.[9]

Jefferson made his first parallel edition of extracts from the Gospels at this time, and tried to get Priestley and Benjamin Rush to publish the claims of Jesus' superiority to pagan sages, claims that he could not circulate in his own name but that he believed it important for the republic to acknowledge.[10] As Jefferson told Benjamin Rush in 1803, his views were

> very different from that anti-Christian system imputed to me by those who know nothing of my opinions. To the corruptions of Christianity I am indeed opposed; but not to the genuine precepts of Jesus himself. I am a Christian, in the only sense in which he wished any one to be; sincerely attached to his doctrines, in preference to all others; ascribing to himself every human excellence; and believing he never claimed any other.[11]

Later, when Jefferson was preparing to make his more ambitious (multilingual) arrangement of Gospel extracts, he confessed to a correspondent his desire to make the world "see the immortal merit of this first of human sages."

> I believe it may even do good by producing discussion and, finally, a true view of the merits of this great reformer. [12]

While Jefferson was compiling his larger version of the Gospel extracts, he wrote to Vine Utley: "I never go to bed without an hour or half hour's previous reading of something moral, whereon to ruminate in the intervals of sleep." [13]

As Jefferson became more ardent for the ethical doctrines of Jesus, his anger at priests for distorting his message was intensified. He hoped for the day when the authentic portrait he had assembled would be widely accepted. As he told Mrs. Samuel H. Smith, "there would never have been an infidel if there had never been a priest." [14] He took comfort from the growth of Unitarianism, an escape from what he considered the "polytheism" of trinitarian doctrine. He wrote to Timothy Pickering in 1821:

> If nothing had ever been added to what flowed purely from his [Jesus'] lips, the whole world would at this day have been Christian. . . . Had there never been a Commentator, there never would have been an infidel. [15]

And to Thomas Whittemore, in 1822:

> Had his doctrines, pure as they came from himself, been never sophisticated for unworthy purposes, the whole civilised world would at this day have formed but a single sect. [16]

To Benjamin Waterhouse, in 1822:

> I rejoice that in this blessed country of free enquiry and belief, which has surrendered its creed and conscience to neither kings nor priests, the genuine doctrine of one only God is reviving, and I trust there is not a young man now living in the U.S. who will not die an Unitarian. [17]

To James Smith, in 1822:

> The pure and simple unity of the creator of the universe is now all but ascendant in the Eastern states; it is dawning in the West, and advancing towards the South; and I confidently expect that the present generation will see Unitarianism become the general religion of the United States. [18]

Jefferson was not indifferent to the religion held by Americans. He wanted the true deism (monotheism) preached by Jesus to prevail. That religion has political consequences. The religion of Jesus was democratic, since it let people maintain custody of their own consciences, not turning them over to priests, who base an authority over the conscience on mystification and ritual:

> The Christian priesthood, finding the doctrines of Christ leveled to every understanding, and too plain to need explanation, saw, in the mysticisms of Plato, materials with which they might build up an artificial system which might, from its indistinctness, admit everlasting controversy, give employment for their order, and introduce to it profit, power and pre-eminence. The doctrines which flowed from the lips of Jesus himself are within the comprehension of a child; but thousands of volumes have not yet explained the Platonisms engrafted on them; and for this obvious reason, that nonsense can never be explained.[19]

Jesus "corrected the deism of the Jews," returning them to the core of their monotheistic belief, apart from Temple cult and ritual.[20] But then the church councils of the third and fourth century brought back hocus-pocus, debating the double nature of Christ, the immateriality of spirit, the polytheistic trinity (the Athanasian paradox that one is three).[21]

But progress, Jefferson answered John Adams, will lead to a "euthanasia for Platonic Christianity, and its restoration to the primitive simplicity of its founder."[22] Jefferson was prepared to help along practitioners of the less corrupt forms of Christianity—the Presbyterians, for instance, or Quakers, who renounced bishops and priests—against the more super-stitious (like Roman and Anglican Catholics):

> The mild and simple principles of the Christian philosophy would produce too much calm, too much regularity of good, to extract from its disciples a support for a numerous priesthood, were they not to sophisticate [con-taminate] it, ramify it, split it into hairs, and twist its texts till they cover the divine morality of its author with mysteries and require a priesthood to explain them. The Quakers seem to have discovered this. They have no priests, therefore no schisms. They judge of the text by the dictates of common sense and common morality.[23]

The politics of reformed Christianity versus episcopal Christianity lay behind Jefferson's uses of religion in the struggle for independence. Those who think he kept an absolute separation between his politics and religion will be shocked, as John Quincy Adams was, at the way he "cooked up" a religious protest at the British treatment of the colonies:

> We were under conviction of the necessity of arousing our people from the lethargy into which they had fallen as to passing events; and thought

that the appointment of a day of general fasting and prayer would be most likely to call up and alarm their attention. No example of such a solemnity had existed since the days of our distresses in the [French and Indian] war of '55, since which a new generation had grown up. With the help therefore of Rushworth [records of Cromwell's days], whom we rummaged over for the revolutionary precedents and forms of the Puritans of that [War of '55] day, preserved by him, we cooked up a resolution, somewhat modernizing their phrases, for appointing the first day of June, on which the Port bill was to commence, for a day of fasting, humiliation prayer, to implore heaven to avert from us the evils of civil war, to inspire us with firmness in support of our rights, and to turn the hearts of the King and parliament to moderation and justice. To give greater emphasis to our proposition, we agreed to wait the next morning on Mr. [Robert Carter] Nicholas, whose grave and religious character was more in unison with the tone of our resolution and to solicit him to move it.[24]

Going back to the French and Indian War was a shrewd move, since fear of Catholicism in Canada, and of convert Indians fighting with the "priest-ridden" French, had been a powerful motive in that war. And since England still had its own bishop-ruled liturgy, antipapal rhetoric could be turned against England during the Revolution—and it was. Jefferson himself was astonished at the success of his call for national prayer, and he kept that reaction in mind when it came time to write the Declaration of Independence.[25]

The revival of antipapal rhetoric during the Revolution was successful because of colonial resentment at the Quebec Act of 1773. England won Canada from France in the French and Indian War, which the colonies had treated as a crusade against the menace of Roman Catholicism on this continent, yet England granted Catholic Canadians the right to continue practicing their religion, even under the rule of an England that had an established Protestant religion. American zealots considered that a capitulation to "the Whore of Babylon." According to the puritan preacher Samuel Sherwood, in a famous Election Day sermon, the Quebec Act proved that "the ministry and parliament of Great Britain, which appears so favorable to popery and the Roman Catholic interest, [is] aiming at the extension and establishment of it."[26]

So strong was resentment against this act that New Englanders had made sure it was put in the colonies' declaration of rights at the First Continental Congress of 1774—even though it took some stretching to say that Parliament's toleration of a religion in one British province violated the rights of those in another province. Here is how the bill of rights stated the colonies' interest in the matter: Their rights had been taken away, according to the text, by

> the act passed in the same [parliamentary] session [as the Force Acts] for establishing the Roman Catholic religion in the province of Quebec, abolishing the equitable system of English laws, and erecting a tyranny there, to the great danger, from so total a dissimilarity of religions, law, and government to the neighboring British colonies, by the assistance of whose blood and treasure the said country was conquered from France.[27]

Though the delegates were careful to include the suspension of other British laws in Quebec, it is clear that the core grievance was the practice of Catholicism in contaminating proximity to the New England colonies. Naturally, the same congress put the Quebec Act in its petition to the king for redress of grievances, denouncing Parliament for "establishing an absolute government and the Roman Catholic religion throughout those vast regions [of Quebec], that border on the westerly and northerly boundaries of the free protestant English settlements."[28] The king would have to abolish the form of government in that other part of his dominion before the colonies would consider their rights restored.

Jefferson, knowing the power of this grievance among the Northern colonists, included it in his 1775 Declaration of the Causes and Necessity for Taking Up Arms: "They [Parliament] have erected in a neighboring province, acquired by the joint arms of Great Britain and America, a tyranny dangerous to the very existence of all these colonies."[29] He does not expressly mention religion, though that was the understood basis of complaint. In his own rough draft of the Declaration of Independence, he did not include the Quebec Act in his list of grievances, perhaps considering it not worthy of the international scrutiny that document would undergo. But members of the drafting committee (which included John Adams of Massachusetts) must have convinced him that important interests would not suffer it to be omitted. So the draft he submitted to Congress read this way:

> He [King George] has combined with others [Parliament] to subject us to a jurisdiction foreign to our constitutions and unacknowledged by our laws, giving his assent to their [Parliament's] pretended [illegitimate] acts of legislation . . . for abolishing the free system of English laws in a neighboring province, establishing therein an arbitrary government, and enlarging its boundaries, so as to render it at once an example and fit instrument for introducing the same absolute rule into these colonies.[30]

Congress made no change in this part of Jefferson's draft except to regularize his idiosyncratic spelling and to substitute *states* for the last word in the item. Thus America declared its independence by—among other things—deploring the grant of free exercise to a religion held to the north of the aggrieved colonies.

Jefferson did not separate religion and politics while agitating for independence. Yet this was the very time when he was revising Virginia's laws to include religious freedom. How can we reconcile these activities on his part? Presumably he thought he could use Protestant fears of a hieratic and priestly church because he considered the latter inimical to freedom. But how could he, simultaneously, plan for the freedom of religion (including the Catholic religion) south of the Canadian border?

❖ T H I R T Y ̵ T W O ❖

Jefferson:
The Protection of Religion

NOT LONG AGO, IT WAS WIDELY HELD THAT JEFFERSON PROPOSED FREEDOM of religion in order to help mankind escape religion—that he considered it a retardative force in history, a darkness to be dispelled, and wanted to free the state from its power.[1] But even if he felt that, he could hardly *say* it in a country that was still very religious. He had to pretend, if nothing else, that he was freeing religion in order to help religion, not hurt it; to protect it from compromising association with secular power. And he did this so well that his arguments for freedom of religion were later quoted by his friends when they had to oppose the charge of Jefferson's atheism.

Jefferson wanted his 1779 statute for religious freedom to be included in the select list of his finest achievements—along with his drafting of the Declaration and his founding of Virginia's university.[2] Yet the arguments he made for it were insincere, according to those who believe he wanted to hinder religion. His professions, at least, were of respect and concern for retaining or regaining religious purity. His rhetoric was as favorable to religion as was that of Roger Williams—and the passages cited in my last chapter suggest this was no mere pose on his part. Still, even if it were a pose, the arguments he advanced for his statute remain the legislative rationale for it. Legislative intent is voiced in such public ways. Legislative motive may be secret and perverse—one may propose a law in order to embarrass government with its absurdity, but one cannot make that the professed aim of the law. Assume, if you will, that Jefferson's own dark motive was to hamper religion; nonetheless, his open and declared *intent* was to free it. To see this, all we need do is look at the terms he used in proposing the statute:

Well aware

1) that the opinions and belief of men depend not on their own will, but follow involuntarily the evidence proposed to their minds;

2) that Almighty God hath created the mind free, and manifested his supreme will that free it shall remain by making it altogether insusceptible of restraint;

3) that all attempts to influence it by temporal punishments, or burthens, or by civil incapacitations, tend only to beget habits of hypocrisy and meanness;

4) and are a departure from the plan of the holy author of our religion, who being lord both of body and mind, yet chose not to propagate it by coercion on either, as was in his Almighty power to do, but to extend it by its influence on reason alone;

5) that the impious presumption of legislators and rulers, civil as well as ecclesiastical, who, being themselves but fallible and uninspired men, have assumed dominion over the faith of others, setting up their own opinions and modes of thinking as the only true and infallible, and as such endeavoring to impose them on others, hath established and maintained false religions over the greatest part of the world and through all time;

6) that to compel a man to furnish contributions of money for the propagation of opinions which he disbelieves and abhors, is sinful and tyrannical;

7) that even the forcing him to support this or that teacher of his own religious persuasion, is depriving him of the comfortable liberty of giving his contributions to the particular pastor whose morals he would make his pattern, and whose powers he feels most persuasive to righteousness;

8) and is withdrawing from the ministry those temporary rewards which, proceeding from an approbation of their personal conduct, are an additional incitement to earnest and unremitting labours for the instruction of mankind;

9) that our civil rights have no dependence on our religious opinions, any more than our opinions in physics or geometry; [point 1 above, repeated in order to introduce the further point] that therefore the proscribing any

citizen as unworthy the public confidence by laying upon him an incapacity of being called to offices of trust and emolument, unless he profess or renounce this or that religious opinion, is depriving him injuriously of those privileges and advantages to which, in common with his fellow citizens, he has a natural right;

10) that it tends also to corrupt the principles of that very religion it is meant to encourage, by bribing, with a monopoly of worldly honours and emoluments, those who will externally profess and conform to it;

11) that, though indeed these are criminal who do not withstand such temptation, yet neither are those innocent who lay the bait in their way;

12) that the opinions of men are not the object of civil government, nor under its jurisdiction;

13) that to suffer the civil magistrate to intrude his powers into the field of opinion and to restrain the profession or propagation of principles on supposition of their ill tendency is a dangerous fallacy, which at once destroys all religious liberty, because he being of course judge of that tendency will make his opinions the rule of judgment, and approve or condemn the sentiments of others only as they shall square with or differ from his own;

14) that it is time enough for the rightful purposes of civil government for its officers to interfere when principles break out into overt acts against peace and good order; and finally,

15) that truth is great and will prevail if left to herself; that she is the proper and sufficient antagonist to error, and has nothing to fear from the conflict unless by human interposition disarmed of her natural weapons, free argument and debate; errors ceasing to be dangerous when it is permitted freely to contradict them.[3]

It is clear that Jefferson gave the arguments in this preamble careful thought. He took care to distribute his text widely, as he did his own draft of the Declaration of Independence. He wanted the views expressed in it to prevail, and he wanted credit for advancing them. So the bill appears in his *Notes on the State of Virginia* (addressed primarily to a French audience), in correspondence with men he respected, and in the composition of his own epitaph.[4] We should expect, then, a thoughtful arrangement of the arguments here, as in the list of grievances in the Declaration of Independence (a list that moved logically from executive acts of the British government to joint legislative-executive acts, and from those to recent war atrocities, before reaching a summary final count against king and Parliament).[5]

Yet the order of arguments prefaced to the Bill for Religious Freedom is not perspicuous—not, at any rate, to a superficial glance. Some points seem repetitive (e.g., numbers 1 and 9), and others look as if they could as appropriately appear somewhere else in the list. To see what reason Jefferson had for his arrangement, it is best to look at the core concerns of each clause. Jefferson maintains that politically enforced religion would

A. 1) ignore the structure of the mind, and so
   2) offend the God who structured that mind;
   3) promote hypocrisy, and so
   4) offend the God who requires sincerity;
B. 5) impose mainly false religions;
   6) be sinful (making people act against conscience) and tyrannical (a form of taxation without consent);
   7) discourage the search for convincing moral guides;
   8) make for a lax clergy;
   9) unjustly bar dissenters from public office;
   10) corrupt the enforced church with bribes to belief;
C. 11) make the enforcers complicitous in the bribing process;
   12) make conscience the object of civil government;
   13) make temporal rulers the judges of religion's truth;
   14) anticipate civil disorders before they arise; and, last,
D. 15) weaken truth, which fares best in contest with error.

The first four points in this list (A) concern the individual's nature and that nature's relation to God. The next six points (B, points 5 through 10 inclusive) deal mainly with the health of religion and the good of the churches. Jefferson begins this section with an argument, taken from Locke, that is tailored to a Protestant audience: If establishment is the proper course, it has mainly enforced the *Catholic* (i.e., false) religion in Europe's history—or, in the sweep of world history, non-Christian religions.

Only in the third section of his list (C, points 11 through 14, four items) does Jefferson turn to the proper aims and healthy performance of the state. Nor can anyone argue that this is the climactic part of the catalogue, saving the most important matter for last. The summary concluding point looks back, rather, to the structure of the individual's intellect, and to the claims of truth upon the mind, which had opened the list.

The conscious way Jefferson organizes his approach in the bill can be assessed if we look at an earlier structuring of his arguments for religious freedom. We have the notes for his address to the legislature in support of the forerunner to this bill, his 1776 disestablishment proposal. These notes afford us a rare glimpse of the way Jefferson spoke in deliberative assembly. He rarely made formal addresses, and his lack of success in this debate of 1776 became a further reason for his diffidence as an orator.[6] But the carefully prepared notes for his presentation tell us how he approached the task when he felt that his own intervention was imperative.

The situation should be kept in mind. Jefferson comes before his fellow Virginia legislators as a member of the commission they have appointed to revise the laws after their separation from the English system. The religious bill is just one of the revised statutes Jefferson is submitting at the time (though the one he cared about most deeply). He begins by stressing the enormities that will stay in effect if the old laws are not changed. I expand the abbreviations in his notes: "Before entering on proper redress, [we should] see what is [the] injury—the state of religious liberty [under the laws on the books]."[7] This gives Jefferson an opportunity to list the gruesome persecutions Virginia would inflict if it observed all the English statutes against apostasy, heresy, recusancy (failure to swear the oath of allegiance to the Church of England's Thirty-Nine Articles), papacy, profaneness, and failure to support the church financially. It is a dark picture Jefferson draws of an English heritage of suppression: "Gentlemen will be surprised at [the] detail [of] these persecuting statutes. Most men imagine [that] persecution [is] unknown to our lands. [The] legal status [of] religion [is] little understood."

Such laws have not been recently enforced, not because they were removed from the books, but because "happily the spirit of [the] times [is] in favor of [the] rights of conscience." But those expressly charged with revising the law should not rely on "the spirit of the time" to keep ferocious laws from being retained. Here Jefferson anticipates an objection from his listeners: The old rigors of law are allowed to stand only *in terrorem*—to intimidate possible offenders. Jefferson answers this objection at length:

> Acts *in terrorem* [are] not justifiable. Men presume they will be executed. [They] leave everyone at [the] mercy of [a] bigot. Everyone should know under what law [he] lives. [He] should not be obliged [to have] recourse to [the] spirit of [the] time for protection. This is not [the way to] secure government, but [it leaves things to the] mercy of events. [The] spirit of [the] time may alter. [A] single zealot may undertake [a] reform [by enforcing the laws]. [It is] a bad compliment [i.e., compliance] to law that people discern iniquity and not exterminate it.[8]

This was as impassioned as Jefferson was likely to get in legislative debate. His last words about exterminating the inequity of persecution call to

mind Voltaire's cry, *"Ecrasez l'infâme."* But even here Jefferson has made
a special plea to the Protestants in the assembly room. England's older
laws would, if successfully enforced, have "prevented [the] Reformation."
They would, in fact, resemble laws used to enforce Islam in other lands.

After this introduction on the state of the present law, to which Jefferson
appends a list of English and Virginian enactments,[9] he proceeds to his
four main arguments, in this order:

> 1) The state has no right to force religious opinions on the free con-
> science, which can only submit to evidence.
>
> 2) A state religion is not expedient, since it is neither desirable nor
> attainable.
>
> 3) If a state religion were desirable and attainable, there would be no
> way to ascertain *which* religion should be imposed.
>
> 4) It is advantageous to religion not to impose one set of beliefs.

Under the second heading, Jefferson proves that establishment is not
desirable by recurring to the argument that "the Glorious Reformation"
had to shake off the established Catholic religion, that "Mohammedism
[is] supported by stifling free inquiry," and that "in Rom[a]n Cath[olic]
countr[ies is] most infidel[i]ty."

These passages show that "our religion," referred to in point 4 of the
final bill, was clearly *Christian Protestantism* when Jefferson argued before his peers in the legislature. Religious establishment is presented as
a remnant, not sufficiently adverted to, of *popish* days. In Jefferson's last
argument before the assembly, which *is* climactic for persuasion purposes,
he appeals to the Protestant view of history to show that state support
weakens the Christian religion: "Christianity flourished three hundred
years without establishment. [As] soon as [it was] established [under the
Emperor Constantine, it] declined from [its] purity."

Jefferson even quotes, twice, the Christian Bible to make his case for
religion's independence from the state. He uses the same scriptural verse
in both cases—Matthew 16.18, which says that the "gates of hell" will
not overcome the church Christ founded. Jefferson uses the passage to
answer a foreseeable argument: "Objection: Religion will decline if not
supported [by the state]. Answer: '[The] gates of hell shall not prevail . . .' " Then, in a final argument for the advantages given religion
by disestablishment, Jefferson made this appeal: "[It] betrays [a] want [of]
confidence in [the] doctrines of [the] church to suspect that reason or
intrinsic excellence [is] insufficient [to support it] without [a] secular prop.
'The gates of hell shall never prevail.' "

Jefferson is obviously using an argument he had found in Locke, one that is not (in Locke's text) an argument for the state's *neutrality* toward all forms of religion. Locke believed that toleration would actually *favor* true religion, since that is the only kind that neither takes nor wants support from secular coercion. The first sentence of Locke's *Epistola de Tolerantia* (which Jefferson studied and took extensive notes from in 1776) says that tolerance is "the principal distinguishing feature of the true church [*praecipuum verae ecclesiae criterium*]."[10]

This attitude lies behind point 5 in Jefferson's bill, which makes the interesting assertion that "impious presumption" in past legislatures "hath established and maintained false religions over the greatest part of the world and through all time." This is not the language of later secularists, who would not themselves presume to distinguish true from false religions, or let the state entertain such hypothetical categories. Jefferson's bill is not neutral in its list of the reasons for denouncing links between church and state. He unequivocally says that his move is preferential toward one form of religion—the true religion.

Jefferson's own religion was quite different from Locke's. Locke believed in a number of things Jefferson rejected—miracles and inspired scripture, to name just two.[11] And it is obvious that the Virginian was even farther from the evangelical piety of Roger Williams. But all three men agreed that the true religion (whatever that might be) would never, because of its own purity, use secular power to coerce belief. Williams thought one cannot command the grace of God, which alone leads people to a saving belief. Locke and Jefferson believed one cannot honor God by defying "the laws of Nature and of Nature's God," violating the nature of the mind's response to evidence.

Jefferson considered himself a theist (which is simply the Greek form of the Latin *deist*) and a "true Christian" (one who believed Jesus the supreme moral teacher within human history). He obviously thought other religions true insofar as they approximated this religion; and one criterion (to use Locke's word) of *any* religion aspiring to truth is its refusal to violate the structure of conscience. Thus Jefferson, however secular, was not a relativist. He was convinced that he knew the truth, and could distinguish true religion from false, and could even legislate on the basis of that distinction, putting an attack on "false religion" into the statute book of the state of Virginia.

Jefferson's bill claims to favor true religion not only in this all-important point of honoring the law of God about the workings of conscience, but in many *practical* ways. At the time when he was reading Locke's religious writings, he also read "A Letter Concerning Enthusiasm," in Lord Shaftesbury's *Characteristics*—which argued that freedom of speech on the subject of religion is a healthy thing, exposing religion to the purifying influence of satire, which castigates excess and purges corruption. In his notes from Shaftesbury, Jefferson wrote again that the Protestant Reformation depended on the freedom of attack that could identify "Romish follies." Thus religion is served by "free argument, raillery, and even ridicule [that] will preserve the purity of religion."[12]

Jefferson used another Shaftesbury argument when he said that *competition* between religious teachers makes for an improved religious product. In his notes for speaking to the legislature in 1776, he said that freedom of religion will "strengthen [the] church," since it will "oblige its ministers to be industrious [and] exemplary." He asked "whether dependence [on the state] or independence [is] most likely to make [them] industrious," and cited the parallel case of lawyers and physicians.[13]

This argument for a "free market" of religious teachers is put negatively in the text of the bill itself. In point 7, we are told that establishment deprives the citizen "of the comfortable [invigorating] liberty of giving his contributions to the particular pastor whose morals he would make his pattern, and whose powers he feels most persuasive to righteousness."

The same principle of free competition lies behind points 10 and 11 in the bill, according to which a "monopoly" on religious teaching leads to an impure product (to people profiting from religion while they "externally profess and conform to it") as well as to corruption of the state (to officers who "lay the bait" for feigning ministers and believers).

Jefferson went farther in his tolerance than Locke had—noting that "where he stopped short, we may go on."[14] But it is significant that Jefferson did *not* go farther than Roger Williams had. Locke, while denying the state any instruments of coercion, would allow it the tools of exhortation to religious duty.[15] Roger Williams, who could not find real "apostles" even among *religious* teachers, denied that the *state* had any religious light at all to share with others. Locke's state would not tolerate atheists, but Williams included every kind of chaff and "tares" in the world, since the worldly can only govern others by worldly devices. In practical terms, Jefferson was closer to Williams than to Locke; and even in terms of principle he was closer to the New England preacher than has been generally suspected. Thus, in his arguments for disestablishment, Jefferson told Virginia's legislators that New England ministers, who *competed* for their posts, were better than the bishop-appointed curates of their native state.[16]

Naturally, Jefferson did not know or admire the work of Williams. But the success of his own bill depended on its congruence, in the eyes of those accepting it, with religious values Williams had championed. Williams believed, as surely as Locke and Jefferson, that the civil competence of the state did not reach to any person's private acts of belief. For Williams, such acts were matters of commerce between the individual and the converting Spirit. Yet the Spirit uses the divinely created machinery of human intellect to effect the "soul's persuasion from the Scripture."[17] The only true belief grows out of that inner conviction which no other human can effect for the individual. Even the natives of America cannot be coerced into European beliefs. Rather, "they must judge according to their Indian or American consciences, for other consciences it cannot be supposed they should have."[18] Since each person's belief is private, all the establishment of religion does is impose the conscience of one person, or of one set of persons—the ruler or his magistrates—on everybody else. In that case, officials "judge and punish as *they* are persuaded in their *own* belief and conscience (be their conscience paganish, Turkish, or Antichristian)."[19]

This part of Williams's argument coincided perfectly with Locke's and Jefferson's views. Locke said an established religion is simply one that "appeals to the prince [*quae principi placet*]."[20] Since "every man is his own rule of faith [*sibi quisque orthodoxus est*]," a *public* religion is simply one form of *private* religion imposed where it has no place.[21] This is the argument Jefferson's bill makes in point 5 ("setting up their own opinions and modes of thinking") and point 13 ("make his opinions the rule of judgment"). In his argument to the Virginia legislature, Jefferson noted that the individual, whether ruler or ruled, can answer only for his own belief, "founded on the evidence offered to his mind," since "his own understanding, whether more or less judicious, [is the] only faculty [given by] God."[22]

Williams, considering the problem of tolerance against a theological background very different from Locke's and Jefferson's, agrees with them on the pragmatic reasons for protecting religion from secular corruption—that establishment promotes hypocrisy, for instance, and corrupts both the benefactors and the beneficiaries of secular favor.[23]

Jefferson certainly did not have the zeal of Williams, or even the piety that made Locke join with Newton in a search for God's plan of the world hidden in Scripture. But Enlightenment was not simply a theologically negative matter, for Jefferson, of escaping the superstitions of the past. He saw the need to replace the gloomy and confining doctrines about God with his own highly optimistic view of Nature's Lord. That view would of itself promote freedom, restoring the dignity of self-government to those who must *choose* their form of worship, not have it imposed on them.

Jefferson resorted to religion as a political weapon in the Revolution precisely because the freedom that favors religion did not exist under the British establishment. Jefferson, who opposed the formation of political parties, resorted to partisan tactics in the 1790s, arguing that Federalist oppression called for emergency measures. In the same way, British favors done to priestly hierarchies could be attacked on the way to disestablishing religion. Once freedom of conscience was guaranteed, the truth could be trusted to make its own way. This was not as radical a position as Roger Williams would have taken, but it aimed in its own way at the same protection of religion from corruption.

James Madison, more radical than Jefferson on the separation of church and state, was for that reason even closer to the position of Roger Williams. Madison has a less dramatic impact on people's minds today, but he had a deeper impact on our history, in the matter of religious freedom. And he, too, came to protect religion, not dishonor it, by disestablishment.

❖ T H I R T Y ▪ T H R E E ❖

Madison and
the Honor of God

JEFFERSON IS MORE VIVID IN OUR MINDS THAN MADISON. HE HAS AN AL-most melodramatic gift for getting our attention. Henry Adams thought him cursed with an eloquence that outran its own intent.[1] His statements go to the extreme: Jesus is first a dupe and then the teacher of a "system" that is "perfect"; if trinitarian Christianity is the corrupter of mankind, unitarian Christianity becomes its deliverer. He moves with a swirling of his cloak.

Madison's rhetoric seems pedestrian after Jefferson's; but in the matter of disestablishing religion he was always more absolute, consistent, and effective. He was at the key legislating sessions that Jefferson missed. His efforts were more concentrated on this topic, the one that engaged him most passionately. He maneuvered Jefferson's statute into law after Jefferson had failed. He strengthened the religious freedom clause in the Virginia Bill of Rights (though not as much as he had hoped to). He advanced religious freedom (though not as far as he had hoped) in the federal Bill of Rights. Though he is called the father of the Constitution, he has an even better claim as the father of disestablishment. His own religious views were either more conventional or less disclosed than Jefferson's. He was not widely accused of atheism by his enemies. He has not regularly been called a "deist" by those who equate that adjective with "irreligious." But anyone who dislikes the separation of church and state in America should by all rights be railing at Madison, not at Jefferson.

Madison's long and efficient campaigning on this matter is best suggested by a chronology:

1774: Madison, denouncing the jailing of Baptist preachers in Virginia, concludes that "ecclesiastical establishments tend to great ignorance and corruption."[2]

1776: At Virginia's revolutionary convention, Madison tries to amend George Mason's preamble to the new Virginia constitution, in order to remove all "emoluments or privileges" from religion. He fails at that, but does substitute "free exercise of religion" for "fullest toleration in the exercise of religion."[3] His first important legislative act, undertaken when he is only twenty-five, strikes a blow for religious freedom.

1785: Against Patrick Henry's plan to support religion in general with a tax assessment, Madison publishes his major statement on religious freedom, "Memorial and Remonstrance against Religious Assessments."[4]

1785: Relying on the reaction built up against Patrick Henry's assessment measure, Madison steers Jefferson's statute on religious freedom into law.[5]

1787: As architect of the constitutional drafting convention, Madison promotes a document that goes beyond the Articles of Confederation, which did not require a religious oath for holding office, by *forbidding* such oaths (article VI).

1789: Drafting what will become the First Amendment, Madison proposes not only disestablishment at the national level but that "no *state* shall violate the equal rights of conscience."[6] Passed in the House, this measure is defeated in the Senate. Though disestablishment at the federal level is all he can accomplish in his lifetime, he regularly refers to the First Amendment as opposing "establishments," reflecting *his* original intent.[7]

c. 1817: After retiring from the presidency, Madison writes a long "Detached Memorandum" on "the danger of silent accumulations and encroachments by ecclesiastical bodies," deploring the growth of (untaxed) church wealth, tax-paid chaplains, and religious proclamations like that of Thanksgiving.[8]

1822: In a long letter on religious freedom, he returns to the attack on chaplaincies and proclamations.[9]

This is Madison's record of striving to keep the state innocent of religious involvement. He believed that the national census should not list religious ministry as an occupation, since "the general government is proscribed from the interfering, in any manner whatever, in matters respecting religion; and it may be thought to do this in ascertaining who and who are not ministers of the gospel."[10]

But mere punctilio about the details of separation is less important than the reasons Madison advanced for his purist view. These do not show any hostility to religion. Even more than Jefferson—and, to some people, more persuasively—he says he wants to keep religion free of the state out of concern for its own good. This is emphasized in his most comprehensive statement on the subject, his 1785 "Memorial." In that document, Madison puts a variety of arguments under fifteen headings, moving from his strongest points of principle to weaker ones of prudence or mere convenience. His basic argument is in the complex heading numbered 1. The rest simply apply, amplify, or supplement it.

1) Since faith depends on evidence, not on coercion, man cannot alienate the right to follow conscience, nor can God abrogate his demands on the individual conscience; so that civil society has no cognizance [jurisdiction] over religious faith.[11]

2) If civil society in general has no such cognizance, no organ of it can have any.

3) Partial establishment can lead to absolute establishment.

4) Free exercise of conscience is an equal right for all.

5) Civil magistrates are incompetent to judge of religious matters, even if they had a right to.

6) Religion is not helped by establishment,

7) but is hurt by it,

8) as is civil society.

9) Establishment would hinder immigration,

10) foster emigration,

11) disturb good social relations,

12) and retard Christian evangelizing.

13) Attempts at enforcement would weaken government,

14) since there is no clear public consensus on the matter.

15) To deny religious freedom would weaken other rights.[12]

Since the form of Madison's document is a public petition looking for signatories, he argues like a lawyer, trying whatever will sway the jury. He appeals, therefore, to the convictions of the moment—for example, that immigration is good for Virginia, and emigration bad. There is no implication that the permanent arguments, especially that in point 1, would change with the state's demographics, or in case a consensus were formed against religious freedom. Should we put point 12, where Madison assumes the desirability of Christian evangelizing, on a level with mere preferences, like that for brisk rates of immigration? There are many places on the list, not just this one, where protecting religion is called an aim of disestablishment. Like Jefferson, Madison appeals to the memory of an uncorrupted pre-Constantinian church as the true one. He even offers the goal of confounding "false religions" in point 12, where "the diffusion of the light of Christianity" is offered as a motive for disestablishment.

Like Jefferson, Madison commends those religions—he mentions "Quakers and Menonists" in point 4—that rely on no "compulsive support" to spread their teaching. They avoid what are called, in point 7, the fruits of establishment—"pride and indolence in the clergy, ignorance and servility in the laity, in both superstition, bigotry and persecution." When civil authority tries to use religious tools, this is, according to point 5, "an unhallowed perversion of the means of salvation." On this Madison agrees with Roger Williams. Madison denounces the use of "religion as an engine of civil policy" (point 5). Williams condemned the effort "to pull God and Christ and Spirit out of heaven and subject them unto natural, sinful inconstant man."[13] Religion, with Madison and Williams, is too sublime a matter to be entrusted to sinful magistrates. Madison makes this almost a part of God's honor, since religion (in point 1)

> is a duty towards the Creator. It is the duty of every man to render to the Creator such homage, and such only, as he believes to be acceptable to Him. This duty is precedent, both in order of time and in degree of obligation, to the claims of civil society. Before any man can be considered as a member of civil society, he must be considered as a subject of the Governor of the Universe; and if a member of civil society, who enters into any subordinate association, must always do it with a reservation of his duty to the general authority, much more must every man, who becomes a member of any particular civil society, do it with a saving of his allegiance to the Universal Sovereign. We [the petitioners] maintain, therefore, that in matters of religion no man's right is abridged by the institution of civil society, and that religion is wholly exempt from its cognizance.

Madison does not argue, here, against this or that form of religious establishment, but against *any* jurisdiction in the matter by "civil society" in general—a thing he hammers home in point 2, saying that no particular social unit can have any cognizance if civil society in general does not. In his very first written criticism of establishment (in 1773) he contemplated eliminating it in all the American colonies *and* in the English mother country.[14] He would never, from that point, consider disestablishment a valid goal for one part of civil society (e.g., the federal government) but less important for others (e.g., the states). In his later correspondence he complains that some states have not gone as far as Virginia in the recognition of God's exclusive jurisdiction over matters of conscience. Men cannot tread where God alone holds sway. As he puts it in point 4 of the "Memorial," "If this freedom be abused, it is an offense against God, not against man. To God, therefore, not to man, must an account of it be rendered." *That* is why (in point 5) he says that any political use of religion is "an unhallowed perversion of the means of salvation." It trenches on the domain of God, and derogates from His honor.

Some have used the fact that Madison hesitated about the desirability of the Bill of Rights to claim that disestablishment was not essential to his view of the state.[15] But Madison's fears were that the nation was not yet ready to go far enough (as it proved by rejecting his proposal for state disestablishment). He saw even Virginia failing to live up to the standard Jefferson had set for it. As he wrote to Jefferson in October of 1788:

> There is great reason to fear that a positive declaration of some of the most essential rights could not be obtained in the requisite latitude. I am sure that the rights of conscience, in particular, if submitted to public definition, would be narrowed much more than they are likely ever to be by an assumed power [of the federal government over religion]. . . . In Virginia I have seen the bill of rights violated in every instance where it was opposed to a popular current. Notwithstanding the explicit provision contained in that instrument for the rights of conscience, it is well known that a religious establishment would have taken place in that state if the legislative majority had found, as they expected, a majority of the people in favor of the measure; and I am persuaded that if a majority of the people were now of one sect, the measure would still take place and on narrower ground than was then proposed, notwithstanding the additional obstacle which the law has since created.[16]

Jefferson sought to reassure Madison on this point. Later, when fighting with the federal courts, he would have been horrified at what he wrote at this juncture. But history has proved him right in his first position:

> In the arguments in favor of a declaration of rights, you omit one which has great weight with me, the legal check which, if rendered independent and kept strictly to their own department, merits great confidence for their learning and integrity.[17]

Jefferson goes on to argue that a Bill of Rights is one more brace added to the structural supports of the Constitution, and that later ages will live up to its standard because "our young people are educated in republicanism."[18] Accordingly, Madison argued for the amendments in Congress on the grounds that "they have a tendency to impress some degree of respect for them, to establish the public opinion in their favor, and rouse the attention of the whole community."[19]

So Madison advanced his disestablishment clause not as a final and optimal piece of legislation, but as a move in the right direction, a base from which to vindicate the argument against *any* political infringing of God's sphere. The later history of the doctrine of separation, which makes conservatives lament progressive moves to separate church and state, is just what he and Jefferson were hoping for. And, in fact, the states with established churches did approximate the federal norm in time, even going beyond it in explicit denial of funds for some religious purposes:

> Each of the fifty states has at least one section in its constitution affecting church-state relations. Those sections are as diverse as they are frequent. By far the most usual are clauses that state more fully than the U.S. Constitution a concept of no support for religious groups. For example:
>
>> No money shall ever be taken from the public Treasury, directly or indirectly, in aid of any church, sect, or denomination of religionist, or of any sectarian institution.
>>   —Article I, sec. 1, ch. 2–114 of the Georgia constitution
>
> In other instances the prohibition against establishment is put in terms of the rights of the individual:
>
>> no man ought to, or of right can be compelled to attend any religious worship, or erect or support any place of worship, or maintain any minister, contrary to the dictates of his conscience.
>>   —Chapter I, art. 3 of the Vermont constitution
>
> In many of the state documents one also finds more specific clauses prohibiting aid to religious schools, either through a specific sanction or through a protected public school fund. . . . At least six states prohibit such transportation [of private school students] under the terms of their state constitutions, and several ban the purchase of texts.[20]

So far have the states come in realizing Madison's vision. And this is not a matter of federal court decisions but of the states' own constitutions. The ideal of disestablishment had its seeds in the kind of separation John Winthrop administered, to protect the separate congregations of Massachusetts. The federal Constitution spelled out a more thorough doctrine of separation, and the states have adopted that model.

It is true that the courts have, in recent years, made new applications of the doctrine of separation—going farther, on matters like school prayer, than custom once allowed (though not farther than Madison wished). Some of these cases were brought by atheists like the colorful Madalyn Murray O'Hair, a favorite bogey of the right wing, who almost single-handedly removed the Lord's Prayer from schools.[21] The ACLU, more active, and more effective in the long run, has argued from a secularist viewpoint for strict separation. That is what makes the religious Right see separation as hostile to religion. But when Madalyn Murray O'Hair argues for the same thing that James Madison did, why should we believe that her reasons are more important than his? Roger Williams would conclude that she is doing God's work, without realizing it, when she frees His church from contamination by politics.

And, in fact, various religious groups have joined the litigation that led to recent separation decisions—the National Council of Churches, the Americans United (formerly Protestants and Other Americans United) for Separation of Church and State, the American Jewish Congress, and the Baptist Joint Committee on Public Affairs.[22] Some have considered these groups somehow less legitimate than the "neutralists" of the ACLU, since their agenda aimed at preventing privileges for specific groups.[23] The AJC, for instance, has opposed the institutionalizing of Christianity in schools and public ceremonies. The Americans United and Southern Baptist groups have opposed aid to Catholic schools. But that is in a great American tradition. The churches that want to protect their own ortho-doxy help disestablishment by keeping state support from "heretics." This is what completed disestablishment in Massachusetts: By the 1830s, state money would have gone to Unitarians as well as Congregationalists unless all churches lost their state support—which was the preferable solution.[24] After all, both Jefferson and Madison had argued their case by pointing out the danger of the Catholic religion's winning state support. Nothing could demonstrate better the difference between a religious *motive* for supporting a law and the nonreligious *intent* of the law. Protection of orthodoxy was Roger Williams's motive for disestablishment.

The success of the Madisonian ideal has vindicated Madison's maxim that "religion flourishes in greater purity without [rather] than with the aid of government."[25] America has remained deeply religious while taking ever more seriously the ideal of separation. It is false to think that recent court decisions have made religion less important or effective in America, or even in our politics. The civil rights and antiwar movements of the sixties and seventies show how effective religious leadership remains—

continuing a tradition of "conscience politics" that made the churches strong in the abolition, women's rights, and temperance movements. By contrast, religious complicity with government in the slave states was a blot on the churches, as Forrest G. Wood argues with bitter eloquence.[26]

The same thing might be said of religious complicity in war symbolized by the military chaplain system, in which the clergy take government pay and wear the government's uniform. Madison did not oppose military chaplaincies, as he did the congressional chaplain. He just suggested that the chaplains be voluntary and voluntarily supported. If there is no fervor for such religious tasks, he held, then the state should not create an artificial concern, which serves its own purposes more than the good of religion: "Look through the armies and navies of the world, and say whether, in the appointment of their ministers of religion, the spiritual interests of the flocks or the temporal interests of the shepherds be most in view."[27] The argument for military chaplains often alleges the need for control by military superiors, revealing the actual priority in this matter. When, rarely, a chaplain objects to military actions, he is treated as an ingrate or traitor who has taken the state's money, put on its uniform, and then refused to accept military discipline. Does anyone doubt there would have been more religious freedom to scrutinize the morality of military action if the chaplaincies had been voluntary? Those who insist on government control do not show any such doubt.

If Madison is any guide, our churches are not, even now, too separated from political support. They should be freer still, which would make them more powerful *and*, paradoxically, more political. That is one of the American paradoxes we can be most proud of—that our churches have influence because they are independent of the government. If any people doubt that, let them look to Dr. King.

Conclusion

SINCE THIS BOOK IS ABOUT RELIGION IN AMERICAN POLITICS, IT HAS DEALT primarily with Protestant, and especially evangelical, Christianity. The influence of that form of religion has been so preponderant that only recently has the notion of America as "a Christian nation" become rightly suspect. Justice Sandra Day O'Connor caused a flurry of criticism when she endorsed that notion in 1989.[1] Yet the Supreme Court referred to "this Christian nation" in nineteenth-century cases.[2] Abraham Lincoln regularly used the term.[3]

To understand why the term is now offensive we must recognize exactly what it meant through most of our history. It did *not* mean that "Judeo-Christian heritage" people invoke when they want to defend civil religion of Tocqueville's sort or try to shoehorn prayer back into the schools. The dominant Christianity of America tolerated when it did not encourage anti-Semitism and anti-Catholicism. The "Judeo" part of the mythical Judeo-Christian heritage was a Protestant reading of *its* "Old Testament" as if that were the Jewish Scripture. There is more genuine religious vision, much of it derived from the Jewish tradition, in recent criticism of religious symbols than in condescending praise of the Jews as preparers of the Christian testament. The ancient prohibition on idolatry is a healthy warning against letting "civil religion" appropriate the attributes of God. In most of our wars, as in dubious other matters like slavery, we have indeed "taken God's name in vain."

America was, sociologically, a "Christian (Protestant) nation" by virtue of its dominant cultural values, so long as those values were not effectively challenged by others. Catholics withdrew from the national school system to escape Protestantism, not secularism. Prayers were still said, the Bible still read, in schools that the Catholic hierarchy objected to—only it was the Protestant translation of the Bible that was used, and the Protestant version of the Lord's Prayer. Nineteenth-century Protestantism was not ecumenical. Those harking back to the "good old days" of religion in public life forget just how exclusive that religion was.

America's culture was infused with Protestantism in the same way that, according to Cardinal Newman, British literature was culturally Protestant. As a Catholic, of course, he did not consider this historical fact prescriptive, the expression of what should have been or had to be or must forever be; but he told his fellows to face it as a historical fact: "We cannot write a new Milton or a new Gibbon."[4] There are some givens of a historical situation—and he was speaking *de facto*, not *de jure*. Catholics should not deny the facts, he argued. They should face the obvious: "We cannot destroy or reverse it [the Protestant character of classical English literature]; we may confront and encounter it, but we cannot make it over again."[5]

In the same way, there is no denying the Protestant consensus with which this nation began—the anti-Catholicism expressed even in the Declaration of Independence, the long exclusion of Jews from "Christian organizations," the nativist resistance to other cultures. A Protestant God led armies into war against the devil-worshiping Native Americans. African gods could not be worshiped on America's soil when slaves were brought here. Yet the first insights into the need to separate church and state also came from Protestants—from people like John Endecott, Roger Williams, and the Baptists. There were Protestant critics of slavery as well as defenders—Anthony Benezet, for instance, in colonial and revolutionary Philadelphia, breaking the law to teach slaves how to read. We have a double heritage, even from the Protestant background that dominated our culture for so long.

But few, even Protestants, want that exclusive aspect of our culture to be maintained. That is why our history has been selectively rewritten, foisting on us a premature ecumenism and mythical amity of "Judeo-Christian" elements. But it is our task, in a society of increasingly complex articulation, to complete the effort of Madison in removing religion from state ceremony and proclamations. We appreciate better than Lincoln's contemporaries did his use of religious language to question the complacent view that God is in agreement with armies that invoke him. We value more those who follow conscience to deny that a once-Christian culture must have a Christian state. A modern prophet like Dr. King makes us understand the witness of those who found the "Christian state" ungodly in its blessing of things like slavery.

Despite the Protestant presuppositions of our culture (many of them unspoken), we have had a professed ideal of constitutional separation. That gave to religion an initial, if minimal, freedom from crippling forms of cooperation with the state. That, more than anything else, made the United States a new thing on the earth, setting new tasks for religion, offering it new opportunities. Everything else in our Constitution—separation of powers, balanced government, bicameralism, federalism—had been anticipated both in theory and practice. The framers aptly defended their handiwork with citations from Polybius and Montesquieu and Hume, and with references to the history of constitutional monarchies, ancient republics, and modern leagues. We combined a number of these features in a way that was suitable to our genius, as the drafters put it—to what Montesquieu called the national *esprit*. But we invented nothing, except disestablishment.

No other government in history had launched itself without the help of officially recognized gods and their state-connected ministers. It is no wonder that, in so novel an undertaking, it should have taken a while to sift the dangers and the blessings of the new arrangement, to learn how best to live with it, to complete the logic of its workings. We are still grappling with its meaning for us. But, at the least, its meaning has been one of freedom—the free exercise of the churches, free not only from official obstruction but from compromising favors. A burden was lifted from religion when it ceased to depend on the breath of princes, when it had nothing by way of political office with which to lure or tempt people into the fold or into the ministry. Thrown back on themselves, the churches were encouraged to search for their own essence, make their moral case on truly religious grounds, reward people in the proper spiritual currency. The contradictory goals of political advancement and religious vocation were not an omnipresent problem.

Corruption of church and state is a mutual infection, whether mild or extreme. Even in mild form, it leads to the quiet agony of Trollope's Warden (Septimus Harding), baffled by pygmy clergy seeking preferment.

At its worst, it leads to the horror of the medieval papacy, Lord Acton's own example of "absolute power [that] corrupts absolutely."[6]

Our American churches have escaped the worst element of that partnership—the effort to maintain theological consistency through changes of political regimes; the cleansing of mud from ecclesiastical skirts after official scandal; the labor to maintain spiritual strength in captivity, like Samson stirring in his chains; the spectacle of disappointed clerics who dwindle into bitter courtiers. Purity of teaching and practice is easier to demand, and not always impossible of achievement. Mercenary desires, though they can creep in on ministers from all other sides, are at least not obtruded by the state. We stumble on no remnants of *cuius regio eius religio* (each region its own religion), as even Queen Elizabeth II does, obliged to change identities in moving from one realm to another: Head of the English church south of the Scottish border, she becomes head of the Presbyterian kirk north of it.

The fear, of course, was that a church freed of official power would be neutered. But no careful look at our history can support such fear. Religion has, admittedly, been a powerful force for social stability, supporting indirectly the regime that offers free exercise to all beliefs; but it has also been a prophetic voice of resistance to power when that is unchecked by moral insight. The cleric in jail is an American tradition, the conscientious objector, the practitioner of civil disobedience. The Quaker Anthony Benezet denounced slavery to Patrick Henry, war to General Howe, and the treatment of Acadians to his local Philadelphia rulers.

Carrie Nation, like Ronald Reagan a Disciple of Christ, made fervent war on saloons. The Underground Railway was run by holy criminals. Religious radicals have extraordinary staying power—like Dorothy Day, who went to jail for women's rights with Alice Paul in the 1920s, and with Ammon Hennacy to protest nuclear war in the 1950s, feeding the poor and defying the powerful, decade in and decade out. Of all the communes formed in the wake of the 1960s, only religious ones seem to have survived into the 1990s—Jonah House, Sojourners, the Committee for Creative Non-Violence. The sanctuary movement offered a new underground railway for those fleeing oppression in El Salvador and Guatemala.

The sanctuary movement of the 1980s renewed a religious drama played out, over and over, in our supposedly secular world—the nocturnal gathering for prayer, then the flight from police. The FBI sent bugged informers into sanctuary churches. It paid spies like Jesús Cruz to smuggle refugees alongside the movement's organizers, then to testify against them in the Phoenix trial of 1985–86.[7]

Jesús Cruz was an interesting name in this context, both the first and the last name (*cruz* means "cross"—Jesús Cruz always wore one around his neck). I think of him at Mass with the refugees, repeating that Last Supper at which Jesus said the one who dipped a hand in the bowl with him would betray him. In Cruz's case, the price was not thirty pieces of silver but eighteen thousand dollars of tax-collected money. Here, as so often, the church was not only separate from the state, but opposed to the state, castigating it, breaking its laws, as Dr. King did, and Dorothy Day, and Anthony Benezet. It is a part of our history we can be proud of, though our elected representatives play the villains in the story. Roger Williams knew that true religion must always be, in some measure, an underground affair.

Notes

INTRODUCTION

[1] Karl Marx, "The Eighteenth Brumaire of Louis Bonaparte," in *Karl Marx and Friedrich Engels: Selected Works* (International Publishers, 1969), p. 104.

[2] *The Washington Post*, May 3, 1990, p. A25.

[3] Seymour Martin Lipset, *The First New Nation: The United States in Historical and Comparative Perspective* (Norton, 1973), p. 144.

[4] Ibid., pp. 145–50.

[5] George Gallup, Jr., and Jim Castelli, *The People's Religion: American Faith in the 90's* (Macmillan, 1989), p. 4. A different reading of the statistics confirms the same general pattern: Andrew M. Greeley, *Religious Change in America* (Harvard, 1989). When the Social Science Research Council assigned the latter book to Greeley, "its letter assumed that one of the major tasks of a study of religious indicators over the last half-century would be to document the 'secularization' of the American population" (p. 3). Greeley demonstrates that no fair reading of the data could lead to that conclusion.

[6] Gallup and Castelli, op. cit., p. 75.

[7] Ibid., pp. 33, 48.

[8] Ibid., p. 45.

[9] Ibid., p. 47.

[10] Ibid., p. 186.

[11] Paul Kleppner, *The Cross of Culture: A Social Analysis of Midwestern Politics, 1850–1900* (The Free Press, 1970).

[12] Gallup and Castelli, op. cit., pp. 227, 249. Andrew Greeley (op. cit., p. 50) notes that "strength of affiliation with either party does indeed correlate with strength of churchgoing propensity."

[13] Greeley, op. cit., p. 91.

[14] *The New Republic*, November 13, 1989.

[15] Yet "37 percent of Americans say they would be more likely to vote for a candidate who said Jesus was his savior" (Gallup and Castelli, op. cit., p. 228).

[16] *Newsweek*, April 30, 1990, p. 19: "Nancy and I are sorry to hear about your illness. Our thoughts and prayers are with you. God bless you." Addressed to Augusta Lockridge, a character going blind in *Santa Barbara*.

[17] At 1 Peter 1.23, Christians are said to be "born anew, not of mortal parentage but of immortal, through the living and enduring word of God." At Matthew 18.3, it is said that only those who "turn round and become like children" can enter the kingdom of heaven.

[18]Gallup and Castelli, op. cit., p. 93. Evangelicals are not a separate denomination of Christians but those, especially within the "low church" denominations, who emphasize the personal experience of being saved. They make up 57 percent of Baptists, 32 percent of Methodists, 29 percent of Lutherans, 27 percent of Presbyterians, but only 14 percent of Episcopalians. The church with the lowest number of evangelicals (1 percent) is not, as one might expect, the Catholic but the Mormon. Blacks are overrepresented among evangelicals, and Hispanics are leaving the Catholic church in increasing numbers for more evangelical forms of worship (ibid., pp. 93–94). See also George Gallup, Jr., and Jim Castelli, *The American Catholic People: Their Beliefs, Practices, and Values* (Doubleday, 1987), pp. 139–48, and Andrew Greeley, *The Catholic Myth: The Behavior and Beliefs of American Catholics* (Charles Scribner's Sons, 1990), p. 120: "Catholics of Hispanic origin are defecting to Protestant denominations at a rate of approximately 60,000 people a year."

[19]George Marsden, *Fundamentalism and American Culture: The Shaping of Twentieth-Century Evangelism, 1870–1925* (Oxford, 1980), p. 6.

[20]Nathan O. Hatch, *The Democratization of American Christianity* (Yale, 1989).

[21]Paul Rader, of the World Wide Gospel Couriers, was a predecessor of Billy Graham in his broadcasts of revivals on the radio. Nixon made his decision for Christ at a Los Angeles revival Rader conducted in 1926, as he recalled in Graham's journal *Decisions*, in the issue of November 1962.

[22]Jay P. Dolan, *Catholic Revivalism: The American Experience, 1830–1900* (Notre Dame, 1978).

[23]Princeton Religious Research Center study of the decade's most admired persons, reported by Ari L. Goldman in *The New York Times*, April 7, 1990, p. 9. Other religious figures frequently named were Archbishop Desmond Tutu, Rev. Terry Waite, and (on the women's list) Mother Teresa: cf. Gallup and Castelli, *The People's Religion*, p. 209.

[24]See, for instance, Nathan O. Hatch, *The Sacred Cause of Liberty: Republican Thought and the Millennium in Revolutionary New England* (Yale, 1977).

[25]Timothy Egan, "Thousands Plan Life Below, After Doomsday," *New York Times*, March 15, 1990.

[26]One shining exception to journalists' ignorance of religion in recent politics is Taylor Branch's study of the civil rights movement, *Parting the Waters: America in the King Years 1954–63* (Simon and Schuster, 1988).

[27]For fundamentalists making up roughly 20 percent of the population, see Greeley, *Religious Change*, p. 19. Fundamentalists, though generally evangelical, place greater emphasis on preserving orthodox doctrine (the Fundamentals) than do evangelicals more centrally interested in the religious *experience*—of rebirth (revivalists), marked holiness (perfectionists), or gifts of the Spirit (Pentecostalists).

[28]There was a falloff in church attendance in the 1960s, entirely attributable to changes in Catholics' views on the obligation to attend Mass every Sunday. See Greeley, *Religious Change*, pp. 44–50.

[29]Gallup and Castelli, *The People's Religion*, pp. 16–17, 25–27.

[30]The influx of evangelicals into the Republican electorate in 1984 reflected less a growth of evangelicals than an increase of activism in those who already existed, or their massive switch from Democratic to Republican voting habits, especially in the South. This switch among evangelicals did not occur earlier, in connection with the desegregation struggle, but between 1980 and 1984, as disillusionment with Jimmy Carter gave way to admiration for Ronald Reagan. A balanced treatment of this is contained in Jerome L. Himmelstein, *To the Right: The Transformation of American Conservatism* (University of California, 1990), pp. 119–28. Evangelical support changed from 40 percent Democratic, 37 percent Republican in 1980 to 45 percent Republican, 29 percent Democratic

in 1984. Evangelical leaders (ministers) went from 29 percent Republican in 1980 to 66 percent in 1984.

³¹See, for instance, Michael d'Antonio, *Fall From Grace: The Failed Crusade of the Christian Right* (Farrar Straus Giroux, 1988).

³²John Henry Newman, "Waiting for Christ," in *Parochial and Plain Sermons*, vol. 6 (reprinted by Ignatius Press, 1987), p. 1326.

³³Evangelicals were alerted to the "false religion" of the Catholic evolutionist Teilhard de Chardin by their respected leader, the late Francis Schaeffer (see chapter 28). Since then, Teilhard's demonic role in the New Age cults has been described by Dave Hunt and Tom McMahon (*The Seduction of Christianity*, Harvest House, 1984), Douglas R. Groothuis (*Unmasking the New Age*, Intervarsity Press, 1986), and Texe Marrs (*Dark Secrets of the New Age*, Good News, 1987).

PART I. SIN AND SECULARITY

Chapter One. New Moral Language

¹Jack W. Germond and Jules Witcover, *Whose Broad Stripes and Bright Stars? The Trivial Pursuit of the Presidency, 1988* (Warner Books, 1989), p. 195.

²Washington, as an unmarried soldier going into battle, professed love for a married woman, but proposed to do nothing dishonorable about his infatuation then or later. See Garry Wills, *Cincinnatus: George Washington and the Enlightenment* (Doubleday, 1984), pp. 133–35.

³The scurrilous journalist James Callendar made a number of accusations against Jefferson, ranging from atheism to corrupt favors. Only one of the sexual charges involved a possible adultery, and it came to nothing: Before his own marriage Jefferson made an overture to a married woman and was rebuffed. If his love for Maria Cosway, after his own wife's death, was ever consummated, Callendar knew nothing about it, since Jefferson and Mrs. Cosway met only in France. The most famous charge, that Jefferson had a slave mistress, would not involve adultery if it were true, and the best Jefferson scholarship, ever since Douglass Adair's pioneering essay of 1960, has rightly questioned that myth. See Adair, "The Jefferson Scandals," in *Fame and the Founding Fathers* (Norton, 1974), pp. 160–91.

⁴Robert V. Remini, *Andrew Jackson and the Course of American Freedom, 1822–1832* (Harper & Row, 1981), pp. 133–34.

⁵Allan Nevins, *Grover Cleveland: A Study in Courage* (Dodd, Mead, 1932), pp. 162–65.

⁶Though it is now a popular myth that Franklin Roosevelt had affairs while in the White House (with "Missy" LeHand and/or Lucy Mercer Rutherford), the two biographers with personal experience of polio and the widest acquaintance with the literature on polio conclude that Roosevelt was celibate after 1921. See Hugh Gregory Gallagher, *FDR's Splendid Deception* (Dodd, Mead, 1985), pp. 130–44, and Geoffrey C. Ward, *A First-Class Temperament* (Harper & Row, 1989), pp. 709–15. Mr. Gallagher even argues that the prepolio affair with Miss Mercer (as she was then) was unconsummated. For Kennedy's "poon days" note, see Lloyd Grove, "Candidate JFK Scribbles from the Trail," *The Washington Post*, May 27, 1987, p. B4.

⁷Gary Hart, *Right from the Start: A Chronicle of the McGovern Campaign* (Quadrangle, 1973), p. 243.

⁸Germond and Witcover, op. cit., pp. 170–83, 199–200.

⁹Hart, op. cit., p. 161.

[10]Gary Hart, *The Strategies of Zeus* (William Morrow, 1987), pp. 29–30. When early explanations of his movements with Donna Rice were challenged, Hart said they *had* to be true since, as a spy novelist, he could have invented more probable things if he meant to lie. It is true that trysts and evasions between lover-conspirators occur in *The Strategies of Zeus*. It is said of the hero: "He now assumed his privacy was being violated by one or more sides fairly regularly" (p. 308), and he tells his heroine, when they are being chased: "When we leave, just follow me. We'll move quickly and be out before anyone knows" (p. 283). But the heroine of the novel is a Russian intellectual, not Donna Rice, and his trysts are meant to save the world from nuclear disaster. He seems to have had no ingenuity left over for less noble-minded clandestinity. The title of the spy novel is a quote from Aeschylus (*Agamemnon* 677) which says that human rescue must come from divine contrivance, which the book's lovers are presumably furthering.

[11]Jeane Kirkpatrick, *The New Presidential Elite: Men and Women in National Politics* (Russell Sage Foundation, 1976).

[12]Hart, *Right from the Start*, p. 222. The McGovern team showed that it was not committed to the insurgents when it tried to persuade Mayor Daley's Illinois delegation to stay at the convention, in a compromise with the challengers led by William Singer and Jesse Jackson. Daley's intransigence made that bargain fall through, not any lack of flexibility in the McGovern camp (ibid., pp. 227–28).

[13]Ibid., p. 221.

[14]Rick Stearns, taped interview in *Fear and Loathing on the Campaign Trail '72* by Hunter S. Thompson (Straight Arrow Books, 1973), p. 307.

[15]Hart, *Right from the Start*, p. 269.

Chapter Two. Holiness and Gary Hart

[1]Gail Sheehy, *Character: America's Search for Leadership* (William Morrow, 1988), p. 46.

[2]The Greek verb *tellomai* means "to complete (a circuit, ceremony, journey)"—cf. Hjalmar Frisk, *Griechisches etymologisches Wörterbuch* (Carl Winter, 1969), pp. 869–73. The adjective *teleios* means "complete" in several senses—finished, properly carried out (of ceremonies), perfect, or *inclusive*. The latter meaning is established by context in both Matthean uses (5.48 and 19.21). Thus the New English Bible translates 5.48 as "There must be no limit to your goodness, as your heavenly Father's goodness knows no bounds," and 19.21, "If you wish to go the whole way . . ."

[3]Norman Cohn, *The Pursuit of the Millennium* (Essential Books, 1957), pp. 149–94, 233–35. Adamites take as applicable to themselves St. Augustine's speculations about what sex would have been like without original sin. Cf. Wilhelm Fränger, *The Millennium of Hieronymus Bosch*, translated by Eithne Wilkins and Ernst Kaiser (Hacker Art Books, 1976), p. 13. Bosch, the Adamite painter, was influenced by illustrated editions of Augustine's *City of God*. Cf. D. Bax, *Hieronymus Bosch*, translated by M. A. Bax-Botha (A. A. Balkema, 1979), pp. 320–24.

[4]The best brief treatment of the Holiness Movement in America is in chapters 6–11 of George M. Marsden's *Fundamentalism and American Culture: The Shaping of Twentieth-Century Evangelicalism* (Oxford, 1980). The American who had gone to Keswick to launch the movement, Robert Pearsall Smith, part of a preacher team with his wife, Hannah, had to drop out of the founding meeting because of a sex scandal. See Marsden, op. cit., p. 77.

[5]Richard Collier, *The General Next to God: The Story of William Booth and the Salvation Army* (Collins, 1965), pp. 21–26.

[6]Unlike the more decorous modern Army, the "corybantic" Salvationists, protesters against taverns, were thrown into jail for civil disobedience. There were many real-life

equivalents of Shaw's Major Barbara, including Booth's flamboyant daughter, Kate, who was known in France as La Maréchale. See Carolyn Scott, *The Heavenly Witch: The Story of the Maréchale* (Hamish Hamilton, 1981).

⁷David Edwin Harrell, Jr., *Oral Roberts: An American Life* (Indiana University Press, 1985), p. 20. Nathan Hatch has studied the earlier encounter of evangelicals with industrial poverty: "While Progressive prophets attacked structures that permitted poverty and need, it was Pentecostals, Nazarenes and Fundamentalists that founded churches among the dirt-poor farmers of Oklahoma, the automobile workers of Detroit, and the mill hands of Gastonia. Although these movements had their share of charlatans and autocrats, they were remarkably effective in forging moral communities among the poor, the sick, the ignorant, and the elderly—those most vulnerable in a rapidly industrializing society" (Nathan O. Hatch, *The Democratization of American Christianity*, Yale, 1989, p. 216). Urban missions had a special meaning for evangelicals in America, as a heroic form of Christian witness. As William Jennings Bryan said of them: "It takes a man who has been saved from the depths to reach men like these [in slums]." Quoted by Ray Ginger in *William Jennings Bryan: Selections* (Bobbs-Merrill, 1967), p. xxx.

⁸The authoritative history of the Nazarenes is Timothy L. Smith's *Called unto Holiness* (Kansas City, 1962).

⁹Ibid., pp. 237–42. George Sharpe, the Scot who brought his country's Holiness churches into the Nazarene movement, had spent time in America, where he (typically) collaborated with L. Milton Williams of the Salvation Army. Nazarenes and the Army had many points of contact and cross-influence. Currently, the Nazarenes are growing. Their numbers rose by 22 percent between 1973 and 1983 (George Gallup, Jr., and Jim Castelli. *The People's Religion: American Faith in the 90's.* Macmillan, 1989, p. 17).

¹⁰In this the Nazarenes resembled an earlier "pure gospel" movement, the Disciples of Christ, who formed schools with literary academies and courses in practical management. One of these schools, which incorporated other academies, was Eureka College of Illinois, which President Reagan attended during the Depression. See Garry Wills, *Reagan's America* (Doubleday, 1987), pp. 36–52.

¹¹Material on the Ludwigs is taken from the Nazarene Archives at the church's national headquarters in Kansas City. A good survey of S. T. Ludwig's career is contained in "The History of Bethany Nazarene College," by Roy H. Cantrell, Ph.D. dissertation, Seminary Hill, Fort Worth, Texas, 1955.

¹²The Hartpence paper is the lead selection in a student publication of the school's Social Science Club, *The BNC Historian*, for 1956–57. Its title is "The Origin of the Company of Jesus, Their [sic] Founder and Contribution to the Counter-Reformation."

¹³Charles Edwin Jones, a lifelong friend of Oletha Ludwig, went on from Bethany to get his doctorate in history at the University of Wisconsin, and wrote an important book on the Holiness Movement, *Perfectionist Persuasion*, published by the American Theological Library Association in 1974 with an introduction by the renowned scholar William G. McLaughlin. Dr. Jones, who is now an Episcopalian deacon, was especially helpful with information about the Nazarenes' Bethany College, the Ludwig family, and Professor Johnson's Philosophy Club.

¹⁴W. H. Auden, "Søren Kierkegaard," in *Forewords and Afterwords* (Random House, 1973), p. 179.

¹⁵Søren Kierkegaard, "The Immediate Erotic Stages, or the Musical-Erotic," in *Either/ Or, Part One*, edited and translated by Howard V. Hong and Edna H. Hong (Princeton, 1987), pp. 63 (reverse incarnation), 102 (age of Don Giovanni), and 88 (spirit of flesh).

¹⁶Ibid., p. 92.

¹⁷Ibid., p. 93.

¹⁸Ibid., p. 97. Kierkegaard expands this point in "A Cursory Observation Concerning a Detail in *Don Giovanni*," in *The Corsair Affair*, edited and translated by Howard V.

Hong and Edna H. Hong (Princeton, 1982), pp. 28–37: "What is so profound and so Greek [is] that Don Giovanni stumbles over a straw, over a little Zerlina."

[19]Kierkegaard, *Either/Or*, p. 129.

[20]John Updike, "The Fork," in *Kierkegaard: A Collection of Critical Essays*, edited by Josiah Thompson (Doubleday Anchor, 1972), p. 173.

[21]Ibid., p. 178.

[22]"Luther has actually done incalculable harm by not becoming a martyr" (*Søren Kierkegaard's Journals and Papers*, edited by Howard V. Hong, Indiana University, 1975, vol. 3, p. 97).

Chapter Three. Fatal Composure

[1]Hjalmar Frisk, *Griechisches etymologisches Wörterbuch* (Carl Winter, 1968), s.v. *sōs*.

[2]Aristotle, *Politics* 1253a.

[3]Helen North, in her book on *sōphrosynē*, translates the word that describes Hippolytus' virtue as "chastity," but argues that Hippolytus has a cramped version even of that negative virtue. See Helen North, *Sōphrosynē, Self-Knowledge and Self-Restraint in Greek Literature* (Cornell, 1966), pp. 79–81.

Chapter Four. Jeremiad: The Extreme Center

[1]Leonard I. Sweet, "Nineteenth-Century Evangelicalism," in *Encyclopedia of the American Religious Experience*, edited by Charles H. Lippy and Peter W. Williams (Charles Scribner's Sons, 1988), vol. 2, pp. 890–91. The first party convention was held in Baltimore by the Antimasons, a party with a strong evangelical and populist resentment of Masonry as "an infidel society at war with true Christianity" (Leonard L. Richards, *The Life and Times of Congressman John Quincy Adams*, Oxford, 1986, p. 43).

[2]*The Poetry of Vachel Lindsay*, edited by Dennis Camp (Spoon River Poetry Press, 1984), vol. 1, p. 345.

[3]*William Jennings Bryan: Selections*, edited by Ray Ginger (Bobbs-Merrill, 1967), p. 41.

[4]Ibid., pp. 45–46.

[5]Ibid., p. 40.

[6]Ibid., p. 39.

[7]Ibid., p. 46.

[8]Richard Hofstadter, *The American Political Tradition* (Vintage, 1948), p. 186.

[9]Lindsay, op. cit.

[10]Robert G. Pope, "New England Versus the New England Mind: The Myth of Declension," in *Puritan New England*, edited by Alden T. Vaughan and Francis J. Bremer (St. Martin's Press, 1977), pp. 314–25. For ways the perception of decline may have led to moral renewal, cf. Emory Elliott, *Power and the Pulpit in Puritan New England* (Princeton, 1975).

Chapter Five. A Theology of Willie Horton

[1]*William Jennings Bryan: Selections*, edited by Ray Ginger (Bobbs-Merrill, 1967), p. 4.

[2]Ibid., p. 189.

[3]*Papers Relating to the Foreign Relations of the United States: The Lansing Papers* (Government Printing Office, 1939), vol. 1, p. 373.

[4]Ibid., p. 378.

[5]Ibid., p. 438.

[6]Ibid., pp. 392, 411, 377.

[7]Thomas A. Bailey and Paul B. Ryan, *The "Lusitania" Disaster: An Episode in Modern Warfare and Diplomacy* (The Free Press, 1975), p. 257. Wilson's first major biographer, Ray Stannard Baker, found Bryan "the statesman of largest calibre" among Wilson's advisers on neutrality (*Life and Letters*, Doubleday, 1927–39, vol. 5, pp. 300–301).

[8]Lawrence W. Levine, *Defender of the Faith: William Jennings Bryan, The Last Decade, 1915–1925* (Oxford, 1965), p. 15.

[9]Kendrick A. Clements, *William Jennings Bryan: Missionary Isolationist* (University of Tennessee, 1982), p. 185.

[10]Andrew Delbanco, *The Puritan Ordeal* (Harvard, 1989), p. 220.

[11]Steve Burkholder, "The Lawrence *Eagle-Tribune* and the Willie Horton Story," *Washington Journalism Review*, July/August 1989, pp. 14–19.

[12]Jack W. Germond and Jules Witcover, *Whose Broad Stripes and Bright Stars? The Trivial Pursuit of the Presidency, 1988* (Warner Books, 1989), pp. 10–12, 157–64.

[13]Catharine A. MacKinnon, *Feminism Unmodified: Discourses on Life and Law* (Harvard, 1987), p. 81.

[14]*Final Report of the National Commission on the Causes and Prevention of Violence* (Government Printing Office, 1969), p. 210.

Chapter Six. Playing to Win

[1]Fred H. Harrison, *Athletics for All: Physical Education and Athletics at Phillips Academy, Andover* (1983), p. 272.

[2]Donnie Radcliffe, *Simply Barbara Bush: A Portrait of America's Candid First Lady* (Warner Books, 1989), p. 133.

[3]Ibid., p. 134.

[4]Chris Evert on *Late Night with David Letterman*, September 1989.

[5]Radcliffe, op. cit., p. 6.

[6]Judy Bachrach, "That Old Voodoo Haunts a New Bush," *Washington Star*, September 23, 1980. Story confirmed by Marianne Means and Pete Teeley.

[7]Radcliffe, op. cit., p. 177.

[8]George Will, "George Bush: The Sound of a Lapdog," *Washington Post*, January 30, 1986.

[9]Charles F. Shepard, *Forgiven: The Rise and Fall of Jim Bakker and the PTL Ministry* (Atlantic Monthly Press, 1989), pp. 346–47.

[10]Jack W. Germond and Jules Witcover, *Whose Broad Stripes and Bright Stars? The Trivial Pursuit of the Presidency, 1988* (Warner Books, 1989), p. 151.

[11]Winn, "Inside the Atlanta Explosion," *Washington Journalism Review*, January-February 1989, p. 20.

[12]Michael d'Antonio, *Fall From Grace: The Failed Crusade of the Christian Right* (Farrar Straus Giroux, 1989), p. 41.

[13]Nat Hentoff, "Sweet Land of Liberty," *Washington Post*, June 10, 1989.

[14]Nat Hentoff, "Sweet Land of Liberty," *Washington Post*, July 2, 1988.

[15]Nat Hentoff, "Sweet Land of Liberty," *Washington Post*, February 25, 1989.

[16]William A. Donohue, *The Politics of the American Civil Liberties Union* (Transaction, 1985). An older assault on the ACLU treated it as a dupe or worse of Communists; William H. McIlheny II, *The ACLU on Trial* (Arlington House, 1976).

[17]"Rhode Island Declares Witchcraft a Religion," Associated Press, August 8, 1989.

Chapter Seven. Secular Innocence

[1] Henry Steele Commager, *The American Mind: An Interpretation of American Thought and Character Since the 1880's* (Yale, 1950), pp. 342–45, 339–40.

[2] Schlesinger's speech, delivered at the inauguration of Vartan Gregorian as the president of Brown, was printed in *The New York Times Book Review* of July 23, 1989, where it stimulated a large response in the correspondence column.

[3] Louis Hartz, *The Liberal Tradition in America* (Harcourt, Brace and Company, 1955).

[4] The High Table Test Snow applied to his two cultures involved the discovery, at Yale, of "what is usually known as the non-conversion of parity." To his disappointment, this did not set the Cambridge table on a roar: "If there were any serious communication between the two cultures, this experiment would have been talked about at every High Table in Cambridge." C. P. Snow, *The Two Cultures and A Second Look* (Cambridge, 1964), p. 16. Cf. the explanatory note on page 102: "Almost all college High Tables contain Fellows in both scientific and non-scientific subjects." The word *contain*, which looks clumsy at first, has a certain justice on further consideration.

[5] Though professing evenhandedness, Snow stacks the deck in his distinction of the scientific community (with "the future in their bones," p. 10) and the reactionary others (p. 8). His difficulty in naming the nonscientific "culture" shows he was looking less at what positively animates it than at its perceived hostility to science. Sometimes it is called the camp of "intellectuals" or of "academics" (expressing the scientists' sense of exclusion in their own setting). Sometimes it is "literary people," though social scientists are often in this camp. Sometimes it is "Luddites," showing Snow's insensitivity to the class aspects of his analysis.

[6] Peter Steinfels, "Library's Choice of Priest Is Debated," *New York Times*, April 2, 1989.

[7] Gay Talese, Letter to the Editor, *New York Times*, March 1, 1989.

[8] Joseph Heller, Letter to the Editor, *New York Times*, March 31, 1989.

[9] For a typical presentation of the evangelical case against "secular humanism," see Tim LaHaye, *The Race for the Twenty-first Century* (Nashville, 1986). Justice Potter Stewart gave legal support to the evangelicals' forced description of irreligion as a form of religion in his dissent from the Pennsylvania school prayer decision of 1963:

> [A] compulsory state educational system so structures a child's life that if religious exercises are held to be an impermissible activity in schools, religion is placed at an artificial and state-created disadvantage. . . . And a refusal to permit religious exercises is thus seen, not as a realization of state neutrality, but rather as the establishment of a religion of secularism (*Abingdon School District v. Schempp*, 374 U.S. 313).

[10] The seventeenth-century skeptic Pierre Bayle used to claim that he was a Protestant because he protested the existence of all religion. That would not have placated Increase Mather.

[11] Pat Robertson, *What I Will Do as President*, audiocassette widely distributed during his 1988 presidential campaign.

[12] Frances FitzGerald, *America Revised: History Schoolbooks in the Twentieth Century* (Little, Brown, 1979), p. 193.

[13] Frances FitzGerald, *Cities on a Hill: A Journey through Contemporary American Cultures* (Simon and Schuster, 1986).

[14] Surveys show that opposition to religion is strong in the "soft" (social) sciences, but not, to some people's surprise, in the "hard" (physical) sciences. One study, for instance, found that 41 percent of social scientists called themselves atheists, as opposed to only

20 percent of the physical scientists. Fred Thalheimer, "Religiosity and Secularization in the Academic Professions," *Sociology of Education* 46 (1973), pp. 183–202.

PART II. BIBLE BEGINNINGS
Chapter Eight. The Superman Trial

[1]Ray Ginger, *Six Days or Forever? Tennessee v. John Thomas Scopes* (Beacon, 1958), p. 7.

[2]Ibid., p. 180. Cf. John T. Scopes and James Presley, *Center of the Storm* (Holt, 1967), pp. 60–62: "To tell the truth, I wasn't sure I had taught evolution." The school principal was the normal biology teacher (Scopes just helped some students review for a test), but the principal, married and with children, did not want to face arrest.

[3]Richard Hofstadter, *The American Political Tradition* (Vintage, 1948), pp. 198–99.

[4]Robert W. Cherny, *A Righteous Course: The Life of William Jennings Bryan* (Little, Brown, 1985), pp. 202–3.

[5]Edward J. Larson, *Trial and Error: The American Controversy over Creation and Evolution* (Oxford, 1985), p. 28.

[6]Lawrence W. Levine, *Defender of the Faith: William Jennings Bryan, the Last Decade* (Oxford, 1965), p. 357.

[7]Irving Stone, *Clarence Darrow for the Defense* (Doubleday, 1941), p. 464. In his later memoirs, Darrow more decorously attributed Bryan's death to a "too generous meal" (*The Story of My Life*, Charles Scribner's Sons, 1932, p. 270).

[8]Levine, op. cit., p. 261. Bryan's quickening of interest in evolution from 1916 into the twenties is charted by Ferenc Morton Szasz, *The Divided Mind of Protestant America, 1880–1930* (University of Alabama, 1982), pp. 107–16.

[9]Levine, op. cit., p. 175.

[10]Larson, op. cit., p. 188.

[11]George M. Marsden, *Fundamentalism and American Culture: The Shaping of Twentieth-Century Evangelicalism, 1870–1925* (Oxford, 1980), p. 185.

[12]Levine, op. cit., p. 263.

[13]Richard Hofstadter's *Social Darwinism in American Thought* (George Braziller, 1944) was the best-known book in a body of work—by Talcott Parsons, Merle Curti, and others—that treated social Darwinism as legitimating "rugged individualism." Robert C. Bannister and Howard L. Kaye have responded that Hofstadter did not sufficiently separate the actual thought of Herbert Spencer, William Graham Sumner et al. from popular misconceptions, nor ground those misconceptions in the actual defenses made of their conduct by entrepreneurs. "The charge of social Darwinism was . . . a means for reformers to discredit their political opponents and to claim Darwin for themselves" (Kaye, *The Social Meaning of Modern Biology: From Social Darwinism to Sociobiology*, Yale, 1986, p. 25). But Hofstadter agreed beforehand that popular views of social Darwinism were distorted, and Bannister says of Bryan in particular that "his identification of Darwinism, irreligion, and *political reaction* was both natural and compelling in light of the popular belief that Darwin was destroying American ideals" (*Social Darwinism: Science and Myth in Anglo-American Social Thought*, Temple University, 1979, p. 245, italics added). A good discussion of the elasticity of the term *social Darwinism* is contained in Gertrude Himmelfarb's *Darwin and the Darwinian Revolution* (Norton, 1968).

[14]H. L. Mencken, *The Philosophy of Friedrich Nietzsche* (Kennikat Press reprint of 1908 edition, 1967), pp. 102–3, where Mencken interprets Nietzsche as saying: "The masses have no right to exist on their own account; their sole excuse for living lies in their usefulness as a sort of superstructure [sic] or scaffolding, upon which a more select race

of beings may be elevated." Bannister tries to make Mencken "the exception that proved the rule" about social Darwinism's benignity. But already in 1905 William Travers Jerome was out on the Chautauqua circuit defending corporations by saying: "This is business, and business is war. This is commerce, this is competition—it is war and strife. I do not say that this is moral. It is immoral" (*New York Times*, July 8, 1905). Compare Mencken's words in *The Atlantic* (1914): "Barbarous? Ruthless? Unchristian? No doubt. But so is life itself. So is all progress worthy the name." Reprinted in *The Young Mencken: The Best of His Work*, collected by Carl Bode (Dial, 1973), p. 440.

[15]Larson, op. cit., p. 46.

[16]Mencken, *Philosophy of Friedrich Nietzsche*, p. 138.

[17]Ibid., pp. 176–77.

[18]Ibid., p. 177. Cf. p. 187: "The participation of women in large affairs, he [Nietzsche] argued, could lead to but one result: the contamination of the masculine ideals of justice, honor, and truth by the feminine ideals of dissimulation, equivocation, and intrigue. In women, he believed, there was an entire absence of that instinctive liking for a square deal and a fair fight which one finds in all men—even the worst."

[19]Ibid., p. 186.

[20]Ibid. Later Mencken would attack the similar myth of "so-called wifebeating" (*In Defense of Women*, Knopf, 1922, p. 174).

[21]Levine, op. cit., p. 243.

[22]Mencken, *Philosophy of Friedrich Nietzsche*, pp. 85–86.

[23]Ibid., p. 238. For Jews as the inventors of the crippling "theory of humility," cf. *H. L. Mencken's Smart Set Criticism*, selected and edited by William H. Nolte (Cornell, 1968), p. 197.

[24]Larson, op. cit., pp. 65–66.

[25]Mencken, *Philosophy of Friedrich Nietzsche*, p. 195. For Bryan's record on blacks, cf. Cherny, op. cit., pp. 197–99.

[26]Bode, op. cit., pp. 438–39.

[27]Ibid., p. 434.

[28]Ibid., p. 440. According to Mencken (*Philosophy of Friedrich Nietzsche*, p. 435), Nietzsche's *Thus Spake Zarathustra* was the new Germany's Magna Charta.

[29]Marsden, op. cit., p. 149. The evangelicals were not alone in their interpretation of German militarism. In England, the Elizabethan scholars Wallace Notestein and E. E. Stoll had argued a similar thesis at the beginning of the war. The liberal Rex Stout revived the charge in World War II (*New York Times*, January 17, 1943). Nietzsche makes a good culture-villain, as Allan Bloom would prove in the 1980s.

[30]Marsden, op. cit., pp. 169–70.

[31]Larson, op. cit., p. 47; Szasz, op. cit., p. 109.

[32]Clarence Darrow, *Plea in Defense of Loeb and Leopold*, the final address to the jury republished in pamphlet form by Darrow's friend Haldeman-Julius (1924 and frequent revisions)—the pamphlet Bryan read from during the Scopes trial. I have quoted from pp. 44–49.

[33]Stone, op. cit., p. 345.

[34]Kevin Tierney, *Darrow: A Biography* (Thomas Crowell, 1979), p. 74.

[35]Darrow, *The Story of My Life*, p. 246.

[36]Ibid., p. 249.

[37]Ibid., pp. 268–69.

[38]For the alliance of evangelicals and progressives in the early years of the century, see Szasz, op. cit., pp. 43ff.

Chapter Nine. Scopes: Who Won?

[1] Carl Bode, *Mencken* (Southern Illinois University, 1969), p. 265.

[2] Ibid.

[3] Ibid., p. 268.

[4] William Manchester, *Disturber of the Peace: The Life of H. L. Mencken* (Harper & Brothers, 1951), p. 164.

[5] Charles A. Fecher, *Mencken: A Study of His Thought* (Knopf, 1978), pp. 8–9, 179.

[6] Manchester, op. cit., p. 185.

[7] Ray Ginger, *Six Days or Forever? Tennessee v. John Thomas Scopes* (Beacon, 1958), pp. 144–45.

[8] Clarence Darrow, *The Story of My Life* (Charles Scribner's Sons, 1932), pp. 270–71.

[9] Edward J. Larson, *Trial and Error: The American Controversy over Creation and Evolution* (Oxford, 1985), p. 190.

[10] Darrow, op. cit., pp. 249, 277.

[11] John T. Scopes and James Presley, *Center of the Storm* (Holt, 1967), pp. 143–47, 209–16. Bryan was "the most outstanding speaker the country has produced" (p. 209).

[12] Larson, op. cit., pp. 68, 188.

[13] *The Young Mencken: The Best of His Work*, collected by Carl Bode (Dial, 1973), p. 434.

[14] Quoted in Richard Hofstadter, *Anti-intellectualism in American Life* (Knopf, 1963), pp. 209–10.

[15] Ginger, op. cit., p. 90.

[16] Hofstadter, op. cit., pp. 211–13.

[17] Ibid., p. 128.

[18] Ginger, op. cit., pp. 193–99. The union even tried to get Felix Frankfurter, the famous Harvard law professor, to intervene in a friendly way and dissuade Darrow from pursuing the appeal.

[19] Darrow, op. cit., pp. 268–69.

[20] Ginger, op. cit., p. 209.

[21] Judith Grabiner and Peter Miller, "Effects of the Scopes Trial," *Science* 185 (1974), pp. 832–35; Ronald L. Numbers, "Creationism in Twentieth-Century America," *Science* 218 (1982), pp. 539–42; Dorothy Nelkin, *The Creation Controversy: Science or Scripture in the Schools* (W. W. Norton, 1982), pp. 32–34.

[22] Ferenc Morton Szasz, *The Divided Mind of Protestant America, 1880–1930* (University of Alabama, 1982), p. 123. In 1963, Richard Hofstadter noticed that most high school students told pollsters they did not learn the concept of evolution from their textbooks, though "the evolution controversy seems as remote as the Homeric era to intellectuals in the East" (Hofstadter, op. cit., pp. 129–30).

[23] Larson, op. cit., p. 88.

Chapter Ten. Refighting Scopes

[1] Bellah's paper on civil religion was delivered at a *Daedalus* symposium in 1966, though it was not published in that journal until 1967.

[2] On these developments, Frances FitzGerald's book is useful: *America Revised* (Little, Brown, 1979).

[3] The texts were called the *Biological Sciences Curriculum Study*, and BSCS became a four-letter word to its critics. Cf. Dorothy Nelkin, *The Creation Controversy: Science or Scripture in the Schools* (Norton, 1982), pp. 44–47.

[4] Ibid., pp. 47–57.

[5]Nelkin, op. cit. In 1974, use of the *MACOS* text dropped by 70 percent. In 1975, Senator Jesse Helms and others brought about the cancellation of federal funds for *MACOS* and began a review of the whole NSF education program. The House even passed Congressman Robert Bauman's amendment to give Congress a veto over future grants. (The Senate rejected this as unmanageable.) Nelkin, op. cit., pp. 127–32.

[6]Michael Ruse, *Darwinism Defended: A Guide to the Evolution Controversies* (Addison-Wesley, 1982), p. 292.

[7]Henry M. Morris, *History of Modern Creationism* (San Diego: Master Book Publishers, 1984), pp. 60–61, 79–82.

[8]Ibid., p. 147.

[9]Henry M. Morris and Duane T. Gish, *The Battle for Creation: Acts/Facts/Impacts* (San Diego: Creation-Life Publishers, 1976), pp. 130–44.

[10]Wendell Bird published his first proposal for creationist legal tactics while he was still a law student at Yale: "Freedom of Religion and Science Instruction in Public Schools," *Yale Law Journal* 87 (1978), pp. 515–20. He followed that up with an article in the *Harvard Law Review*, and, after writing bulletins and drafting "equal-time" proposals he defended in state trials and before the Supreme Court, he published his two-volume *summa creationistica*, *The Origin of Species Revisited* (Philosophical Library, 1989).

[11]Justice Antonin Scalia, joining Chief Justice William Rehnquist in a dissent from *Aguillard*, wrote: "We have no basis on the record to conclude that creation science need be anything other than a collection of scientific data supporting the theory that life abruptly appeared on the earth" (*Edwards* v. *Aguillard*, 107 S.Ct. 2595).

PART III. BIBLE ENDINGS

Chapter Eleven. Fundamentals

[1]Leslie Allen, *Bryan and Darrow at Dayton* (A. Lee & Company, 1925), p. 134.

[2]Ibid., p. 146.

[3]Ibid., p. 153.

[4]Ibid., p. 155.

[5]Neil Forsyth, *The Old Enemy: Satan and the Combat Myth* (Princeton, 1987), p. 427.

[6]St. Augustine, *Genesis Taken Literally* 1.2, 1.9.

[7]Ibid., 1.10.

[8]Some have tried to reconcile Darwin and the Bible by taking Augustine's *rationes seminales* as evolutionary tendencies. But Henry Woods, S.J., shows that this is a distortion of Augustine's meaning; see *Augustine and Evolution: A Study in the Saint's* De Genesi ad Litteram *and* De Trinitate (Universal Knowledge Foundation, 1924). The *rationes seminales* had a long life in Western culture. They are "Nature's germens" in Shakespeare. For these inmost "seeds" of things to change is Shakespeare's ultimate vision of disorder in the universe. So Macbeth vows he will let

> the treasure
> Of Nature's germens tumble all together
> Even till destruction sicken. . . . (4.1.74–76).

And Lear says

> Crack Nature's moulds, all germens
> spill at once. . . . (3.2.8)

Florizel says, in *The Winter's Tale,*

Let nature crush the sides o' th' earth together
And mar the seeds within. (4.4.478–79).

The "seed-reasons" of things are the most *stable* elements in a world of flux, not *evolving* elements.

⁹*The City of God* 11.9.

¹⁰Luther says that Augustine and Hilary "abandon the historical account, pursuing allegories and fabricating I don't know what speculations. . . . We do not exalt them as do the monks" (*Lectures on Genesis, Chapters 1–5*, translated by George V. Schick, Concordia, 1958, p. 121).

¹¹*City of God* 8.1.

¹²*The Princeton Theology: 1812–1921*, edited by Mark A. Noll (Presbyterian and Reformed Publishing Company, 1983).

¹³Curtis Lee Laws, editor of *The Watchman Examiner*, a Baptist paper, first used the term *fundamentalist* as a rallying call. Cf. George M. Marsden, *Fundamentalism and American Culture: The Shaping of Twentieth-Century Evangelicalism, 1870–1925* (Oxford, 1980), p. 159.

¹⁴Ibid., pp. 216–17.

¹⁵*City of God* 20.7.

¹⁶*Miliast* and *chiliast* were interchangeable terms in the seventh century according to Isidore the etymologist (G. W. H. Lampe, *A Patriotic Greek Lexicon*, Oxford, 1961, p. 1525).

¹⁷Lou Cannon, private communication.

¹⁸Some scholars think this is an early forgery of a letter from St. Paul—partly because they think the code can be somewhat deciphered if the letter is moved back twenty years or so. The prejudice that apocalyptic accumulates on the original Gospel, rather than launches it, is at work here. See, for instance, I. Howard Marshall, *1 and 2 Thessalonians* (Eerdmans, 1983), pp. 28–45.

¹⁹Garry Wills, "Jefferson's Jesus," *New York Review of Books*, November 24, 1983.

Chapter Twelve. America's Miliast Founders

¹H. R. Trevor-Roper, "The General Crisis of the Seventeenth Century," in *Crisis in Europe*, edited by Trevor Astin (Anchor Books, 1967), p. 64. Also see Christopher Hill, *Antichrist in Seventeenth-Century England* (Oxford, 1971), p. 5, for the meaning of the Antichrist as a Counterchrist.

²Quoted by Perry Miller in *Errand into the Wilderness* (Harvard, 1956), p. 114.

³Cotton Mather, *Magnalia Christi Americana* (1702, reprinted in the 1852 edition by Atheneum, 1967), vol. 1, p. 51.

⁴Charles Francis Adams, *Three Episodes of Massachusetts History* (1903, revised edition reprinted by Russell and Russell, 1965), p. 12.

⁵"A Map of Virginia" (1612), in *The Complete Works of Captain John Smith*, edited by Philip L. Barbour (The Institute of Early American History and Culture, 1986), vol. 1, p. 168.

⁶Howard Mumford Jones, *O Strange New World: American Culture, The Formative Years* (Viking, 1952), pp. 57–60.

⁷Richard Baxter and John Higginson joined Mede in his theory of the transport of peoples by the devil (perhaps, in fact, from India!). See Kenneth Silverman, *The Life and Times of Cotton Mather* (Harper and Row, 1988), pp. 108, 239, 439, 448. Cf. Stephen J. Stein, "Transatlantic Extensions: Apocalyptic in Early New England," in *The Apocalypse in English Renaissance Thought and Literature*, edited by C. A. Patrides and Joseph Wittreich (Cornell, 1984), pp. 266, 275, 281, and Katherine R. Firth, *The*

Apocalyptic Tradition in Reformation Britain, 1530–1645 (Oxford, 1979), pp. 223–24.

[8]J. F. Maclear, "New England and the Fifth Monarchy: The Quest for the Millennium in Early American Protestantism," *William and Mary Quarterly*, 1975, pp. 243ff.

[9]Mather, op. cit., vol. 1, p. 42.

[10]Ibid.

[11]William Bradford, *Of Plymouth Plantation, 1620–1647*, edited by Samuel Eliot Morison (Knopf, 1966), p. 84.

[12]Ibid., pp. 204–10. Cf. Charles Francis Adams's edition of *The New English Canaan of Thomas Morton* (Prince Society, 1883; original edition published 1637).

[13]Perry Miller, *Orthodoxy in Massachusetts* (Harvard, 1933), p. 213.

[14]Norman Cohn, *Europe's Inner Demons: An Enquiry Inspired by the Great Witch-Hunt* (Basic Books, 1975), pp. 253–54. Also H. R. Trevor-Roper, *The European Witch-Craze of the Sixteenth and Seventeenth Centuries* (Harper Torchbooks, 1967), pp. 90–192.

[15]George Lyman Kittredge, *Witchcraft in Old and New England* (Atheneum, 1972), pp. 362–63.

[16]For witches and "the fifth column of Satan," see Trevor-Roper, *European Witch-Craze*, p. 96.

[17]Silverman, op. cit., p. 239.

[18]Christine Leigh Heyrman, "Specters of Subversion, Societies of Friends: Dissent and the Devil in Provincial Essex County, Massachusetts," in *Saints and Revolutionaries: Essays on Early American History*, edited by David D. Hall, John M. Murrin, and Thad W. Tate (Norton, 1984), p. 60.

[19]Christopher Hill, op. cit., p. 40.

[20]"Râle, Sébastien," *Dictionary of National Biography*. Francis Parkman has an interesting chapter on Father Râle in *A Half-Century of Conflict* (1892), as does William Carlos Williams in *Against the American Grain* (New Directions, 1956), but he has been largely neglected by more recent historians until James Axtell took him up in *The Invasion Within: The Contest of Cultures in Colonial North America* (Oxford, 1985).

[21]Cf. Christine Leigh Heyrman, op. cit., pp. 48–60.

[22]Miller, *Errand*, p. 145.

[23]Perry Miller, *Roger Williams: His Contribution to the American Tradition* (Atheneum, 1953), p. 139. Morton admitted that Indian medicine men were witches, but denied they were as powerful as the other settlers claimed (*New English Canaan*, Charles Francis Adams edition, pp. 150–51).

[24]Robert V. Beverley, *History and Present State of Virginia*, edited by Louis B. Wright (University of North Carolina, 1947), p. 38.

[25]Rolfe's letter printed from the copy in the Bodlerian Library as appendix 3 in Philip L. Barbour's *Pocahontas and Her World* (Houghton Mifflin, 1970), pp. 247–52.

[26]Cf. Neal Salisbury, "The Praying Indians of Massachusetts Bay and John Eliot," *William and Mary Quarterly*, 1974, pp. 32, 40, 54.

[27]Mather, op. cit., vol. 2, pp. 629–30.

[28]The standard work is Ernest Lee Tuveson, *Redeemer Nation: The Idea of America's Millennial Role* (University of Chicago, 1968).

Chapter Thirteen. Reagan and "the Prophecies"

[1]See, for instance, Sacvan Bercovitch, *The Puritan Origins of the American Self* (Yale, 1975) and *The American Jeremiad* (University of Wisconsin, 1978).

[2]Nathan O. Hatch, *The Democratization of American Christianity* (Yale, 1989), p. 184.

[3]Ruth H. Bloch, *Visionary Republic: Millennial Themes in America's Thought, 1756–1800* (Cambridge, 1985).

[4]Garry Wills, *Reagan's America* (Doubleday, 1987), pp. 18–25.

[5]Ernest R. Sandeen, *The Roots of Fundamentalism: British and American Millenarianism, 1800–1930* (University of Chicago, 1970), p. 42; Hatch, op. cit., p. 184.

[6]Leon Festinger, Henry W. Riecken, and Stanley Schachter, *When Prophecy Fails* (University of Minnesota, 1956); Leon Festinger, *A Theory of Cognitive Dissonance* (Stanford University Press, 1962). Festinger developed his theory of cognitive dissonance—a widely used sociological tool—from his study of miliasts' ability to keep on believing in the world's end after the world has refused to end.

[7]Barbara Grizzuti Harrison, *Visions of Glory: A History and a Memory of Jehovah's Witnesses* (Simon and Schuster, 1978), pp. 185–86.

[8]J. Gordon Melton, *The Encyclopedia of American Religions* (McGrath Publishing Company, 1978), vol. 1, p. 411. Ernest Sandeen would define modern fundamentalism as nothing but Darbyism (premillennial dispensationalism), though George M. Marsden qualifies that view in *Fundamentalism and American Culture: The Shaping of Twentieth-Century Evangelicalism, 1870–1925* (Oxford, 1980). The movement is both broader and narrower than that—broader because other streams fed it and narrower because there are dissident fundamentalists who believe, unlike Darby, that the Rapture will come during or after the time of Trial. Cf. Gleason L. Archer, Jr., Paul D. Feinberg, Douglas J. Moo, and Richard R. Reiter, *The Rapture: Pre-, Mid-, or Post-Tribulational?* (Zondevan, 1984), and Hal Lindsey, *The Rapture* (Bantam, 1983), pp. 27–38.

[9]Broadcast excerpt on National Public Radio cassette *Ronald Reagan and the Prophecy of Armageddon* by Joe Cuomo.

[10]Ibid.

[12]Francis Wright Beare, *The Gospel According to Matthew: A Commentary* (Basil Blackwell, 1981), p. 171.

[13]Raymond E. Brown, *New Testament Essays* (Doubleday Image, 1968), pp. 275–320.

[14]Raymond E. Brown, *The Gospel According to John* (Doubleday, 1970), vol. 2, p. 761.

[15]Raymond E. Brown, *The Epistles of John* (Doubleday, 1982), pp. 303–4, on 1 John 2.13, giving all the New Testament references to the devil as *ho Poneros* (five times in the first letter of John).

[16]Brown, *New Testament Essays*, pp. 305–7.

[17]Brown, *The Gospel According to John*, vol. 1, p. 468.

[18]St. Augustine, *City of God*, book 20.

[19]Joe Cuomo, op. cit.

[20]Answer to Marvin Kalb in 1984 presidential debate.

[21]The miraculous Shroud of Turin was a favorite subject in what Reagan has called his favorite magazine, *National Review*. For Reagan's personal interest, see the Patrick Buchanan interview in *God in the White House: How Religion Has Changed the Modern Presidency* by Richard G. Hutcheson (Collier Books, 1988), pp. 170–71: "He's very interested in the Shroud of Turin. . . . I know, because he called a friend of mine, Ann Higgins, who's a very devout Catholic. She said [something about] it in a book. He was very interested in it, and he talked to her about it."

[22]Brown, "The Pater Noster," p. 280.

Chapter Fourteen. Fundamentalism and the Quayles

[1]R. B. Thieme, Jr., *Mental Attitude Dynamics* (1974), p. 8. All Thieme booklets are published by R. B. Thieme, Jr., Bible Ministries, Houston, Texas.

[2]Elinor J. Brecher and Robert T. Garrett, "Marilyn's Thieme," *New Republic*, November 14, 1988, p. 24.

[3]Ibid., p. 23.

[4]The total perdition of the sinner affects Thieme's view of modern criminals: "Before a person becomes a criminal, he has entered the last stages of reversionism—blackout of the soul and scar tissue—where he is totally influenced by evil." R. B. Thieme, Jr., *Divine Establishment* (1988), p. 36.

[5]R. B. Thieme, Jr., *Christian Integrity* (1984), p. 21.

[6]Hal Lindsey with C. C. Carlson, *Satan Is Alive and Well on Planet Earth* (Bantam, 1974), pp. 169–91.

[7]Louis Moore, "Berachah's Colonel," *Houston Chronicle*, December 1, 1979, and "Berachah Church," *Houston Chronicle*, December 8, 1979.

[8]Joe Layton Wall, "Bob Thieme's Teachings on Christian Living," Ph.D. dissertation, Dallas Theological Seminary, printed by Church Multiplication, Inc., Houston, Texas, 1982, pp. 18–20. Cf. Stewart Custer, *What's Wrong with the Teaching of R. B. Thieme* (Bob Jones University Press, 1972).

[9]R. B. Thieme, Jr., *Isolation of Sin* (1976), p. 19. Thieme so fiercely opposes demonstrative religiosity that he attacks people for saying "God bless you" (*The Integrity of God*, 1987, p. 99).

[10]R. B. Thieme, Jr., *Tongues* (1974), p. 52.

[11]Ibid., pp. 55–58; R. B. Thieme, Jr., *The Integrity of God* (1987), p. 106.

[12]R. B. Thieme, Jr., *King of Kings and Lord of Lords* (1974), p. 3.

[13]Thieme, *Integrity of God*, p. 77; R. B. Thieme, Jr., *Daniel, Chapters One, Two, and Three* (1988), pp. 66–69.

[14]"The religious Jews were always up to something! Typical of the evil of religion, they were very particular about the superficialities of life. . . . They had destroyed their own souls with mental attitude sins of hypocrisy. In effect, they had become little better than animals" (R. B. Thieme, Jr., *The Blood of Christ*, 1989, pp. 18–19).

[15]R. B. Thieme, Jr., *Levitical Offerings* (1973), pp. 5–6.

[16]R. B. Thieme, Jr., *Daniel, Chapter Six* (1975), p. 21.

[17]Thieme, *Integrity of God*, pp. 120–21.

[18]Only Jesus seems to be more bloodthirsty than David: "Jesus Christ Himself was the Commander in Chief of the Jewish Armies . . . , Jesus Christ issued instructions to annihilate the enemy—to spare neither man, woman, child nor animal. . . . The Lord Jesus Christ holds the record for slaughtering the enemy. . . . He will break His own record in this application of righteous violence at the close of the Tribulation" (Thieme, *Divine Establishment*, p. 22).

[19]*Larry King Live*, October 21, 1988.

[20]Thieme, *King of Kings*, p. 2. The UN is the new Tower of Babel in *Tongues*, p. 5, and an expression of Satanic internationalism in *Divine Establishment*, p. 39. The National Council of Churches is "an evil and antibiblical organization" in *Divine Establishment*, p. 75.

[21]R. B. Thieme, Jr., *The Divine Outline of History: Dispensations and the Church*, edited by Wayne F. Hill (1989).

[22]Thieme, *Integrity of God*, pp. 61–64, 77–79.

[23]Thieme, *Mental Attitude Dynamics*, p. 42.

[24]Cheryl Lavin, "Marilyn Quayle," *Chicago Tribune*, January 15, 1989.

Chapter Fifteen. Coffee-Cup Apocalypse

[1]James West Davidson, *The Logic of Millennial Thought: Eighteenth-Century New England* (Yale, 1977), pp. 25–36, 75–80.

[2]C. M. Robeck, Jr., "Azusa Street Revival," in *Dictionary of Pentecostal and Charismatic Movements*, edited by Stanley M. Burgess and Gary B. McGee (Regency Reference Library), pp. 31–36.

[3]J. R. Zeigler, "Full Gospel Business Men's Fellowship International," in Burgess and McGee, op. cit., pp. 321–22.

[4]David Edwin Harrell, Jr., *Pat Robertson: A Personal and Political Portrait* (Harper & Row, 1987), pp. 42–43.

[5]Ibid., pp. 35–38.

[6]John B. Donovan, *Pat Robertson: The Authorized Biography* (Macmillan, 1988), pp. 89–98.

[7]Harrell, op. cit., pp. 126–28.

[8]Charles Richard Eberhardt, *The Bible in the Making of a Minister: The Theological Basis of Theological Education: The Lifework of Wilbert Webster White* (Associated Press, 1949).

[9]Donovan, op. cit., pp. 124–25.

[10]Susan D. Rose, *Keeping Them out of the Hands of Satan: Evangelical Schooling in America* (Routledge, 1988).

[11]Jeffrey K. Hadden and Anson Shupe, *Televangelism: Power and Politics on God's Frontier* (Henry Holt, 1988), pp. 192–93.

Chapter Sixteen. Campaigning

[1]John B. Donovan, *Pat Robertson: The Authorized Biography* (Macmillan, 1988), p. 155.

[2]Jeffrey K. Hadden and Anson Shupe, *Televangelism: Power and Politics on God's Frontier* (Henry Holt, 1988), p. 189.

[3]David Edwin Harrell, Jr., *Pat Robertson: A Personal, Religious, and Political Portrait* (Harper & Row, 1987), pp. 93–96.

Chapter Seventeen. "Claiming"

[1]Pat Robertson and Jamie Buckingham, *Shout It from the Housetops: The Story of the Founder of the Christian Broadcasting Network* (Logos International, 1972), p. 195.

[2]Ibid., p. 196.

[3]Ibid.

[4]Letter of September 29, 1949; this and the letters quoted subsequently in this chapter are in the A. Willis Robertson papers in the library of the College of William and Mary. The papers are not to be published, but the portions dealing with his son's military service were brought into the public domain through legal depositions in a lawsuit Pat Robertson filed against ex-congressman Pete McCloskey. McCloskey had accused Robertson of requesting special favors during the Korean War. Robertson withdrew his suit during his presidential campaign.

PART V. POLITICS AND BLACK RELIGION

Chapter Eighteen. African-American Miliasm

[1]Jon Butler, *Awash in a Sea of Faith: Christianizing the American People* (Harvard, 1990), pp. 290, 129, 130, 157.

[2]Ibid., p. 158.

[3]The pseudo-Pauline letters are strong on slave obedience. See Colossians 3.22–25 and Ephesians 6.5–8. The church was settling into a longer wait for the Parousia.

[4]Butler, op. cit., p. 134.

[5]For the miliast inspiration of Nat Turner, see Donald G. Mathews, *Religion in the Old South* (University of Chicago, 1977), pp. 231–36.

[6]Ibid., p. 204.

[7]Ibid., p. 186.

[8]Ibid., p. 227.

[9]John W. Blassingame, *The Slave Community: Plantation Life in the Antebellum South*, revised edition (Oxford, 1979), p. 133.

[10]Lawrence W. Levine, *Black Culture and Black Consciousness: Afro-American Folk Thought from Slavery to Freedom* (Oxford, 1977), p. 52.

[11]R. Nathaniel Dett, *Religious Folk-Songs of the Negro* (Hampton Institute Press, 1927), p. 58.

[12]James Weldon Johnson and J. Rosamund Johnson, *The Book of American Negro Spirituals* (Viking, 1925), p. 40.

[13]See, for instance, Dett, op. cit., pp. 81, 189, 220, 229, Appendix 7, or William Francis Allen, Charles Pickard Ware, and Lucy McKim Garrison, *Slave Songs of the United States* (Peter Smith, 1951), p. 51:

When de ship is out a-sailin',
O Jesus got de hellum.

[14]Johnson and Johnson, op. cit., p. 39.

[15]Dett, op. cit., p. 139.

[16]Ibid., p. 126.

[17]Johnson and Johnson, op. cit., p. 41.

[18]Levine, op. cit., p. 39.

[19]Mary Allen Grissom, *The Negro Sings a New Heaven* (University of North Carolina, 1930), p. 67.

[20]Allen, Ware, and Garrison, op. cit., p. 104.

[21]Ibid., p. 9.

[22]Johnson and Johnson, op. cit., p. 41.

[23]Ibid., p. 168.

[24]For John Jasper, see Mathews, op. cit., pp. 216, 221. For Vernon Johns, see Taylor Branch, *Parting the Waters: America in the King Years, 1954–63* (Simon and Schuster, 1988), pp. 1–26.

[25]G. K. Chesterton, *Charles Dickens: Last of the Great Men* (Schocken, 1965), p. 40.

[26]Robert Weisbrot, *Father Divine and the Struggle for Racial Equality* (University of Illinois, 1983).

[27]*Abraham Lincoln: Speeches and Writings, 1832–1858*, edited by Don E. Fehrenbacher (Library of America, 1989), pp. 74, 360.

Chapter Nineteen. Lincoln's Black Theology

[1]John Milton, *On Reformation*, book 1, in *The Prose of John Milton*, edited by J. Max Patrick (Doubleday, 1967), p. 44. The "light to the nations" comes from Isaiah 42.6–7.

[2]John Winthrop, "A Model of Christian Charity," in *The American Puritans*, edited by Perry Miller (Doubleday, 1956), p. 83.

[3]Cotton Mather, *Magnalia Christi Americana* (Russell and Russell, 1967).

[4]Perry Miller, *Errand into the Wilderness* (Harvard, 1956), p. 145.

5Jean H. Baker, *Mary Todd Lincoln* (W. W. Norton, 1987), pp. 218–22.

6Franklin Kelly, *Frederic Edwin Church* (Smithsonian Institution Press, 1988), pp. 118–25.

7*Abraham Lincoln: Speeches and Writings, 1832–1858*, edited by Don E. Fehrenbacher (Library of America, 1989), pp. 339–40. Henceforth *AL, 1832–1858*.

8Ibid., pp. 32–33.

9Revelation here draws on Isaiah 63.3 and Joel 3.13–15. The spiritual is derived from the favored book, Isaiah:

> It looks like Jesus, yes,
> Glorious in His appearance, yes,
> Treadin' the wine press, yes, Lawd,
> Time is drawin' nigh.

(Mary Allen Grissom, *The Negro Sings a New Heaven*, University of North Carolina, 1930, p. 55).

10*AL, 1832–1858*, p. 400.

11Ibid., p. 456.

12Ibid., p. 340. Cf. "to the latest generation" in *Abraham Lincoln: Speeches and Writings, 1859–1865*, edited by Don F. Fehrenbacher (Library of America, 1989), p. 415 (henceforth *AL, 1859–1865*).

13See, for instance, the insistent return of the phrase in his 1860 New Haven speech (*AL, 1859–1865*, pp. 141, 142, 147).

14*Collected Works of Abraham Lincoln*, edited by Roy Basler (Rutgers University Press, 1953), vol. 4, p. 169.

15*AL, 1832–1858*, p. 40.

16Ibid., p. 398.

17Ibid., p. 399.

18*AL, 1859–1865*, pp. 136–37.

19Ibid., p. 597.

20Ibid., p. 565.

21See, for instance, the letter to Schuyler Colfax (ibid., p. 224) and also pp. 193 and 471.

22Ibid., pp. 195, 298, 385–87, 435, 420, 446–47, 478–79.

23Ibid., pp. 238, 471–72.

24Ibid., pp. 530–31.

25Ibid., p. 329.

26Ibid., p. 642.

27Ibid., p. 687.

28Ibid., pp. 521, 520.

29Ibid., p. 637.

30Ibid., p. 264.

31Ibid., p. 687. *Bondman* is a biblical term for "slave" (e.g., see Deuteronomy 15.15, 16.12, 24.18).

32Ibid., p. 361. Lincoln was usually chary about claims to know, ahead of time, God's will in history. He tried to do right "as God gives us to see the right" (p. 687), or "in the best light he gives us" (p. 627), or "as we understand it" (p. 130). By the same hedging instinct, the most he could bring himself to say of Americans was that they are "an *almost* chosen people" (p. 209).

33Ibid., p. 589.

34Ibid., p. 627.

35Ibid., p. 627. Cf. p. 359.

36Ibid., p. 586.

[37]The songs are at Isaiah 42.1–4, 49.1–6, 50.4–11, 52.13, and 53.12. Cf. John L. McKenzie, S.J., *The Second Isaiah* (Doubleday, 1968), pp. 1–1v.

[38]*AL, 1858–1865*, p. 210.

[39]Ibid., p. 213.

[40]Ibid., p. 212.

[41]Ibid., p. 211.

[42]Ibid., p. 207.

[43]Ibid., p. 628: "In regard to this Great Book, I have but to say, it is the best gift God has given to man. All the good the Saviour gave to the world was communicated through this book."

[44]Ibid., p. 665.

Chapter Twenty. Marginal Man

[1]Henry G. Mitchell, *Black Preaching* (Harper & Row, 1979), p. 115.

[2]James Baldwin, *Go Tell It on the Mountain* (Laurel, 1980), p. 114. The reference is to Genesis 21.10 and Galatians 4.30.

[3]Bob Faw and Nancy Skelton, *Thunder in America* (Texas Monthly Press, 1986), p. 11.

[4]David J. Garrow, *Bearing the Cross: Martin Luther King, Jr., and the Southern Christian Leadership Conference* (William Morrow, 1986), p. 409.

[5]Ibid., pp. 392–93.

[6]Barbara Reynolds, *Jesse Jackson: America's David* (JFJ Associates, 1985), pp. 54–55.

[7]Quoted in Theodore H. White, *The Making of the President 1972* (Atheneum, 1973), p. 165.

[8]Abernathy published an irenic account of the breakup in 1989, after Jackson's successes in the 1988 campaign: *And the Walls Came Tumbling Down* (Harper & Row, 1989), pp. 400–411. He had lent his name to harsher accounts, as when he wrote the introduction to *Jesse Jackson and the Politics of Race* by Thomas H. Landess and Richard M. Quinn (Green Hill, 1985).

[9]Ernest R. House, *Jesse Jackson and the Politics of Charisma: The Rise and Fall of the PUSH/Excel Program* (Westview Press, 1988), pp. 21–23.

[10]Ibid., p. 15.

[11]Garrow, op. cit., p. 454.

[12]Landess and Quinn, op. cit., pp. 188–91.

[13]Adolph L. Reed, Jr., *The Jesse Jackson Phenomenon: The Crisis of Purpose in Afro-American Politics* (Yale, 1986), pp. 89–105.

[14]Faw and Skelton, op. cit., pp. 61–62.

[15]Reed, op. cit., p. 102.

[16]Landess and Quinn, op. cit., pp. 99–100.

[17]Lucius J. Barker, *Our Time Has Come: A Delegate's Diary of Jesse Jackson's 1984 Presidential Campaign* (University of Illinois, 1988), p. 155.

[18]Ibid., p. 156.

[19]Faw and Skelton, op. cit., pp. 193–94.

[20]Reed, op. cit., p. 42.

Chapter Twenty-one. Preacher Jesse

[1]Adolph L. Reed, Jr., *The Jesse Jackson Phenomenon: The Crisis of Purpose in Afro-American Politics* (Yale, 1986), pp. 44, 46, 55, 57, 60. Reed anticipates with secular relish the fading of religion as a force in the black community. But predictions of such an event seem less certain, even, than similar pronouncements about religion in general.

As George Gallup and Jim Castelli put it: "American blacks are, by some measures, the most religious people in the world. In 1981, for example, Gallup International organizations conducted surveys on religious beliefs in twenty-three nations. One question asked respondents to rank the importance of God in their lives, with 10 the top score. The highest score recorded was by American blacks—9.04. . . . And while 83 percent of all church members say they would invite someone to attend their church, 95 percent of black church members say they would extend an invitation. . . . Blacks are more likely than other Americans to read the Bible frequently and half (48 percent) read it at least once a week" (*The People's Religion: American Faith in the 90s*, Macmillan, 1989, pp. 122–23).

[2]Reed, op. cit., pp. 3, 33, 34.
[3]Ibid., p. 74.
[4]Ibid., pp. 8, 30.

Chapter Twenty-two. Preacher Andy

[1]David J. Garrow, *Bearing the Cross: Martin Luther King, Jr., and the Southern Christian Leadership Conference* (William Morrow, 1986), p. 464.
[2]Lucius J. Barker, *Our Time Has Come: A Delegate's Diary of Jesse Jackson's 1984 Presidential Campaign* (University of Illinois, 1988), p. 67. The Young affair was treated earlier by Barker and Jesse McCorry in *Black Americans and the Political System* (Winthrop Publishers, 1980), pp. 334–42.
[3]Wolf Blitzer, "Andy Young's Undoing," *New Republic*, September 15, 1979, p. 12.

Chapter Twenty-three. What Did Jesse Want?

[1]Christine M. Black and Thomas Oliphant, *All by Myself: The Unmaking of a Presidential Campaign* (The Globe Pequot Press, 1989), p. 166.
[2]Bob Faw and Nancy Skelton, *Thunder in America* (Texas Monthly Press, 1986), p. 205.
[3]Robert H. Bork, *The Tempting of America: The Political Seduction of the Law* (The Free Press, 1990), p. 337.
[4]Ibid., pp. 337, 341, 343.
[5]Ibid., pp. 343, 337, 136.
[6]Ibid., p. 273.
[7]Ethan Bronner, *Battle for Justice: How the Bork Nomination Shook America* (Norton, 1989), p. 69.
[8]Ibid., p. 196.
[9]Robert H. Bork, "Neutral Principles and Some First Amendment Problems," *Indiana Law Journal*, Fall 1971, pp. 23, 35. Bork offered his 1963 views on segregation as legal "heresy" ("Civil Rights, A Challenge," *The New Republic*, August 31, 1963, p. 22).
[10]Ronald Dworkin, "The Bork Nomination," *New York Review of Books*, October 8, 1987, pp. 59–61.
[11]Bork, "Civil Rights," pp. 21–24.
[12]Bork, "Neutral Principles," p. 22; "The Supreme Court Needs a New Philosophy," *Fortune*, December 1968.
[13]Bork, *Tempting*, pp. 23–24.
[14]Ibid., p. 43.
[15]Ibid., pp. 42–43.
[16]Ibid., pp. 44–49.
[17]Ibid., pp. 49, 61.
[18]Ibid., p. 116.

[19]Ibid., p. 128.

[20]Bronner, op. cit., p. 258.

[21]Ibid., pp. 258–59.

[22]Ibid., p. 260.

[23]Ibid., p. 251.

[24]In his book (p. 309) Bork denies that he had ever spoken out on school prayer, but the friends of that idea could count on a man who said, in 1985, "A relaxation of currently rigid secularist doctrine would in the first place permit some sensible things to be done. . . . I suspect that the greatest perceived change would be in reintroduction of some religion into schools and some greater religious symbolism in our public life" (Bronner, op. cit., p. 93).

[25]Ibid., pp. 189, 298–99, 186.

[26]Ibid., p. 301. According to the CBS/New York Times poll, public opinion was 26 to 16 percent against Bork. According to the NBC/Wall Street Journal poll it was 42 to 34 percent against.

[27]Ibid., p. 185. For evangelicals joining the anti-Bork forces, see George Gallup, Jr., and Jim Castelli, The People's Religion: American Faith in the 90's (Macmillan, 1989), p. 95.

[28]Bork, "Civil Rights"; Bronner, op. cit., p. 233; Bork, Tempting, pp. 52, 53: "People who found state regulation oppressive could vote with their feet. . . . If another state allows the liberty you value, you can move there."

[29]David Hume, Essays Moral, Political, and Literary, edited by Eugene F. Miller (Liberty Classics, 1985), p. 475.

[30]Bronner, op. cit., p. 236.

[31]Keep Hope Alive: Jesse Jackson's 1988 Presidential Campaign, edited by Frank Clemente and Frank Watkins (South End Press, 1989), pp. 35–36.

[32]Ibid., p. 214.

[33]For Jackson's populism as a missed opportunity for the Democrats in 1988, see Kevin Phillips, The Politics of Rich and Poor: Wealth and the American Electorate in the Reagan Aftermath (Random House, 1990), pp. 47–50.

PART VI. POLITICS AND PORNOGRAPHY

Chapter Twenty-four. "With Ladies Present"

[1]Robert H. Bork, The Tempting of America: The Political Seduction of the Law (The Free Press, 1990), p. 124.

[2]Robert H. Bork, "Neutral Principles and Some First Amendment Problems," Indiana Law Journal, Fall 1971, p. 20.

[3]Bork, Tempting, p. 333.

[4]Ibid., p. 123.

[5]Bork, "Neutral Principles," pp. 9, 10.

[6]Ronald Dworkin, "The Bork Nomination," New York Review of Books, August 13, 1987, pp. 3–10; Philip Kurland, "Bork: The Transformation of a Conservative Constitutionalist," Chicago Tribune, August 18, 1987.

[7]Allan Bloom, The Closing of the American Mind (Simon and Schuster, 1987), p. 75.

[8]Ibid., p. 99.

[9]Ibid., p. 100.

[10]Jane J. Mansbridge, Why We Lost the ERA (University of Chicago, 1986).

[11]Ibid., p. 104; Midge Decter, "The Boys on the Beach," Commentary (September 1980); Gore Vidal, Pink Triangle and Yellow Star (Granada, 1983), pp. 206–7.

[12]George Gilder, *Sexual Suicide* (Quadrangle, 1973).

[13]G. Jonathan Liebersohn, "The Reality of AIDS," *New York Review of Books*, January 16, 1986.

[14]Ethan Bronner, *Battle for Justice: How the Bork Nomination Shook America* (Norton, 1989), p. 87.

[15]Ibid., p. 89.

[16]Bork, *Tempting*, p. 120.

[17]Ibid., p. 122.

[18]Ibid., pp. 95–97.

[19]Ibid., p. 117.

[20]Bronner, op. cit., p. 87.

[21]Ibid.

[22]William Bradford, *Of Plymouth Plantation, 1620–1647*, edited by S. E. Morison (Knopf, 1966), pp. 320–21.

[23]D. H. Lawrence, "A Propos of Lady Chatterley's Lover," in *Sex, Literature, and Christianity*, edited by Harry T. Moore (Twayne, 1953), p. 94.

[24]Edmund Morgan, "The Puritans and Sex," *New England Quarterly* 15 (1942), pp. 591–607.

[25]Because the penalties were severe, evidence of misconduct had to be spelled out, by two eyewitnesses. In one case that lacked a second witness, a pig was considered the beholder of its own deflowering, and it shared the gallows for the crime it testified to. See John Murrin, "Trial by Jury in Seventeenth-Century New England," in *Saints and Revolutionaries: Essays on Early American History*, edited by David D. Hall et al. (Norton, 1984), pp. 177–78.

[26]Alexis de Tocqueville, *Democracy in America*, the Reeve-Bowen text revised by Phillips Bradley (Knopf, 1976), vol. 1, p. 304.

[27]Ann Douglas, *The Feminization of American Culture* (Knopf, 1977).

[28]Nathan O. Hatch, *The Democratization of American Religion* (Yale, 1989).

[29]On elite permissiveness, see Richard S. Randall, *Freedom and Taboo: Pornography and the Politics of a Self Divided* (University of California, 1989), pp. 147–67.

[30]For Tocqueville on usefully feigned belief, see *Democracy*, 1.305 (even revolutionaries "are obliged to profess an ostensible respect for Christian morality"), 1.308 (fervor in the "outward duties of religion"), 1.313 (even the unbeliever, though "he does not admit religion to be true, still considers it useful," so that "those who do not believe conceal their incredulity"). Religion usefully restrains individualism (2.21–22, 2.28), skepticism (2.149–51), and hedonism and materialism (2.26, 2.134–35, 2.143–48). It provides social cohesion (1.311–14, 2.7, 2.22). It does this by standing over against the political, in a relation of

> society to government (1.311)
> custom to law (1.304)
> morality to politics (1.304)
> home to state (1.304)
> manners to policy (1.304)
> authority to force (1.309)
> influence to power (1.310–12).

This separation is healthy, necessary, and to be preserved (1.301, 1.308–9, 2.23, 2.27), since "Christianity must be maintained at any cost in the bosom of modern democracies" (2.147), for its service to the state it both undergirds and checks, providing it stability precisely *because* it fixes its limits.

[31]Alexis de Tocqueville, *De la démocratie en Amérique*, edited by François Furet (Garnier-Flammarion, 1981), vol. 1, p. 396. The Reeve-Bowen-Bradley version misses

the play of connectives and the irony of language for dominion (*"pouvoirs sur les âmes, exerce le plus d'empire"*) and liberation.

[32]John D'Emilio and Estelle B. Friedman, *Intimate Matters: A History of Sexuality in America* (Harper & Row, 1988), pp. 156–61; Randall, op. cit., pp. 171–74.

[33]For Hollywood's obeisance to the family values of Catholic censors, see Leonard J. Leff and Jerold L. Simmons, *The Dame in the Kimono: Hollywood Censorship and the Production Code from the 1920s to the 1960s* (Grove Weidenfeld, 1990). At some studios, an alliance between homage to Jewish mothers and to the Virgin Mary made "Mom" the most inviolable icon on the screen.

[34]According to Marcuse, an anything-goes society leads to "the systematic moronization of children and adults alike" ("Repressive Tolerance," in *A Critique of Pure Tolerance*, Beacon, 1965, p. 83).

[35]According to Baudrillard, there is an "absolute repression" in absolute permissiveness: "by giving you a *little too much*, one takes away everything." *Seduction*, translated by Brian Singer (St. Martin's, 1979), p. 30.

[36]Donald Alexander Downs, *The New Politics of Pornography* (University of Chicago, 1989).

[37]Michel Foucault, *The History of Sexuality, Volume 1: An Introduction*, translated by Robert Hurley (Pantheon, 1978), pp. 17–35, 77.

[38]Jules Feiffer, "Smut," in *Men Confront Pornography*, edited by Michael S. Kimmel (Crown, 1990), p. 24; Susan Stewart, "The Marquis de Meese," *Critical Inquiry*, Autumn 1988, pp. 162–92.

[39]Edward Donnerstein, whose work was used by the Meese Commission, protests that he was misrepresented, since research has still not established pornography's power to induce crime. See Edward Donnerstein, Daniel Linz, and Steven Penrod, *The Question of Pornography: Research Findings and Policy Implications* (Free Press, 1987), p. 172. Cf. Garry Wills, "Measuring the Impact of Erotica," *Psychology Today*, August 1977, pp. 30–34, 74–77.

[40]Margaret Atwood, *The Handmaid's Tale* (Fawcett Crest, 1987). The dystopia follows on a social condition that was seen as too free: "We were a society dying, said Aunt Lydia, of too much choice" (p. 34)—cf. Marcuse (note 34 above) and Baudrillard (note 35 above). That world was ended by the burning of pornographic books (pp. 50–51). Though prostitution is retained in the new order, it is used to punish successful women not easily returned to the feminine ideal: "That one there, the one in green, she's a sociologist. Or was. That one was a lawyer, that one was in business, an executive position" (p. 309).

Chapter Twenty-five. In Praise of Censure

[1]As Shylock preserves the story for a later time:

> And when the work of generation was
> Between these wholly breeders in the act,
> The skilful shepherd peeled me certain wands,
> And in the doing of the deed of kind
> He stuck them up before the fulsome ewes,
> Who then conceiving, did in eaning time
> Fall parti-colour'd lambs. . . . (*Merchant of Venice* 1.3.81–87)

[2]The medical writer Soranus, quoted in St. Augustine, *Against Julian* 5.9.

[3]G. P. Lomazzo, *Treatise on the Arts* (1584), quoted in David Friedberg, *The Power of Images: Studies in the History and Theory of Response* (University of Chicago, 1989), p. 1.

[4]Plutarch, introduction to *The Paired Lives of Timoleon and Aemilius Paulus* (introduction prefixed to one or other of the two lives, according to edition).

[5]William Griffitt, "Sexual Stimulation and Sociosexual Behavior," in *Love and Attraction*, edited by Mark Cook and Glenn Wilson (Pergamon, 1979).

[6]Georges Bataille, *Eroticism: Death and Sensuality*, translated by Mary Dalwood (City Lights, 1986), p. 7.

[7]Denis Diderot, *Le Neveu de Rameau* (Editions Gallimard, 1951), p. 396.

[8]Plato, *Symposium* 189–93.

[9]Denis Diderot, *Rêve de d'Alembert* (Editions Gallimard, 1951), p. 908.

[10]Blaise Pascal, *Pensées sur la religion*, edited by Louis Lafuma (Éditions du Luxembourg, 1951), no. 809, p. 433. Cf. Victor Hugo, *Les Misérables* (Garnier-Flammarion, 1979), vol. 3, p. 12: "There is something in the very makeup of this life that makes one grasp it all as punishment." Sartre says that the experience of shame suggests an original fall. See *Being and Nothingness*, translated by Hazel E. Barnes (Methuen, 1957), p. 289.

[11]St. Augustine, *City of God* 14.12–13.

[12]Ibid., 14.15. Augustine finds the height of the involuntary in a friend who experienced orgasm from a mere sexual image (*The Trinity*, 11.4).

[13]Ibid., 14.16. On this Augustine agrees with the erotic Latin poet Martial (*Epigrammata* 3.70, 5.83, 6.23).

[14]St. Augustine, op. cit., 14.16.

[15]Ibid., 14.20.

[16]Mercutio's words at *Romeo and Juliet* 2.4.91–93 (cf. *All's Well That Ends Well* 4.5.27). On the shape and sexual meaning of the bauble, cf. William Willeford, *The Fool and His Sceptre* (Northwestern University, 1969). Michelangelo gives the bauble comically heroic treatment on the Sistine ceiling (carried by Obeth in the fifth lunette on the right wall looking toward the altar).

[17]*The City of God* 14.24. Elaine Pagels claims that rightful desire and performance *never* come together in sex for St. Augustine ("desire can never cooperate with will," p. 112), one of the many ways she misunderstands this part of *The City of God*. Her lack of humor is as much at fault as her scholarship. She should have pondered the significance of wiggled ears and tuneful farts. Cf. Pagels, *Adam, Eve, and the Serpent* (Random House, 1988).

[18]Bataille, op. cit., p. 18. Sartre (op. cit., 289), describes nakedness as defenselessness.

[19]Ibid., p. 17.

[20]Ibid., p. 198.

[21]Psychologists note a period of sexual latency in children, when they repress in order to control their earliest sexual information. Violation of this would be an invasion. See Richard S. Randall, *Freedom and Taboo: Pornography and the Politics of a Self Divided* (University of California, 1989), pp. 113–14.

[22]Bataille, op. cit., pp. 224–25.

[23]Deposition of Rose Kailair, in Paul Dinnage, *The Marquis de Sade: Selections from His Writings* (John Calder, 1962), p. 214.

[24]Simone de Beauvoir, "Must We Burn Sade?" in Dinnage, op. cit., p. 31. Democritus compared orgasm to epilepsy, a point Clement of Alexandria repeated when contrasting orgasm with the Stoic ideal of imperturbability (*ataraxia*): "The shudder it involves racks and crumples the whole frame's fittings" (*Pedagogue* 2.95).

[25]Roland Barthes, *Sade, Fournier, Loyola*, translated by Richard Muller (Hill and Wang, 1976), p. 27: "Sadian practice is ruled by a great noting of order: 'irregularities' are strenuously regulated, vice is unbridled but not without order (at Silling, for example, all debaucherie irrevocably ends at 2 A.M.)."

[26]Sade, "Philosophy in the Bedroom," in Dinnage, op. cit., p. 135. It is no wonder

that Sade refers to "rape, so rare and so hard to prove" (p. 142), since he takes the classic attitude that women "really want it" (p. 137). For Sartre (op. cit., p. 399), Sadism appropriates others by obliterating their right to themselves.

[27]Ibid., p. 136.

[28]De Beauvoir, op. cit., p. 61.

[29]Tipper Gore, *Raising PG Kids in an X-Rated Society* (Abingdon Press, 1987), p. 55.

[30]Nanette Varian, "Terry's Rights and Yours," *Penthouse*, July 1989, p. 93: "What she [Terry Rakolta] is engaging in is not free speech. It's yelling 'fire' in a crowded theater [the classic case of unprotected speech] in order to close down what she doesn't care for." Cf. Frank Zappa with Peter Occhiogrosso, *The Real Frank Zappa Book* (Poseidon, 1989), p. 270, deploring terrorism from "The Wives of Big Brother."

[31]George Gallup, Jr., and Jim Castelli, *The People's Religion: American Faith in the 90's* (Macmillan, 1989), pp. 133–35.

[32]Garry Wills, "Blood Sport," *New York Review of Books*, February 18, 1988, pp. 5–7.

[33]Rechy in interview with Stanley Crouch, *Notes of a Hanging Judge* (Oxford, 1990), p. 124. Ageism, promiscuity, and the cult of vapid beauty are as little admirable among gays as straights. As Rechy says:

> You've got to have a certain type of beauty. Increasingly, there are signs, especially in California [circa 1980], which say, "No Fats, No Thins, No Over 35s." Along with those signs, there is a tacit understanding that ethnic minorities will be excluded—blacks, Mexicans, and, most of all, Orientals. To avoid suits, there are no explicit signs, but when ethnic gays appear at the doors of chic gathering places, they will be told there is no more room, then some pretty blond gay will be allowed in (ibid., p. 122).

Crouch adds: "Heterosexual men who chase after or idealize teenage girls are assumed immature until proven otherwise" (p. 125).

[34]Camille Paglia, *Sexual Personae: Art and Decadence from Nefertiti to Emily Dickinson* (Yale, 1990), p. 239.

Chapter Twenty-six. A Theology of Erotica

[1]Victor Hugo, *Les Misérables* (Garnier-Flammarion, 1967), vol. 1, pp. 373–75.

[2]Motion Picture Production Code, reprinted in Leonard J. Leff and Jerald L. Simmons, *The Dame in the Kimono: Hollywood Censorship and the Production Code from the 1920s to the 1960s* (Grove Weidenfeld, 1990), p. 285.

[3]Ibid., pp. 95–96.

[4]Thomas Eakins, perhaps America's greatest painter, was forced out of the Pennsylvania Academy of Fine Art in 1886 for including women students in his life classes from the nude. See Lloyd Goodrich, *Thomas Eakins* (Harvard, 1982), vol. 1, pp. 282–94.

[5]St. Augustine, *True Religion* 77.

[6]Ibid., and *Against Faustus* 21.6.

[7]*The Nature of the Good* 14.

[8]*City of God* 21.8.

[9]Ibid., 22.24.

[10]*The Trinity*, 9.11. Cf. Søren Kierkegaard, *Fear and Trembling and Repetition*, translated by Howard V. Hong and Edna H. Hong (Princeton, 1983), pp. 148–49.

[11]Simone de Beauvoir, "Must We Burn Sade?" in Paul Dinnage, *The Marquis de Sade: Selections from His Writings* (John Calder, 1962), p. 47.

[12]Sade quoted in Edmund Wilson, "The Vogue of the Marquis de Sade," in *Eight Essays* (Doubleday, 1954), p. 178.

[13]De Beauvoir, op. cit., p. 45.

[14]Wilson, op. cit., p. 178.

[15]Ibid., p. 179.

[16]Ibid., pp. 180, 171.

[17]Jean Baudrillard, "The Ironic Strategy of the Seducer," in *Seduction*, translated by Brian Singer (St. Martin's Press, 1979), pp. 98–118. Cf. Douglas Kellner, *Jean Baudrillard: From Marxism to Postmodernism and Beyond* (Stanford, 1989), p. 146, on "Kierkegaard's highly masculist and misogynist text," and Andrew Ross, "Baudrillard's Bad Attitude," in *Seduction and Theory*, edited by Dianne Hunter (University of Illinois, 1989), p. 217, on "Baudrillard's inability to recognize the urgency of a wide range of feminist strategies."

[18]Søren Kierkegaard, *Either/Or, Part One*, translated by Howard V. Hong and Edna H. Hong (Princeton, 1987), pp. 386, 412, 440.

[19]Ibid., p. 445.

[20]Ibid., p. 444.

[21]Ibid., p. 381.

[22]Andrew M. Greeley, *Religious Change in America* (Harvard, 1989), chapter 9, "Religious Images," pp. 94–111. According to Kierkegaard, Job's "uppityness" to God came from a conviction that God is not a tyrant but a lover, and Job "will be sufficiently noble to go on loving him . . . even when God is tempting the lover" (*Repetition*, p. 207).

[23]For the treatment of pederasty in Dickens see Garry Wills, "Love in the Lower Depths," *New York Review of Books*, October 26, 1988, pp. 60–67.

[24]George Gallup, Jr., and Jim Castelli, *The People's Religion: American Faith in the 90's* (Macmillan, 1989), p. 75.

[25]René Girard's treatment of possession could be a description of the Humbert-Quilty relationship: "Possession is not an individual phenomenon. . . . There are always at least two beings who possess each other reciprocally. . . . Each is the other's demon" ("The Demons of Gerasa," in *The Scapegoat*, translated by Yvonne Freccero, Johns Hopkins, 1986, p. 172). Cf. Jean Starobinski, "La Démoniaque de Gerasa," in *Analyse structurale et exégèse biblique* (Neuchâtel, 1971), pp. 63–94. The word *diabolos* means, in Greek, "the divider," "the setter-at-odds" (*dia-ballein*).

[26]For William Blatty's *The Exorcist* as a form of spiritual pandering, cf. Garry Wills, "The Devil," in *Lead Time* (Doubleday, 1983), pp. 320–26.

[27]"Anactoria." Cf. Job 13.15. For "Anactoria" as Swinburne's masterpiece, with its blasphemous central section, see Camille Paglia, *Sexual Personae: Art and Decadence from Nefertiti to Emily Dickinson* (Yale, 1990), pp. 472–78.

[28]*Scorsese on Scorsese*, edited by David Thompson and Ian Christie (Faber and Faber, 1989), pp. 120–22.

[29]*Time*, August 15, 1988, pp. 34–36; Erwin W. Lutzer, "*The Last Temptation of Christ*": *Its Deception and What You Should Do About It* (Moody Press, 1988).

[30]John Henry Newman, "Mental Sufferings of Our Lord in His Passion," *Discourses to Mixed Congregations* (1849). This Lenten sermon, remarkable for its insights into various forms of suffering, was preached in Birmingham during the cholera plague of 1849, the fear of which it refers to when discussing the fears of Jesus. As such, the sermon ranks with other works of Christian art created during or after catastrophes that tried people's faith. Newman, asked to send a priest of his order to the plague center at Bilston, went himself, despite the pleas of his followers that he was indispensable in Birmingham. It is reasonable to assume that it was through his own fear, his sensitivity to the fears of others, and the pitiable nature of the confessions he was hearing in such a time of panic that he was able to interpret the fears of Jesus in the garden and the temptation to turn away from his ordeal (Meriol Trevor, *Newman: The Pillar of the Cloud*, Macmillan, 1962, pp. 498–502).

[31]Shusaku Endo, *Silence* (Taplinger, 1980), p. 116.

[32]For Endo's Catholic fiction, see Garry Wills, "Embers of Guilt," *New York Review of Books*, February 19, 1981. Carl Dreyer, the great Swedish director who meant to film a life of Jesus, made Judas the collaborator with Jesus, as one sees from the script he prepared (Carl Theodore Dreyer, *Jesus*, Delta, 1971, pp. 253, 272).

PART VII. POLITICS AND ABORTION

Chapter Twenty-seven. Catholics: Mario Cuomo

[1]Technically, Catholics annually took a pledge in their parishes to observe the Legion of Decency ratings, so that what bound them was their word—as happened in "taking the pledge" not to drink before age eighteen (or twenty-one). But the impression given in parochial schools was that the *church* condemned movies, and that going to a "condemned" one was a mortal sin to be confessed.

[2]Robert S. McElvaine, *Mario Cuomo: A Biography* (Charles Scribner's Sons, 1988), pp. 92–93.

[3]Ibid., p. 94.

[4]Ibid., p. 93.

[5]Cuomo made a neat retort to this analogy, so far as his clerical critics were concerned, by pointing out that the Catholic bishops of America did not speak out against slavery before emancipation. See the reprint of Cuomo's speech in *The New York Review of Books*, October 25, 1984, p. 34. Forrest G. Wood spells out the bad record of America's bishops (who were themselves slaveholders) on the slavery issue in *The Arrogance of Faith: Christianity and Race in America From the Colonial Era to the Twentieth Century* (Knopf, 1990), pp. 356–61.

[6]Polls reported in Andrew Greeley, *The Catholic Myth: The Behavior and Beliefs of Catholics* (Charles Scribner's Sons, 1990), pp. 92–93.

[7]A sociological study of the "clerical rebellion" is in John Seidler and Katherine Meyer, *Conflict and Change in the Catholic Church* (Rutgers, 1989), pp. 94–95, 109–27.

[8]Greeley, op. cit., p. 97.

[9]Catholic views have changed rapidly on abortion (if Hispanic Catholics are separated out). George Gallup, Jr., and Jim Castelli, *The People's Religion: American Faith in the 90's* (Macmillan, 1989), pp. 167–79.

[10]St. Augustine, Epistle 19.15. Catholic theologian Bernard Haring used the number of fertilized eggs that do not achieve nidation (perhaps half) to suggest, as recently as 1970, that life cannot begin at fertilization. See John T. Noonan, Jr., *The Morality of Abortion: Legal and Historical Perspectives* (Harvard, 1970), p. 130.

[11]St. Augustine, Epistle 166.12.

[12]Robert J. O'Connell, S.J., argues that Augustine always inclined to Origen's view. At any rate, he shows how that view puzzled and tempted and returned to Augustine in his long, unsuccessful search for the mode by which souls enter bodies. See O'Connell, *The Origin of the Soul in St. Augustine's Later Works* (Fordham, 1987).

[13]St. Augustine, Epistle 166.22.

[14]St. Augustine, Epistle 190.5. Even when Augustine was taunted for his ignorance on the point, he refused to give up his dubiety (*cunctatio*), suggesting that it may be sinful to aspire to a knowledge not offered in Scripture (*The Soul and Its Origin* 4.5). Augustine condemned contraception and abortion, but not on the grounds that the latter was homicidal, since he did not know whether a human soul was involved in destruction of the fetus (Noonan, op. cit., pp. 15–16).

[15]Aristotle, *Animal Generation* 2.2 (736a–737a).

[16]Noonan, op. cit., p. 23.

[17]Ibid., p. 23.

[18]William J. Jordan, *Panama Odyssey* (University of Texas, 1984), p. 316.

[19]John Locke, *The Second Treatise of Government*, no. 23.

[20]Mario Cuomo, "Joining the Debate," *Commonweal*, March 23, 1990: "In Tucson, I said I felt presumptuous talking about the terrible, hard judgment women make with regard to abortion. I do. I am very uncomfortable with having to make decisions about abortion. I do think there is an element of the absurd or incongruous in men making laws about something they can never experience—pregnancy." Legislators deal with many things they may never, individually, experience—drug addiction, religious mysticism, combat, higher learning.

Chapter Twenty-eight. Evangelicals: Francis Schaeffer

[1]Augustine surveyed texts of possible relevance in Epistle 190 and *Genesis Taken Literally* 10.6–22, and he took up other texts proposed by his critics in *The Soul and Its Origin* 1.17–30. Vincentius Victor, speaking for the Pelagians, called Augustine the thoughtless beast of Psalm 49.12 for lingering in his ignorance over the subject of life's beginnings.

[2]This text is often read at Operation Rescue rallies. The intellectual case for it is made in Paul B. Fowler, *Abortion: Toward an Evangelical Consensus* (Multnomah Press, 1987), pp. 143, 149–53; C. Hassell Bullock, "Abortion and Old Testament Prophetic and Poetic Literature," in *Abortion: A Christian Understanding and Response*, edited by James K. Hoffmeier (Baker Book House, 1987), pp. 67–68; Randall A. Terry, *Operation Rescue* (Whitaker House, 1988), p. 138.

[3]St. Augustine, *Confessions* 3.6.

[4]Mitchell Dabood argues that this text describes the soul's preexistence in Sheol. See *The Anchor Bible: Psalms* (Doubleday, 1970), vol. 3, p. 295.

[5]James K. Hoffmeier, "Abortion and the Old Testament Law," in Hoffmeier, op. cit., pp. 57–61; Terry, op. cit., pp. 138–39.

[6]E. A. Speiser, *The Anchor Bible: Genesis* (Doubleday, 1964), p. 297.

[7]Fowler, op. cit., pp. 24–26, 65–94. Randall Terry frequently tells his audiences that they must act in a spirit of repentance for evangelicals' earlier indifference to abortion. It was not until two years after the legalization of abortion by the *Roe* v. *Wade* decision that evangelical leaders, meeting at Billy Graham's home, set up the Christian Action Council to oppose abortion.

[8]George Gallup, Jr., and Jim Castelli, *The People's Religion: American Faith in the 90's* (Macmillan, 1989), p. 178: "The backbone of the antiabortion movement comes increasingly from white Evangelicals, not Catholics. . . . There may be no other issue that so clearly differentiates the views of white Evangelical and white non-Evangelical Protestants."

[9]David O. Beale, *In Pursuit of Purity: American Fundamentalism Since 1850* (Unusual Publications, 1986), pp. 163–70.

[10]Francis A. Schaeffer, *The Complete Works of Francis A. Schaeffer: A Christian World View* (Crossway Books, 1982), vol. 1, pp. 14–17. On the mythical Kierkegaard of Schaeffer's system, see Ronald W. Ruegsegger, "Francis Schaeffer on Philosophy," in *Reflections on Francis Schaeffer* (Academic Books, 1986), pp. 118–20.

[11]Schaeffer found Teilhard in essential agreement with Marx (Schaeffer, *Complete Works*, vol. 1, p. 45), with Dalí (p. 72), with Leopold Senghor (p. 89), with Tillich (p. 94), with Julian Huxley (p. 243), and with Darwin (p. 266).

[12]Schaeffer, *Complete Works*, vol. 1, pp. 8–9, 27–36, 40–41, 76; vol. 3, pp. 385–86.

For an evangelical estimate of Schaeffer's unfamiliarity with art and music, see Harold M. Best, "Schaeffer on Art and Music," in Ruegsegger, op. cit., pp. 131–72.

[13]Schaeffer, *Complete Works*, vol. 1, pp. 138, 141–42.

[14]Ibid., pp. 6–8. For the role of Cornelius Van Til in Schaeffer's intellectual formation, see Forrest Baird, "Schaeffer's Intellectual Roots," in Ruegsegger, op. cit., pp. 56–58.

[15]Baird, op. cit., pp. 60–61; *Francis A. Schaeffer: Portraits of the Man and His Work*, edited by Lane T. Dennis (Crossway Books, 1986), pp. 209–10.

[16]Dennis, op. cit., p. 136.

[17]Schaeffer, *Complete Works*, vol. 1, pp. 209–16; vol. 5, pp. 103–17. For the inadequacy of Schaeffer's acquaintance with St. Thomas Aquinas, see Baird, op. cit., pp. 112–15.

[18]Schaeffer, *Complete Works*, vol. 5, pp. 473–79. Schaeffer asserts the influence of Rutherford and Witherspoon without ever citing a single actual passage from either man. Cf. Timothy D. Hall, "Rutherford, Locke, and the Declaration," Th.M. thesis, Dallas Theological Seminary, 1984. On Catholic immigration as the solvent of American religion, see Ronald A. Wells, "Schaeffer on America," in Ruegsegger, op. cit., pp. 225, 236.

[19]Donald W. Dayton, *Discovering an Evangelical Heritage* (Harper & Row, 1976), pp. 45–62; Mark Belz, *Suffer the Little Children: Christians, Abortions, and Civil Disobedience* (Crossway Books, 1989), pp. 85–104.

Chapter Twenty-nine. Feminists and Fundamentalism

[1]Ronald and Beverly Allen, *Liberated Traditionalism: Men and Women in Balance* (Multinomah Press, 1985), p. 25: "We wish to join the sentiment of Concerned Women for America in rejecting the arrogance of such feminist groups as the National Organization for Women (NOW) in their presumptuous claims that they speak for the women of America. If for no other reason than to cry foul against an unfair tactic, traditionalists such as Beverly LaHaye, the president of Concerned Women for America and the wife of Moral Majority cofounder Tim LaHaye, and Phyllis Schlafly, the president of Eagle Forum and an outspoken foe of the women's movement, should be applauded. Millions of women (and men) are neither sympathetic to nor supportive of the goals of the secular feminist movement." For Phyllis Schlafly's Catholic antifeminism, see "Catholics and Fundamentalists against the ERA," chapter 9 of *Politics, Power, and the Church: The Catholic Crisis and Its Challenge to American Pluralism* by Lawrence Lader (Macmillan, 1987), pp. 121–33. Joseph Scheidler of the Catholic Pro-Life Action League regularly refers to feminists as "NOW cows."

[2]William F. Orr and James S. Walther, *The Anchor Bible*, vol. 32: *Corinthians I* (Doubleday, 1976), p. 108.

[3]Wayne Meeks, *The First Urban Christians* (Yale, 1983), pp. 49, 60, 79, 217. Phoebe and Apphia (Philemon 2) are called "sister," a term that means "co-worker" (Orr and Hay, op. cit., p. 100).

[4]Ibid., p. 59. The household of Chloe is Paul's later listening post at Corinth. Cf. Edward Schillebeeckx, *The Church with a Human Face: A New and Expanded Theology of Ministry* (Crossroad, 1988), pp. 53–54.

[5]Scholars now hold that Galatians 3.26–28, the great "Christian charter of freedom," is an early baptismal formula subscribed to by Paul:

For you are all children of God,

for all of you are baptized in Christ
are clothed with Christ.

There is no longer Jew nor Gentile,
there is no longer slave nor free man,

There is no longer man nor woman
but you are all one in Christ Jesus.

Cf. Edward Schillebeeckx, op. cit., pp. 37–38. St. Augustine denied that I Corinthians 11.8 could mean that woman was less "the glory of God" than man, expressing the "feminist" view that there is a male and a female component in each person (*The Trinity*, 12.7).

[6]Francis A. Schaeffer, *The Complete Works* (Crossway Books, 1982), vol. 2, p. 137. Cf. p. 127: "This statement is crucial because it affirms as a historic statement the fact that Adam came first and Eve came from Adam."

[7]George Marsden, *Reforming Fundamentalism: Fuller Seminary and the New Evangelism* (William B. Eerdmans, 1987), p. 281.

[8]Ibid., pp. 286–87.

[9]An earlier crisis at the school had been concerned with women's role there (ibid., pp. 123–28): "Keeping women in their place, though honoring them there, had become part of the fundamental ethos."

[10]Ronald and Beverly Allen, op. cit., p. 152. One difficulty that fundamentalists cause for themselves is their need to believe that the traditional ascriptions of authorship, so long as they are themselves contained in Scripture, are also unerring. So David had to write the Psalms, and Solomon the Book of Wisdom, and Paul the pastoral letters. Thus a later discipline for women, like that in the Epistle to Timothy, has to be reconciled with that in Galatians. The Allens exercise their interpretive ingenuity, making 1 Timothy 2.15 apply to "women who have given birth to illegitimate children through their pagan cultic experience" (p. 153), something as far as possible from ordinary Christian life.

[11]Susan D. Rose, *Keeping Them out of the Hands of Satan* (Routledge, 1988), pp. 34, 37, 60–68, 93, 137, 180.

[12]Ken Ham and Paul Taylor, *The Genesis Solution* (Master Books, 1988), p. 75: "He made a man and a woman, not a man and another man." Modern scholars are coming to the position that Jewish law called homosexuality unclean for the reason Mary Douglas finds in all the ritual purity legislation—to prevent any "mixing of kinds" (even to two different fibers in a fabric). Cf. L. William Countryman, *Dirt, Greed, and Sex: Sexual Ethics in the New Testament and Their Implications for Today* (Fortress Press, 1988), pp. 24–28, 109–23.

[13]Forrest G. Wood, *The Arrogance of Faith: Christianity and Race in America from the Colonial Era to the Twentieth Century* (Knopf, 1990), pp. 106–11.

[14]For titles in the early church, see Meeks, op. cit., pp. 134–36. He notes that all the descriptions are of "functions rather than offices"—emissaries (*apostoloi, angeloi*), prophets, leaders, evangelizers, overseers (*episkopoi*), shepherds, teachers, interpreters, ministrants (*diakonoi*), admonishers, patrons, guides, workers, co-workers, donors, pedagogues. Cf. Schillebeeckx, op. cit., pp. 55–61, and *Ministry: Leadership in the Community of Jesus Christ* (Crossroad, 1981), pp. 6–16, 55–59; also see Raymond E. Brown, *Priest and Bishop: Biblical Reflections* (Paulist Press, 1970), pp. 13–19.

[15]Raymond E. Brown, op. cit., pp. 40–41.

[16]Schillebeeckx, *Human Face*, pp. 119, 145–46; Schillebeeckx, *Ministry*, pp. 48–50.

[17]Schillebeeckx, *Human Face*, pp. 241–43; Schillebeeckx, *Ministry*, pp. 85–88; Peter Brown, *The Body and Society: Men, Women, and Sexual Renunciation in Early Christianity* (Columbia University, 1988), pp. 377–78.

[18]Countryman, op. cit., p. 29; Peter Brown, op. cit., p. 145.

[19]Peter Brown, op. cit., pp. 80–81, 118.

[20]Ibid., p. 266.

21Ibid., pp. 288, 332.

22Schillebeeckx, *Human Face*, pp. 163, 176.

23Ibid., p. 164; Schillebeeckx, *Ministry*, pp. 56–59.

24Schillebeeckx, *Human Face*, pp. 171–76.

25Ibid., pp. 240–49; Schillebeeckx, *Ministry*, pp. 88–89.

26Andrew M. Greeley, *The Catholic Myth: The Behavior and Beliefs of American Catholics* (Charles Scribner's Sons, 1990), pp. 202, 217. Eighty percent of the priests favored optional celibacy—30 percent more than the laity (in 1974), though 70 percent of laypeople said they would accept married clergy (p. 220).

27Excluding people from one's table at the Eucharist was one of the faults in Corinth that Paul called desecrating the Lord's body. It is a point the pope, who uses Paul's name, should meditate on: "The taboo view of the [eucharistic food] elements demands sacred officials to handle them, and the salvation of the recipient is in jeopardy if they are improperly handled. This, then, involves discipline. So what should be the very sign and seal of the unity of the church becomes a perpetual cause of its disruption" (Orr and Walther, op. cit., p. 269).

28Greeley, op. cit., p. 217.

29Ibid., p. 224.

30Ibid., p. 218.

31Peter Brown, op. cit., p. 52.

32Meeks, op. cit., pp. 117–30.

PART VIII. CHURCH AND STATE

Chapter Thirty. Religious Separatism

1See, for instance, Elaine C. Huber, *Women and the Authority of Inspiration: A Re-Examination of Two Prophetic Movements from a Contemporary Feminist Perspective* (University Press of America, 1985).

2David D. Hall, ed., *The Antinomian Controversy, 1636–1638: A Documentary History* (Wesleyan University, 1968), p. 316.

3Cf. Jean Hering, *The Second Epistle of Saint Paul to the Corinthians*, translated by A. W. Heathcote and P. J. Allcock (Epworth, 1967), pp. 79–80.

4Edmund S. Morgan makes Winthrop's battle with religious separatists the center of the political life of Winthrop and the early colony: *The Puritan Dilemma: The Story of John Winthrop* (Little, Brown, 1958).

5Hall, op. cit., pp. 349–87.

6Emery Battis, *Saints and Sectaries* (University of North Carolina, 1963), pp. 264–69.

7Charles Francis Adams, *Three Episodes of Massachusetts History* (Russell and Russell, 1965), vol. 2, pp. 560–65.

8Hall, op. cit., pp. 337–38.

9Ibid., p. 387. Cf. Larzer Ziff, *The Career of John Cotton: Puritanism and the American Experience* (Princeton, 1962), pp. 145–46.

10James Boswell, *Life of Johnson*, Hill-Powell edition (Oxford, 1934), vol. 1, p. 397.

11John Winthrop, *The History of New England*, edited by James Savage (Boston, 1825), vol. 1, p. 162; Cotton Mather, *Magnalia Christi Americana* (Russell and Russell, 1967), vol. 2, pp. 497–98.

12*The Complete Writings of Roger Williams* (Russell and Russell, 1963), vol. 7, p. 37. The best brief treatment of Williams's attitude toward converting Indians is the editorial note by Glenn W. LaFantasie in *The Correspondence of Roger Williams* (Brown University, 1988), vol. 1, pp. 141–44.

[13]Williams, *Complete Writings*, vol. 5, pp. 412, 350, 134. Williams also used *the little foxes* of the Song of Songs to ridicule Fox.

[14]Ibid., pp. 50, 211, 99, 242, 261, 211, 134. Williams even differed with the Foxians on the taking of oaths, though he had his own objections to that practice (ibid., pp. 408–13).

[15]Ibid., pp. 41, 260.

[16]Ibid., p. 307.

[17]In 1665, Lydia Wardell walked naked in Salem's streets and Deborah Wilson went naked into Newberry's meetinghouse.

[18]Williams, *Complete Writings*, vol. 5, pp. 59–62; also pp. 28, 134, 241–42.

[19]Ibid., p. 62. George Fox defended his nude Quakers against Williams's attack: "We do believe thee, in that dark persecuting bloody Spirit that thou [Williams] and the New England priests are bewitched in, you cannot believe that you are naked from God and his clothing, and blind, and therefore had the Lord in his power moved some of his sons and daughters to go naked. And so they were true prophets and prophetesses to the nation, as many sober men have confessed since, though you and the old persecuting priests in New England remain in your blindness and nakedness" (George Fox, *A New England Fire-Brand Quenched*, pp. 229–30).

[20]Williams, *Complete Writings*, vol. 1, p. 64, on the papistical "gross abominations" Luther retained.

[21]Letter from John Winthrop to John Endecott, January 3, 1633, in *Proceedings of the Massachusetts Historical Society*, February 1873, p. 344.

[22]Williams, *Complete Writings*, vol. 4, p. 205.

[23]Ibid., vol. 5, pp. 350, 246–57.

[24]Ibid., pp. 403–04. There was a touch of popishness in the way Fox asked James Naylor to kiss his foot.

[25]Ibid., p. 206. Fox answered in kind, denouncing "Roger Williams's envious, malicious, scornful, railing, false accusations, and blasphemies, which he foully and unchristianlike hath scattered and dispersed through his book" (*A New England Fire-Brand Quenched*, "Catalogue"). In those days theologians ventured out only in heavy armor. Since Fox wrote his attack on Williams in the home of William Penn, three revered religious leaders were hovering over this pious scrimmage.

[26]Williams, *Complete Writings*, vol. 5, pp. 191, 260. In Williams's account, the Quaker doctrine of inner light works against the primacy of Scripture as much as does the papist doctrine of church authority (ibid., pp. 49–50, 149, 200–03, 251–52).

[27]Ibid., p. 362.

[28]Augustine, *The City of God*, 19.21–24 (passages discussed in Garry Wills, *Confessions of a Conservative*, Doubleday, 1979, pp. 187–99). For the importance of Augustine to Puritans in general, see Perry Miller, *The New England Mind: The Seventeenth Century* (Harvard, 1939), p. 4: "[Augustine] exerted the greatest single influence upon Puritan thought next to that of the Bible itself, and in reality a greater one than did John Calvin." So great was the admiration for "Austin" that some Puritans continued calling him St. Austin when they had indignantly denied that title to other fathers canonized by Rome (ibid., p. 22). For the importance of Augustine to Roger Williams in particular, see Perry Miller, *Roger Williams: His Contribution to the American Tradition* (Atheneum, 1962), pp. 35–36.

[29]Williams, *Complete Writings*, vol. 3, pp. 249–50.

[30]Williams, *Writings*, vol. 3, pp. 35 ff.

[31]Williams, *Complete Writings*, vol. 3, pp. 311–63.

[32]Martin Marty, "The Virginia Statute Two Hundred Years Later," in *The Virginia Statute for Religious Freedom: Its Evolution and Consequences in American History*, edited by Merrill D. Peterson and Robert C. Vaughan (Cambridge, 1988), p. 17.

[33]St. Augustine, *The City of God* 4.33, 5.17, 18.47–48, 20.2.

[34]Ibid., 4.8, 6.9, 8.27. Williams, too, rejected providential arguments for worldly success—all too familiar in modern evangelists' "prosperity theology" (*Complete Works*, vol. 3, pp. 189–90). Puritans even opposed gambling because, like astrology, it trivialized God's providence as "luck" (Perry Miller, *The New England Mind: The Seventeenth Century*, Harvard, 1983, p. 16).

[35]St. Augustine, op. cit., 18.52–53, 20.7–8.

[36]Ibid., 18.48, 20.5, 20.9; Williams, *Complete Writings*, vol. 3, pp. 29, 97–119, and 169–74, and vol. 4, pp. 114–55.

[37]Williams rightly caught Augustine up on his defenses of persecution (*Complete Writings*, vol. 3, pp. 207–8).

[38]*Thomas Jefferson: Writings*, edited by Merrill D. Peterson (Library of America, 1984), p. 510.

[39]Williams, *Complete Writings*, vol. 1, p. 108.

[40]Ibid., vol. 3, p. 98.

[41]*Thomas Jefferson: Writings*, p. 285.

[42]Perry Miller, 1963 introduction to Williams, *Complete Works*, vol. 7, pp. 9–10.

[43]Ibid.

[44]William G. McLaughlin, *Rhode Island* (Norton, 1978), p. 5.

[45]Ibid., pp. 74–75.

[46]G. B. Warden, "The Rhode Island Civil Code of 1647," in *Saints and Revolutionaries: Essays on Early American History*, edited by David D. Hall, John M. Murrin, and Thad Tate (Norton, 1984), p. 149.

[47]Mark DeWolfe Howe, *The Garden and the Wilderness: Religion and Government in American Constitutional History* (University of Chicago, 1965), p. 7.

Chapter Thirty-one. Jefferson: The Uses of Religion

[1]Gary T. Amos, *Defending the Declaration: How the Bible and Christianity Influenced the Writing of the Declaration of Independence* (Wolgemuth & Hyatt, 1989), pp. 140–50. The book was endorsed by *National Review* (April 30, 1990, pp. 50–51): "Happily for us, as Mr. Amos proves in this small book, all the embarrassing old [religious] junk that liberals are furiously stuffing into the historical trunks was coveted and used by Jefferson himself." The extent of Jefferson's religious writings does not protect him from distortion even after their publication in scholarly editions—which Amos does not consult.

[2]*Thomas Jefferson: Writings*, edited by Merrill D. Peterson (Library of America, 1984), p. 1123. Cf. pp. 1082, 1404. Gary Amos, in the book cited above (note 1), weirdly claims (on p. 195) that Jefferson published his version of the Gospels in 1816. That compendium was not published till 1902. Cf. *Jefferson's Extracts from the Gospels*, edited by Dickinson W. Adams (Princeton, 1983), pp. 125–26. The "Syllabus" was published anonymously (not by Jefferson) in 1816 and received no public notice.

[3]*Jefferson's Literary Commonplace Book*, edited by Douglas L. Wilson (Princeton, 1989). For the importance of this edition, see Garry Wills, "Booked Up," *The New Republic*, January 22, 1990, pp. 41–42.

[4]Jefferson, *Commonplace Book*, pp. 38–40.

[5]Ibid., p. 35.

[6]Jefferson, *Writings*, p. 1121. The reference to Jesus as a "master workman" reflects Jefferson's reading of a Masonic author: "He says, no one ever laid a surer foundation for liberty than our grand master, Jesus of Nazareth" (ibid., p. 1077).

[7]Ibid., p. 903. This is from a letter to Jefferson's nephew, Peter Carr, advising him on his studies. Carr is told to read the Bible skeptically, as he would any work of secular history, and to consider whether Jesus was a supernatural miracle-worker or the deceived man described in the words just quoted.

[8]Eugene R. Sheridan, "Introduction," in Jefferson, *Extracts*, pp. 3–42.

[9]Ibid., p. 330.

[10]The first Jefferson "edition" of the New Testament, "The Philosophy of Jesus," is lost, but Dickinson Adams has ingeniously reconstructed it from the books from which he clipped his extracts.

[11]Jefferson, *Writings*, p. 1122.

[12]Jefferson, *Extracts*, p. 369.

[13]Jefferson, *Writings*, p. 1417. Eugene Sheridan justifiably concludes that the Gospel extracts were a staple of this night reading.

[14]Ibid., p. 1404.

[15]Jefferson, *Extracts*, p. 403.

[16]Ibid., p. 404.

[17]Ibid., pp. 405–6.

[18]Ibid., p. 409.

[19]Ibid., p. 359.

[20]Ibid., p. 334.

[21]Ibid., pp. 347, 350, 401 ("the metaphysical insanities of Athanasius"), 405, 409 ("the Athanasian paradox"), 413.

[22]Jefferson, *Writings*, p. 1302.

[23]Ibid., p. 1090. Some Quakers among his political opponents made Jefferson later qualify his approval of these "Protestant Jesuits" (ibid., pp. 1408 and 1215). For Presbyterians, see *The Papers of Thomas Jefferson*, vol. 1, edited by Julian P. Boyd (Princeton, 1950), p. 552.

[24]Jefferson, *Writings*, p. 8.

[25]Ibid., p. 9: "The people met generally, with anxiety & alarm in their countenances, and the effect of the day thro' the whole colony was like a shock of electricity. . . ."

[26]Samuel Sherwood, *The Church's Flight into the Wilderness: An Address on the Times* (1776), p. 33.

[27]Bill of Rights (1774), in A *Decent Respect to the Opinions of Mankind: Congressional State Papers 1774–1776* (Library of Congress, 1975), p. 56.

[28]Petition to the King (1775), in A *Decent Respect*, p. 76.

[29]*The Papers of Thomas Jefferson*, vol. 1, edited by Julian P. Boyd (Princeton, 1950), p. 200.

[30]Ibid., p. 317.

Chapter Thirty-two. Jefferson: The Protection of Religion

[1]See, for instance, Mark DeWolfe Howe, *The Garden and the Wilderness: Religion and Government in American Constitutional History* (University of Chicago, 1965), p. 19.

[2]*Thomas Jefferson: Writings*, edited by Merrill D. Peterson (Library of America, 1984), p. 706.

[3]Ibid., pp. 346–47.

[4]*The Papers of Thomas Jefferson*, vol. 2, edited by Julian P. Boyd (Princeton, 1950), pp. 550–51.

[5]On the arrangement of the Declaration's grievances, see Garry Wills, *Inventing America* (Doubleday, 1978), pp. 65–73.

[6]Jefferson called this debate on disestablishment the occasion for "desperate contests,"

so he prepared his own argument with care, anticipating the objections to all major points. Cf. "The Autobiography," in Jefferson, *Writings*, pp. 34–35.

[7]The abbreviated notes are in Jefferson, *Papers*, vol. 1, pp. 535–39. The model for expanding the abbreviations is on p. 529.

[8]For *compliment* as *compliance*, see *Oxford English Dictionary* s.v. *complyment* and *complier*, meaning 2.

[9]*Jefferson Papers*, vol. 1, pp. 539–44.

[10]John Locke, A *Letter Concerning Toleration: Latin and English Texts*, revised and edited with variants and an introduction by Mario Montuori (Martinus Nijhoff, 1963), p. 6. For Jefferson's 1776 notes on Locke's *Epistola* (and on his *The Reasonableness of Christianity*), see Jefferson, *Papers*, vol. 1, pp. 544–48, 549–51.

[11]For Locke's study of scriptural prophecy, in conjunction with his friend Isaac Newton, see *The Correspondence of Isaac Newton*, edited by H. W. Turnbull and J. F. Scott, vol. 3 (Cambridge, 1967), pp. 147, 152, 214, 216. Jefferson excised all forms of miracle, prophecy, and the supernatural from his own version of the New Testament.

[12]Jefferson, *Papers*, vol. 1, p. 549.

[13]Ibid., pp. 538–39. Shaftesbury's argument for a "free market" of the mind comes from the part of *Characteristics* called "*Sensus Communis*: An Essay on the Freedom of Wit and Humor":

> For wit is its own remedy. Liberty and commerce bring it to its true standard. The only danger is, the laying of an embargo. The same thing happens here, as in the case of trade. Impositions and restrictions reduce it to a low ebb. Nothing is so advantageous to it as a free port.

(Anthony, Earl of Shaftesbury, *Characteristics of Men, Manners, Opinions, and Times*, edited by John M. Robertson, Bobbs-Merrill, 1964, vol. 1, pp. 45–46).

[14]Jefferson, *Papers*, vol. 1, p. 548. Locke, for instance, would not tolerate atheists in his state. Locke, op. cit., pp. 54, 92.

[15]Ibid., pp. 18, 80.

[16]Jefferson, *Papers*, vol. 1, pp. 538 (on "Northern Clergy"), 539 (on "N. Engld.").

[17]*The Complete Writings of Roger Williams* (Russell and Russell, 1963), vol. 3, p. 313.

[18]Ibid., p. 250.

[19]Ibid., p. 201.

[20]Locke, op. cit., p. 50.

[21]Ibid., p. 6.

[22]Jefferson, *Papers*, vol. 1, p. 537.

[23]Williams, op. cit., pp. 138–39, 369.

Chapter Thirty-three. Madison and the Honor of God

[1]Henry Adams, *History of the United States during the Administrations of Thomas Jefferson and James Madison* (Library of America, 1986), p. 100: "He was curiously vulnerable, for he seldom wrote a page without exposing himself to attack."

[2]*The Papers of James Madison*, edited by William T. Hutchinson et al. (University of Chicago, 1962–77), vol. 1, p. 105. The editors conclude that "it was religious issues, more than tax and trade regulation disputes with England, which were rapidly luring JM away from his beloved studies" (p. 107).

[3]Ibid., pp. 171–79. Whether he knew it or not, Madison was returning Mason's draft toward the proposed form Jefferson had sent down from Philadelphia, which called for "full and free liberty of religious opinion" and outlawed public support for "any religious institution" (*The Papers of Thomas Jefferson*, edited by Julian P. Boyd et al., vol. 1, Princeton, 1950, p. 353).

⁴Madison, op. cit., vol. 8, pp. 295–305.

⁵Ibid., pp. 399–401, 473.

⁶Ibid., p. 202.

⁷Leonard Levy thinks Madison's use of the word *establishments* can refer to "a church school or any religious institution" as well as to a "national religion" (*Original Intent and the Framer's Constitution*, Macmillan, 1988, p. 180). But the frequent use of the word *constitutions* for the *state* charters shows that *establishments* would mean state churches.

⁸Elizabeth Fleet, "Madison's 'Detached Memoranda,' " *William and Mary Quarterly*, 1946, pp. 554–62.

⁹Gaillard Hunt, *The Writings of James Madison* (G. P. Putnam's Sons, 1910), vol. 9, pp. 100–103. Madison admits he yielded to popular pressure for proclamations during his presidency, especially in the patriotic fervor around the War of 1812, but he regrets those lapses, even though he made his documents vague recommendations, not orders. He honors Jefferson for refusing to issue such proclamations.

¹⁰Irving Brandt, *James Madison, Father of the Constitution, 1787–1800* (Bobbs-Merrill, 1950), p. 272.

¹¹For the legal sense of *cognizance*, see *The Oxford English Dictionary*, meaning 3a. The young Madison, who was not a lawyer, may have met the term in his religious readings. Locke refers, in his *Third Letter on Tolerance*, chapter 10, to "magistrates whose duty it is to punish faults under their cognizance." For Jefferson's use of the legal term, see his letter to Gouverneur Morris, August 16, 1793: "The Admiralty declined cognizance of the case."

¹²Madison, op. cit., vol. 8, pp. 295–306. Resemblances to Jefferson's statute, which Madison was about to advance through the Virginia legislature, are partly explained by their independent study of the same texts from Locke (ibid., p. 305).

¹³*The Complete Writings of Roger Williams* (Russell and Russell, 1963), vol. 1, p. 101.

¹⁵For instance, Willmoore Kendall, in *The Basic Symbols of the American Political Tradition* (Louisiana State University, 1970), p. 128, and in *Willmoore Kendall Contra Mundum* (Arlington House, 1971), p. 316.

¹⁶Madison, op. cit., vol. 11, pp. 297–98.

¹⁷Ibid., vol. 12, p. 13.

¹⁸Ibid., p. 15.

¹⁹Ibid., pp. 204–5.

²⁰Frank J. Sorauf, *The Wall of Separation: The Constitutional Politics of Church and State* (Princeton, 1976), pp. 25–26.

²¹Despite the animosity she arouses on the right, Mrs. O'Hair is a kind of Horatio Alger figure who shows what one person can do against "the system": "Without holding any office or seeking any, without any formal political support or allies, without, indeed, very much support or status of any kind, and with only modest expenditures and a somewhat inexperienced attorney . . . she fundamentally altered the relationship of religion to the state in American life" (ibid., p. 130).

²²Ibid., pp. 31–53.

²³Ibid., p. 23.

²⁴Leonard Levy, *The Establishment Clause: Religion and the First Amendment* (Macmillan, 1986), pp. 34–38.

²⁵Hunt, op. cit., vol. 9, p. 103.

²⁶Forrest G. Wood, *The Arrogance of Faith: Christianity and Race from the Colonial Era to the Twentieth Century* (Knopf, 1990).

²⁷Fleet, op. cit., p. 559.

CONCLUSION

[1]Alan M. Dershowitz, "Justice O'Connor's Second Indiscretion," *New York Times*, April 2, 1989.

[2]*People* v. *Ruggles* (1811): "we are a Christian people." Justice Brewer in *Church of the Holy Trinity* v. *United States* (1892): "This is a Christian nation." Cf. Mark DeWolfe Howe, *The Garden and the Wilderness: Religion and Government in American Constitutional History* (University of Chicago, 1965), pp. 14, 29.

[3]See Lincoln's order for Sabbath observance by the military, out of "deference to the best sentiment of a Christian people," in *Abraham Lincoln: Speeches and Writings, 1859–1865*, edited by Don F. Fehrenbacher (Library of America, 1989), p. 382. Also the resolution of slavery, as disqualifying the South from entry "into the family of christian and civilized nations" (ibid., p. 445—and cf. pp. 223, 433, 597, 627).

[4]John Henry Newman, "English Catholic Literature," in *The Idea of a University* (Oxford, 1976), p. 255.

[5]Ibid., p. 259.

[6]Acton's famous axiom was formulated in a letter of 1887 to Mandell Creighton, a historian of the papacy. See *Selected Writings of Lord Acton*, edited by J. Rufus Fears (Liberty Classics, 1985), vol. 2, p. 383.

[7]Cf. Miriam Davidson, *Convictions of the Heart: Jim Corbett and the Sanctuary Movement* (University of Arizona, 1988), pp. 115–17; Robert Tomsho, *The American Sanctuary Movement* (Texas Monthly Press, 1987), pp. 159–67, 204–5.

INDEX